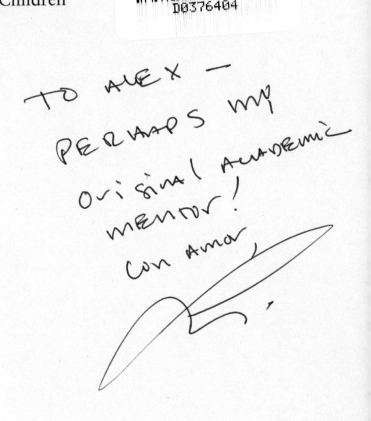

TO ALEX —
PERHAPS MY
ORIGINAL ACADEMIC
MENTOR!
Con Amor,

La Llorona's Children

Religion, Life, and Death in the
U.S.–Mexican Borderlands

Luis D. León

UNIVERSITY OF CALIFORNIA PRESS
Berkeley · Los Angeles · London

Quotations from the following poems or songs appear by courtesy of their authors or publishers: "*La encruci-jada*/The Crossroads," by Gloria Anzaldúa, from *Bor-derlands/La Frontera: The New Mestiza,* 2nd ed. (San Francisco: Aunt Lute Press, 1999), 102; "Oralé," by Rimbault-Dodderidge-Simon-El Vez, performed by El Vez, from the compact disc *Boxing with God* (Gra-ciasland Music BMI, n.d.); and "Many Burning Questions Remain," by Guillermo Gómez-Peña, in Guillermo Gómez-Peña, Enrique Chagoya, and Felicia Rice, *Codex Espangliensis: From Columbus to the Bor-der Patrol* (San Francisco: City Lights Books, 2000).

University of California Press
Berkeley and Los Angeles, California

University of California Press, Ltd.
London, England

Library of Congress Cataloging-in-Publication Data

León, Luis D., 1965–
    La Llorona's children : religion, life, and death in the
U.S.-Mexican borderlands / Luis D. León.
        p.   cm.
    Includes index.
    ISBN 0-520-22350-0 (cloth : alk. paper).—ISBN
0-520-22351-9 (pbk. : alk. paper)
    1. Mexican American Catholics—Religious life.
I. Title.
BX1407.M48L46 2004
277.3'083'0896872—dc21   2002019426

Manufactured in the United States of America

13   12   11   10   09   08   07   06   05   04
10   9   8   7   6   5   4   3   2   1

The paper used in this publication is both acid-free and totally chlorine-free (TCF). It meets the minimum requirements of ANSI/NISO Z39.48-1992 (R 1997) (*Permanence of Paper*).♾

Contents

Preface

The United States–Mexican borderlands is home to a distinct grand pattern of the eternal return: it is a place constituted by multiple crossings and mixings. Hence, its religious expressions reflect the tensions and ambiguities of a place in constant (r)evolution. Take, for example, the saint known as Juan Soldado, who is enshrined in a cemetery on the Tijuana side of the border. He exists as one of many "unofficial" saints in the Mexican and Chicana/o sacred pantheon and is the embodiment of what I call religious poetics.[1] In 1938, Soldado, then known as Juan Castillo Morales, was tried and convicted in a Mexican court for the rape and murder of a young girl.[2] A very popular myth has judged Soldado innocent, a victim of his military superior. As such, God has favored him as the "victim intercessor." Thus others who suffer injustice flock to his shrine seeking understanding and help.[3] On 24 June, the feast of Saint John the Baptist, devotees gather at the tomb of Soldado as if the calendar of saints actually recorded his name. The story of Soldado's unjust death and his sacred recompense serves as a discourse around which to imagine a community that does not depend on institutional support.[4] Indeed, according to Father Salvador Cisneros, rector of the Sacred Heart Seminary in Tijuana, "The church does not have a very high opinion of Juan Soldado; the Church views it as something closer to a superstition, or a false gospel, than an authentic religious movement."[5]

This is but one of the many examples in the U.S.–Mexican borderlands in which religion is a tool to invert justice and injustice and to rewrite the

religious, cultural, and mythical maps in ways that privilege those outside
the official cartography of history; in the case of Soldado, his mythology
demonstrates a preference for the poor, the undocumented border
crossers.[6] But Chicanos, too, pray to Juan Soldado, and they come from
all over the southwestern United States to venerate him. The fact that Soldado's story rings plausibly in the ears of millions on both sides of the border should give us occasion to pause and reflect.[7] This book is a series of
such reflections on borderlands religious phenomena.

Perhaps the first reflection should concern the question of religion itself, a question to which this book returns again and again. Suffice it to
say that my research and writing here stemmed in part from my frustra-
tion with the increasing limitations in the study of religion and from my
desire for a continuous critique of the definition of religion and its place
inside and outside the human community. In short, religion is a system
of symbols that are constantly contested, negotiated, and redefined. In
the words of one anthropologist, "The complexity and uncertainty of
meaning of symbols are sources of their strength."[8] But most important
for me is the way in which "material and symbolic resistance," as James
Scott has demonstrated, "are part of the same set of mutually sustaining
practices."[9] Too often, historians and social scientists dismiss symbolic
manipulation, and/or religious initiative and defiance, as simply a form
of compliance with an oppressive social order. In this way—because such
poetics do not submit to the classical models of revolutionary political
change inherited from the Enlightenment West and are thus beyond the
scope of academic recognition—the political action of borderlands
agents as expressed in religious poetics can be interpreted as simple repli-
cation of the status quo. This is yet another form of what Renato Rosaldo calls "imperialist nostalgia."[10]

In 1972, Davíd Carrasco lamented the fact that scholars "lack a
methodology to investigate, criticize, and understand [Chicano] Catholic
traditions and folk religious practices. (The reasons for this lacuna in academic programs would be a fascinating study in itself.)"[11] Let's take a
look at some possible reasons.[12] At its core, in the words of Rudy Busto,
"the genesis of American religious historiography is related to the project
of nation building and a triumphalist Protestant American exceptional-
ism," and this historiography remains largely so committed today—even
in some of its most revisionist efforts.[13] Localizing itself on the cities of
the eastern seaboard, particularly the New England states, American religious cartography seemingly ends in the Puritan mind of the early twentieth century; too often, the Southwest is neglected.[14]

Working in postcolonial studies in religion, Laura Pérez deftly illuminates the colonial mentality behind the erasure of Chicano/a religion from academic texts, arguing that Chicana spiritual/cultural production "suggests that the trivialization and privatization of spiritual belief that is socially empowering to the exploited is, perhaps, the most powerful sleight of hand of all."[15] Indeed, manifestations of the divine in the feminine face/body/soul were central to the imagined communities of Mesoamerica long before the Spanish fertilized indigenous soil with the seed of the male Godhead that grew the culture of the colonizers. But even inasmuch as colonialism attempted to eradicate indigenous traditions, the cosmology would not be erased. Strategic and tactical religious resistance in the borderlands is guided not so much by calculated reason but by what Pierre Bourdieu calls a "feel for the game."[16] I trace this "feel for the game," or *habitus* or soul, especially through sacred and symbolic practice or ritual performances.[17]

Lamentably, religious thought and practice throughout the borderlands remain largely "undocumented" in primary texts. Thus they escape the academic gaze of recent religious-studies writing that issues from the genre that I call "positivism light": a reliance on searching for answers to religious questions through a textual record that may or may not exist. But material culture acts as cultural texts and discloses types of "data" about religiosity. To unearth borderlands religion, I simply learned as much as possible about a particular "religion" (or religious practice) through archival and bibliographic research, and, in addition, I examined cultural products that disclosed information valuable for understanding a religious way of life and how that way of life is thought about and represented. Thus, key parts of this narrative rely on literature and film, which, while not providing "ethnographic data," offer more intimate glimpses of culture and, as Margaret Miles claims, insight into how "a society reveals itself to itself," asking, "How should we live?"[18]

Following Clifford Geertz's methodology, I have tied my interpretations to a particular referent—a type of text—from which arises a hermeneutic.[19] However, whereas Geertz held that religion is a cultural system, borderland religions demonstrate that culture is instead a religious system; this simple fact is illustrated throughout the following pages. I spent nearly ten years in formal research on this project, and many more in personal experience. From my doctoral degree program in religious studies at the University of California, Santa Barbara, I drove the ninety miles to East Los Angeles several times a month to attend religious ceremonies and other related events, to interview people, and to record my impressions.[20] Between the filing of the dissertation (on the feast day of the Virgin of Guadalupe, 12 December 1997) and the publication of this book, I traveled to my original California sites of research several times a year; I also traveled to Mexico City six times, three to witness and participate in the Guadalupe pilgrimage, on 12 December, and once for Holy Week. In addition, my visits to Mexico City included more general research, and in June 1999 I participated in the First International Congress on Religion in Latin America, where I had the great fortune of presenting my research to an international group of scholars.

This book would not have been realized without the aid of numerous individuals and institutions. Because it grew out of my doctoral research in religious studies at the University of California, Santa Barbara, perhaps my greatest debt of gratitude is owed to Richard Hecht, my advisor. He convinced me of the importance of comparison in Chicana/o religions and that a broad history-of-religions approach could shed fresh light on a long-overlooked phenomenon. Similarly, Mario Garcia and Charles Long provided invaluable guidance and support. Catherine Albanese meticulously read drafts of the dissertation and offered detailed criticism for which I am deeply grateful. Also at UCSB, Denise Segura, director of the Center for Chicano Studies Research, made monies available for several research trips to Mexico City, and the Humanities Center and the Graduate Division supported study.

Davíd Carrasco gave direction to the manuscript from the beginning and read and commented on its development. Indeed, my work is possible because of his pioneering research and writing on Mesoamerican-Chicano religious studies. I am grateful also to Bob Orsi and José Saldívar for carefully reading the manuscript and offering extensive suggestions for its improvement. Laura Pérez appeared at the eleventh hour to read the entirety of the manuscript for proper Spanish usage and more. To her I am very grateful. Wade Clark Roof and Stephen Warner's ethnographic expertise was particularly valuable in my fieldwork research.

I wish also to thank Doug Arava and Reed Malcolm at the University of California Press.

Carleton College's faculty in the Department of Religion provided valuable collegial support, and the dean's office graciously supported the project with research money. I am grateful especially to Carleton's Laurence Cooper and Jay Levi for their warm friendship, criticism, and powerful insights into Nietzsche. My gratitude goes also to Arizona State University.

I thank Professors Tony Stevens Arroyo and Ana María Díaz-Stevens at the Program for the Analysis of Religion among Latinos (PARAL) for funding travel to conferences. I owe gratitude also to the Cushwa Center at the University of Notre Dame for making funds available for the sections of this work on *curanderismo*. Much of the research and writing of this project took place while I was on summer grant from the National Endowment for the Humanities during the summer of 1998 and while I was on a research leave, during the fall of 2000, funded by the Hispanic Theological Initiative at Princeton Seminary—I feel blessed to know the HTI directors, Zaida Maldonado Perez and Joanne Rodriguez.

I have been blessed also by the companionship of good and smart friends in ethnic and religious studies: Rudy Busto, Gilbert Cadena, Gaston Espinosa, Santos Humo, Roberto Lint-Sagarena, Tim Matovina, Alberto Pulido, Vicki Ruíz, and Miguel de la Torre. I am especially thankful to Jon Armajani, Saint Jon, for the many insane hours we spent on the phone talking about nothing but keeping me sane during the isolated hours of writing. Gary Laderman, "G.," has taught me much, and I look forward with appreciation to our continued collaboration and close friendship. Lara Medina and Jane Iwamura have become like academic and soul sisters to me, and for that I am grateful.

My birth sister, Laura León-Maurice, has given financial and emotional support and, together with my brother, Leonardo León, has supplied the sort of unconditional love and joy only siblings can bring. My mother, Ruth León, rose to the difficult challenge of raising and teaching me, and while the opportunities I enjoyed were denied to her because of her Puerto Rican ancestry, she would not let anything be denied to her own children. I am eternally inspired by her courage. In life, my father, the child of Mexican immigrants, the Reverend Daniel León, was perhaps the holiest man I've known. He continues to inspire, support, and teach me even from the other side. It is to him, to my mother, and to the ancestors that this book is dedicated.

In Search of La Llorona's Children

Reimagining Religion

There are no revolutions without poets.
  Rodolfo "Corky" Gonzales, *I Am Joaquín/*
  Yo Soy Joaquín: An Epic Poem

"The future" will belong to the *mestiza*. Because the future depends on the breaking down of paradigms, it depends on the straddling of two or more cultures. By creating a new mythos—that is a change in the way we perceive reality, the way we see ourselves, and the ways we behave—*la mestiza* creates a new consciousness.
  Gloria Anzaldúa, *Borderlands/La Frontera: The New Mestiza*

This world is the will to power—and nothing besides! And you yourselves are also this will to power—and nothing besides!
  Friedrich Nietzsche, *The Will to Power*, ed. and trans.
  Walter Kaufmann and R. J. Hollingdale

Today once again, today finally, today otherwise, the great question would still be religion and what some hastily call its "return."
  Jacques Derrida, "Faith and Knowledge," from *Religion: Cultural Memory in the Present*, trans. Samuel Weber

During the fall of 1999, for the first time in over four hundred years, La Virgen de Guadalupe, patron saint of Mexico, crossed the border into the United States. Her Los Angeles Archdiocese Web page made it clear: "Tuesday, September 14, 1999, will be a historic occasion for the residents of Los Angeles. Arriving via train, a replica of Our Lady of Guadalupe, blessed by Pope John Paul II, will arrive in the City of Angels." "Her Arrival," or "Su Llegada," as the event was dubbed, promised to be a "multicultural" and "multilingual" affair. Appropriately, reenacting the journey taken by millions of Mexicans, the Virgin's first stop would be Plaza Olvera, site of La Placita Church, and Olvera Street—the historic Mexican downtown.[1]

La Virgen's tour promoters admonished: "Be present as the Sacred Image is carried into Plaza Olvera and officially welcomed by officials from the City of Los Angeles, the Roman Catholic Archdiocese of Los Angeles, and the sponsoring organization, Pueblo Corporation."[2] Guadalupe would tour California for three months before returning to Mexico to embark upon more pilgrimages throughout the Americas. The original image of Guadalupe, emblazoned upon the cape of Juan Diego, to whom she first appeared, is now framed in gold and hangs in the ultramodern basilica at Tepeyac. Though it is common for other Mexican Virgin images, whether paintings or small free-standing sculptures—*bultos* or *santos*—to tour the pilgrimage circuit throughout the Mexican Americas, this particular image of Guadalupe, the most sacred icon of

Mexico, had not left Mexico City since her first apparition to the Indian Juan Diego in 1531.

Her *gran despedida,* or grand farewell, was scheduled for Saturday, 11 December 1999, and was expected to draw over one hundred thousand *guadalupana/os* to the Los Angeles Memorial Sports Coliseum for six long hours. The event began with a giant procession from downtown Los Angeles, was broadcast live on the major Spanish network, and was featured as a special episode by Spanish television's talk-show diva Christina, who also served as emcee. Emma Perez of Los Angeles spoke for the attendees: "This is a holy day for us. . . . She [Guadalupe] is the mother of God, and she's our mother. And we're here to show how much we love her."[3]

The picture of Guadalupe that traveled to Los Angeles was not, in a literal sense, the image that hangs over the most sacred altar in Mexico, the shrine church of Guadalupe at Tepeyac. Rather, it was a digitized exact replica of the painting, generated by a computer program. Nonetheless, judging by the throngs of people who gathered to see her, Guadalupe's apparition was the real thing: after nearly two centuries of anticipation and pilgrimages back to the motherland, and with the global village as a witness, La Virgen de Guadalupe, La Patrona of Mexico and Queen of the Angels, reigned—if only briefly—in one of the nation's most powerful and glamorous cities: Los Angeles, City of the Angels.

The accompaniment of La Lupe's replicated image in Los Angeles created the opportunity for Latinas and Latinos, especially Mexicans, to "presence" themselves in a grand and spectacular way, creating a wildly public "transcript" of influence and sacred and civil authority—which, sponsors anticipated, would foreground social change.[4] In other words, La Lupe's visit was not, as it might seem to some, another show of her divine quality of symbolic and literal omnipresence, but rather it was a triumph, in a broad sense, of what I call religious poetics: through a strategy of performed and narrated religious discourse, *tactics,* and strategies, social agents change culturally derived meanings and, indeed, the order of the phenomenal world by rearranging the relationships among symbols and deftly inventing and reinventing the signification of symbols—especially those held sacred.[5] As a persistent social and historical phenomenon, this process is described by Nietzsche as the *transvaluation* of morals, wherein ethics, values, and norms are mutated, inverted, and ultimately transformed to favor the disempowered.[6] In the fall of 1999, the symbol of *mexicanidad,* Guadalupe, captivated the mind of Los Angeles, the center of world fantasy, not only normalizing Mexican and

Latina/o Catholic presence in Los Angeles but *sacralizing* it—a triumph of the hyper-reality characterizing current public imaginaries.

In sacred poetics, religious actors can manage the often harsh and potentially overwhelming conditions they confront—the battle for survival and more, dignity, love, freedom—by deploying the most powerful weapons in their arsenal: signs, myths, rituals, narratives, and symbols. And, empowered by their freshly perceived role in the cosmic drama, agents of social change appeal to, create, and reinvent religious institutions and their place in the lives of constituents. Religious practice, in the borderlands and elsewhere, is of course not singularly triumphant and comedic. It is often tragic. Tragedy is signaled by the spectral presence of La Llorona, the weeping woman whose myth tells of endless searching for her slain children. La Llorona's memory is birthed in *consejos* or *dichos* (proverbs or sayings) that poetically narrate the world as part of a larger theology and system of ethics always under construction but always returning to the basic principles of "conscience," the good, and the virtuous.

My thesis in this book is that in the Mexican Americas, religious belief and practice are continuously redefined by devotees of various traditions that started in and were transformed by, brought to and found, throughout the borderlands as a creative and often effective means to manage the crisis of everyday life. When the promises of religion, as they are meted out by institutions and by what Pierre Bourdieu calls official "religious specialists," are insufficient to meet expectations and to quiet the fears, confusion, pain, and agonies of people on the margins of power, then the meanings of religious symbols can be "redirected," "reinterpreted," or conjured anew to fill the gap between what "ought" to be and the way it actually is.[7] Poetic, creative religious practice does not occur only at the boundaries of institutions, but within, parallel to, and sometimes in direct conflict with established traditions. In short, religion—broadly and personally defined—in addition to serving power as an ideological mechanism of social control, exploitation, and domination, is also effectively deployed in attempts to destabilize those very same forces by people who have access to only the bare resources that constitute conventional power. As one postcolonial theorist describes it, the religious or "symbolic is not a residual dimension of purportedly real politics; still less is it an insubstantial screen upon which real issues are cast in pale and passive form. The symbolic is real politics, articulated in a special and often powerful way."[8]

Within the last decade, anthropological studies of myth and ritual have emerged to argue for the strategic potential of religion.[9] Chicana and Chicano scholars stress the power of cultural symbols in the social arena; they have for some time now recognized the force of cultural and religious production in foregrounding, if not producing, historical change. Historian of Religions Davíd Carrasco has called this type of resistance and change "the lyrics of Chicano spirituality." José Saldívar argues that the power of border songs and *corridos* "lies in lyrics that always tell truths and that depict the problematic of unequal power relationships."[10] The inequality of power relationships is exploited for social change in cultural strategies by what Chela Sandoval describes as "differential movement." This type of semiotic and narrative movement enables a performative and rowdy critique of the nation's social arrangements, what Laura Pérez names *el desorden*.[11] Focusing on twentieth-century Mexican-American women, Vicki Ruíz has described the process of "cultural coalescence" as "picking and choosing," while adapting and creating, cultural forms.[12] José Limón's cultural poetics and erotics figure issues of *mexicano* culture into fresh idioms of resistance, struggle, and change.[13] But the work at hand, an elaboration of cultural poetics and erotics, is a significant departure if only for its framing of religion.

The poetics of religion in the borderlands is perhaps best described by Gloria Anzaldúa, who remembers her religious socialization through stories; not ordinary stories, but poetic ones, "stories where things aren't what they seem—supernatural powers, the ability to fly, changing form, transforming shape. . . . These stories are indigenous, where a man becomes a cougar, a snake, or a bird. Very much like the don Juan books by Carlos Castañeda—stories of transformation, about powers and abilities existing and manifesting themselves in the wind, the ability to feel a presence in the room."[14] She concludes by defining what constituted the sacred for her: "My religion was the stories my mother would tell which had to do with spirits, with devils, I'd feel their presence. The folk myths like La Jila, La Llorona."[15] For Anzaldúa and others, then, the motherly figure of La Llorona is disembodied—she is a specter who travels the earth in search of her children across the borderlands. As such, her searching is a framing metaphor for the present work.

TOWARD A GENEALOGY OF LA LLORONA

Perhaps the earliest American recounting of the story of La Llorona comes in the form of the "highest" Aztec goddess, who was said to be Cihuacoatl, or Snake Woman: "By night she walked," claims the Aztec

Florentine Codex, "weeping, wailing; also was she an omen of war." And yet she also embodied the light: "And as she appeared before men, she was covered with chalk, like a court lady. . . . She appeared in white, garbed in white, standing white, pure white. Her womanly hairdress rose up." That she symbolized duality is apparent in her face, which "was painted one-half red, one-half black." Generally, Cihuacoatl was thought to be a malevolent force: "She was an evil omen, she brought misery to men."[16] Cihuacoatl assumes various forms in ancient and contemporary Mexican mythology. She was transformed in the cultural imagination into La Llorona during the Spanish conquest of Mexico.

According to this Aztec codex, just a few years before Spanish ships first landed on the Mexican coast of Vera Cruz in the sixteenth century, a woman circled the walls of the great Aztec city of Tenochtitlán. Late at night she was heard weeping in mourning for the impending destruction of the great Mexican civilization, and especially for her children: "My children, we must flee far from this city!"[17] The Aztecs took this as the sixth of eight omens warning of their imminent ruin. Because of her signaling doom, the Weeping Woman, or La Llorona, became a perennial avatar of Snake Woman.

Another account of La Llorona comes to us from Mexico City, where in 1550 a woman was heard weeping—a siren wailing loudly—especially on moonlit nights. In response, residents of the great city daringly crept into the streets looking for the source of the intense lamentations.

> There they saw a woman, dressed in very white garments, with a thick veil, also white, covering her head. With slow and soft steps she walked through many streets of the sleeping city, each night choosing a different route to the Plaza Mayor where she turned her veiled face toward the east. Falling to her knees she gave a last long agonizing moan. Then, rising, she continued with slow and measured steps in the same direction, and, on arriving at the edge of the brackish lake, which at that time extended into some of the suburbs, she disappeared like a shadow.[18]

La Llorona is often sighted near bodies of water, especially rivers; and it was from the east that the Spaniards came and arrived on the coast of Mexico.

The weeping-woman myth survived colonialism and crossed the border into the United States. Based on one folklorist's field investigations conducted in the 1940s, the "legend" of Llorona "is continually refreshed by contact with Mexican sources, either social or literary—by visiting back and forth across the border and then among Arizona and California families."[19] La Llorona is a transnational symbol who thrives and is reproduced in several types of movements. In this way she epitomizes transnational culture in the Mexican Americas—inhabiting both sides of the border.

From the Mexico side, Octavio Paz conjures La Llorona as a continuation of La Malinche, and a continuation also of the grand colonial metaphor:

> Who is the *Chingada* [Violated Woman]? Above all, she is the mother. Not a Mother of flesh and blood but a mythical figure. The Chingada is one of the Mexican representations of Maternity, like *La Llorona* or the "long-suffering Mexican mother" we celebrate on the tenth of May. The Chingada is the mother who has suffered—metaphorically or actually—the corrosive and defaming action implicit in the verb that gives her her name. It would be worthwhile to examine that verb.[20]

Let's examine that verb. *Chingar,* "to violate," is not only the ultimate act of individual rape but also connotes the ultimate effect of colonialism: Paz poetically reiterates the mass psychic images of Mexican domination (La Malinche/La Llorona) and salvation (La Lupe) in relation to the most sacred Mexican archetype: motherhood.

But, as Limón, among others and more recently, has keenly observed, the myth of La Llorona serves especially as a vehicle for women to narrate the order of the world. In Santa Fe, New Mexico, for example, a story was told of a man who was setting a bad example for his children. He stayed out drinking until the early morning hours and refused to attend church. He was bad-tempered and stubborn. Then, when he was coming home one morning from a drunken escapade, "La Llorona stopped him and lectured him about his not being a good father." She tied him to the door of the church on several occasions until he not only followed her advice but encouraged the men in the town to behave more responsibly as well! According to the storyteller/poet/mythmaker, "So that's how a miracle occurred in that particular neighborhood."[21] That La Llorona is dead matters but little to the narrators, for she continues to be a powerful response to quotidian problems, especially the everyday matters of gender, sexuality, and love.

The public history of Mexican diva and Hollywood film star Lupe Vélez, the original "Mexican Spitfire," bears an uncanny resemblance to the myth of La Llorona. On 15 December 1944—just three days after the start of the Guadalupe holy days—Vélez's corpse was discovered in her Beverly Hills apartment. She had committed suicide, thus taking the life of her unborn child as well.[22] The apparent motive for her act was that, like Medea of Greek myth, she had been painfully rejected by her lover, a Frenchman of another class and culture. Like La Malinche—the indigenous woman who was Hernán Cortéz's lover and translator, who was used and rejected by a European male—Vélez was tossed aside.

THE GODDESS TRINITY AND THE DEVIL

On 1 December 2000, before a global audience, the newly elected president of Mexico, Vicente Fox, kneeled before Mexico's queen, La Virgen de Guadalupe, and received her blessing just prior to celebrating a series of inaugural events and ceremonies that opened a spellbinding drama of radical national transformation. Not only had Mexico's political power changed hands for the first time in nearly a century, but for the first time since the "godless" Mexican Revolution, Mexico, Catholicism's prodigal child, had come home. It's as if the changing of the millennium itself heralded the transformation of Mexico's political system, a change marked not so much by individual personal confession (for Fox is a man of few, carefully chosen words, a man of action) as by ritual: Vicente Fox defied Enlightenment mandates and prayed at the altar of Mexico's most revered mother, the nation's biggest star and most fashionable of all exports, the Virgin of Guadalupe. Fox is a good son.

However, Fox is not the first of Mexico's First Sons to exhibit a spiritual life after the Revolution (1910–17). Francisco Madero himself is said to have been an avowed spiritist—a movement in Mexico closely associated with spiritualists. (The two movements differ in terms of founders, origins, and beliefs.) And in 1938, Plutarco Calles, who had been a Marxist and persecutor of the Catholic Church, is said to have traveled north to the obscure town of Espinazo, Nuevo León, seeking the healing powers of El Niño Fidencio, who, somewhat ironically, is often imagined as an incarnation of La Virgen de Guadalupe. Reportedly, Fidencio stripped Calles naked, rubbed him with honey, and beat him with a squirrel. The cure worked.[23] More recently, Carlos Salinas de Gotari reputedly consulted regularly with a *curandera* (a healer of spiritual and/or physical illness). In July 2002, both the Pope and Fox submitted to a *limpia,* or traditional spiritual cleansing.

Mexico, however, is a state more officially secular than is the United States. The paradoxical mixture of Mexico's public and private religion is perhaps best embodied by Guadalupe and company. In the traditional Mexican collective representation, the male God-triad is symbolically answered by La Virgen de Guadalupe/La Malinche/La Llorona. Each one has a distinct mythology, yet they are remarkably similar in ways that meet in their uncanny aspects. La Virgen de Guadalupe is the mother of Jesus—she is an Indian and Mexican regional manifestation of Mary.[24] Since what was ostensibly her primordial appearance in Mexico as an Aztec mother goddess in 1531, the Virgin of Guadalupe, now the "Queen of Mexico," has functioned in Mexican and Chicano history as a powerful cultural symbol of highly idealized—virgin—motherhood.

Daughters are warned not to become women of loose virtue, the "whore" *(puta)*, symbolized in *mexicana/o*-Chicana/o traditions by La Malinche.[25] She was the indigenous Mexican woman who acted as Hernán Cortéz's translator and lover and proved essential to Spain's conquest of the Americas in the sixteenth century. For this, she has become the great traitor in Mexican cultural myths: the emblematic "Jezebel" who is Guadalupe's binary pole and reversal. She is the structural opposite of Guadalupe. Together, Guadalupe and La Malinche circumscribe the traditional possibilities for ethnic Mexican women's identities. Octavio Paz writes of La Malinche: "In contrast to Guadalupe, who is the Virgin Mother, the *Chingada* [violated one] is the violated Mother."[26]

La Llorona, who mediates between the two, has a spotty history, dating back to the sixteenth-century Mesoamerican pantheon of goddesses. As the ghostly apparition of the weeping woman, reputedly guilty of infanticide, she appears in anguish, searching for her children. She is history/myth/legend and more: siren calling, crying evil, decrying injustice: remorse, regret, pain, change: sorrow, suffering, lamenting: she wants another chance, to right a wrong.[27] She is a universal symbol of the eternal soul who never completely disappears but whose form, whose shape, is shifted and changed; even while her essence answers to the vicissitudes of life, it remains unchanged. There are multiple versions of La Llorona, as is characteristic of religious poetics, and equally numerous variations of her motivations and culpability: the way in which La Llorona's children die depends on the context of the narration and the narrator's purpose in enacting the myth.

In the words of José Limón, "La Llorona's critical efficacy [is] as a powerful, contestative female symbol. In contrast to the male dominated promotion and circulation of these 'official' legends, La Llorona remains largely *in the hands of women*. . . . Women control this expressive resource, and it therefore speaks to the greater possibility that it is articulating their own symbolic perceptions of the world."[28] And more, all of these legends, "official" or otherwise, are in the hands of women, men, and children; the "laity" become, in Bourdieu's phrase, their own "religious specialists," articulating a distinct set of logics within the religious field.[29]

Take, for example, the feminist recuperation of La Malinche. History records the birth of the figure who came to be known as La Malinche around the year 1502, in Coatzacoalcos, a Mesoamerican province in the Valley of Mexico. "La Malinche is believed to have originally been named Malinal after 'Malinalli,' the day of her birth, as was the custom at the time. As daughter of an Aztec cacique, or chief, she was a member of a privileged, educated class."[30] Because she served as translator for Cortéz, she was the first to narrate and translate the conquest. She was given to Cortéz, bore him children, and was passed on to one of Cortéz's men. Malinche came to be known as La Lengua, or "the Tongue," and consequently she attained some status in Spanish eyes and was addressed as "doña Marina and Malintzin," *doña*, of course, signifying respect. She disclosed Aztec beliefs and battle plans to the Spanish, thus providing them with a tremendous military advantage. Consequently, subjugation of the Aztecs came at much too low a cost to Spain: in 1521 the final Aztec resistance was overwhelmed and the great Aztec capital, Tenochtitlán, lay in ruins—for which Malinche is blamed.

According to Paz, Malinche gave birth not only to a new breed of half-European Americans but to a race of colonized people: "Sons of La Malinche," a figuration in which La Malinche conveys betrayal itself, and more, violation, submission, passivity, and fall—the great whore of Mexico.

La Guadalupe continues, as well as reverses, Malinche narratives. Guadalupe has been called the New Eve, the woman described in Saint John's Revelation, mother of a new creation, Spanish and Indian, a creation underwritten by Indian patrimony. Chicana feminists have reclaimed and contested the Christian mythos of Malinche as a Mexican Judeo-Christian Eve—a woman who is damned and brings the condemnation of generations. In a feminist revision, Guadalupe is not the redemption of Malinche but her counterpart: Malinche is the alpha-woman signaling death to the old and bringing life to the new.[31]

Each of these symbolic women attains power from her dialectic exchange with the other. It is around this discursive and symbolic movement that Mexican cultural norms take shape and coalesce into various modes of social codes, idioms, expectations, forms of resistance, and modes of submission. This poetic discourse circulates within, without, and between many institutions, but perhaps its primary institutional locus is the Catholic Church. Still, observes Octavio Paz, "it is no secret to anyone" that "Mexican Catholicism is centered about the cult of the Virgin of Guadalupe." As we shall see, throughout parts of the Catholic Mexican Americas, La Lupe is bigger than Jesus. Perhaps her popularity can be explained in part by her primordial roots in Mexican soil. Paz explains how Guadalupe discontinues earlier roles of female deities. "The Catholic Virgin is also the Mother (some Indian pilgrims still call her Guadalupe-Tonantzin), but her principal attribute is not to watch over the fertility of the earth but to provide refuge for the unfortunate. . . . The Virgin is the consolation of the poor, the shield of the weak, the help of the oppressed. In sum, she is the mother of orphans."[32] As José Saldívar points out, Paz's "vantage point" is that of a "bourgeois intellectual from the South"; he is fully enfranchised in the Mexican nation.[33] Paz labored in the 1950s as a Marxist who was heavily influenced by Freud. For Paz, then, the obsessive mother figure frames the Mexican imaginary and collective psyche. His analysis of Guadalupe unfolds the discussion of the Oedipal family drama that I adumbrate in my discussion of the Tepeyac pilgrimage (see chapter 2). La Malinche, in Paz's writing, is colonization itself—she is the mythical physical embodiment of the act of sexual/spiritual/psychic violation—*chingar*.

Deena Gonzalez reponds: "This fascinating story of this remarkable sixteenth-century woman might be read as an account of the prototypical Chicana feminist." She says, "La Malinche embodies those personal characteristics—such as intelligence, initiative, adaptability, and leadership—which are most often associated with Mexican-American women unfettered by traditional restraints against activist public achievement. By adapting to the historical circumstances thrust upon her, she defied traditional social expectations of a woman's role. Accordingly, the exigent demands placed on her allowed La Malinche's astonishing native abilities to surface."[34]

As a concomitant to Malinche's transformation, Guadalupe is experiencing transitional movements herself—especially transsexual ones. "The feminist writers place emphasis on recapturing Our Mother's omnipotence, retrieving the feminine face of God," writes Ana Castillo in the introduction to a collection of essays on Guadalupe.[35] Some Chicana critics reinscribe Guadalupe with a forceful sexuality, reversing her desexualized virgin reputation. In a brief personal reflection, "Guadalupe the Sex Goddess," Sandra Cisneros laments the alienation and fear that swelled within her at the sight of her own body when she was a young girl. She attributes her emotions to cultural prescriptions that are regrettably traceable to Guadalupe: "Religion and our culture, our culture and religion, helped to create that blur, a vagueness about what went on 'down there.' " She laments:

> What a culture of denial. Don't get pregnant! But no one tells you how not to. This is why I was angry for so many years every time I saw la Virgen de Guadalupe, my culture's role model for brown women like me. She was damn dangerous, an ideal so lofty and unrealistic it was laughable. Did boys have to aspire to be Jesus? I never saw any evidence of it. They were fornicating like rabbits while the Church ignored them and pointed us women toward our destiny—marriage and motherhood. The other alternative was *puta* hood [whoredom]. . . . As far as I could see, *la Lupe* was nothing but a goody two shoes meant to doom me to a life of unhappiness. Thanks but no thanks.[36]

Instead of the Guadalupe handed down by the Church, Cisneros poetically reconstructs Guadalupe, melding her into a pre-Columbian fertility goddess—female deities who were venerated for the power invested in them through their close kinship to the cosmos and the ability to create life—and expressing what has for so long remained silenced: "My Virgen de Guadalupe is not the mother of God. She is God." Cisneros's concluding doxology brings fully to bear the spirit of religious poetics: "When I see *la Virgen de Guadalupe* I want to lift her dress as I did my dolls' and look to see if she comes with *chones* [underwear], and does her *panocha* [vagina] look like mine, and does she have dark nipples too? Yes, I am certain she does. She is not neuter like Barbie. She gave birth. She has a womb. *Blessed art thou and blessed is the fruit of thy womb.* . . . Blessed art thou, Lupe, and, therefore, blessed am I."[37]

Similarly, Carla Trujillo has written of the advantages Guadalupe could gain, in her own words, "If La Virgen de Guadalupe, or 'Lupe,' as I would affectionately call her, decided to spend some time with me as my woman, I would make sure that life would be different and much more fulfilling for her."[38] Trujillo paints a poetic and ironic picture of life in full human union with the Indian/*mestiza* mother of God.

These authors share a particular cultural location—a *place*—out of which their stories arise; they also share this cultural space with the women who tell stories about Guadalupe and religion to their children, family, and friends every day. That is, these narratives capture the essence of religious poetics from the various social-economic-political levels from which they arise. In the words of Lupe Reyes, a Chicana from East Los Angeles, "We come to pay homage to Our Lady of Guadalupe who gives us strength."[39]

The third and perhaps mediative figure in the symbolic triad is an earthbound specter, La Llorona, who travels the Mexican Americas searching for her dead children. Like Medea, Llorona's story is a myth of infanticide. The standard premise of the myth condemns the weeping woman for killing her children to spite her lover; some have said La Llorona is actually a synecdoche for La Malinche, who purges the soul of the New World, as well as her own soul, of colonial excess by destroying the patrimony of Cortéz: the first mixed-race children, or *mestizos*.[40]

Here, then, is the birth of tragedy—that impulse in religious poetics that does not ignore but confronts the reality and drama of suffering and orders, narrates, and ultimately resolves it. Limón describes this tragic impulse in the symbol of the devil—particularly the apt allegory of dancing with the devil:

> I also came to know my scholarly precursors and my people's capacity to culturally critique and bedevil those who have dominated the working-class Mexican people of the United States. I would, however, add a distinctive theme in these pages, and that is the capacity of my people to bedevil themselves, always under the constraining conditioning of the sociocultural Other. I will also speak here of how this community's self-questioning led to a greater sense of political and cultural freedom, with its cultural poetics as a primary form of interrogation.[41]

In "religious poetics"—perhaps both a more specific and a more elaborate form of "cultural poetics"—the devil and evil manifest in the tragic drama of suffering.

RELIGIOUS POETICS: BASED ON A TRUE STORY

In her account of the spiritual channeling practices of a Mexican woman named Esperanza, Ruth Behar argues that "there is no *true* version of a life after all. There are only stories told about and around a life." These stories about lives occur in political contexts, in real worlds. For that reason, like the cultural poetics of James Clifford, religious poetics assume that the "poetic and the political are inseparable." Scholarship is a political act; it cannot be dissociated from the conditions of its production.[42] The field of religious studies is inherently political, and it too has real implications in real worlds. As Pérez puts it, "What individuals and groups perceive and represent as the spiritual—that having to do with the s/Spirit(s)—is a socially and politically significant field of differences and contention, as well as of resonances, crossings, and even hybridization."[43] Not only is the religious field politically charged; it is amorphous, multiply manifest, comprised of both spiritual and material matters, and in no way absolutely and/or entirely described.[44]

While considering religion a distinct element of culture, a *cultural* history of religions treats it broadly as *sui generis,* of its own kind, not reified as an entity of its own essence but a cultural phenomenon with its own discrete set of logics—rather than an epiphenomenon reduced to a product of another invented and reified *disciplined* post-Enlightenment academic discourse. Inasmuch as economics, political science, sociology, or history requires suspension of disbelief, broad generalizations, and a set of idioms that capture and contain ambiguity and contradiction likely unrecognizable to the people whom they purportedly describe while facilitating the circulation of ideas whereby various "data" point to various "truths," religion too is of that kind.[45]

For its pragmatic inclination, the following study asks: How do people survive and make meaning under conditions of discrimination, poverty, and deprivation? How do they negotiate racism, sexism, and general hatred? How do they resolve conflict? How do they love, and how do they die? What diseases do they get, and how do they heal them? How do they raise children? What salvation narratives appeal to their passions and desires? What is borderland religion? How can it be researched, represented, and theorized? As a starting place, I propose a spiritual survey of the religious ecology that exists between Mexico and the United States, based around the religious stories of the borderlands—its religious poetics. Like the Esperanza of Behar's border crossing, the poetic impulse in religious narration "suggests that a woman [or man] from the margins of the other America can also be a thinker, a cosmologist, a story teller," or, as I see it, a prophet.[46]

Hence, I search for La Llorona's children in different religious places and forms throughout the Mexican Americas, guided by what Renato Rosaldo calls "narrative analysis," or gleaning meaning from various cultural stories.[47] Each encounter yields a genealogy. The result of this study is a series of *fragmented* and *incomplete* genealogies that reveal, when placed in relation to one another, uncanny similarities, as well as, of course, significant differences.[48]

This book is concerned with the distinct "parts" that together constitute a religious system, following the definition of Emile Durkheim, which turns on a social and categorical delineation of the sacred and profane, subsequently delimited into phenomenological structures, whereby "religion is a totality of religious phenomena, and the whole can only be defined in terms of its parts."[49] Such an approach allows for a broad range of human activities to emerge as "religious." I examine these "parts" in devotion to Guadalupe, *curanderismo, espiritualismo,* and evangelical Protestantism, spanning Mexico City and East Los Angeles, and areas across the U.S. Southwest. More specific foci include "pilgrimage" and "prophecy." Focusing first on the pilgrimage tradition to Guadalupe, I come to an understanding of the ritual and place of pilgrimage as an "arena for competing discourses."[50] I take issue, then, with the consensual model of liminality (for liminality fosters conflicts) and question also the notion of *communitas*—wherein all social hierarchies are eradicated and pilgrims experience each other equally in a state of temporary utopia.[51]

Since her first apparition in Mexico Guadalupe has served as a spiritual healer, or *curandera.* But even prior to Guadalupe's emergence, religious healers across the borderlands established followings, arising socially as charismatic prophets, *pace* Weber. "Charisma" is the human endowment of extraordinary powers; it can be either inherited or conferred—but only the first type is "fully merited" and is therefore of greater value and power. Its avatar, says Weber, is a "purely individual bearer of charisma, who by virtue of his mission proclaims a religious doctrine or divine commandment." Weber echoes Nietzsche, who believed fresh religious formations emerge when a prophet figure emphasizes existing but neglected elements of a tradition.[52] Healers continue to appear within and around Christian traditions, including and especially evangelicalism. In fact, the voluntary establishment and growth of *evangélico* churches in Mexican communities around the Southwest is tantamount to a pilgrimage phenomenon. I. M. Lewis argues that "pilgrimage is not only a matter of visiting designated sacred places and shrines. Pilgrims also throng to seek the blessing of particular holy men [and women]—sacred persons who in certain periods and settings may challenge the power of long-established shrines."[53]

Religious competition has been a fact of the borderlands for centuries, and beginnings are also continuations, so the lines "between a 'renewer of religion' who preaches an older revelation, actual or supposititious, and a 'founder of religion' who claims to bring completely new deliverances" is actually murky and indeterminate.[54] Prophecy, as Weber argues, occurs when a charismatic figure claims, *de facto,* autonomous religious authority and speaks on behalf of the poor and oppressed: a poetics of salvation as if a divinely fresh revelation but emerging also from memory.

The recovery of borderlands prophecy and memory is framed here allegorically as a search for La Llorona's children. "Religious poetics" is used in the Greek, Aristotelian sense of poetry as performance,[55] from the Greek *poesis,* doing or acting. This is true particularly for religious terms, or for the religious context. Perhaps the best known of the early recorded uses of the term appears in the canonized Christian scriptures, James 1:25: "He will be blessed in his doing." Similarly, the Greek *poetes* signifies one who does something, or the maker of a poem.

But my deployment of this term comes mostly from the Aztecs, for only in the poetry of *flor y canto,* flower and song, was truth, whether provisional or eternal, to be found for the Mesoamericans. In keeping with this discourse, central to the following study is the return of *poesis* as a viable method not only to study and understand the way people attempt to make sense of themselves, others, and religion, but also to do, make, and achieve *religion* itself. Rather than constructing a genealogy of borderlands poetics as a "return" after an absence, in the first chapter I construct it as an instance of the Nietzschean eternal return.

"Religion" is a difficult term to define outside a common "faith" setting (other than academic) with any degree of consensus—and often even then it can prove a devilish task. "We know what religious things are. What distinguishes them from all others," claims Durkheim, "is the way in which they are pictured in people's minds."[56] In short, what I mean by "religion" is often (re)produced by, but not limited to, institutional settings, rigorously defined and explicitly stated "religious movements," or even ancient traditions that have been thought of as "great" or not so great. I also mean the emotional, psychological, physical, spiritual, imaginative, real, dogmatic, ambiguous, semiotic, mystical, mundane, ordered, and disordered stuff that emerges when humans try to make sense—*make history*—out of the fantastic forces of their world, of their *unchosen* conditions.

Religion emerges in memory—bearing out Milan Kundera's famous proposition that the struggle of freedom against oppression is the struggle for memory against forgetting.[57] Memory is the glue that binds together the spiritualities of the borderlands. The colonial enterprise is never a *fait complait,* and the influence of earlier discourses, especially religion, continue to inform the consciousness and lives of social agents. The result has been described by Daniel Cooper Alarcon as the "Aztec Palimpsest," wherein the cultural text serving as the template for identity is continuously erased and reinscribed, but the resulting text and its attendant social formation are a composite of the current inscriptions and the stubborn remnants of what has come before it.[58] Religion in the borderlands is unfolded to long mythical/historical memory, enacted through body and place. But, as Henri Bergson argues, sense stimulation and memory are similarly experienced neurologically and are therefore phenomena belonging to the present more than to the past.[59]

BORDERLAND RELIGION(S):
MEMORY, THE BODY, AND PLACE

Experienced through physicality and the body, memory—knowledge, knowing—as a physical phenomenon is more a matter of present experience than of the time marking the occurrence remembered. Walter Benjamin contends that "memory is not an instrument for exploring the past but its theater." Memory is intensely embodied, and as a result, as Lawrence Sullivan has argued, "The knowledge of the body is central to the history of religions because these physiologies are religiously experienced and religiously expressed." "The study of religion is thus a materialist enterprise," argues Bryan Turner, "since our corporeality is constitutive of our experience of the parody of existence."[60]

For the ancient Aztecs, the human body reproduced cosmology: the body was a microcosm.[61] Moreover, the belief that the body is subject to both debilitating and empowering spiritual forces is an inheritance common to the various traditions in this study.[62] This principle alone (though I discuss many others) is potentially subversive to modernity's power structures, for it reclaims physical self-control and relocates it outside a scientifically vouchsafed language of domination articulated through colonialism, Enlightenment, and modernity. Instead, it is sanctioned by the sacred—that which is both interior to and outside of language. The body connects and divides borderland religions.

But human corporeality exists within a discursive field that controls its maintenance; it has a history, an episteme, and an attendant narrative: in Foucault's words:

> The body is also directly involved in a political playing field; power relations have an immediate hold upon it; they invest it, mark it, train it, torture it, force it to carry out tasks, to perform ceremonies, to emit signs. . . . Its constitution as labour power is possible only if it is caught up in a system of subjection. . . . The body becomes a useful force only it if is both a productive body and a subjected body.[63]

The body was the pivot upon which turned a logic of subjugation prefiguring modernity.

From the earliest European-American encounters, the bodies of the indigenous were thought to signal deprivation and sin; the colonial perspective confused the question of the humanity of the Native Americans. As Charles Long observes, "In the midst of this ambiguity, for better or for worse, [Native Americans'] experiences were rooted in the absurd meaning of their bodies, and it was for these bodies that they were regarded not only as valuable workers but also as the locus of the ideologies that justified their enslavement."[64] Understandings of nonwhite bodies were used to advance strategies of social control, which were thought to exist outside of language, in a state of nature, in a condition prior to language.

When Thomas Jefferson reflected on the presence of Native Americans and Africans in eighteenth-century Virginia, he arrived at the proposition that there are multiple conditions of humanity, determined not only by social and political factors but, more importantly, by "the real distinctions which nature has made . . . which are physical and moral. The first difference which strikes us is that of colour." He says of blacks in particular: "In general, their existence appears to participate more of sensation than reflection. . . . It appears to me that in memory they are equal to whites; in reason much inferior."[65] The meaning of race—its economic and political implications—was determined by linguistic speculation after people had studied differences in "color" and was collectively decided upon by people with access to the determining international conversation: race is a social construction.

Thus, the idea of a social contract that binds together citizens in a democracy is actually better understood as many different contracts between each type of inhabitant and the state. Women, children, men, immigrants, migrants, the poor, the powerful, the weak, Christians, and non-Christians—all with variable physical capacities and forms—are subject to different sets of laws, depending upon their condition at birth and at any given subsequent moment. The racial component of this system has been described as "racialization"—a designation that depends on the grammar of the modern human body.[66]

The social construction of race undercuts the very premise of Enlightenment American conceptions of self and other. By the nineteenth century, argues Ronald Takaki, Euroamericans "were substituting technology for the body"; modern civilization became a process of "dissociating themselves even further from their bodies as they sought to become 'mind' and thus 'perfection.' . . . They set themselves further and further apart from peoples of color, they were directing toward nature and toward Indians, Mexicans, and Asians the violence and 'boisterous passions' that the domination of ascetic rationality had been stoking."[67]

Colonized peoples in the Americas, however, never entirely surrendered control of the body, memory, and place; their control remained partially in the realm of the spiritual. Indeed, as one postcolonial theorist has argued, "In this, its true and essential domain [the spiritual], the nation is already sovereign, even when the state is in the hands of the colonial power. The dynamics of this historical project is completely missed in conventional histories in which the story of nationalism begins with the contest for political power."[68] Religions are shaped and reshaped in the struggle for political power. For Durkheim, "It is not in human nature in general that we must seek the determining causes of religious phenomena; it is in the nature of the societies to which they relate."[69]

Though its analytical and practical tactics are mobile and transferable, religious poetics is a product of the extended history of the borderlands—spiritual advances and returns. Like the myth of La Llorona, symbolic narratives in Chicano culture are continually adapted and shaped to their places—their spatial and temporal locations—to confront, explain, and resolve moral, cognitive, and material issues that might otherwise immobilize movement. La Llorona's children are dead, but despite this "cultural" and "psychic" death, they *haunt* the places that are occupied by Mexican-Americans.[70] In the same way, Mexican-Americans, and especially undocumented immigrants, long overlooked by American institutions—except, of course, by the I.N.S.—exist among the invisible ones of U.S. society, who haunt and persist despite incessant attempts to remove them. If they cannot exist in the realm of the seen, they haunt the unseen, or memory.

Memory is tied to place and to the body: it is enacted through the body—a physical imprint or sensation—when it is triggered by a place. Certainly, claims Benjamin, "just as there are plants . . . [that] confer the power of clairvoyance, so there are places endowed with such power."[71] Structures, odors, and climate impact the body and evoke sensations associated with the original experience. The experience of cities affects the psyche/soul. Benjamin illustrates the power of cultural memory in Berlin: "Here I am talking of a space, of moments and discontinuities. For even if months and years appear here, it is in the form they have at the moment of recollection."[72] This fact, he argues, leads to a powerful form of what Derrida refers to as "possession in memory."[73]

La Llorona is a possession of group memory, a product of a place and a historical experience. Catholic and Protestant children alike are told this tragic tale of Indian memory, the repetition of which orients them not only to the abiding interpretations of the story but to the facts of ethics and religion taught in domestic storytelling. La Llorona is a guiding metaphor in this work, as I have already stated, because she embodies several issues that bear directly upon the attempt to describe and interpret ethnic Mexican religions. First, of course, is the theme of death itself, which (as in many religions) is central to many Chicana/o and *mexicana/o* religious traditions. La Llorona's children are deceased but vivid spiritual actors who motivate and perform religious improvisation and change—a religious poetics. In the following pages I encounter La Llorona's children and witness to having glimpsed them. I hope that others will have similar visions.[74]

CHAPTER I

The Terror
of Postcolonial History

Eternal Returns in the Borderlands

Does man possess any truth?
If not, our song is no longer true.
Is anything stable and lasting?
What reaches its aim?

> Nehuactoactl (1402–72), Aztec
> poet, warrior, and sage, quoted in
> Miguel León-Portilla, *Aztec
> Thought and Culture: A Study of
> the Ancient Nahuatl Mind*, trans.
> Jack Emory Davis

In ancient Mesoamerica, philosophers, the *tlamatinime,* who were both wise men and women and poets, made questions of truth, existence, and the nature of the cosmos and of the self central to their conceptual architecture of the Americas. And yet, despite its geography and chronology, the penetrating thought of Mesoamericans is deemed irrelevant to discourses on "Western philosophy." The discursive male Godhead brought by the Renaissance Spanish to Mesomerica did not discover empty and fertile religious soil to germinate. Instead, the Aztec religious terrain was drenched in complex and ancient tradition: the philosophy of Mesoamerica thrived in a rich environment and continued to evolve once the Spanish covered Aztec worldviews with Christian veneer. *Tlamatinime* debated religion with their European conquerors and did not accept the singularity of Christianity, even officially, until more than a century after contact.

This chapter adumbrates a selected genealogy of religious poetics—from Mesoamerica to the borderlands—by asking how, in what ways, and to what extent, the gods and goddesses of ancient Mexico fell victim to the Christian sword. What are the origins of religious practices in their extant forms? And, intimately related to this question, what are the limits of colonial religious powers? How completely can a colonial religious system replace a former system? What are the historical and material conditions that enable religious practice to emerge?

Rather than conceive of these issues as "syncretism," "dissimulation," or a singular conversion, I propose multiple, continuing, inchoate, and progressive "conversions." "Colonialism was a dialogue," claims Ramón Gutiérrez, "not a monologue."[1] Inasmuch as Catholicism changed Mexico, so too Mexico changed Catholicism—another sort of conversion. A key to the reading of religion throughout what we now designate as Mexico and the U.S. Southwest is understanding that previously accepted assumptions about even formal, if not essential, superficial Christianization of natives must be regarded suspiciously and interrogated. J. Jorge Klor de Alva charts colonial conversions to Christianity on a continuum ranging from rejection to belief, most falling in the middle, ranging between "accommodation" and "resistance." But in traditional Mesoamerican scholarship, writes Klor de Alva, "the acceptance of some external Christian forms has been seen as tantamount to conversion; the integration of Christian values and world views [has] been taken for granted."[2]

The impossibility of documenting spiritual resistance does not make it possible to conclude, solely on the authority of texts, that the poetic-religious philosophy of the *tlamatinime* was eradicated by Christianity. Gloria Anzaldúa puts forth the following proposition:

> The religion of the Mexicans—Catholicism—is just a veneer. I don't know with white people, but with Mexicans it's a veneer for the old gods and goddesses. People only go to church, believe in Christ, and eat the host because that was happening in the Aztec religion: they ate the flesh of the sacrificial victim. If you eat part of a bear, you become fierce like a bear. That's what I meant about Catholicism being loose: it allows other religions to survive and it builds in the sacred places of the older religions.[3]

Both Anzaldúa and Klor de Alva conclude that the colonial situation engendered a condition described as *nepantla,* an Aztec term, originally from the Nahuatl language, for the land of the "in between." One of the earliest recorded examples of *nepantla* was described by Renaissance Franciscan ethnographer Fray Diego Dúran. He expressed great dismay at the practices of his "converts," who, according to his records, continued their indigenous traditions together with those of the colonizer: "Once I questioned an Indian regarding certain [religious] things . . . and he answered, 'Father, do not be astonished; we are still *nepantla.*' "[4] Miguel León-Portilla has defined *nepantlaism,* in the words of Klor de Alva, "as that situation in which a person remains suspended in the middle between a lost or disfigured past and a present that has not been assimilated or understood."[5]

Anzaldúa defines *nepantlaism* as "an Aztec word meaning torn between ways," a condition that she says is central to *la mestiza,* a woman of mixed Indian and Spanish ancestry who "is a product of the transfer of the cultural and spiritual values of one group to another. . . . Cradled in one culture, sandwiched between two cultures, straddling all three cultures and their value systems, *la mestiza* undergoes a struggle of flesh, a struggle of borders, an inner war."[6] Rudy Busto writes, "I would like to consider the idea of *nepantla* religion as a way to illuminate the predicaments that have dogged U.S. Latino cultures and religions . . . *nepantla* . . . as the root element *nepan-* conveys a sense of mutuality or reciprocity."[7]

The world in which the Aztecs lived, which was divided into at least twelve levels, reflected the concept of *nepantla:* The upper levels, known as *omeyocan,* consisted of several distinctions; and the lower layers, or "under" world, *mictlan,* was also divided into many layers of life. The Aztec plane, *nepantla,* was in the middle. It was, as a result, a product and producer of the other realms—as it was the mediative space between beings who occupied the territories above and below. In light of the colonial religious field, the condition of *nepantla* describes that paradoxical place that is in neither the world of pre-Hispanic traditions nor entirely the religious world of the Hispanic, but is in both at once. Klor de Alva cautions, however, "*Nepantlaism* should not be confused with syncretism, which is, in both a historical and a psychological sense, the consequence of *nepantlaism* when it is resolved under conditions that make a full conversion [to Christianity] impossible."[8]

Spaces of resistance remained *nepantla,* especially the women's sphere. As June Nash argues:

> The Spanish conquest reinforced the gendered division of labor and subordination of women in New Spain that had begun in the conquest states of Middle America. The heritage of conquest for women was the burden and responsibility for providing the basic needs of the conquerors as well as their own families. This ensured the greater survival of elements of women's culture related to domesticity in the supernatural as well as the mundane world.

Though women under Aztec rule did not assume political leadership positions, a right they had held under the previous Toltec rule, Nash argues that they nonetheless "possessed property and rights within the *calpulli* [community] organization. They were curers as well as priestesses. Their skills in weaving and pottery provided basic metaphors for talking about creative forces."[9]

"Full conversion" to Christianity would be possible only if natives could grasp the singularity of Christianity, an idea inimical to the traditions of the Aztec empire, which built upon older traditions and were progressive at their core, not exclusive. Overall, the Aztecs' view of the cosmos emphasized the principles of movement and return.

OLLIN: EL QUINTO SOL (MOVEMENT: THE FIFTH SUN)

The ancient Nahuas, too, held that the world was in constant cycles of regeneration and movement. In patterns of motion the Nahuas addressed their destiny. They believed that four temporal periods of life had existed prior to the Aztecs, whose period, the fifth—during which they erected grand cities and colonized millions—was destined to end in catastrophe as the previous four had.

According to the Aztec "cosmogonic myth," writes León-Portilla, "there had been four historical ages, called suns." These eras corresponded to the four elements—earth, wind, fire, and water—and each of them had ended in cataclysmic destruction. "The present epoch was that of the Sun of Movement, *Ollintonatiuh*."[10] It was only through the movement of the Sun that the totality of life forces was pushed in its relentless revolution. The "cyclical evolution of the foundations of the world" was an organizing paradigm for the Nahuas. León-Portilla writes: "The earth, created by Ometéotl, is not static, it is ever moving. Subjected to the influence of the cosmic forces, it becomes the field of action for these forces. When there is an equilibrium of forces, an age or Sun exists."[11] The instability and uncertainty that drove Aztec thought was expressed through their myths, poetry, and sacrifices. Davíd Carrasco has demonstrated how "cosmic order and destiny" were maintained by the Aztecs in their ritual sacrifices. Human blood was necessary to mitigate the cosmic forces, reenact the primordial moment of creation (through sacrifice), and regenerate the cosmos, all to stave off the destruction of their present era of the fifth sun, the sun of movement.[12]

The Nahuatl poetic trope and symbol to represent development was *ollin*, movement, part of a continuous loop. Mayan and Aztec calendars represented the dual ideas of progress and return. Tzvetan Todorov explains, "Among the Mayas and Aztecs . . . the cycle prevails over linearity: there is a succession within the month, the year, or the 'cluster' of years; but these latter, rather than being situated in a linear chronology, are repeated exactly from one to the next. There are differences within each sequence, but one sequence is identical with the next, and none is situated in an absolute time."[13] Nahua thought made central the idea that death is necessary for rebirth and regeneration: the Nahuas held a conceptualization of life that made spiritual and material revival necessary for the full circular rotation of cosmic existence.

Questions of the cosmos, truth, life, and death flourished in Mesoamerica, especially in the twelfth century, during the reign of the Mayan civilization based in the Yucatán region of southern Mexico. This era, known as the "classical period" of the Mesoamerican world, witnessed the burgeoning of several poetic movements. The idea of movement captivated the ancient Mesoamerican world and, as in ancient Greece, in Mesoamerican philosophy this idea was partly based on empirical, observable laws of stasis and movement, natural elements, sensations, and especially the human body.

In fact, within the arts of speech and poetics, discourses of truth and certainty dominated. One argued that truth on earth is elusive, that destiny may be scripted or random but positive knowing is beyond the realm of the living condition, and that to strive after veracity is futile. Truth, therefore, was an illusion; reality, for many, was a dream state of obfuscation in which only fleeting moments of truth were possible. Death, then, awakened consciousness to reality. Most of the elders held that life was a dream and that death, paradoxically, was awakening. León-Portilla classifies the following Nahuatl lamentation under the category "The Thought of the Sages":

> although it be Jade, although it be gold,
> it too must go to the place of the fleshless.
> It too must go to the region of mystery;
> we all perish,
> no one will remain!

> We came only to be born.
> Our home is beyond:
> In the realm of the defleshed ones.
> I suffer:
> Happiness, good fortune never comes my way.
> Have I come here to struggle in vain?
> This is not the place to accomplish things.
> Certainly nothing grows green here:
> Misfortune opens its blossoms.

> It is true that we leave, truly we part,
> We leave the flowers, the songs, and the earth.[14]

Death was necessary for the soul's movement, which, for the Nahuas, included movements between the levels of earth, underworld, and sky; and, of course, the movement and regeneration of the cosmic forces. Poetic thought and verse captured the idea of these movements. According to many of the wise elderly statesmen and women, or *tlamatinime*, truth emerges in poetry: flower and song—*flor y canto*. There is truth in beauty, and certainty in suffering. Flower and song, according to León-Portilla, allegorized "nature" and "personality." Epistemology consisted in a rendering of the incongruity of the cosmos as a hopeless dissonant duality of flower and song: thus, duality and dissonance, or what the Nahuas called *difrasismo*, was at their religious-philosophical base. The term *difrasismo* described the philosophical quest for explanation, religious poetics, but was used also as a metaphor for poetry or poem.

The qualities of *difrasismo* and duality were structured into the Aztec cosmology, particularly in the supreme being, Ometéotl. León-Portilla explains: "Behind the apparent confusion of the entire Nahuatl pantheon, was the ever present Ometéotl. . . . In their quest for a symbol, through 'flower and song,' what might lead them to comprehend the origin of all things and the mysterious nature of an invisible and intangible creator, the *tlamatinime* conceived the most profound of all their '*difrasismos*,' [Ometéotl] Lord and Lady of duality."[15] In its singularly progenitor forms, Ometéotl was Omecihuatl and Ometecuhtli. Hence, conceptions of the sacred embodied the Aztec predicament of *nepantla*: the root of the name Ometéotl comes from the word *omeyotization*, which means "dualization." The binary gender of the primary divinity is a *difrasismo* poetic.

Religious forms emergent during various periods of colonialism and nationalism (and into the present day) are largely continuations of *difrasismo* poetics that reimagine and rework conceptions of space, time, and the body. When the Aztecs encountered and conquered other tribes, they aggregated the religious artifacts they discovered into their own cosmology; religious change responded to the inevitable vicissitudes of quotidian life. This practice continued when the Aztecs themselves were colonized, creating what Carrasco identifies as "jaguar Christians." He writes: "Religious change never occurs in a void. Albeit no religion is ever simply a static, given monolith, it is however true that the past, rooted, shared traditions of a given religion carry an important weight: they furnish the chief ingredients to be reworked and transformed in the processes of religious change; they circumscribe and somewhat steer the efforts toward innovation; they narrow and restrict the possibilities of reformation."[16]

MANIFEST DESTINY ZERO: THE MISSION

First contact between the Spanish leader Hernán Cortéz and the Indians was akin to a collision of planets: contact engendered numerous questions and responses from both parties, the experience of what Stephen Greenblatt calls "wonder" in the practice of colonization. Such a response exists outside of language and disorients all involved. The Spanish conquistadores were able to resolve the dilemma only through possession: "To wonder is to experience both the failure of words—the stumbling recourse to the old chivalric fables—and the failure of vision, since seeing brings no assurance that the objects of sight actually exist. The assurance comes rather from violence."[17] The Spanish attempted to understand their "others" by figuring them into extant medieval and Renaissance myths; among other European impositions, for example, natives were figured as the twelve lost tribes of Israel.[18] Both the Spanish and the Indians engaged in what Greenblatt calls "the assimilation of the other." For the Indians, such conceptual assimilation yielded tragic consequences.

Many Mexican natives assimilated the arrival of Cortéz and his troops into their own cosmology as perhaps the grandest of all returns in Aztec society, narrated through the poems, myths, and histories of Quetzalcoatl, of which there are many variations.[19] The "irony" of Aztec history, as Carrasco puts it, is that in 1519, some Nahuas believed that Cortéz was Quetzalcoatl, a returning *hombre-dios*, or divine-human king. It was taught that a great Toltec priest-king named Quetzalcoatl was banned from an earlier civilization, but he was prophesied to return during the calendar year One Reed—which coincided exactly with Cortéz's landing on the shores of what is now central Mexico![20] Cortéz capitalized on the confusion, and by the time the Aztecs learned of his deception it was too late: Tenochtitlán, the Aztec imperial capital and sacred city, was already destined to fall to a powerful alliance, formed by Cortéz, that included over ten thousand indigenous warriors.

When Christian colonizers later heard tales of Quetzalcoatl in exile, they speculated that he might have been Christ or Saint Thomas. These colonizers claimed that the similarities between Quetzalcoatl and Christian holy men were uncanny, including physical characteristics and messages of redemption and return.[21] Another remarkable similarity was in the blood: the colonizers saw a parallel between blood from Quetzalcoatl's penis and that from Christ's stigmata—now depicted in Mexican popular art as originating within the groin of the penitent Christ.[22] Periodically, during the last five centuries, Mexicans have claimed that Quetzalcoatl was soon to return and restore the spiritual and political excellence of the ancient Toltecs. In fact, some indigenous peoples believed that the Pope's visits to Mexico are camouflaged returns of the Feathered Serpent, Quetzalcoatl.

Nash reports that still today for the indigenous of Mexico, "Linked with the Virgin of Guadalupe is Saint Thomas, who in turn is identified with Quetzalcoatl. The coupling of the Christian Virgin of Guadalupe and Saint Thomas invoked the Lord and Lady of Duality, who were identified with the submerged macehualtin, or commoners, not with the elites, whose gods were toppled along with their empire."[23] That is, the subaltern realm of nonofficial religious practices sheltered symbols and narratives and thus protected them from the fatal Christian sword of the colonizers.

Spanish attempts to incorporate the Indians into European cosmology had special concern for the matter of Indian souls. Initially during the colonial period, the Church's authority over colonial subjects, Indians particularly, proved a weighty matter of debate. Spaniards debated whether Indians possessed souls, whether they were fully human—if they were capable of "reason," of becoming *gente de razón,* people of Christian reason, in Spanish classificatory systems—and whether they could therefore participate in Christian salvation. If not, then the Spaniards could "justifiably" enslave the Indians based on an interpretation of Aristotelian theories of master/slave relations.[24] The Indians found their champion in Fray Bartolomé de las Casas, proponent of Indian salvation. His opponent, Juan Ginés de Sepulveda, argued that Indians were "natural slaves."

The fiery polemic between these two sides climaxed in an audience before the Spanish king in Valladolid during the years 1550–51. Bartolomé de las Casas argued that, during the forty years of colonization, "in truth, I believe without trying to deceive myself that the number of slain is . . . fifteen million." De las Casas does not attribute the genocide to the conquerors' desire to spread Christianity:

> [The Spanish] reason for killing and destroying such an infinite number of souls is that the Christians have an ultimate aim, which is to acquire gold and to swell themselves with riches in a very brief time and thus rise to a high estate disproportionate to their merits. It should be kept in mind that

their insatiable greed and ambition, the greatest ever seen in the world, is the cause of their villainies. And also, those lands are so rich and felicitous, the native peoples so meek and patient, so easy to subject, that our Spaniards have no more consideration for them than beasts. And I say this from my own knowledge for the acts I witnessed. But I should not say "than beasts" for, thanks be to God, they have treated beasts with some respect. I should say instead like excrement on the public square.[25]

In the end, Indians were thought of as a simpler form of humanity, in need of paternal Christian care. It was decided, as Todorov puts it, that the Indians were "inferior beings, halfway between men and beasts. Without this essential premise, the destruction could not have taken place."[26] Figuring the Indians in this way justified what Enrique Dussel calls "an irrational praxis of violence." At the core of this "mythical" legitimizing discourse is a process wherein "as the civilizing mission produces a wide array of victims, its corollary violence is understood as an inevitable action, one with a quasi-ritual character of sacrifice."[27]

But already by 1514, in the document known as Requerimiento ("Summons"), the rules for taking Indian lands had been established, following the mandates of the Patronato Real, or powers of "royal patronage," granted by the pope and claimed by the Spanish crown through divine right. The Requerimiento supposedly protected Indians if they accepted the authority of Christ, Saint Peter, the pope, and the Spanish crown, respectively. If not, they could be enslaved through the *encomienda* ("commission"), empowering Spanish to collect tribute from lands that remained in native hands. The *repartimiento* ("delivery") allowed Spaniards to benefit from compulsory Indian labor.[28] Throughout the seventeenth and eighteenth centuries, Christianized Indians were herded onto Spanish missions, which functioned, in effect, as forced-labor camps. Early in the conquest, the compulsory movement of Indians into European spatial arrangements was called the *congregación;* that is, the process of congregating Indians in spaces of European design, under Church control, to nurture their volatile salvation.

But even well after the conquest, Indians questioned and rejected Spanish attempts at religious, social, and political order. Colonial ethnographers recorded several examples of Indian resistance; de las Casas observed: "Not once but many times a Spaniard would ask an Indian if he was a Christian, and the Indian would reply: 'Yes, sir, I am a bit Christian because I have learned to lie a bit; another day I will lie big, and I will be a big Christian.' "[29] One of the best-known and earliest Indian revolts occurred among the Pueblo peoples of New Mexico in 1680. The

Spanish reconquered them in 1692, and this event, known as the Re-
conquista, is still commemorated today in a religiously and politically
contested ceremony.[30] But the New Mexico Indian revolt itself is instructive, for it was religiously and politically motivated, organized by
holy men, and directed against the Franciscans: Christian icons were
profaned—destroyed and smeared with feces.[31] Pedro Naranjo, an
eighty-year-old man who was a native of the San Felipe pueblo, the
Queres nation, was a participant in the revolt. He testified before the
Franciscans:

> Asked for what reason they so blindly burned the images, temples, crosses,
> and other things of divine worship, he stated that the Indian, Popé, came
> down in person, and with him El Saca and El Chato from the pueblo of Los
> Taos, and other captains and leaders and many people who were in his
> train, and he ordered in all the pueblos through which he passed that they
> instantly break up and burn the images of the Holy Christ, the Virgin Mary
> and the other saints, the crosses, and everything pertaining to Christianity,
> and that they burn the temples, break up the bells, and separate from the
> wives whom God had given them in marriage and take those whom they
> desired. In order to take away their baptismal names, the water, and the
> holy oils, they were to plunge into the rivers and wash themselves with
> amole, which is a root native to the country, washing even their clothing,
> with the understanding that there would thus be taken from them the char-
> acter of the holy sacraments.[32]

One hundred and thirty years later, the Indians of central Mexico
staged a holy war of a different kind—led by a priest and intended to
crown their *mestiza* goddess, Guadalupe, as Queen of Mexico: the Mexican War of Independence (1810–21). The next chapter revisits this
episode in some detail, including the central role of La Virgen de
Guadalupe, but the resistance manifested in that war began percolating
years earlier. William Taylor reports:

> At first in isolated instances and then throughout central and western Mex-
> ico, the Virgin of Guadalupe became attached to an idea of millennial re-
> conquest. . . . In a regional Indian uprising . . . in 1769, the leaders called
> for the death of Spanish bishops and the creation of an Indian priest-hood.
> . . . The leader of their theocratic utopia called himself the New Savior, and
> his consort was known as the Virgin of Guadalupe.[33]

Taylor further reports that during the eighteenth century it was not uncommon for Indians to violently attack priests—indicating, for Taylor, if
not a rejection of the Church, then certainly an eschewing of Christian-

ity as mediated by the priests and a fragmentary acceptance of Christian images on indigenous terms.

The expulsion of the Jesuits from New Spain in 1767, and, after the Louisiana Purchase of 1803, the westward encroachment of the French and Russians onto what Spain had claimed as its northern frontier, necessitated Mexico City's northward expansion. Spanish expansion occurred largely through the mission efforts of the Franciscan Order, and migration to California took place initially as a movement from south to north. Father Junípero Serra (1713–84), now prominent in official California mythology and currently in the beatification stage of canonization in the Catholic Church, headed the missionization of California until his death. In 1769, the first Alta California (now the state of California) Catholic church and mission was founded in San Diego. By 1846, the time of the American invasion of northern Mexico, there were twenty-one missions stretching from San Diego to Sonoma (slightly southwest of Sacramento). The mission movement, as opposed to permanent parishes, was California's first official introduction to Catholicism. Spain originally planned to convert the missions to parishes and give Indians half of the mission land, with the provision that they could not sell it. This ambition, however, was never fully realized.

"Conversion" of the Indians at the missions was dubious; many Indians escaped the missions, continued practicing their old religions, or simply died at the hands of the Spanish. Officially, individual Native Americans were only to be attached to the missions for ten years, but the actual time of the commitment proved much longer. Howard Lamar asks rhetorically, "Was the American West and the Western frontier more properly a symbol of bondage than freedom when it came to labor systems?"[34]

Although exact numbers are not available, demographers have widely accepted that at the time of Spanish settlement of California, 310,000 native inhabitants lived there. This figure is much higher than the first Spanish census enumerations.[35] During the missionization period, the nonindigenous population of California, according to the census counts, was small but increasing: California had approximately 900 residents in 1790, 2,000 in 1810, and 3,500 by 1821. This population, like Spanish colonial society itself, was highly racialized. Census data from the colonial period indicate a *calidad,* or condition, for each of its residents: Spanish, *mestizo*, mulatto, Indio, Coyote, Negro, Morisco (Spanish Moor), and Pardo.

According to the foundational myth of Los Angeles, on 2 August 1769 Spaniards Father Serra and the explorer Visitador José Galvez, accompanied by a team of Indians and soldiers, camped near an Alta California river, naming it El Río de Nuestra Señora la Reina de los Angeles de Porciúncula (River of Our Lady Queen of the Angels of Portiuncula). Later, the city was to be known by two words, "the Angels." In 1781, California's governor, Felipe de Neve, dispatched a settlement to California from Mexico City that included forty-four civilians and four soldiers, eleven families in all. The racial composition of this group was eight mulattos, nine Indians, two Negroes, one *mestizo*, and one Chino (Spanish for Chinese).[36]

The unwelcoming desert separating California from Mexico City made traveling north difficult, and settlement in California was slow in spite of the generous land grants parceled out by the Spanish government. Thus, Mexico City began exiling teams of people to California between the years 1791 and 1846. These expeditions were comprised of Mexico City's rejects: prison convicts and orphans. These *pobladores,* or settlers of the pueblos, were the earliest nonnative, nonmilitary, and nonreligious occupants of southern California. The Spanish military fortresses, *presidios,* and the large *ranchos* rounded out the institutional presence in colonial California. Spanish soldiers were instructed to populate California. They were offered large plots of land and were encouraged to exploit Indian labor. In this way, many formerly impoverished Spanish military men accumulated vast fortunes. It is from this newly enfranchised, elite *ranchero* class, the "Californios," that the myths of Spanish frontier California are drawn: there were six *ranchos* during Spanish California (1769–1821), and approximately two hundred developed during the Mexican years. Each segment of mission California (1769–1834) depended on the others for survival: The *rancheros* depended on the goods produced by the missions, the protection of the *presidios,* and the labor of the Indians. The missions depended on trade with the *rancheros* and especially with the *presidios,* as well as Indian labor. The *presidios* would have been unable to function had it not been for the manufactured goods and foodstuffs produced by the missions. And all, in turn, depended on Indian work.

The Indians experienced the attempted conversion of California as profound reorientations of space, time, and bodies. Following the disruption of indigenous life ways, the monks' strategy to convert the Indians consisted of offering them basic enticements, including food, shelter, and Christian salvation, while waiting for the Indians to enlist themselves in the service of the missions. However, the "waiting game," as Roberto Lint-Sagarena notes, "was a rather inefficient means for the conversion of a territory the size of Alta California. These milder methods soon gave way to quicker and more violent means. Conversion soon went from somewhat voluntary . . . to physical coercion (beatings, abduction, and murder). This transition didn't take long."[37] Douglas Monroy has forcefully illuminated the differences between Indian and European patterns of work and play, especially as these were individually and culturally embodied.[38] The Indians were connected physically to the rhythms of nature—working steadily during planting and harvesting seasons and tending the crops at other times. Pueblo tribes throughout the Southwest had developed similar temporal, spatial, and physical rhythms. Gutiérrez has noted the design of the New Mexico pueblo, which consisted of a series of concentric circles, the innermost being the *kiva,* or sacred space, which was enveloped by the space of fertility— women, family, and crops—and the outermost sphere, which was the place of hunting, warfare, and danger.[39] This design was in direct contrast to Spanish colonial architecture, whose blueprint expressed the purpose of converting the Indians into *gente de razón.* Reducing the Indian "heathendom," instructed a representative of the Spanish crown in 1768, required: "First, the Indians 'must no longer live vagrant in the mountains,' . . . to be *de razón* they must be 'reduced socially into arranged pueblos' because concentrated thus, 'the Christian religion will establish itself in their hearts.' " Monroy notes that for Indians to internalize and learn "European ways of production [and consumption], it was of utmost importance for schedules and clocks to guide their labors."[40]

Mission San Gabriel, twelve miles east of present downtown Los Angeles, was one of the most prosperous in all of southern California. At the time of the death of Father Serra, it housed 1,019 neophytes. By the time of California's Mexican period in 1821, Mission San Gabriel was a lucrative enterprise, owing especially to neophyte labor. In 1826, the mission was visited by two American explorers with Indian guides. One of the Americans, Harrison Rogers, recorded the lavish way in which he and his American colleague were treated by the friars, but his Indian guides, meanwhile, were imprisoned. He describes the layout of the mission:

> 4 rows of houses forming a complete square, where there is [*sic*] all kinds of macanicks at work; the church faces the east and the guard house the west; the N. and S. line comprises the work shops. They have large vineyards, apple and peach orchards, and some orange and some fig trees. They manu-

facture blankets, and sundry other articles; they distill whiskey and grind their own grain, having a water mill, of a tolerable quality; they have upwards of 1,000 persons employed, men, women, and children, Inds. [Indians] of different nations. The situation is very handsome. . . . and this mission has upwards of 30,000 head of cattle, and horses, sheep, hogs, etc., in proportion. . . . They slaughter at this place from 2 to 3,000 head of cattle at a time; the mission lives on the profits.[41]

Neophytes who escaped from the missions would be hunted down, returned to the missions, and punished by beatings. Rogers recounts a disciplinary incident catalyzed by some Indians' refusal to work on 10 December of the same year:

Sunday. There was five Inds. [Indians] brought to the mission by two other Inds, who act as constables, or overseers, and sentenced to be whiped [sic] for not going to work when ordered. Each received from 12 to 14 lashes on their bare posteriors; they were all old men, say from 50 to 60 years of age, the commandant standing by with his sword to see that the Ind who flogged them had done his duty. Things in other respects similar to the last sabbath.[42]

Carey McWilliams notes the uncanny symmetry between California and the southern United States during the same period: "The Indians were the slaves, the gente de razón were the plantation owners or 'whites,' and the Mexicans [mestizos] . . . were the poor whites."[43]

In 1834, Californians received the edict to secularize the missions and to distribute the land among the Indians. Instead, Pio Pico, the governor of California, "sold off the last of the mission lands in 1845 and 1846 to his compañeros. The missions were transubstantiated into ranchos, Indians and all."[44] Once again in California, the ownership of the means of production changed hands but racialized work patterns remained in place.

MANIFEST DESTINY ONE:
THE PROTESTANT/CAPITALIST MISSION

Narratives appropriated from Hebrew scriptures, describing "election" and the "Promised Land," prompted Protestants to usurp what is now the eastern United States during the seventeenth and eighteenth centuries, a pattern that also manifested as discourses of "divine right" when Euroamericans took their destiny west, to northern Mexico.[45] Diatribes against Mexicans and Indians charged that fertile land was being wasted that could otherwise be put to good use in industrial, modern, white hands. One of the best known of these claims was penned by Harvard undergraduate Richard Henry Dana, who in 1835 visited California as a seaman on leave from his studies. His notes from the voyage, *Two Years before the Mast,* fueled the fires of American continental consumption: Dana's narrative was wrought with contempt for the people he encountered in California. "The Californians are an idle, thriftless people," he wrote in disgust, "and can make nothing for themselves." Dana, however, admired the aesthetic qualities of the Californio *mexicanos,* which seemed lamentably foreign to the Protestant New Englander. He exclaimed, "In fact, they [Californios] sometimes appeared to me to be people on whom a curse had fallen, and stripped them of everything but their pride, their manners, and their voices."[46]

Hubert Howe Bancroft, a nineteenth-century historian of colonial California, describes the *mexicano* population of California in highly racialized terms, "halfway between savagism and civilization . . . a race halfway between the proud Castilian and the lowly root-digger of the Coast Range valleys."[47] These representations were accented by nineteenth-century anti-Catholic sentiments. The priests, Bancroft writes,

> possessed little learning or intelligence, and this little they devoted to the crushing and plundering of their people. They were dissolute and unscriptural, fatherly in too literal a sense, bringing too much of heaven to earth as if such is the kingdom of heaven; and loving . . . the water of life, more than the bread of life. For the laity, they were the largest order of animals then known, as well as the dirtiest; a people wholly lying in wickedness and lacking soap. They were supercilious, yet ignorant and superstitious, and full of beastly habits.[48]

Californio society was class-stratified; the *ranchero* class controlled land and natural resources, while the lower classes worked as artisans, shop owners, and ranch hands. Bancroft makes no distinction with respect to race and class, however, but only describes degrees of religious piety. "Indeed, among the more pious life was one continuous petition, or series of petitions, to the almighty powers for favors desired, and calamities to be averted. The most insignificant of everyday affairs were referred to the manager of the universe, to be passed upon and adjusted."[49] This echoes the sentiments of one of the priests in Mexico two centuries earlier. When describing the *abusos* of the Indians, the colonial priest remarked in dismay: "There is nothing for which someone does not pray."[50] The spirit of religious poetics, which involves God in the details, was nurtured from this condition—*nepantlaism*—halfway between the Spanish and Indian, between Catholicism and indigenous religions.

Westward expansion and colonization was not only racialized but gendered. Antonia Castañeda has shown how California's women were more likely to be associated with Spanish *qua* pure Spanish civilization and thus held up as the standard-bearers of civilization on the frontier. Their male counterparts, however, were dismissed outright as "mongrels," Mexican and savage. Castañeda uncovers a poem published in Boston in 1846:

THEY WAIT FOR US

The Spanish maid, with eyes of fire
At balmy evening turns her lyre,
And looking to the Eastern sky,
Awaits our Yankee Chivalry
Whose purer blood and valiant arms,
Are fit to clasp her budding charms.

The *man,* her mate, is sunk in sloth—
To love, his senseless heart is loth;
The pipe and glass and tinkling lute,
A sofa, and a dish of fruit;
A nap some dozen times a day;
Sombre and sad, and never gay.[51]

In fact, marriage between Mexican California women and Yankee settlers was not uncommon, as the newly invented Californio class seized the opportunity that the American presence occasioned to further distinguish themselves from the more common Mexicans.

Generally, sentiment regarding the U.S. colonists was divided along class lines, the lower castes feeling greater solidarity with Mexico. The first Yankee shots of war against the Californios galvanized many at different socioeconomic levels, but still some of the elite assisted the Anglo-Americans in their conquest. At the first instance of U.S. military action, Governor Pico issued a decree intended to congeal Mexican loyalties: "This is the most unjust aggression of late centuries undertaken by a nation which is ruled by the most unheard-of ambition. . . . [The Americans] formed the project of authorizing robbery without disguising it with the slightest shame."[52]

In 1848, Mexico and the United States signed the Treaty of Guadalupe Hidalgo, which ceded California and the states now referred to as the U.S. Southwest, including parts of Colorado and Wyoming, for 1.5 million dollars. At the time of the U.S. invasion,

Catholicism in California was in a disordered transformation: from a Franciscan mission system, nationalized and in decline, to a more permanent parish system.

MANIFEST DESTINY TWO: THE MISSION (CONTINUED)

In 1836 the Mexican congress officially approved the request for a discrete California diocese that would stretch from San Diego to Monterey. Concomitant to the creation of a separate diocese, the Mexican government ejected Spanish clergy and began replacing them with Mexicans. The bishop of both Californias, Francisco Garcia Diego y Moreno, a Franciscan named as bishop in 1840, reached Santa Barbara, the seat of his new diocese, in 1842. At that time there were only seventeen Franciscans in the entire state. Bishop Diego y Moreno died in 1846, but not before opening the seminary of Our Lady of Guadalupe near Santa Barbara. He actively recruited Mexicans for the seminary, and he saw six of them ordained. For lack of administrative interest, Our Lady of Guadalupe Seminary closed its doors in 1861. After the brief revival of California Catholicism generated by Diego y Moreno, the Church in southern California declined steadily—especially during and as a result of American military aggression.

In 1847, in the midst of the U.S. invasion of California, a representative of the queen of England lamented the plight of the Catholic Church:

> The clergy of California consists of six Franciscan friars, and four curates ordained by the late Bishop Garcia Diego; and with this very limited number of pastors, who in one single place only, dedicate their attention to the religious instruction of their flock, Your Reverence will readily perceive how deplorably prostrate must be the state of intellect and how mortifying must be the feelings of enlightened Catholics to see the pure and divine doctrine of Christ so neglected.[53]

By the time the American military usurpation of California was complete in 1848, there were only sixteen priests (eleven Franciscans and five regular) in the diocese, and only three to serve all of southern California. Of these few, Jonathan Stevenson, a colonel in the American army hailing from New York, wrote as follows:

> There is but one who appears to render any service whatever, and his character is so notoriously profligate that his influence and respect is entirely gone; he is a Spaniard, old and somewhat infirm and has been 29 years in this country, his name is Blaz Ordaz. The other, Antonio Rosales, quite a young man and well educated, but constantly sick (Hypochondriac) and

confined to his house, these are the only officiating Priests from this to some two hundred miles below. The other, José Maria Jimenez is also a young man of unsteady mind and constantly urging the people of the country to resort to violent measures to rid themselves of the American authorities.[54]

Isolation from official centers and curators of Catholicism allowed for a community-based devotion to flourish in California and throughout the Southwest.

Consequently, what emerged was a religion based in medieval Spanish ritual, the apotheosis of the Virgin Mary, and devotion to the saints, all of which had been transported to Mexico from Spain prior to the reforms initiated by the Council of Trent (1545–63).[55] Indigenous traditions, not so unlike medieval Spanish Catholicism, were characterized by a philosophy that separated life forces into good and evil, a rich pantheon of gods and goddesses, pilgrimage, devotion, prayer, healing, apocalyptic narratives, salvation dramas, and myths of return.[56] California Indians helped shape the cultural arrangements of Mexicans and also informed "Christian" culture. Indians taught colonists "their foods, medicines, games, and languages. . . . By 1850, through the processes of missionization, secularization, intermarriage, adoption, and employment, remnants of the local Indian way of life had become a living part of the Hispanic culture of Los Angeles."[57]

At the close of 1850, recruitment of priests from Europe and Oregon boosted the total number of Catholic clergymen in California to thirty-five. However, the number of Mexican priests in California dwindled thereafter, until in 1856 only one remained; most of them had died, but others had returned to Mexico. According to the 1850 census, Los Angeles County had a population of 1,610, of which 85.3 percent were classified as Mexican natives, 9.6 percent U.S.-born, and 4.2 percent European. By 1880, Mexicans accounted for 25.6 percent of the California population, Mexican-Americans 19.4 percent, Euroamericans 38.7 percent, and 16.3 percent were "other."[58] Catholics were counted as 21,000 people, with 39 priests, of whom 12 had "Spanish surnames." Although Catholic and Protestant numbers in California by 1880 were virtually even, Protestants had control of the major institutions. In 1930, Los Angeles was a metropolis of 1,283,000 people, among whom 301,775 Catholics were served by 490 priests. Of these priests, 59, or 12 percent, had Spanish surnames, which is a significant decline from the nearly one-third of priests who had Spanish surnames in 1880.[59] In 1967, 1,640,167 Catholics were counted in Los Angeles; they were served by 1,496 priests, of whom 108—or 7.2 percent—had Spanish surnames. The data show a marked decline in the percentage of priests with Spanish surnames serving Mexican-American communities since the U.S. conquest of California.

The American Catholic Church that inherited California as an orphan charge was suffering its own crisis in the late nineteenth century. The ancient aesthetics and doctrines of Catholicism seemed alien to a land that was only beginning to invent its history, imagining itself as a civilization that surpassed the monarchism of European institutions. In 1850, the "Know Nothing" party crystallized these sentiments, accusing Catholics of antidemocratic Republican values. In his *Syllabus of Errors* (1864), Pope Pius IX condemned the separation of church and state, religious freedom, individualism, liberalism, and rationalism—values at the core of American civilization. In 1870, the formal declaration of papal infallibility further encouraged Protestant fears of Vatican domination over American Catholics.

Even more, additional waves of European immigration—largely of Catholics—were crashing onto eastern shores to swell the tide of xenophobia sweeping the nation.[60] The institutional brand of Catholicism that was overtaking the Southwest originated oceans away from the more flexible Mexican Catholic ethos. According to Catherine Albanese, "It was Irish Catholics who, by the sheer power of their numbers—almost one million by 1850—and their willingness to enter ecclesiastical service, came to dominate the hierarchy of the American church."[61] Between the years 1850 and 1910, 322 priests served California. Of these, 83 percent had Irish surnames and 53 percent of them were trained in Ireland.[62] The Church's mission to the newly acquired territories was "Americanization," which, at this initial point, tried to normalize and institutionalize Catholics across the continent.[63]

Throughout California, Mexicans were made "to sit in special pews in the back of the church; other churches had signs reading: 'Mexicans prohibited.'" As Jay Dolan has noted, "Another common practice was to have one mass on Sunday for Mexicans, and if they attended any other mass, they would be asked to leave. Even at the special early morning Mass they would have to wait outside church until all the Anglos had entered, and only then could they enter and take their place in the back of the church."[64]

The first American bishop of California, Joseph Sadoc Alemany, a Spanish Dominican, worked for the meaningful participation of Mexicans in the Church upon arriving in California in 1850. However, in

1852 he was transferred to the newly created San Francisco archdiocese, which covered all of California north of San Jose, and was replaced by another Spaniard, Bishop Thaddeus Amat, C.M., who did not arrive in the state until 1855. Upon his arrival he "faced serious challenges," reports Michael Engh. "There were only sixteen members of the clergy scattered across the diocese; legal title to religious property was clouded; communication was poorly developed; the cost of living was exorbitant; and diocesan financial resources were negligible."[65] Amat worked quickly to institute his no-nonsense Catholicism.

During his first year Amat issued a pastoral letter upping the ante among Mexican Catholics. He exhorted the clergy of southern California to require a minimum level of normative church ritual among lax Mexican parishioners—or let them suffer damnation. He decreed that "All the faithful of one or the other sex, who have arrived at the use of discretion, should confess at least once a year; and receive the body and blood of Jesus Christ at least at Easter; and with much rigor I order, that you should deny entrance to the church in life and later in death the ecclesiastical burial to those who do not comply."[66] Amat's letter speaks to the *institutional* laxity of Mexican Catholicism. The bishop also expressed concern for the decay of the churches and admonished the priests to solicit money for their care. He then attempted to dissolve Mexican Catholic sensibilities by regulating practice.

Engh describes Mexican California Catholicism as a system of "personal and communal customs" that "effectively brought religion within the daily experience of the ordinary person. The rosary, novenas, promesas (personal vows of devotion), altarcitos (domestic shrines), public processions, and other devotions were developed out of necessity in regions where priests were few in number and frequently absent from the pueblo or distant from the far-flung ranchos."[67] In 1861, the council fathers in Los Angeles put an end, at least officially, to many of the Mexican devotional practices.

Throughout the Southwest, American encroachment spelled trouble for Mexican Catholicism. Upon his appointment to Brownsville, in south Texas, Father Dominic Manucy expressed his outrage in a letter, commiserating: "I consider this appointment as Vicar Apostolic of Brownsville the worst sentence that could have been given me for any crime. The Catholic population is composed almost exclusively of Mexican greasers—cattle drovers and thieves. No money can be got from these people, not even to bury their fathers." Yet, as Timothy Matovina has shown, devotion to Guadalupe tied Tejanos, Mexicans of Texas, together throughout waves of colonialism.[68] Simultaneously, New Mexico and Colorado were developing a lay-based Catholicism organized around fraternal brotherhoods—Los Hermanos Penitentes. The lesser-known women's counterpart to the Penitentes was known as the Carmelitas.[69] Racism, isolation, and centuries of colonialism had strained relations between the Church and the laity, and thus fraternities based in *moradas,* de facto churches, dotted the landscape, as did the crosses that penitents used to dramatically reenact the passion of Christ. In Arizona, the traditions of the Pimeria-Alta Desert continued to exert their pervasive influence as Yaqui Indians built their own churches and celebrated their own version of the Christian calendar in ceremonies conducted from shrines adjacent to the "main" parish churches.[70]

Back in California, on 10 March 1926, the *San Francisco Chronicle* published a letter written by the archbishop of San Francisco, Edward Hanna, to a California congressman, urging him to oppose Mexican immigration. Among the reasons given by the archbishop were that Mexicans drain Catholic charities, are given to criminal activities, spread disease, are of "low mentality," decrease the total number of whites, and "remain foreign." Hanna's tirade echoed the sentiments of much of the non-Mexican population of California.[71] California was virtually a Catholic territory, but one that the Protestants characterized as entirely "unreligious."[72] One Presbyterian missionary, upon his leaving Los Angeles with little success, quipped, "The name of this city is in Spanish the City of Angels, but with much truth it might be called the city of demons."[73]

MANIFEST DESTINY THREE: HOME MISSIONS

In 1917, one Euroamerican Protestant missionary compared his work in Mexico to his mission among Mexican-Americans in the Southwest; the latter population he deemed more resistant to his gospel. He attributed this to "the peculiar evil influences encountered here, particularly in the cities, influences of an antireligious nature rarely met with in Mexico, and which are extremely injurious to the ignorant, simple-minded *peón* class, already out of sympathy with the church of their fathers." Such "influences" included exposure to "lower-class 'Americans' [who] are often Italians, Portuguese, or French."[74] Protestants engaged in "home-mission" activities sought to convert Catholic Mexicans to Protestantism but considered them an inferior variation even of their European counterparts, whom Protestants already held in low regard.

Largely as a result of Protestant efforts and public discourses, Catholics renewed their efforts among ethnic Mexicans in Los Angeles and began aggressively instituting social-welfare programs throughout the barrio. The expressed mission of the Catholic Church into the 1920s and beyond was the "Americanization" of Mexicans, which meant inculcating them with the language, customs, and "manners" of the Euroamerican middle class. Patrick McNamara explains that "both Protestant and Roman Catholic clergy in Los Angeles established settlement houses and welfare institutions with an overtly assimilative philosophy," the goal of which, for Catholics, according to the Bureau of Catholic Charities in 1919, was to make Mexicans "better Catholics" and thus make them "better citizens."[75] In the words of George Sánchez, " 'Americanization' was an enigmatic, yet often nativist, ideology which failed to appeal to the majority of Mexican newcomers."[76] Many of these newcomers were the one million who fled the Mexican Revolution for the United States after 1910. This group, dubbed by Mario Garcia the "immigrant generation" (1880–1930), imagined they would return to Mexico; they kept their packed bags by the door as they waited breathlessly for the first sign that the internecine struggles had abated.[77] Sánchez says that "Even those who had decided to settle permanently in the United States rarely wanted to give up their ethnic heritage and cultural values. Mexicans were wise enough to accept medical services and employment opportunities without abandoning their cultural values."[78] This group considered themselves *mexicanos de afuera*—foreign Mexicans, Mexicans outside of Mexico.

By the 1930s, Los Angeles was the home of 97,116 Mexicans, but only a small percentage were legal citizens. Before long, Mexicans began realizing that they would not return to Mexico: a generation of Mexicans was coming of age in the United States. Consequently, Mexico, in the words of Richard Griswold del Castillo, became more of a "spiritual" rather than a "geographical" homeland.[79] Mexicans needed to rethink adjusting their former Mexican customs to life in the north, and thus reviving and/or producing salient cultural expressions. Political machinations became a prime focus of their energies, and so a tradition of Mexican-American activism came to life. Sánchez argues that this "Mexican American generation" was characterized by what he calls "ambivalent Americanism," dualistic in cultural practices and loyalties.[80] Mexican conversions to Americanism were vastly incomplete. And yet, inasmuch as this generation was ambivalently American, they were at least equally ambivalently Mexican—betwixt and between Mexican and North American: dual loyalties, a new form of *nepantlaism*.

THE WORLD SYSTEM IN THE MEXICAN AMERICAS: INTERNAL COLONIALISM AND BARRIOIZATION

The narrative of Chicano *qua* Mexican-American history traditionally begins in 1848, when the U.S. border crossed illegally into Mexico. With the end of the Mexican and American War, marked by the signing of the Treaty of Guadalupe Hidalgo, the heretofore northern Mexican states fell under the auspices of the United States and were later fully incorporated into the union. Scholars have described this act as "forced entry" into the union and have made it the first instance of a model for interpreting the experiences of U.S. minorities, called "internal" or "domestic" colonialism. Robert Blauner was one of the originators of the domestic-colonialism model and has classified it using four primary components:

> Colonization begins with a forced, involuntary entry. Second, there is the impact on culture. The effects of colonization on the culture and social organization of the colonized people are more than the results of such "natural" processes as contact and acculturation. The colonizing power carries out a policy that constrains, transforms, or destroys indigenous values, orientations, and ways of life. Third is a special relationship to governmental bureaucracies or the legal order. The lives of the subordinate group are administered by representatives of the dominant power. The colonized have the experience of being managed and manipulated by outsiders who look down on them. The final component of colonization is racism.[81]

One of the main provisions of the Treaty of Guadalupe Hidalgo guaranteed that Mexicans still living in the areas occupied by the United States ("occupied Mexico") would enjoy status as American citizens.[82] Nonetheless, people of Mexican descent were systematically dispossessed of their lands.[83] In Los Angeles and southern California, existing Mexican land titles, as well as land disputes, had to be validated in local courts. This process had dire results for the ethnic Mexican population, as many lost their lands due to their inability to communicate in English and their lack of familiarity with American laws. Additionally, Euroamericans would boldly occupy lands held by Mexican-Americans, in practices known as "squatting." The courts decided the majority of these cases in favor of the Euroamerican squatters, owing especially to their race and proficiency with the English language and American litigation. To make matters worse, extended droughts in California during the 1850s made it difficult to keep cattle alive, and many of the fortunes of the ranchers dried up and gave way to fresh Euroamerican money.

In Los Angeles and throughout the Southwest, Mexicans of all classes were dispossessed of their lands, brought together in the least desirable sections of towns, and cemented into the lowest sectors of the American labor pyramid: this is the historical process of *barrioization*. Historians have tied the systematic dispossession of Mexico, and subsequently of Mexican-Americans, to the formation of economic "cores" and "peripheries," reflecting concentration of capital worldwide.[84]

By the turn of the century, Los Angeles's downtown plaza (now adjacent to Olvera Street), the site of Our Lady Queen of the Angels Catholic Church, became the nucleus of the once-sprawling Mexican community. Because most of the immigrants there came from the Mexican state of Sonora, the historic plaza came to be known as Sonoratown. In a sense, ethnic Mexicans in California experienced the annexation of Mexico's northern territory as the shift from identities defined by class to those defined by ethnicity, which therefore functioned simultaneously as a political classification. In other words, as a result of the incorporation of Mexican northern territories into the United States, class differences among Mexicans were all but dissolved and subsumed under the definition "Mexicans," an ethnic, racial, and class identity. Thus, the primary signifier for the semioticized body shifted from class, in relatively homogenous space, to "race," signified by Mexican ancestry contextualized in tightly controlled and highly articulated configurations of space. This process illustrates something about how bodily subjection is continuous with spatial oppression and economic and political disenfranchisement.

As noted above, by the dawn of the 1930s, the Mexican-American population in Los Angeles had swelled, owing especially to people fleeing the internecine struggles characterizing the Mexican Revolution. With the industrial development of downtown and the establishment of a rail line, Mexicans spilled east of Sonoratown and across the river into the communities of El Sereno, Lincoln Heights, and Boyle Heights, now collectively referred to as East Los Angeles.[85] For many Mexican-Americans, confronted by discrimination and poverty, East Los Angeles was the only available place in which to live. Still others chose to live in East Los Angeles because of the succor they received from being with their Mexican kin. Ethnic Mexicans created a vital community in the barrio, replete with rich cultural expressions. They also formed labor organizations; mutual aid societies, or *mutualistas;* and religious institutions. "As a result," in the words of Sánchez, "parents and children alike forged an ambivalent Americanism—one distinguished by a duality in cultural practices and a marked adaptability in the face of discrimination. . . . Mexican-American cultural adaptation occurred without substantial economic mobility, particularly since it was rooted in the context of the Great Depression."[86] This ambivalence, *nepantla,* was the condition, again, for the articulation of an evolving politics and poetics of identity.

THE FAILURE OF THE COSMIC RACE

In 1925, Mexican philosopher José Vasconcelos (1882–1959) introduced the term "La Raza Cósmica," the Cosmic Race, into discourses on culture, race, and the nation. "La Raza Cósmica" was a term that meant the ultimate result of a cosmic combination of peoples. Mario Garcia reports that La Raza Cósmica became a concept around which Spanish-speaking workers in the United States organized during the 1930s. Andrés Guerrero concurs, suggesting that by the late 1930s and into the 1940s "the Cosmic Race" was employed generally by Latinos throughout the Americas. Since then, the term has become a perennial trope in narratives on cultural identity, deployed in the rhetorics of the Chicano movement and in more recent Latino theologies. In 1982, Guerrero made the principle of Cosmic Race central to his *Chicano Theology.* Similarly, Roberto Goizueta has recuperated aspects of Vasconcelos's advanced aesthetic theory.[87]

Vasconcelos was a widely respected philosopher in Mexico, the United States, and Europe. He ran for the Mexican presidency in 1929 but was defeated by Plutarco Calles. Vasconcelos was a firm supporter of the Mexican Revolution (1910–17), and until his death he was a vocal critic of corruption in Mexican politics. In his later life, however, he became a supporter of the Franco project, a leader in support of the "recuperation" of the conqueror Cortéz, and he apologized generally for the "errors" he had made in his work on the Cosmic Race. He died while he was president of the International Congress of Philosophy. The title of his autobiography indicates how this man wanted to be remembered: *A Mexican Ulysses.*[88]

In the prologue to the posthumously published 1979 English translation of *La Raza Cosmica,* Vasconcelos states, "The central thesis of this book is that the various races of the earth tend to intermix at a gradually increasing pace, and eventually will give rise to a new human

type, composed of selection from each of the races already in existence."
He explains further, "This prediction was first published at a time when
the Darwinist doctrine of natural selection, which preserves the fittest
and dooms the weak, was still prevalent in the scientific world; a doctrine which, applied to the sociological field by Gobineau, gave origin
to the pure Aryan theory, supported by the English and carried to aber-
rant imposition by Nazism."[89] Vasconcelos's apologetics were not out of
place, considering his mission of arguing that racial miscegenation
would create the Cosmic Race. The result was a very disturbing racial
theory:

> The Black could be redeemed, and step by step, by voluntary extinction,
> the uglier stocks will give way to the more handsome. Inferior races, upon
> being educated, would become less prolific, and the better specimens would
> go on ascending a scale of ethnic improvement, whose maximum type is not
> precisely the White, but that new race to which the White himself will have
> to aspire with the object of conquering the synthesis. The Indian, by graft-
> ing onto the related race, would take the jump of millions of years that sep-
> arate Atlantis from our times, and in a few decades of aesthetic eugenics,
> the Black may disappear, together with the types that a free instinct of
> beauty may go on signaling as fundamentally recessive and undeserving,
> for that reason, of perpetuation. In this manner, a selection of taste would
> take effect, much more efficiently than the brutal Darwinist selection, which
> is valid, if at all, only for the inferior species, but no longer for man.[90]

Vasconcelos proposes a "new science," claiming that "if we do not first
liberate the spirit, we shall never be able to redeem matter."[91]

Vasconcelos's romanticism leads him to subordinate Matter to a
Hegelian Spirit, a dialectic destined to triumph in the form of a perfected
master race: "No contemporary race can present itself alone as the finished model that all the others should imitate," writes Vasconcelos. "The
mestizo, the Indian, and even the Black are superior to the White in a
countless number of properly spiritual capacities. Neither in antiquity,
nor in the present, have we a race capable of forging civilization by itself."[92] The racial synthesis he proposes must occur in the Americas because, he argues, the Latin Americans offer land, space, and the "mal-
leability" of their characters. Vasconcelos closes by summarizing:

> At any rate, the most optimistic conclusion that can be drawn from the
> facts here observed is that even the most contradictory racial mixtures can
> have beneficial results, as long as the spiritual factor contributes to raise
> them. In fact, the decline of Asiatic peoples can be attributed to their isola-
> tion, but also, and without doubt, primarily to the fact that they have not
> been Christianized. A religion such as Christianity made the American Indi-

ans advance, in a few centuries, from cannibalism to a relative degree of civilization.[93]

Vasconcelos provided a morphology to describe and understand the experiences of the *mexicanos de afuera*—and his ideas were widely popularized, absenting the racist component.

During the 1930s, East Los Angeles was inhabited by both Mexican-Americans and Jews. Vicki Ruíz has documented the ways Jewish and Mexican-American women forged bonds that tied both groups together in mutual struggles around labor practices.[94] Chicanas and Jews experienced similar modes of alienation from the dominant L.A. Anglo-Protestant culture and comparable levels of exploitation in the workplace. Eventually, however, because most Jews had moved out of East Los Angeles by the 1960s,[95] the area was left to foster a distinctively Mexican-American consciousness, one that required its own myths, symbols, and narratives of identity as well as new ways to determine "affinity and estrangement," to distinguish "us" from "them." The limits of this cultural identity were drawn through a return to an ancestral identity, a myth, which amounted to a push for a postmodern recognition of a multiple and complex identity—well before such notions had become fashionable. The method for formulating identity was *difrasismo* poetics. Alurista, crowned the Chicano poet laureate, explains:

> In the face of flagrant institutional racism and ethnocentrism, Xicanos now sought to redefine themselves on their own terms—that is to say, in terms other than those ascribed by the white, Anglo-Saxon, male Protestant state to "keep Mexicans in their place." Much of the literature that had flowed from the pens of Anglo-American novelists, social commentators, journalists, and academicians since 1848 had rendered the Mexican in the United States as lazy, ignorant, criminally prone, and definitely not worthy of trust. After many years and many generations of Xicano subordination to Anglo world views and values, the socialization process had clearly begun to take its toll, instilling in many children the notion that for some "divine" reason, Xicanos were not quite as human as Anglo-Americans.[96]

Mexican-Americans would have to rely on a poem to change this notion of "divine" reason.

YO SOY JOAQUÍN

In 1967, Rodolfo "Corky" Gonzales published his epic poem *I Am Joaquín*, a myth based on a historical figure, Joaquín Murieta.[97] Joaquín

Murieta is the *mexicano* social bandit who has enjoyed the greatest no-
toriety and popularity, even outside of California, especially in Mexico
and Chile, and he has been memorialized in popular *corridos,* or storytelling poems, sung to the rhythm of an acoustic guitar. Born in Sonora,
Mexico, Murieta came to California sometime in 1850. It wasn't long
before he experienced the racism of the Anglo miners firsthand. During
the Gold Rush period, Mexicans were lynched, flogged, branded, and
ultimately forced from their claims. This conflict between the Anglo and
Mexican miners undoubtedly contributed to the rise of Joaquín—the
"bloody bandit." The ultimate disgrace that Murieta suffered was the
rape and killing of his wife by Anglo miners, who, additionally, stole his
mining claim. According to the mythology, Murieta consequently
turned to a life of brigandage, especially horse thievery and murder.
Murieta's actions were retaliatory and subversive. He warred against
the oppression of Mexicans and became a symbol of Mexican-American
resistance following the Mexican and American War (1846–48).[98]

> I am Joaquín,
> Lost in a world of confusion,
> Caught up in a whirl of an
>   gringo society,
> Confused by the rules,
> Scorned by attitudes
>
> I am Cuauhtémoc,
> Proud and Noble
>   Leader of men,
> King of an empire,
> civilized beyond the dreams
> of the Gachupín Cortéz,
> Who is also the blood,
>   the image of myself.
> I am Nezahualcoyotl,
> Great leader of the Chichimecas.
> I am the sword and flame of Cortéz
>   the despot.
>
> I am Joaquín.
> I rode with Pancho Villa,
> I am Emiliano Zapata.
> I ride with Revolutionists
>   against myself.
>
> I am the masses of my people and
> I refuse to be absorbed.
>   I am Joaquín

I am Aztec Prince and Christian Christ
    I SHALL ENDURE!
    I WILL ENDURE![99]

Editions of the poem proliferated, and a short film was made wherein the poem is read to various images. One Chicana historian recalls that the poem "expressed the collective rage of our generation."[100] Again, Joaquín crystallized and iterated the multiple subject positions of Mexican-Americans—well before the naming of postmodern subjectivities, that is, the idea of multiple selves, had become common parlance.

However, as I see it, the poem failed to make space and place central to the mythology of cultural identity. At one point the protagonist claims, "The ground was mine," but that line is not developed further. John Chávez explains that "the desire of Southwest Mexicans for recovery of the region has always been tied to their desire for cultural, political, and economic self-determination, a self-determination they believe can only be achieved through control of the space they occupy."[101] Subsequently, the poetic myth of Aztlán emerged and took center stage in Chicano identity performances. In it, space was to be reclaimed and made into a homeland place.

EL PLAN ESPIRITUAL DE AZTLÁN: MYTH IN CHICANO HISTORY

The poet Alurista is credited with authoring the myth of Aztlán, or what is formally called the "Spiritual Plan of Aztlán," and accordingly he has been dubbed the poet laureate of Aztlán. Aztlán is the mythical Aztec homeland; it was (re)introduced into Chicano consciousness in 1969. Alurista explains:

> I think Chicanos for a long time, ever since 1848, were subjected to a number of modern myths, such as the Christian myth, which said the kingdom of heaven is for the poor and the meek; or the American dream, the notion that America and its thirteen colonies are the future of the world and whoever wants to join it, join it; whoever doesn't like it leave it. Manifest Destiny, the notion that the United States was the savior, not only of this continent, but of the world. . . . So these are myths that I think Chicano people have been trying to fight back against, and I don't think that Christian mythology helped us any. I mean I don't think that Catholic mythology assisted us in coming up with a myth of resistance.[102]

The pivotal event in the construction of Chicano identity and for the emergence of Aztlán occurred in Denver in 1969, at the first National Chicano Youth Liberation Conference. The conference was convened by a boxer-politician, Rodolfo "Corky" Gonzales, head of the Denver-based Chicano youth organization that had fashioned itself as a front line of the Chicano Power Movement. But, according to Carlos Muñoz, "It was no surprise that the majority of the participants [in the conference] came from California, because that was where the rapidly developing Chicano student movement first came to maturity."[103] Luis Leal contends that finding the "historical" origin of Aztlán is less important than "documenting the myth in Chicano thought. It is necessary to point out the fact that before March, 1969, the date of the Denver Conference, no one talked about Aztlán," although Alurista ". . . during the Autumn of 1968, had spoken about Aztlán in a class for Chicanos held at San Diego State."[104]

The ideological underpinning of Aztlán was known then, as it is now, as Chicano "cultural nationalism," which at that time was also called "Chicano chauvinism," a conviction that only Mexican cultural artifacts were valuable in ordering Chicano lifeways. In the words of Corky Gonzales, "Nationalism is the key to our people liberating themselves."[105] Memory, or the invention of memory, was key to the mythological and poetic plan of liberation. Michael Pina explains that the Mexican and Chicano desire for historical justice and the myth of Aztlán "merged to form the living myth of Chicano nationalism. This myth spanned the diachronic chasm that separates the archaic contents of cultural memory from the contemporary struggle for cultural survival."[106]

The goal of cultural nationalism, says Muñoz, was a "pride in Mexican ethnicity and culture. *It was reasoned that all Mexican Americans, regardless of how indoctrinated they were with the dominant values of US society, ultimately nurtured such pride.* Nationalism, therefore, was to be the common denominator for uniting all Mexican Americans and making possible effective mobilization."[107]

Aztlán, then, emerged to provide Chicanos with an *authoritative* sacred narrative of ancestry, delineating a map for ritual and world production that could *ground* a claim to authenticity. The mytho-poetic preamble to the "Plan," which is indeed the most widely recognized part of the document, reads as follows:

> In the spirit of a new people that is conscious not only of its proud historical heritage but also of the brutal "gringo" invasion of our territories, *we,* the Chicano inhabitants and civilizers of the northern land of Aztlán from whence came our forefathers, reclaiming the land of their birth and consecrating the determination of our people of the sun, *declare* that the call of our blood is our power, our responsibility, and our inevitable destiny.

We are free and sovereign to determine those tasks which are justly called for by our house, our land, the sweat of our brows, and by our hearts. Aztlán belongs to those who plant the seeds, water the fields, and gather the crops and not to the foreign Europeans. We do not recognize capricious frontiers on the bronze continents.

Brotherhood unites us, and love for our brothers makes us a people whose time has come and who struggles against the foreigner "gabacho" who exploits our riches and destroys our culture. Before the world, before all of North America, before all our brothers in the bronze continent, we are a nation, we are a union of free pueblos, we are *Aztlán*.[108]

In the *Los Angeles Times,* Ruben Salazar wrote that "at the final session of the revolutionary-rhetoric-filled conference [in Denver] the plan of Aztlán was read to the cheering youths from California, Arizona, Texas, New Mexico and Colorado. Aztlán is the Indian word for Northern Mexico."[109]

In the preface to his now classic 1973 book on Chicano identity, *Aztecas del Norte: The Chicanos of Aztlán,* Native-American studies professor Jack Forbes claimed that Chicanos, whether they realized it or not, were inhabitants of Aztlán, and that "the Chicanos of Aztlán are currently engaged in the most significant kind of struggle, the struggle of mind, the development, in fact, of a filosofía Chicana, a philosophy of Aztlán."[110] Under the heading "Program," the plan calls for "a nation autonomous and free—culturally, socially, economically, and politically—[which] will make its own decisions on the usage of the lands, the taxation of our goods, the utilization of our bodies for war, the determination of justice (reward and punishment), and the profit of our sweat."[111]

Aztlán reified a stable identity in an imagined Aztec past, which, fittingly, is how the myth was used originally by the Aztecs, who invented a reflexive sacred genealogy to gain legitimacy. The tribes who developed into the Aztec empire arose not from a royal lineage but from an itinerant band of hunter-gatherers. As a result, the Aztecs told of their providential journey from their homeland, Aztlán, sometime between the ninth and eleventh centuries C.E. According to Diego Dúran, colonial writer and Dominican priest, Aztlán was a paradise for the Aztecs, where poetry and art flourished and harmony reigned. It was known variously as the Land of Seven Caves, the Land of Herons, and the Place of Whiteness.[112]

Davíd Carrasco explains the invented mythology of the Aztecs:

The historical reconstruction of a people struggling to fit into the developed world of the lakes is a far cry from the glorious mythological story of divine

guidance that appears in the sacred histories of Tenochtitlán. . . . Faced
with overwhelming evidence of their predecessors' monumental achievements, sacred genealogies, and complex social structures, the Aztecs felt im-
mensely inferior and strove to construct a city, mythology, and destiny in
order to impress and intimidate others and to legitimate themselves . . . to
establish the social truth that the Aztecs had divine sanction to be where
they were and to do what they did—ritually, politically, and culturally.[113]

Aztlán is a myth of place that is reiterated through memory in so-
ciopolitical contexts—across temporal borders and against colonial
structures. But in the Chicano movement, Aztlán did not realize the
utopia it promised to bring. Chicana feminists were alienated from the
hypermasculine images of the Aztec warrior, as were lesbians and gays,
who did not figure into the fresh identity configuration. Poet and play-
wright Cherríe Moraga has refused to abandon Aztlán and returns to the
poem as the central place of struggle:

> But it is historically evident that the female body, like the Chicano people,
> has been colonized. And any movement to decolonize them must be cultur-
> ally and sexually specific. Chicanos are an occupied nation within a nation,
> and women and women's sexuality are occupied within Chicano nation. If
> women's bodies and those of men and women who transgress their gender
> roles have been historically regarded as territories to be conquered, they are
> also territories to be liberated. . . . The nationalism I seek is one that decol-
> onizes the brown and female body as it decolonizes the brown and female
> earth. It is a new nationalism in which la Chicana Indígena stands at the
> center, and heterosexism and homophobia are no longer the cultural order
> of the day. I cling to the word "nation" because without the specific naming
> of the nation, the nation will be lost.[114]

But it was Gloria Anzaldúa who radically shifted the location of
Aztlán—from a homeland to the borderlands.

BORDERLAND RELIGIONS: A CONDITION OF *NEPANTLA*

Anzaldúa shifted Aztlán both ideologically and spatially, from a fixed
and reified place, male-dominated and hypermasculinized, to a mobile,
decentered Aztlán whose meanings are fluid and shifting. As Rafael
Pérez-Torres notes, she moved Aztlán from the "homeland" to the "borderlands."[115] Embedded in the trajectory of Chicano history, the borderlands thesis suggests that, for many Mexican-Americans, cultural production occurs betwixt and between Mexico and the United States and
is thus characterized by liminality, or the processual state of in-between-

ness, of becoming.[116] The organizing principle of the borderlands thesis focuses on how the international boundary between Mexico and the United States, as well as adjacent regions, creates a distinctive cultural space that paradoxically links yet divides people on either side of the border. The borderlands is not only a physical place but also a poetic device for describing perennially emergent and multiplex individual, social, and cultural formations.[117]

The grand symbol of the border looms large in the Mexican imaginary, and the reality of its daily transgression by people who may be otherwise religious and law-abiding is cause for deep reflection. Mexicans who come to the United States put their faith in the "cross," the act itself that becomes a symbol. Metaphorically, a border-crossing consciousness means living daily with the impulse to surpass institutional, religious, legal, spatial, and symbolic barriers that keep the marginal away from centers of power. Borders of all kinds are central and formative places in the production of religion, but they also serve as peripheries that must be surpassed to arrive at a place with greater promise—a meaningful and better orientation for cultural and religious migrants.

The incessant illegal crossing of Mexicans into the United States should give us pause. Each year 1.5 million Mexicans are arrested for crossing the border, and many suffer a worse fate: in the year 2000 alone, the cross killed nearly 400 people. Crossers face hatred, discrimination, criminalization, cultural dislocation, violence, death, and more. But still they come. What drives them? What gives them hope, the sheer bravado to defy the laws of two national jurisdictions, to risk the terror of the *coyotes,* the mystery of the desert, or the currents of the rivers?

The subjectivity that emerges from the experience of the cross is what Anzaldúa calls the "new mestiza." *Mestizaje* (literally, "miscegenation") is used idiomatically in Mexico to denote the human synthesis of Spanish and Indian. Virgilio Elizondo explains that Chicano history is framed within two discrete convergences of cultures, both grounded in successive *mestizajes:* "But the confrontation of parent cultures also produced a new ethnos, a new people: the Spanish-Indian confrontation gave birth to the Mexican people; the Anglo-American-Mexican confrontation gave birth to the Mexican American people." But Elizondo reminds us that "the birth of a new people from two preexistent peoples . . . *could* come about in various ways. But de facto it has most often come about through military conquest, colonization, and religious imposition."[118] He describes the Spanish colonization of Mexico as the "first *mestizaje,*" and the "second *mestizaje*" he deems the U.S. conquest of Mexico. "The movement between Mexican and American cultures is not so much a world of confusion, but rather a place of opportunity and innovation," argues George Sánchez. "Mexicans, long accustomed to cultural blending and creation, continue this custom in the United States, now incorporating aspects of the 'others' they find in a multicultural setting like Los Angeles. To be Chicano, in effect, is to be betwixt and between."[119]

In an earlier formulation, Anzaldúa asks us to think of her "as Shiva, a many armed and legged body with one foot on brown soil, one on white, one in straight society, one in the gay world, the man's world, the women's, one limb in the literary world, another in the working class, the socialist, and the occult worlds. A sort of spider woman hanging by one thin strand of web."[120] This is what Anzaldúa describes as a *mestiza* or "mixed blood" consciousness.[121] Chela Sandoval explains that "*la consciencia de la mestiza,*" or *mestiza* consciousness, "is born of life lived in the 'cross roads' between races, nations, languages, genders, sexualities, and cultures: It is a developed subjectivity capable of transformation and relocation, movement guided by the learned capacity to read, renovate, and make signs on behalf of the dispossessed in a skill that Anzaldúa calls 'la facultad.'"[122]

It is from *la facultad,* or *mestizaje* consciousness, that new religious innovations arise. In *la facultad* Anzaldúa teaches an existential philosophy, wherein existence precedes essence. Carrasco reads Anzaldúa as figuring a shamanic space, "a religious vision which she shares with many Chicanos, be they politically conservative, liberal or radical, English dominant or Spanish dominant, urban or rural, straight or gay. . . . This religious vision perceives our shared but complex reality as a borderlands that is at once geographical, political, ethnic, gendered but also profoundly mythic." For Carrasco, Anzaldúa's shamanism is akin to borderland religious practice, which "straddles, balances, shifts lines of vision, plays two ends against the middle, middles against the ends, and works to make what have been peripheral concerns into new centers of interest, power, and signification."[123] As we shall see in the chapters that follow, this border-crossing impulse, *la facultad,* is central to religious poetics.

CHAPTER 2

Virtual Virgin Nation

Mexico City as Sacred Center of Memory

The Mexican people, after more than two centuries of experiments and defeats, have faith only in the Virgin of Guadalupe and the National Lottery.

> Octavio Paz, foreword to Jacques Lafaye, *Quetzalcoatl and Guadalupe: The Formation of Mexican National Consciousness, 1531–1813,* trans. Benjamin Keen

We want to tell you that we are very grateful to return to the heart of this country—which is this city; to be with you, and to tell you that you are blessed because you are centered in the center of the heart of Mexico which is La Virgen de Guadalupe. Her vision is the same vision of all the hearts that the day will come when there will be no flags [*banderas*], no borders [*fronteras*], and no wallets [*carteras*]. What will exist is what exists in heaven [*el cielo*]—compassion, light, harmony, and compassion, compassion, compassion.

> Carlos Santana, *Sacred Fire: Live in Mexico City,* trans. Luis D. León

He has not done so for any other nation.

> Psalm 147:20

According to the foundational myth of the *mestizo* Mexican people, on Saturday morning, 9 December 1531, a humble Aztec Indian, Cuauhtlatoatzin, known by his Christian name, Juan Diego, was visited by Mary, the Mother of God, at the hill called Tepeyac on the outskirts of Mexico City. Central to this myth is that the Virgin Mary spoke to Juan Diego in his native tongue, Nahuatl, and manifested herself in the form of a brown-skinned Indian. In this encounter between the Virgin, ostensibly of Spanish/European origin, and the Mexican Indian, two competing conceptualizations of time, space, and corporeality interfaced with each other and coalesced: a primordial sacred human mix, or *mestizaje.* Henceforth, this meeting and its place have become central to the imagined communities of Mexico and Mexican-Americans, and indeed to the greater Latin Americas. On his visit to Mexico in 2002, Pope John Paul II declared 12 December a holy day in the Americas.

What follows advances the method and theory of religious poetics by focusing on the uses of Guadalupe—as narrative and symbol—that create a well of historical memory, or public myth, upon which working-class Mexicans and Mexican-Americans draw to manage their social, psychic, and spiritual conditions. Guadalupe quickens hope; of that we can be certain. However, the style in which the discourse and image of Guadalupe are imagined to make community is the focus of this chapter. Today, an estimated 90 percent of Mexico's eighty-five million people identify themselves as Catholic. The Virgin of Guadalupe is the primary symbol of Mexican-Catholic identity.

The appeal of Guadalupe is most salient at the level of the culturally sublime: she entreats the poor and the oppressed, in spirit, emotion, and body, to trust in a myth that is centuries old, to hope for that which is beyond the visible, to believe in and be transformed by the mysteries of life—to demand a miracle. Her charm is universal, offering to all who suffer the ineffable assurance that only a mother can bring; the chance to suckle at the bosom of hope, to imbibe the milk of life, mother's milk, as pure as it is white, and unconditionally given. Indeed, she is transcendent: she transcends the borders of religion, class, race, genders, and sexualities—in short, the limitations of space, time, and consciousness. She signifies salvation and transformation, a new beginning for the human race. It is utterly significant that her being is a *mestiza*. Even more, she is a single woman, barely fifteen years old, who is pregnant and must boldly deceive the world so that she may give life to a creation so unique it marks a reversal in historical time: she is a forceful agent in history. La Lupe, Mexico's mother, is dually marginal, for she is racialized and poor to boot. In her, Mexico's conflicted history and dire present conditions intersect and melt into an uneasy representation that is unequivocal: the people know her as La Patrona, the Queen of Mexico, and Queen of the Angels. As Sandra Cisneros puts it, she is not the mother of God; she *is* God.[1]

Guadalupe's current symbolic "capital" emerged in complex spatial, historical, and political processes. It wasn't until 1754 that the Vatican officially declared Guadalupe the patroness and protectress of New Spain, even though Mexicans had declared her their queen seventeen years earlier, after her agency was credited with saving Mexico City from an epidemic in 1737. The efficacy of Guadalupe was born from the pain of Mexican history with which she was inseminated: Guadalupe arose as the mother of Mexico precisely when Mexico needed a mother most. Guadalupe's myth and memory thrive in that interstitial *nepantla* space of associations and ruptures: she is implicated in the Spanish colonization of Mexico, in the formation of the Mexican nation-state, in the Mexican Revolution, and in the challenge to the Institutionalized Revolutionary Party (PRI).[2]

Guadalupe first emerged as a countersymbol that publicly signaled the divine election of the Mexicans—Indians, *mestizos,* and *criollos* (Spaniards born in Mexico)—as distinct from Spanish colonizers (*qua* born in Spain). Yet she has since been continuously coopted to serve different causes, including and especially Mexican nationalism, and so, for the most part, she has maintained a resistant and often counterhegemonic location through time. Initially, she deposed La Virgen de los Remedios, who functioned as the protectress of the Spaniards on their colonizing missions. Since then, as we shall see, she has occupied a paradoxical place—both peripheral and central—where she can be used as a prophetic voice and sign to enable the voiceless, the subaltern, to speak and signify in public life.

The following is a fragmented genealogy of Guadalupe that traces the story from her 1531 origins in Mexico to her current situation. First I survey texts and traditions, then conclude with a treatment of the Guadalupe pilgrimage at Tepeyac, Mexico City. Tepeyac is three miles north of the center of Mexico City; originally it was not within city limits but on the city borders, although today the city has swelled to envelop Tepeyac. In no small way, Guadalupe's prominence is indissolubly bound to her locus, the capital of Mexico, Mexico City, known to *mexicanos* simply as Mexico—*as if it were the nation itself.* "Mexico" is sacred in multiple (re)visions: city of Aztec emperors and goddesses, the capital of the Mesoamerican world, the seat of the Spanish colonial empire, and the capital of the Mexican nation. Guadalupe draws from Mexico City, and Mexico is in turn supported by her vast following. The thesis in this chapter is that Guadalupe devotion is a border tradition, straddling and blurring lines of religious demarcation. As such, it lends itself to the tactics and strategies of religious poetics.

Culminating this chapter is a reading of the pilgrimage to Guadalupe at Tepeyac, attended by a reported two million devotees. I have attended these 11–12 December events on three separate occasions (and have visited the basilica dozens of times). Though what happens at the church is serious spiritual reality, in a broader sense it is also what I call "religious play," the carnivalesque, wherein social norms are inverted, new registers of value are created, and class boundaries are redrawn.[3] But even more, people go to the church because it is fun. On any typical Mexico City warm and breezy day, the plaza at the basilica is filled with schoolkids in uniforms and vendors of food, art, and devotional kitsch. How did this powerful institution make its place in Mexico?

THE VIRGIN AND THE INDIAN: NARRATING GUADALUPE

The earliest text for the Guadalupe apparition is entitled *Imagen de la Virgen María, Madre de Dios de Guadalupe,* published in 1648 by

Miguel Sánchez. However, the most commonly accepted Nahuatl source is purportedly based on the testimony of Juan Diego; it is commonly referred to as *Nican mophua,* or "Here it is recounted," the first words of the text.[4] It was first published in 1649 by Luis Laso de la Vega, who dated the interview and inscription of the text back to 1552.

This official foundational myth of the Virgin of Guadalupe is narrated in five distinctive movements. In the first apparition—*eruption*—the Virgin appears to Juan Diego at Tepeyac. Then the incredulous Archbishop Zumárraga, to whom Juan Diego tells his vision, disbelieves or does not understand Juan Diego and sends him away twice, thinking he may be intoxicated. Zumárraga asks for a sign. After another exchange, the Virgin gives Juan Diego a sign to present to Zumárraga as proof of her agency: a bounty of fresh roses in the middle of winter and an imprint of the Virgin on Juan Diego's coarsefiber cape. In the final movement, the Virgin appears to and heals Juan Diego's ailing uncle, Juan Bernardino, whose anticipated death had previously distracted Diego from keeping an appointment with Guadalupe.

Nican mophua begins with the claim that the events therein are narrated exactly as they occurred. It then situates the story within the colonial context. "Ten years after the taking of the city of Mexico, the war was suspended and there was peace in the pueblos, that is how faith began to emerge, the knowledge of the true God, by whom there is life."[5] Guadalupe emanates from Mexico City and is indissociable from the historical period in which her appearance is embedded. Twenty-four million Indians died during the first century of the internecine Spanish colonization of Mexico. The redemptive emergence of Guadalupe responds directly to the situation of colonialism. She is meant to bridge precolonial and colonial contexts and identities: originally Guadalupe arose as the bride and boundary between Christians and Indians.

The official date for the first eruption of Guadalupe is, as noted, 9 December 1531. It is said that Juan Diego was on his way to Tlaltelolco to attend mass. As he was passing at the foot of Tepeyac Hill, he

> saw a brilliant light on the summit and heard strains of celestial music. Filled with wonderment he stood still. Then he heard a feminine voice asking him to ascend. When he reached the top of the hill he saw the Blessed Virgin Mary standing in the midst of a glorious light, attired in heavenly splendor. The beauty of her youthful countenance and her look of loving

kindness filled Juan Diego with unspeakable happiness as he listened to the words which she spoke to him in his Indian language. She told him that she was the Immaculate Virgin Mary, Mother of the True God, and made known to him her desire that a shrine be built there where she could manifest her love, her compassion, her succor and protection. "For I am a merciful mother," she said, "to you and to all your fellow men on this earth who love me and trust me and invoke my help. Therefore, go to the dwelling of the Bishop in Mexico and say that I, the Virgin Mary, sent you to make known to him my great desire."[6]

Guadalupe's opening statement to Juan Diego obliges him: immediately he is involved in religious exchange.

Like Guadalupe, Juan Diego is a border crosser. His Nahuatl name is Cuauhtlatóhuac, or Cuauhtlatoatzin—He Who Speaks Like an Eagle. He is elegant of speech, a poet. After Christian baptism, his name became Juan Diego; he had crossed the indigenous/Christian border. No doubt Juan Diego's conversion was motivated, to some degree, by the desire to survive. He is poor, humble, and, as far as we know from the written tradition, without a partner; he is a survivor of the ravages of war. The Virgin comes to him to comfort but mostly to *heal*. As a convert to Christianity, Juan Diego symbolizes the birth of the new, the transformation possible to the old through death. As such, he is a metonym for colonization and an embodiment of Indian persistence. What emerges in Juan Diego and others like him is a new cultural formation—the first *mestizaje* identity.

Inasmuch as the actors are central to the myth, so is the place, the myth's locus, Tepeyac, on the margins of Mexico City. In this early passage of the myth, Tepeyac is animated: "When he became joined to the hill called Tepeyac, day was breaking; and he heard singing above the hill: it sounded like various precious birds; the voices of the singers were quiet for periods of time; and it seemed that the mountain responded."[7] Juan Diego becomes "joined" with it: *Al llegar junto*. The hill responds to the singing, it becomes animated, it has spirit and life. Tepeyac is a place unlike other places in the world. Juan Diego tries to grasp what is happening to him. " 'Is it for good fortune that I am worthy of what I hear?' 'maybe I am dreaming?' 'should I get up from my sleep?' 'where am I?' 'maybe in the earthly paradise, of which the old men spoke, our elders?' 'maybe already in heaven?' " Significant to this story is Juan Diego's reliance on his pre-Christian memory.

The text continues with Juan Diego following the voice up the hill, "without fear." When he reaches the crest of the hill, he "saw a woman [*señora*], who was standing there and who told him to come closer. Arriving in her presence, he marveled much at her superhuman greatness: her dress was radiant like the sun; the cliff on which she rested her feet, arched by her splendor, appeared like a bracelet of precious jewels shined the earth like an arch rainbow."[8] The place where the Virgin is standing is transformed, so that all the plants shine like "emeralds," "turquoise," and "gold." Tepeyac would never be the same. When Juan Diego arrived at the Virgin's feet, "he bowed in front of her and heard her word, very soft and courteous, that of whom is compelling and esteemed. She said to him: 'Juanito, the least of my children, where are you going?'" The Virgin again conjures an image of Juan Diego—"the least of." The Virgin appears not to the powerful official religious agents but to the most lowly:

> "You the least of my children, I am the eternal Holy Virgin Mary, Mother of the true God for whom there is life. . . . I fervently desire that they build me a temple here soon, for in it I will demonstrate and give all my love, compassion, help, and protection, since I am your merciful mother; to you, to all the inhabitants of this place and the rest who love me who invoke and trust in me; there [I will] hear their laments, and remedy all their miseries, sorrows, and pains. And to realize that for which my compassion strives, go to the palace of the Archbishop of Mexico and you tell him how I sent you to present to him what I very much desire, that here in the clearing they erect a temple to me: you tell him promptly how much you've seen and admired, and what you have heard. Be sure that I appreciate it very much and I will reward [*pagaré*] you, because I will make you happy and you deserve a lot and I recompense the work and fatigue with which you go to do what I have commissioned you. Note that you have now heard my mandate, my son the least of which; be on your way and use all your strength." At this point he bowed in front of her and said: "My Madam, I'm on my way to take care of your command; so now I will take my leave from you [*ti*], me your humble servant." Then he went down, to go and do his commission; and he left by the road that went directly to Mexico.[9]

To put it frankly, the Virgin wants to cut a deal—like the goddesses called Tonantzin, she wants to be propitiated. Guadalupe stresses that she will appreciate and *pay, lo agradeceré bien y lo pagaré* (literally: "I will very much appreciate it and pay [for the work]"). This mandate provides a template for Guadalupe devotion, whereby the extent of one's labor—devotion—determines the extent to which compensation will be paid. Thus is articulated a model of obligation and exchange by means of which Guadalupe devotees call forth her divine intercession. But La Lupe needs work to be done in the world, and also a place for her to meet her people. From there, she rewards. All this and more are materialized in Guadalupe at Tepeyac.

The legacy of this event (and the centuries precipitating the event, in both Mesoamerica and Europe) is that devotees relate to Guadalupe and the saints through relationships of gifting, obligation, and exchange, called either a *promesa,* promise, or *manda,* obligation or errand. One anthropologist has described this tradition as follows:

> A *manda* is an agreement, or contract, between a person and a celestial being. No priest need serve as an intermediary, and no witnesses are required. The *manda* can be made anytime and anywhere. . . . Because this custom is not part of orthodox Catholic ritual, the church has no rules for it. The act of making the *manda,* however, is frequently accompanied by conventional Catholic prayers, gifts of votive candles, or some other church-recognized act of devotion. . . . The very informality of this custom permits people to promise a wide variety of devotional acts. A person may promise to make a pilgrimage to a particular place or shrine; to crawl to the shrine from a certain place . . . or to offer money, candles, flowers, jewelry, fancy pillows—or a *milagro.* Usually the *manda* includes two or more of these acts. When *milagros* or other gifts are promised, all of the effort, travel, time, and money necessary to obtain and bring them to the saint are considered part of the offering.[10]

The discourse emergent between the supplicant and saint is religious poetics.

The material culture of borderlands devotional practices is multiple, including photographs, letters, human hair, crutches, flowers, candles, food, and more. The *retablo* and *milagrito,* two of the most common votive offerings, have developed into a distinct and powerful Southwestern borderlands art form that has reached ultimate vogue in Canada, Europe, and Japan. *Retablos* are small votive oil paintings on tin or metal (typically eight inches by ten inches).[11] Similarly, *milagritos,* used mainly for healing, are tiny, charmlike bronze, silver, or other metal representations of body parts, usually no more than one inch in length, focused specifically on the body. In both the *retablo* and *milagrito,* artists/devotees poetically reimagine images and thus religious discourse: "Although the representation of the holy image must bear some relation to official iconography, the rules of interpretation are loose rather than rigid."[12] Along these lines, doctrines that are Catholic, orthodox boundaries are rewritten in the desires of supplicants who often disregard or challenge official Church teachings—particularly inasmuch as saints are thought of as intercessors and exemplars of behavior. Devotees in Mexico and elsewhere strike bargains with Guadalupe and the saints, negotiating directly, as Juan Diego does.

In the next movement of the myth, for example, Juan Diego tells Guadalupe of his failure before the archbishop and begs her to send another in his place, for he feels himself unworthy to take her message. She responds, "Listen, my son the least of which, understand that there are many of my servants and messengers whom I could obligate to take my message and do my will; but the whole point is precisely that you yourself petition and help and with your mediation my will be realized." Guadalupe thus sends Juan Diego anew to the archbishop, "commanding" him with "rigor." Guadalupe's people are chosen: the humble, the Indians, the poor, the oppressed, "the least of which." She is the heroine of the poor.

Juan Diego returns to Archbishop Zumárraga, who requests a sign from the Virgin. Hence, Juan Diego returns to Tepeyac and informs Guadalupe of Zumárraga's demand. In her third apparition, the Virgin tells Juan Diego to return the next day, Monday, for a sign to take to the archbishop. However, when Juan Diego returns home, he learns that his uncle, Juan Bernardino, has taken ill. Juan Diego is unable to return on Monday; instead, he seeks a "doctor" for his uncle. But the healing efforts prove unavailing; Juan Bernardino's condition has advanced and his prognosis is terminal. The next day, Tuesday, Juan Diego is destined again for Tlaltelolco, this time seeking a priest to administer last rites to his uncle. At Tepeyac, the Virgin appears and asks why he stood her up the day before. Juan Diego's alibi is "the plague." Guadalupe responds:

> "Listen and understand, my son the least of which, that which frightens and distresses you is nothing; don't let your heart be troubled; don't fear that disease, or any other sickness or pain. *Am I not here who is your mother?* Are you not under my shadow? Am I not your health? Are you not fortunate in my lap? What more do you need? Do not be sad and don't worry about another thing, don't be distressed about the sickness of your uncle, because he will not die from it, be certain that he is already well." (And then his uncle got well, according to what he learned later.)[13]

From here, Juan Diego attains the sign, the roses that grew on the sacred hill of Tepeyac only by a miracle, and takes them to Zumárraga. When Juan Diego opens his cape to show the bishop, the roses cascade out to reveal an image of Guadalupe emblazoned upon it. The bishop is convinced by the miracle of the image on the cape. In the final movement of the myth, the image is ceremoniously transported from the center of the city to Tepeyac. On the way there, an Indian falls ill in front of the Guadalupe image and in an instant he is healed: from the beginning, Guadalupe is a healer, a *curandera*/wise woman/medicine woman.

Scholarly debate has raged over the origins and veracity of the myth. As I see it, the opinions roughly follow three paradigms: (1) neocolonial modernist theory, which is heretofore the ruling paradigm; (2) postcolonial theory, articulated primarily in discourses of liberation theology, which sees greater agency in Indian responses; and (3) iconoclastic theory, largely the domain of the Christian political right, which argues that Guadalupe is solely the product of a premodern imagination and ultimately recognizes only the Christian God.

What I describe as the works governed by neocolonial modernist theory have been advanced mostly by Jacques Lafaye in a French-language text that has been translated into Spanish and English. Lafaye presents compelling evidence to suggest that the Guadalupe apparition was a strategy engineered by the Franciscans for the conversion of the Indians. "In all respects," argues Lafaye, "the cult of Tepeyac appears to be a repetition of the cult of Estremadura [Spain]. This does not mean that the former should be considered a simple reflection of the latter. We can only say that in the case of two peoples, inhabiting the same spiritual world, comparable historical ordeals, threatening the existence of the community, inspired the rise of analogous mythical responses at an interval of more than two centuries."[14] Tepeyac assumes great strategic significance in this conspiracy theory, for at Tepeyac the Aztecs were said to have worshipped a fertility goddess, Tonantzin, and celebrated an annual pilgrimage to her there. In Nahuatl, Tonantzin means "Our Lady Mother" and was not an exclusive designation. This resonated, of course, with Guadalupe, who was instantly called "Our Mother." In fact, Indians began using Spanish words to describe indigenous things—including aspects of the sacred.

Lafaye argues that the native Mexicans melded Guadalupe into their sacred pantheon, where she functioned as a symbolic pivot on which colonialism turned, through processes of "syncretism," "continuity," and "transformation." Thus the Guadalupe of history emerges as an instrument of colonization and evangelization, a tool to dupe the Indians into surrendering their spiritual lives and worldviews to the Spanish religious order. For Lafaye, Guadalupe occupies a complex symbolic site that is implicated in dual movements—toward the repression of Aztec religion but also toward its continuation. The appearance of Guadalupe is said to precipitate the mass conversion of Indians to Catholicism. However,

according to historian Jonathan Kendall, "By the 1550s, virtually all natives had been baptized, but it was a sacrament administered without
preliminary instruction. The clergy's main educational efforts were directed at Indian children rather than adults."[15] Indian religious practices
continued, and according to Franciscan colonizer Fray Toribio de Benavente Motolinía, indigenous religious artifacts were ubiquitous in
supposedly Christian spaces.[16] It seems likely, then, that native religions
incorporated Christian symbols, particularly Guadalupe. "Because they
feared this unholy mixture of paganism and Christianity," argues
Kendall, "the missionaries discouraged the Indians from believing in
miraculous apparitions. Too often the natives reported sighting the figures of Christ or the Virgin at locations where Indians had once been
honored."[17]

Virgilio Elizondo offers what is perhaps the first attempt at a postcolonial Guadalupe theology.[18] The Virgin of Guadalupe in this model
ennobles cultural mixing, for she herself embodies and represents the
synthesis of the Indian and the Spanish. God is reimagined in the image
of a *mestiza* via the compound symbolism of Guadalupe. Jeanette Rodriguez summarizes and advances what I call postcolonial Guadalupe theory: "The question as to whether the apparition did in fact occur is in-
consequential," she writes in a theological work based on and intended
for Mexican-American women. "For those who believe, no explanation
is necessary; for those who do not believe, no explanation will satisfy."[19]

The third paradigm in Guadalupe discourse, what I describe as the
iconoclastic, is represented by Stafford Poole's recent work on the "origins" and "sources" of Guadalupe.[20] Poole, a Claretian priest, argues
that the apparition story has no "objective factual basis in history," that
it probably didn't occur, and that Juan Diego likely did not exist. Therefore, as he sees it, Guadalupe is a meaningless symbol. He bases his con-
tentions on the lack of textual sources. "Silence," that is, the lack of *textual* documentation, means that the story was nonexistent until the
seventeenth century, when the *criollos*, Mexican-born Spaniards, "appropriated" the story for themselves as a symbol of their divine election—as a chosen people separate from the Indians and from the Span-
ish-born Mexican residents. Skeptics today still question the validity of
the apparition narrative, that is the *appearances* of Guadalupe to Juan
Diego. Thus, Diego's canonization efforts were stalled for years until
Pope John Paul II made Juan Diego the first indigenous Mexican saint
upon his visit to Mexico City in July 2002. Poole further argues that the

Indians did not become significant in the Guadalupe devotion until the nineteenth century.

The question of the "truth" of the Guadalupe apparitions is best left for Poole and others who have ultimate questions of religious belief and political and personal gain at stake. One Chicano pilgrim to Guadalupe's Mexico home responded to the controversy as follows: "'Whatever Schulemburg says, we are not going to stop believing. And not just Mexicans but the whole Spanish-speaking world,' said Davíd Carrizales, a fifty-two-year-old pilgrim who said he was fulfilling a lifelong promise to visit the shrine from his home in Nuevo Laredo on the Texas border. 'There are millions of people who owe all we have to the Virgin of Guadalupe,' he said. 'Just one person cannot change this.'" Suffice it to say, as one historian of twentieth-century Mexico put it, that Mexicans "are certain whatever learned Vatican theologians might say or do, that the Virgin did indeed appear in Mexico."[21]

MAPPING THE SACRED/HOLY CITY

Today, a ritual plaza at the foot of Tepeyac hill contains the old basilica (opened in 1709) that housed the framed image of Guadalupe until the new basilica opened in 1974, also at the foot of the hill. A history of extra *long duree*, or long duration, focusing on the sacral foundations of Mexico City would show that, while actors came and went, the understanding of the place itself as sacred remained—even while the inspiration for that understanding changed radically. Beginning well before the Aztecs, inhabitants of the valley of Mexico believed themselves to be at the center of the world.[22] The Aztec imperial capital, Tenochtitlán, located in the center of the lake, in the center of the valley, was believed to be literally at the center of the cosmos. This understanding is evident in Aztec poetry:

> Proud of itself
> Is the City of Mexico-Tenochtitlán
> Here no one fears to die in war
> This is our glory

> This is Your Command
> Oh Giver of Life
> have this in mind, oh princes
> Who could conquer Tenochtitlán
> Who could shake the foundation of heaven?[23]

And after the fall,

> Nothing but flowers and songs of sorrow
> are left in Mexico and Tlatelolco,
> where once we saw warriors and wise men.

> We know it is true
> that we must perish,
> for we are mortal men.
> You the Giver of Life,
> you have ordained it.

> We wander here and there
> in our desolate poverty.
> We are mortal men.
> We have seen bloodshed and pain
> Where once we saw beauty and valor.[24]

Davíd Carrasco argues that the city "was eulogized as a proud, fearless, and glorious place, an invincible center that linked the world of fearless warriors with the universal god, the 'Giver of Life.' . . . Tenochtitlán was the point of union between the celestial powers and the underworld. It joined the many parts of the cosmos together."[25]

But the city for the Aztecs was also intimately related to the body. "There is a whole complex of ideas by which the universe was conceived as a projection of the human body," explains Alfredo López Austin,[26] and it was the ceremonial body moving through Aztec landscapes that made place most meaningful. Carrasco illuminates place in Nahuatl religion: "Aztec ritual moved and transformed human experience through colorful, florid, visual displays of images of highly energized relationships between temples and mountains, between social groups, between distinct levels of social status, and between humans and their gods."[27]

What Carrasco has called a "metamorphic vision of place" or "to change place" is particularly instructive for a genealogy of sacred place in the borderlands; the conclusion in this book returns to this discussion. Aztecs held visions of place that were at once fixed and shifting. Hence, Spanish religious spatial overlays not only disrupted Indigenous attachment to place but also continued this attachment in the processes of transformation.

Even before the Guadalupe story, the Spaniards infused the "New World" with Christian symbols combined with discourses of salvation and sacred place that were themselves borrowed from a Jewish conceptualization of Jerusalem. Spanish establishment of empire in the Americas was narrated, in part, as the founding of a New Jerusalem, based in

Mexico City. "A conquest crowned by that glorious moment when the Franciscans," argues Brian Wilson, "acting as a collective David, carried into Tenochtitlán the 'ark of the covenant' into the New World's 'Temple'—that is, the Christian sacraments into the newly erected monastery-church of San Francisco."[28] The apparition of Guadalupe, also referred to as the New Eve, confirmed the holiness of place and reiterated its primordial status in shifting religious cosmologies. According to one Catholic official, "Even though it is only forty meters high, [Tepeyac] is nonetheless the highest summit in America, for it was there the heavens and our land were united, and therefore it is closer to God."[29]

In its shift from Nahuatl to Christian, the valley of Mexico simultaneously underwent a transformation from "sacred city" to "holy city," in the terms delimited by Jeffrey Meyer. Sacred cities, according to Meyer, consist of "orientation, axiality, sacred kingship, and show in addition concrete centralizing symbols at the center of the city, principally the cosmic mountain and the linga." Holy cities, on the other hand, have "religious meaning because it simply is at a certain locus in the environment."[30] The locus is set apart as sacred because of the "hierophany," or the manifestation of a sacred being at a particular place. This describes the changing nature of sacred place in Mexico City.

Bernardino de Sahagún offers a vivid description of Tepeyac, and the continuity of the devotion there:

Close to the mountains there are three or four places where they often make solemn sacrifices, and they come to them from lands very far away. The first of these is here in Mexico, where there is a little mountain that is called Tepeacac [*sic*], and the Spanish call it Tepeaquilla, and now they call it Nstra. Señora de Guadalupe; in this place they had a temple dedicated to the mother of the goddesses who they called Tonantzin, which means Our Mother; there they made many sacrifices in honor of this goddess, and they came to them from places very far away, more than twenty *leguas* [leagues] from all the districts in Mexico, and they brought many offerings; men and women came, and kids to these fiestas; it was a huge gathering of people in those days, and they would all say let's go to the fiesta of Tonantzin; and now that there is built there the Church of our Lady of Guadalupe they also call her Tonantzin, taking the occasion from the preachers who also call Our Lady Mother of God Tonantzin. From where this foundation in this Tonantzin originated is not known for certain, but this we know for certain that the vocabulary signifies from her first imposition on that ancient Tonantzin, and it is something that should be remedied because the proper name of the Mother of God Our Lady is not Tonantzin, but Dios y Nantzin; It seems that this is a satanic invention, to veil idolatry under the error of this name Tonantzin, and they come now to visit this Tonantzin from very far away, as far away as before, the same devotion that is suspect, because there are a lot [of] churches everywhere to Our Lady, and they don't go to them, and they come from far away to this Tonantzin, like they did in ancient times.[31]

This description supports the possibility that Guadalupe was a simulacrum imposed on the place and narrative of Tonantzin, and that both sides, Indians and Spanish, may have been aware of the subterfuge. But, even more, Sahagún attests the mimetic power of the Indians, who at once captured Christian claims to sacred space and reflected them back with indigenous inflections.

The "New World's" holy city, the New Jerusalem, was not erected from a *tabula rasa*; rather, it imposed itself on a place that supported the weight of multiple layers of religious meanings. Contemporary Mexico City, then, is most fruitfully understood as a palimpsest, an ancient text whose original inscription has been erased and multiply reinscribed— while the original meanings are still intelligible. Much to the vexation of the fresh inscriptions, the old ones never quite go away entirely.

GUADALUPE'S NATIONAL BODY: INDEPENDENCE AND REVOLUTION

That Guadalupe was a central and motivating symbol for Mexican independence and nationalism is a topic that has been well covered. Both Eric Wolf and Victor Turner have theorized Guadalupe as a symbolic entity whose incorporation by the Catholic Church is only one of many such claims to ownership of it. William Taylor has meticulously traced Guadalupe's authority to several indigenous revolts against the Church during the eighteenth century. The Mexican nation-state, officially secular, has a history of aggressive socialist anti-Catholicism and, paradoxically, a fierce devotion to the Virgin of Guadalupe.

The Mexican War of Independence was, in many ways, a continuation of the clashes over race and class engendered by the obscenely nuanced and complicated social stratifications that were experienced most keenly as contests over space. By the nineteenth century, the Spanish political power structure was concentrated in Mexico City, which as a result monopolized public resources and managed rural localities by dispersing power centrifugally. Indians were physically barred from entering the center of Mexico City, the Zócalo. In the rural areas resentment grew as church and state continued their unholy alliance of sorts from the Mexican capital. By the early 1800s the Catholic Church owned half of the real estate in Mexico. When the Jesuits were expelled from New Spain in 1767, the government and private entrepreneurs made a fortune from the properties they left.[32]

By 1810, the sparks of Indian, *mestizo,* and *criollo* resentment at colonial racial formations would ignite the War of Independence, led by *criollo* secular priest Miguel Hidalgo (1753–1811).[33] The flames of revolt were also fanned by contemporaneous world events, especially the American and French revolutions and the European Enlightenment, which impacted Mexico mostly in the nineteenth century. The first revolutionary advance, led by Hidalgo, moved from the rural north toward Mexico City. Hidalgo, who was born into a middle-class *criollo* family and is said to have enjoyed gambling and affairs with women, enlisted Indian support with three promises: (1) the expulsion of the *peninsulares* from Mexico; (2) the abolition of tribute to Spain; and (3) the elevation of the Virgin of Guadalupe to empress of Mexico. His ragtag rebel Indian forces fought under the watchful eye of La Virgen de Guadalupe, who blessed their violent rampage from her emblazoned place of prominence on revolutionary banners. Gathering momentum and men as it raced passionately into Mexico City, Hidalgo's Indian/*mestizo* makeshift army repulsed the *criollos. Criollos* thus forged provisional alliances with the *gachupines,* as the *peninsulares* were derogatorily named. After a few key victories and several devastating defeats, the Indians began killing whites at random.

The Indians' sense of indignation and of the righteousness of their cause must certainly have been absolute, propelling the dark hordes of justice seekers moving with frenzy to enshrine their queen anew: the dark Virgin in Mexico City. By capturing the capital, the Indians would not only take control of the center of power in the Americas but in addition would add a mythological overlay to the deeply symbolic ethos of Mexico City. That the Virgin was used effectively in poetic interpretations to galvanize Indian feeling and transform it into action evinces her popularity: by the early nineteenth century, at least, Indians had bonded in a profound and mystical way with their mother, the *morena* goddess, Guadalupe.

In 1811, Hidalgo was tried by the Inquisition for his revolutionary activities and subsequently stripped of his vows, convicted of sedition, shot, and beheaded. In 1821, the Plan of Iguala was signed and Mexican independence from Spain achieved. This, however, was not Hidalgo's Indian revolt; this independence came at a cost to the Indians—especially the noble ideas rejecting racial formations.

Independence under the presidency of Benito Juárez precipitated the effective dismantling of Church power, which would be completed by the later revolution. During 1859 and 1860, Juárez nationalized Church properties in their totality, enabling their auctioning for "public" coffers. Additionally, Juárez declared marriage a civil contract, decreased the number of religious holidays while limiting public religious processions, and secularized cemeteries. The Mexican Revolution (1910–17) would further dismantle any remnants of a church-state union.

Like the War of Independence, the revolution was spatialized in conflicts between the rural areas and Mexico City. The space of the revolution spanned at least two separate revolts, both against Mexico City: one staged by the rebel bands in the north, led by General Pancho Villa, and one by the revolutionaries in the south, led by General Emiliano Zapata. Both revolutionaries made war against the Catholic Church, even while Zapata led his troops into Mexico City flying the banner of La Virgen de Guadalupe. Villa confessed to an American journalist: "I believe in God, but not in religion. I have recognized the priests as hypocrites ever since, when I was twenty, I took part in a drunken orgy with a priest and two women he had ruined. They are all frauds—the priests and their cloth, which is supposed to be a protection, they use to entice the innocent. I shall do what I can to take the Church out of politics and to open the eyes of the people to the tricks of the thieving priests."[34]

In 1911, the thirty-year regime of Porfirio Díaz, known as the Porfiriato, came to a halt when revolutionary Francisco Madero became president. Although the northern revolution had ended, the southern one continued. Madero was an avowed spiritist, and even while he did not undermine the Church during his tenure in office, the revolution had a strong anti-Church current from its beginning, reaching fruition in the constitution of 1917. This constitution, issuing from the revolutionary meeting in Querértaro, reiterated and advanced Juárez's earlier pronouncements. All priests were to register with their local governments so that states could impose ceilings on the number of clergy within their territories, and foreign priests were banned from Mexico. Additionally, the Church's participation in politics was forbidden and all clerics were denied suffrage; education was made entirely secular and churches were denied access to the media. Church buildings were declared under the authority of the state, public celebrations of mass were prohibited, and priests could not wear their sacramental vestments in public. Mexicans and, subsequently, Mexican-Americans inherited these revolutionary attitudes toward the Church, along with a seemingly paradoxical love of Guadalupe. This partly accounts for the character of Chicana/o Catholicism.

GUADALUPE UNDER SOCIALISM

On November 14, 1921, a man apparently praying at the original shrine church of Guadalupe in Mexico City placed a bomb at the feet of an image of Guadalupe. The explosion shattered windows and destroyed marble statuary; the Virgin remained unscathed. But the impact of the Revolutionary anti-Church laws was not fully felt until 1925–26, following the inauguration of President Plutarco Calles (1924–28). Calles was a staunch opponent of the Church and began to enforce the 1917 anti-Church laws aggressively. His campaign against the Church began unofficially when one hundred men disrupted a mass in a working-class Mexico City district, declaring their independence from the Vatican and speaking in the name of the "Mexican Catholic Church." The next day, two men dressed as priests appeared at the church and tried to say mass under the authority of the same entity, the Mexican Catholic Church. Later, these men were identified as policemen—Calles was endeavoring to institute a church under governmental control, forming a distinctively Mexican national religious body.

On 2 July 1926, Calles published an edict ordering the enforcement of the anti-Church constitutional provisions and more. In response, on 24 July 1926, the Mexican Catholic hierarchy published a pastoral letter denouncing the actions of the Calles government and called for an economic "boycott" of all but essential goods and services in an attempt to cripple the economy and force the repeal of the laws. Moreover, the bishops and archbishops announced that, as of midnight on 31 July, all church services performed by priests would cease until the laws against the Church were repealed. Public outcry against this announcement was immediate and massive. A movement that was strongest in the conservative, affluent, rural, white areas—calling itself "Viva Cristo Rey," or "Cristeros"—responded to the situation by waging three years of antigovernment guerrilla tactics, starting in August 1926. This period is known, accordingly, as the Cristero War.[35] At its height, this war involved twenty-five thousand armed acolytes; it was responsible for eight thousand deaths. The Cristero movement was an epitome of a distinct Mexican male devotion (separate from the maternal relationship to Guadalupe)—it was bloody and violent, dedicated to the suffering and sacrificial Christ.

In the capital, Mexican women were holding mass, public requiems of Guadalupe, protesting government actions. Mexican women appealed to the peculiarly feminine religious sensibility by directing a public letter, sent by the Catholic Society of Orizaba, to the wife of the president, Mexico's first *señora* of temporal matters. Tellingly signed by Guadalupe Ortega, the public letter was published on 28 July 1926:

> We propose to permit you to hear the echoes of the voices of the mothers of Mexico. We believe firmly that our letter is a reflection of that mysterious light which flashes from the hearts of good mothers, obedient daughters and faithful wives. We know that there is not one Catholic woman in Mexico who does not think as we do, because we are all educated according to the same principles. Why is our religion so bitterly attacked? What end is being sought in this onslaught on the religion which defends women, which lifts her up to a higher moral level, which places her by the side of the man she loves as a companion and not as a slave? We love Mexico, love her welfare, happiness, progress, and peace. We are optimistic; we believe this crisis will pass because you, Señora, will speak, speak plainly, as the First Lady of the Land should speak.[36]

The idea of sacred motherhood, symbolized by Guadalupe, resonates throughout Mexican culture. The letter continues: "You, Señora, can transform the actual state of affairs, if you wish, through love and sweetness. It is true that a woman has a great influence in the home when she is simple, charitable and loving. Man, more rude, more egotistical, feels the power of a woman."[37]

Women's rank and file relied on ritual discourse, appealing to the premier woman of eternal, spiritual, and symbolic authority—Guadalupe at Tepeyac. On the next day, 29 July 1926, the *New York Times* ran several front-page reports describing the events in Mexico:

> Each day worshippers have come to the Mexico City Cathedral and to the shrine of Guadalupe in increasing numbers, and today they overflowed all the area around the cathedral sweeping in solid streams through all the roads leading to the shrine of the Virgin of Guadalupe, the favorite saint of Mexico and dearest beloved of the Indians throughout the nation. . . . The highways and by-paths leading to the shrine of Guadalupe were alive with Indian families. They had plodded all night long over the ragged roads from remote villages, perhaps snatching a bit of sleep beside the roadside with only a scanty blanket for protection, in order to reach their "shrine of shrines" in time for the first mass at 5 o'clock. For many miles in all directions they trudged through the freshening dawn, and later encamped in the shadow of Guadalupe, where they spent hours at their devotions.[38]

The *Times* stresses the body in the events, particularly the relationship between the body and the city, noting as follows:

> Those of vigorous body were ever ready to aid the crippled, and at times, without assistance, the maimed and blind dragged their weakened bodies to the shrine and added their supplications to the Virgin, who, traditionally, has so often saved Mexico City from peril, so often befriended the Indian, to make manifest again her beneficence. . . . From the entrance gate into the church to the shrine all made the journey upon their knees, many, particularly the aged and infirm, shuffling painfully and proceeding slowly and with difficulty. Upon reaching the church doors, all in the procession lighted candles and continued the journey on their knees frequently pausing to bow their heads until their foreheads touched the floor. Numerous women raised their arms aloft in supreme supplication and lifted their faces to heaven while tears streamed down their cheeks.[39]

This demonstration, the culmination of the church-state conflict in Mexico, is instructive for several reasons. First, it illustrates the responsibility that women have felt for the place of religion in Mexico; all classes of Mexican women led the battle against what some felt was an assault on their religious freedom, and others moved to protect the mother of Mexico, the Virgin of Guadalupe. Women joined in symbolic bodily protest, dressing all in black and wearing black shawls over their heads in mourning. Mexican women's public protests become all the more meaningful and bold in light of the fact that women's national suffrage would not be attained until some twenty-four years later, in 1953, and women would not be given the right to vote in municipal elections until 1947. Not all of Mexican society was unified in opposition to the government's enforcement of the anti-Church laws. It is reported, however without gender distinction, that the male-dominated labor party advocated the government's religious laws.

In 1929 the conflict was resolved when the Church effectively caved in to state pressures, resentfully consenting to the state restrictions. "No longer would creole aristocratic families determine the shape of the Mexican hierarchy," argues historian Robert Quirk. "The future belonged to middle and lower class clerics, to mestizos and even Indians . . . to the people of the dark Virgin of Guadalupe."[40] And indeed, private devotion to Guadalupe, in the annual pilgrimage to Tepeyac, has now been rendered a dramatically public political matter.

AM I NOT HERE? PILGRIMAGE TO MEXICO CITY

Each year on 12 December and during the few days leading up to it, it is estimated that between two and four million pilgrims descend upon the shrine at Tepeyac.[41] They come from all over Mexico, the United States, and the Spanish-speaking world. It is the largest pilgrimage in the Americas.

Pilgrimage to Tepeyac cannot be considered as independent from a pilgrimage to Mexico City—what Diana Eck and Carrasco have called "sacred sight seeing."[42] All roads extending out from the Zócalo are decorated with impressive statuary dedicated to the Aztecs and their pantheon of deities, to Revolutionary War heroes, and to former presidents and other political leaders. Historical memory is created by and structured into the built environment of the city; these statues function as mnemonic devices, at once creating and triggering historical memory, or public myth. The Zócalo itself operates in the consciousness of Mexicans as a shrine, of sorts, to Mexican civil religion.

A pilgrimage path extends outward from the basilica into the middle of the street, stretching the length of several city blocks. Originally, Tepeyac was surrounded by water, and visitors had to cross a land bridge to reach the site encompassing Tepeyac hill. Tepeyac is now a pilgrimage complex spanning approximately two city blocks, referred to as La Villa, the center of which is a flat ritual square, the atrium known as El Atrio de las Americas, which sits an entire story above street level.

La Villa is surrounded by an industrial working-class neighborhood, although certainly not the poorest one in the city. The streets are lined with large shoe stores, restaurants, and beautiful religious-article stores filled with arresting devotional objects and art. There are also a bank, booths to convert currency that continuously display the ever changing rate of exchange with American money, and, as of 1996, a McDonald's restaurant. The sidewalks around the basilica, as in the center of Mexico, are vibrant and alive with movement. Most of the cars halting traffic are Volkswagen Bugs and Nissan Sentras painted green and white and operating as taxi cabs; these can be flagged just about anywhere in the city. During the December pilgrimage, the streets in front of the basilica are blocked by police barricades, and pedestrians crowd the streets, which are also populated by mostly idle police officers and busy medical trucks and tents.

Street vendors sell everything from watches to books, cassette tapes, food, pens, leather bags, shoes, toys, art, and stones, and much more.

Food is also sold in the atrium. As one moves closer to La Villa along the pilgrimage path, the articles become increasingly religious: rosary beads, crucifixes, and prayer cards are everywhere, and the nonreligious items disappear altogether from the gate of the atrium onward. To the side of the atrium, a carnival has set up small rides and games of chance; by playing these games, a pilgrim can determine his or her luck with the Virgin before entering to see her. The most revered image along the pilgrimage path, however, is the image of Guadalupe—she is omnipresent. She is on clocks and framed pictures; she is depicted in four-foot-high statues; she is on pens, key rings, bumper stickers, and "snowballs"; she is a small plastic pendant on a black string necklace filled with chemicals to make her glow fluorescent green ("La Virgen Luminosa—a peso"); she is on a paperweight with Juan Diego at her feet, bearing roses; she is kitsch, a twelve-inch clay image; she is a bookend; she sells insurance and lottery tickets and Gloria Trevi records; and she owns taco stands and blesses telephone booths. As on all streets in Mexico City, vendors aggressively fill the air with lyrical and repetitive sales chants: *Compra joven, a peso, a peso.* During the early weeks of December, more than at any other time throughout the year, La Virgen de Guadalupe goes beyond radical fetishization—she is radically commodified.

The small temple at the base of the Tepeyac hill is the first structure visible from the street near La Villa—it looms over the site. Attached to the Tepeyac church is a cemetery where many nineteenth-century Mexican dignitaries are buried. Directly beneath it on the main plaza sits the old basilica. Built in colonial style, it was erected in 1704. Connected to it is a colonial building, also built in the 1700s, that once functioned as a convent. Both buildings are now defunct, and together they span the length of the atrium, creating one of its lower walls against Tepeyac hill. To the left of the old basilica, as one approaches from the main path, is the new basilica, designed in abstract postmodern style and opened in the late seventies, simultaneous with the erection of other explicitly postmodern Mexican structures. The new basilica marks one end of the atrium. It currently houses the miraculous image, which is denoted by the signifier "the miracle of the continuous preservation" because the image does not fade. Directly across from the new basilica looms an immense crosslike structure sporting Aztec sundials and calendars to echo pre-Columbian architecture. At the center of it a mechanized drama opens at various times to display puppets who reenact the movements of the Guadalupe myth.

Between the convent and the Aztec structure, the pilgrimage path leads around the rose garden and up to Tepeyac, passing two small churches. On the left of the path is a one-room stone structure covered by a tattered green cloth tarp. This is the church of the Indians, built in 1556, where, according to the mythology, Juan Diego lived and is now buried. Hence, it is a favorite stop on the ritual path. Right outside Juan Diego's grave, inside the church, is a poster board on which are pinned many photographs of people, ex-votos in the shapes of various body parts known as *milagritos,* or "little miracles," specifically designed for healing different parts of the body, and narrative petitions to Juan Diego requesting his help in resolving vexing dilemmas of all varieties. The supplicants ask for help in illegal border crossings, for work, to assist those relations who have already crossed over into the First World, and for healing. Here, as throughout the borderlands, material culture and materiality in general are intimately bound to an intense spirituality.

Across from the church of the Indians is another small temple, a waterfall adorned with carved-stone serpents, a rose garden, and a museum. In 1992, a brilliantly painted brass statue was placed in the middle of what is now a waterfall on the hillside. The statue depicts seminaked, prostrate Indians offering small images, "idols," of their gods to Guadalupe. The statue is called "La Ofrenda"—the Offering.

The path up Tepeyac is a wide staircase carved from stone. The center of the city is directly visible from Tepeyac, even through dense smog. It is not difficult to understand why the Aztecs and Spaniards thought of this hill as enchanted: the view of the city from it is spectacular. The climb is arduous for even the most active people because of the altitude and smog—it requires effort to reach the summit of the Americas. The Tepeyac church is small and dark. At its most crowded places, everyone rubs against each other easily. At the pulpit the Empress of the Americas stands with her head bowed. The walls are covered with images narrating the Guadalupe myth. Many of the pilgrims' rituals here are improvised. When I visited in 1994, I saw an elder woman standing in front of the painting that depicts Juan Bernardino's healing, rubbing a one-dollar American bill on the image and then on the foreheads of several children.

The atrium serves as an interactive space where *mexicanos* and Chicanos move from place to place, picking and choosing from historical formations and possibilities, choosing and creating hybrid memory in a historical consciousness. The buildings or cultural and historical artifacts are at once markers of sacrality and identity and nodal points on the identity loop. As *mexicanos* and Chicanos move from location to location in the atrium, they interact with one another and with a place that is both fixed and infinite. Beyond the colonial temple, back in the area of the Aztec sundial, there are reverberations of Aztec ceremonial rites: "metamorphic place." Moving through the atrium brings together landscape, historical imagery, and religious agents in a dramaturgical process that opens and limits avenues to locating one's self on the cosmic map. In one sense, the atrium is a theater where the drama of history is brought together with personal and group identity in public ritual and in the minds of the actors.

Underpinning all of this is the current of individual passages that pilgrims make on their knees, moving from the Aztec sundial to the postmodern basilica. This process, taken in its entirety, symbolizes *mexicano* and Chicano identity. For although Mexican identity is a composite of several historical time periods and processes, its linchpin is the movement from the indigenous to the postmodern, a process in which all the symbols of history get thrown into the mix and managed: hence, the postmodern design of the basilica is an appropriate, salient, and conscious signifier of this process.

11 DECEMBER

Pilgrimage groups mostly come by truck, bus, or bike, or they walk or jog in groups wearing matching warm-up suits. Others, largely those who can't afford more expensive means, take the efficient subway system that extends far out into the city—except the southern part of the city, where the most wealth is concentrated. Many Chicana/os fly in from the United States or drive cars. However people travel, the eleventh of December is the day for arrival, vigil, and actual pilgrimage.

Trucks are popular vehicles for pilgrimage and artistic expression. Big old pickup trucks with wood-framed beds line the streets surrounding La Villa for several city blocks; nearly all are decorated with loud banners, flowers, and giant images of Guadalupe. Pilgrims sleep in, on, and underneath them; indeed, people—perhaps the poorest of the pilgrims— camp out in all corners of the atrium and all around Tepeyac. "Rosa Hernández," a young volunteer at the site, expressed the sentiment popular among the middle classes: "First of all it's about tradition." She was volunteering at the shrine to keep the tradition "alive, so that people will not lose their faith, that they will manifest their faith. It's a very beautiful thing. People arrive here after long pilgrimages, dirty, tired, and hungry; and all they want to do is to see her, and then they fall asleep wherever. The first thing they want to do is to see her."[43]

Pilgrims agree: they are there to see their mother, to honor her, and to ask her for protection—continuing a tradition that is centuries old. One Chicano journalist at the feast in 1994 recorded pilgrims explaining their devotion: "[One pilgrim says,] 'We come to pay her tribute and to petition her, as well.' I speak to a family that's come all the way from East Los Angeles to honor her. 'I want to ask her for better luck with work in the North,' a teenage son, a long-haired rocker, tells me. 'And for her to accompany all Latinos in California now that they've passed 187,' adds his older brother."[44] Guadalupe is opposed to U.S. temporal authorities.

When I asked pilgrims about their motivations for attending the pilgrimage and the meaning of Guadalupe, the answers I received were confirmed by Paolo Giuriati and Elio Masferrer Kan's recent anthropological study of 403 pilgrims. Most answers offered by both women and men of all ages resonate with one another: "To visit our mother at least once a year," "to be closer to her," and the like. There is, however, one key distinction: the middle and upper classes, as well as the clergy, stress the tradition of the pilgrimage, whereas the poorer pilgrims typically have specific material requests, such as personal healing or the healing of a family member, employment, immigration to the United States, or aid for people who have already immigrated. The poorest seekers focus on benefit and retribution pursuant to embarking on a pilgrimage *as* tradition, and not simply on the devotion as a marker of nationality.[45]

Indeed, there are multiple performances on the eleventh of December. Inside the basilica, elegantly dressed Mexican movie stars, politicians, and dignitaries perform for the television cameras as the ceremony is broadcast live throughout the Americas and on a video screen on the opposite side of the atrium (a detail added in 1995). But the video screen may as well be on the other side of the world, because the images it broadcasts—elegantly dressed aristocrats feigning piety while the monsignor exhorts the crowd to "translate" their faith into good citizenship and "fraternity"—could not be further removed from the activities outside the basilica: devotion reifies class divisions. Outside, "Las Mañanitas," the birthday song to La Virgen, is a haunting melody that is ubiquitous on the eleventh.

Local pilgrimage groups, in contrast to those who have traveled long distances, consist largely of coworkers carrying banners; they organize office parties for the occasion. Some of these groups are explicitly political in nature. One tradition, the Great Peregrination of the Workers, marches by candlelight from the Zócalo to the basilica. The flyer for the event in 1995 bore a color likeness of the Virgin and offered the following prayer: "Dark Virgin, give us the strength, the wisdom and the tolerance to shake the yoke, give us the light to recuperate freedom [*la libertad*]." The flyer poignantly demonstrates how the Virgin is used in social contests—how she is poetically renarrated, absorbed, and reflected back in rebellious ways—and it claims that the nation is afflicted by seven plagues: low salaries, high prices, unemployment, lack of security, no job benefits, corruption, and the giving of national patrimony to foreigners.

The all-night prayer vigil/party/political protest on the eleventh is the highlight of the event; the throng of people continues to swell until it nearly implodes by dusk. Sensuality abounds. Pilgrims smoke, drink, eat, dance, pray, scream loudly on carnival rides, gamble, buy, and sell—until daybreak. Indeed, there is an element of play, even of the carnivalesque, to the commemoration. Pilgrims are there to have fun and participate in an ancient Mexican ceremony, while escaping the structure of quotidian life. The crowd has its own energy and independent personality; it becomes a singular life form. It has unique odors that both seduce and repulse, distinct movements and rhythms, and a monotone voice. It demands submission. In return, it offers the uniquely rewarding ability to release the self, to let go of individualism in moments of rapture and *ecstasy*—derived from *ecstatis,* the Greek for stepping outside of one's self. The beating of the drums, the dance, and the smells intoxicate into a radically unique and universal consciousness. That pilgrims experience ecstasy—that sensation beyond language—is confirmed by the Giuriati-Kan study, which concludes that "the majority of the pilgrims confess . . . that the emotions they experience are greater than their ability to express them with words."[46]

The idea of the "carnival" as populist inversion and thus subversion of a capitalist order to serious work provides one way to understand the feast of Guadalupe (and the other traditions discussed in this book). Carlos Monsiváis wryly notes: "Until very recently, only the most paternalistic of statements were ever made about 12 December by institutional Catholicism: 'That's how the people are! Their education merely furthers their excess. They take only their frustrations to the Virgin, their rapture and their filth.'" But Monsiváis ambivalently points to the change in understanding brought by religious study: "This was before, when no one really paid attention to popular religion, or analysed the carnival from a Bahktinian point of view, or talked of sacred spaces and times, or of Christianity's preferential option for the poor."[47]

Religious performance at the Guadalupe pilgrimage challenges competing class and racialized group representations and perceptions by recasting the codes and terms—*symbols*—by which society is constructed.
As a result, the rigid social divisions of Mexican society are symbolically
constructed and replayed. This too is the ideal of the carnival, what Victor and Edith Turner in their description of the pilgrimage called *communitas*. As Monsiváis points out and as I have indicated above, there
are distinct class differences on the pilgrimage. Given the distinct spaces
cordoned off according to race and class, it appears that the pilgrimage
reinscribes class divisions rather than eliminating them.

12 DECEMBER

When the sun rises on the twelfth of December, the crowd has been transformed. It lies still. It is asleep. At about noon the atrium returns to life,
but this time with traditional dancers—mostly Aztec but also regional
dancers with their own costumes, choreography, traditions, and myths;
all, however, mark off a space for themselves within the atrium or below,
on the street, to perform for the crowds. Several enact the theme of the
Spanish and the Moors. Others dress as clowns or perform as tightrope
walkers, and still others exhibit gender transgression—men dressing as
women. Overall, the twelfth is a transgressive performative time, and the
actors who dominate are without question the Indians. The basilica and
the surrounding blocks pulsate with the deafening and hypnotic drum
beat to which two hundred traditional dance groups move in full indigenous regalia.

Dancers undertake their rituals with great seriousness. They must prepare to dance, and while performing they burn copal and other herbs in
small stone holders called *sahumadores*. They recite prayers while waving the smoking offerings in circles, letting the smoke pass onto the
dancers and the spectators. Dancers form circles around the burning incense, a scene that functions as a makeshift shrine approached by audience members for ritual blessings. People crave the smoke, which they
wave onto themselves and their bodies. Medicine women and men set up
shop and on a drop-in basis pray for and anoint seekers with indigenous
herbs and rituals.

A visitor unaware of the shrine's history may wonder how this scene
supports what is ostensibly a Christian phenomenon. "Raul Canizares,"
a dancer in full native regalia, spoke for the dancers during the 1994 pilgrimage, when he explained that he goes to the basilica to dance to honor

the Virgin and the other "Mexican ancestors." He expressed a sentiment widely echoed: "We honor Guadalupe because she is our mother—but we are not Catholic. Still, we respect the Catholic beliefs." He was holding a sign of a spiritualist temple that read (originally in Spanish) "Spiritualist Temple of the Four Powers from the Well of Jacob, Marian Trinitarian," a Mexican spiritualist church (discussed in chapter 5) that prepares year-long for the ceremony.[48]

Dressed as an Aztec and performing the dance, "Fernando Savera," a man probably in his mid-fifties, answered, "Yes and no" when asked whether he was a Catholic. He grounded his ambivalence in history and myth: "When the Spanish conquered Mexico, the Indians began to express their religion through Christian rituals." He argued that Catholicism in Mexico is a synthesis, not "pure Christianity." They worship La Virgen, he said, because she is really Tonantzin. And they don't follow everything that the priests say. He held a banner that read "Unión, Confirmidad, y Conquista, May 3, 1975," which displayed a picture of El Niño de Atocha. When asked what all of this meant, he said, "*Unión* means for us to unite, *confirmar* means for us to confirm, and *conquista* means for us, as Aztecs, to carry on the conquest tradition."[49]

June Nash contends that "the vitality of these [preconquest beliefs] can be seen in the ethnographic descriptions of contemporary communities,"[50] descriptions that have confirmed the perennial influence of Tonantzin-Guadalupe.[51] A modern study of Tonantzin's significance for Nahua Indians in the southern Huasteca region in east-central Mexico found that she is their principal deity, whose annual feast takes place from 20 to 24 December. She is petitioned for many favors, especially for the fertility of the crops and of the women. During her feast, she is ritually imbued with the feminine and the masculine principles—she represents a continuity of both. The Nahua often refer to her in Spanish as "La Virgen de Guadalupe," as if the Christian conquest added only another idiom rather than replacing the old.

All this and more congeals on 12 December, wherein the dramaturgy at the basilica enables the whole of history to be recast—that is, the contact and conquest periods are performed and narrated anew. However, in this playing of the drama of conquest, the Indians are the winners. According to the Giuriati-Kan study:

> In a country like México, in which the State and their corporations are omnipresent, the spaces for worship and for religious ceremonies represent contexts where society can put into practice their own criteria and forms of organization on the margin and outside of State control. It's a place where

leaders are tested and developed, where criteria for respect are developed, consensus and legitimacy, where prestige is gained on one's own merits, where the laity construct the church. True schools of democracy, their roles have been very important in the transformations Mexico has suffered in its long history.[52]

By dusk, the atrium is nearly empty.

MEXICO CITY AS SACRED CENTER OF MEMORY

The truly sacred nature of Mexico City—situated on a high plain that reaches altitudes between 6,800 and 7,900 feet, surrounded by snow-capped volcanoes, and crisscrossed by lakes and streams—was surely confirmed by its initial occupants (approximately fifteen thousand years ago) if only for its majestic beauty. Similarly, today the site is famous for its age and size. Throughout time, groups and individuals have staked competing claims to control not only the space of Mexico City but also its symbolism. Since the time of the Aztecs, the geography of Mexico City has been thought of as a sacred center, with many ritual complexes rounding out its landscape. Today, that original symbolic grammar resonates in the continued narration and symbolization of the city. Mexico City is a center of memory; it is a place where memory is constructed, deconstructed, and poetically reconstructed: the built environment and the mythology are inseparable. Twenty-five million people make it the largest modern metropolis in the world.

There are myriad apparition myths throughout Mexico, yet none has had the force of Guadalupe—because Guadalupe appeared and remains close to the national center. Thus, she is a powerful woman, and those who are also on the margins of authoritative places identify with her symbolic location and are inspired to cross boundaries. To the powerful, she is a symbol of tradition; to the powerless, she is a source of hope and strength. Some devotees make great sacrifices in order to fulfill a pil-grimage to Guadalupe; other Mexicans pass 12 December without even noting the calendar day—and there are many responses in between, impossible to quantify. Suffice it to say that Guadalupe as myth and symbol creates a discourse that is at once powerful and volatile. She is the cement in the construction of Mexico City as a sacred city and capital of the postmodern world.

But time, too, is inflected by the Guadalupe of Mexico City. The Mexican Catholic calendar is delineated by saints and their festivals, which are celebrated by individuals born near the feast of the saint with his or her name—a kind of "birthday." The Christmas season in Mexico begins on 11 December, the most sacred day on the Mexican calendar, and ends on 6 January with the celebration of El Día de los Reyes Magos (Day of the Kings or Magi). Following the 12 December Guadalupe fiesta, the *posadas* begin. *Posadas* are dramas enacted by families and friends, consisting of "a series of night journeys when the Holy Family goes from house to house seeking shelter, being turned down repeatedly until finally (by prearrangement) one family opens its doors," and the family acting as the Holy Family stays the night there, reenacting Christ's birth.[53]

Nowhere do the events of the Christmas season outshine those continuous public events in the nation's capital—and this was true even when the state remained anticlerical *de jure,* until 1989 at least. As part of his campaign to improve Mexico's public image (necessary for the passage of the North American Free Trade Agreement, or NAFTA), Harvard-educated president Carlos Salinas de Gotari declared that he would modernize church-state relations, and in 1992, the anti-Church laws were rescinded. Ironically, modernization in this case meant *reestablishing* Church power! In fact, upon the papal visit in 2002, John Paul II was treated as a state dignitary, President Fox kneeling to kiss the Pope's ring. The *Los Angeles Times* reported on Fox's press meeting as follows: "From off camera, a reporter shouted, 'Mr. President, is Mexico still a secular state?' Fox did not reply."[54]

Mexico City as political and symbolic center has long influenced the people who live on its spatial periphery but nonetheless exist within its radius of command. Not only Mexicans but also Mexican-Americans can find their divine cosmic uniqueness in their election by the Guadalupe of La Capital. In the nineteenth and twentieth centuries, the Guadalupe of Mexico began to hold sway over a new people and periphery: Mexican-Americans in the U.S. Southwest. As historian John Chávez asserts, "Chicanos view their region (despite their practical use of the term Southwest) from the perspective of their cultural center in Mexico City. Furthermore, the current of their history has flowed south and north, not east to west."[55]

Chicana essayist Sandra Cisneros confirms this claim in her account of a poetic encounter with Tepeyac, when her pilgrimage there precipitated a religious regeneration, lifting her out of a deep state of depression. Mexico City, she writes, is the home of her grandparents and ancestors, and in imagining Tepeyac, she extends her U.S./Chicana self into the heart of Mexico, thus expanding the parameters of her individual space into a cosmic universe to which she belongs by blood and memory.[56] Cisneros describes the warmth and familiarity she discovered while on pilgrimage, meeting her ancestry: "I take Abuelito's [grandfather's] hand, fat and dimpled in the center like a valentine, and we walk past the basilica, where each Sunday the Abuela [grandmother] lights the candles for the soul of Abuelito. Past the very same spot where long ago Juan Diego brought down from the *cerro* [hill] the miracle that has drawn everyone, except my Abuelito, on their knees."[57] That "Abuela" lit candles for Abuelo signifies that her communication with her Abuelo is spirit communication: he is dead—Cisneros is consorting with the spirits of the dead who mediate her connection to Tepeyac, to the myth of Juan Diego, and in a profound way to the place of Mexico City. But, "Abuelito" was not brought to his knees—he was not a devotee like his wife.

Cisneros concludes by asking, "Who would've guessed, after all this time, it is me who will remember when everything else is forgotten, you who took with you to your stone bed something irretrievable, without a name."[58] It is Cisneros, unlikely as an American, a Chicana, who remembers the ancestors at Tepeyac; she retrieves what is irretrievable—the patrimony that is the power of the primordial place—now buried in stone. It is that amorphous memory, the nameless—the ineffable—that constitutes Cisneros's vision, her identity, her spirituality: it is grounded in a mythical connection to place mediated by memory. Space can overcome the chasms of time when mediated by the power of memory. In this way, Chicanas and Chicanos who return to Tepeyac return to the primordial wound of *mestizo* birth—to the sacred center, the ground of being. However, only a small number of Chicanos will ever make the pilgrimage to the primordial center of Tepeyac as Cisneros did.

And still, the Mexico City–Los Angeles spatial continuum has served as an interstitial creative space for the dialectical production of two heterogeneous cultures, connecting two communities into one primary symbolization, multiply manifested. According to the *Los Angeles Times,* "In Southern California and throughout the Southwest, devotion to Guadalupe has evolved to become the core of Latino Catholicism. As immigrants from Latin America settled in the U.S. Southwest, the Virgin emerged as a protector and liberator of the poor and marginalized."[59] Let us cross the border now, in search of Guadalupe as she makes her presence felt in Los Angeles.

CHAPTER 3

Religious Transnationalism

A Mexican Virgin in L.A.

Geographically, in fact, the Southwest does resemble the
Mexican deserts and highlands more closely than it does the
plains and woodlands of the eastern United States. To this familiar southwestern terrain the cultural influence of Mexico
City has radiated for over three hundred years.

> John R. Chávez, *The Lost Land: The Chicano Image of
> the Southwest*

To visit Mexico is for a citizen of Los Angeles like a visit to
Home Sweet Home. The traditions that bind us in California
to you in Mexico, are growing stronger year after year.

> John J. Cantwell, Archbishop of Los Angeles, Mexico City (1941),
> in Frances J. Weber, ed., *Documents of California Catholic History*

We ask the church to sacrifice with the people for social
change, for justice, and for love of brother. We don't ask for
words. We ask for deeds. We don't ask for paternalism. We
ask for servanthood.

> César E. Chávez, "The Mexican American and the Church,"
> *El Grito* 4 (Summer 1968)

"My son, there are three things that pertain to our religion," goes an often-cited *consejo* (counsel) from a Mexican-American grandmother. "The Lord, Our Lady of Guadalupe, and the Church. You can trust in the first two, but not in the third."[1] Another devotee, "Señora Inés de la Cruz," *guadalupana* elder in East Los Angeles, explains her devotional practices as distinct from the Church:

> My [home has an] altar for me, and to have La Virgen de Guadalupe there [in my vestibule] is like having a blessing in my home. This is a belief that perhaps those who are not Mexican Catholics will judge and call me crazy, saying, "Crazy woman, how is that picture going to help?" But that is my faith, that is the belief and faith of my family. I never get up without going first to the Virgin. I go to her to continue the day. We, as Latino Catholics, we have faith in the Virgin, and when you have faith in something, that faith is what counts. I believe that in every Mexican Catholic household you will find an image of La Virgen de Guadalupe there. This is the faith that our people have.[2]

These Catholic narratives resonate with centuries of lay attitudes toward institutional Catholicism in the borderlands. Still, and somewhat ironically, in the contemporary U.S. Southwest, Catholicism among Latina/os remains a vital force that emerges from several historical and spiritual movements focused around Guadalupe.

My thesis in this chapter is that Guadalupe functions as a transnational symbol, one that is reimagined in social-political-spiritual movements; La Virgen de Guadalupe is the fulcrum on which religious poetics in Mexican-American Catholicism pivots. She provides a symbolic (and strategic) connection to Mexico City—place, history, and identity— for the diasporic Mexican-American Catholic community. Concomitantly, La Virgen sacralizes peripheral space, rendering it a homeland place, beginning especially and intentionally in Los Angeles. As in Mexico, Guadalupe heads a pantheon of Catholic-origin saints, as well as saints not sanctioned by the Church—community-based or "popular" saints who are called upon to provide various services for devotees in struggles through a poetics of prayer/practice.

Mexican-American attitudes toward Catholicism were inflected by several historical processes, resulting mostly from colonialism. These processes isolated people from urban centers of dogma. Moreover, linguistic differences continue to demarcate distinct regions within Mexico, and many regions were outside each other's spoken language; this condition, added to the trauma of colonialism, rendered translating the idioms and idiosyncrasies of Renaissance Catholicism for a newly conquered population a lofty task indeed. Colonizers relied on performance, the *tableau vivant*—living images—to animate Christian mythologies. Natives, long accustomed to the human performance of cosmic drama, found the images compelling, if they did not clearly understand them. Church and state power were nearly inseparable during the colonial period, and as a result, the poor developed animosities toward the Church, culminating eventually in the Mexican Revolution—a process indelibly stamping Mexican relations with Catholicism. In the United States, barriers of racialization and direct religious competition have added to the difficulties.[3] As a result, in the words of Lawrence Mosqueda, "Given the contradictory signals that Mexicans have received from their church both in Mexico and the United States, it should not be surprising that many Mexicans have developed a strong attachment to the symbols and rituals of Catholicism, while developing a weak commitment to its institutional obligations."[4]

Mexican Catholics are often cautious about becoming Church "fanatics." This idea of "fanaticism" resonates with the discourse of the Porfiriato, *científicos* (the scientific), and was echoed by the Mexicans interviewed in California by Manuel Gamio in the early 1920s.[5] One woman interviewed during the 1920s commented frankly, "I don't believe in the sanctity or in the purity of priests, or that they are invested with superhuman powers. To me they are men like all the rest. That is why I don't pay any attention to their preachings."[6]

But priests, nuns, and churches too occupy central and formative places in Chicana/o Catholicism—witness the overflow crowds at masses all over the Mexican-American Southwest. The patrimony of border-lands Catholicism is a dialectic between the laity as theologians and the clergy; between the institutional site, mostly the site of patriarchy (at least officially), and the home altar, site of matriarchy. At the home altar, as we shall see, devotion to Guadalupe and the saints authorizes those who opt for a Catholic devotional life to become their own "religious specialists" and to create formal political organizations and resist and struggle against power in multiple ways; this is true of women especially.

Men, too, are devotees to La Lupe—one immigrant *mexicano* in Los Angeles during the 1920s confessed: "I'm a Catholic, but the truth is that I hardly follow out my beliefs. I never go to the church, nor do I pray. I have with me an amulet which my mother gave to me before dying. This amulet has the Virgin of Guadalupe on it and it is she who always pro-tects me."[7] But the more pious Catholic men additionally nurture rela-tionships to the passionate Christ, *crucificado/sacrificado*—sacrificed for a greater good. I call this male aspect of devotion "El Lloron," or "the weeping man," a penitent figure who repents and weeps for the cultural sins of machismo and seeks acceptance and love. This is a religious tem-plate that transcends theological boundaries but finds powerful relief in Guadalupe as a nurturing mother. One priest who ministers to Chicano gangs explains that men "have a more complex take on religion that doesn't translate into church attendance. . . . It's not difficult to see they hope protection will come from these images [tattoos of Guadalupe]."[8]

I turn now to a fragmented genealogy, an incomplete surface map-ping, of sites of Catholic-Guadalupe emergence in East Los Angeles, par-ticularly, and throughout the borderlands.

DIASPORA *GUADALUPANOS*, GUADALUPE IN EXILE (CIRCA 1920–60)

The year 1934 was a watershed for *guadalupanos* in Los Angeles. On 9 December 1934, a procession of forty thousand, mostly Mexicans and Mexican-Americans, paraded around Boyle Heights, in East Los Ange-les, from Mount Carmelo Chapel on Ninth and Lorena to the Los An-geles Orphan Asylum on Sixth and Boyle.[9] The procession, ostensibly a commemoration of the apparition of the Virgin of Guadalupe at Te-peyac, was led by traditional Mexican-Indian dancers. Although this was not the first procession of its kind—its humbler beginnings were in

1928—the prodigiousness of this event was unprecedented.[10] The timing for the feast, too, was telling. The Depression years had soured American attitudes toward Mexican immigrants, and nativism had devolved into "repatriation" hysteria resulting in the compulsory deportation of Mexicans *and* Mexican-Americans.[11] Simultaneously, the North American Catholic Church had embarked upon a program of "Americanization" for its immigrant charges, aiming to standardize and modernize U.S. Catholicism. Additionally, Lázaro Cárdenas, president of Mexico in 1934–40, furthered the persecution of the Catholic Church there, enforcing the prohibition of public Catholic ceremony and advancing his commitment to a socialist state. Thus, the center of Guadalupe devotion began to move—for political expediency and survival—to East Los Angeles, which was destined to become the Guadalupe center in the Mexico City periphery. The *Los Angeles Times* reported glowingly on the 1934 procession: "Beautiful Mexican maidens posed as the Holy Virgin of Guadalupe on floats depicting the five appearances of the Virgin to Juan Diego."[12] Later, in December 1937, over one hundred thousand Angelenos—mostly Mexican-Americans—gathered under the leadership of the Archbishop John Cantwell to crown La Virgen de Guadalupe in Los Angeles. The coronation *(la coronación)* marked the two-hundredth anniversary of Guadalupe's ascension to the throne in Mexico City. As mentioned earlier, in 1737, Mexico City officials named Guadalupe the patroness of their city. It wasn't until 1754 that Pope Benedict XIV named her the patroness of the whole of New Spain.

In the years prior to these events, during the Mexican Revolution, over one million Mexicans had entered the United States, the vast majority heading for destinations throughout what had become, just a generation earlier, the U.S. Southwest. By 1920 Mexican congregations had developed throughout Los Angeles, the center of which was Our Lady Queen of the Angels, also known as La Placita Church, in downtown Los Angeles, just across the river from the East Side and adjacent to Olvera Street, in the middle of Sonoratown. In church, women formed a tradition of social work, organizing groups to labor in the Mexican community that paralleled those of Protestant white women. Mexican men and women organized into mutual-aid societies, and La Placita became a center of political praxis and discourse.[13]

Even at La Placita Church, however, Catholicism was not so much accepted as it was meted down through the official sacraments. In 1917, one observer described Our Lady Queen of the Angels as follows: "The 'Little Plaza' of Los Angeles, where hundreds of Mexicans congregate on

Sundays, is often the scene of fiery discourses in Spanish. In these harangues by forceful orators present-day Christianity is ridiculed, and in place of what the church stands for, are presented the crudest and most objectionable theories of socialism."[14]

Guillermo Salorio, one of Manuel Gamio's respondents, spoke for the men who were influenced by modern discourses. This summation deserves lengthy citation here. His wife, he said,

> can have all the saints that she wants in the house and can also pray. I won't bother her but she mustn't interfere with my way of thinking either. I think that all the religions are nothing but a deception which the rich and the strong have of always making the poor work. Although I don't have anything to support my opinion, I don't believe that there is a God for no one has ever seen him. I am not an atheist because I am not educated but I am tending in that direction. I am studying many books. . . . I first became acquainted with these ideas because I went to the square on Sundays and there heard some comrades make some speeches. They said nothing but the truth, that the capital is what steals everything and that money isn't good for anything, that it is necessary for everyone to work. I believe the same in everything and that is why I liked their ideas and I began to read papers and books and I go to the I.W.W. hall.[15]

Señor Salorio reported that he intended to join the most radical of labor organizations, suggesting that during this formative period of reluctant Mexican-American identity formation, labor groups provided men a discourse of union and fraternity, in modern urban idioms. Inside and outside of church, poetics of religious resistance were performed.

Still negotiating relationships to institutions in the United States, *mexicanos* cultivated home-centered Catholicism throughout Chicano communities. A statistical survey of Mexicans in Los Angeles published in 1923 found that

> religious practices in the home are very common, especially among those who find church attendance inconvenient. The ornate improvised altar and religious wall decorations are the rule. . . . The altars are frequently improvised from a lug box shelf, gaudily adorned with colorful crepe paper and the Christmas bells and tinsel which lend their festive air throughout the year. Occasionally a home boasts an elaborately carved altar resplendent with color statues, exquisitely carved from wood by the artistic hand of the owner.[16]

This design is known as *rasquache,* or a form of low-brow bricolage. In 1925, a Protestant missionary characterized the Mexican religious home in Los Angeles as follows:

Here in the corner opposite the door into the "visitors' room" is a crucifix, supposedly of silver. It represents the Lord in agony upon the cross. Before it are two candles which are lighted on certain occasions. Back of the crucifix is a Fe [faith] cloth upon which are some medals and ribbons, reminders of special feast days and dispensations. About the room hang framed chromosome [sic] Maria of the Sacred Heart, picturing the sweet-faced "Queen of Heaven," wearing on her bosom a red heart upon which is a flame of fire. . . . About the room are images of favorite saints, selected by the experiences and occupations of the family. The guardian angel of all these objects of worship is the dear old grandmother who never wears a hat anywhere but always dons her black *reboso* [shawl] since it is not proper to wear a hat in church. One associates this dear little shawl-clad, thin-faced devotee with all the images and shrines and, also, with the religious activities of the whole family. She is its spiritual monitor.[17]

Many Mexican homes in Los Angeles were, in this sense, a sacred center in themselves. Michael Engh notes that during this period "many forms of domestic religiosity continued to flourish within the family circle and included veneration of the saints, the placement of religious pictures and *altarcitos* or shrines in the home. . . . After 1910 images of the Virgin of Guadalupe began to appear in parishes throughout Southern California wherever Mexicans worshipped."[18] Mexico City/Tepeyac was brought into the living rooms of devotees in mail packages from the homeland—devotional images of Guadalupe.

Given this Catholic "priesthood of the believer," it comes as no surprise that the meaning of the Guadalupe celebration in 1934 was publicly contested by the laity. The Catholic clergy in Los Angeles put one spin on the events, publicly declaring that the march was a mass demonstration against the repression of the Church in Mexico. The Mexican consulate in Los Angeles quickly responded by condemning the clerics' statements, supporting the actions of the Mexican president. But once the *mexicano* rank and file got wind of the Catholic declaration and the consulate's response, they rushed to the local Spanish-language daily *La Opinión* and demanded that their voices be heard. They clarified their motivations for the event through four positional statements:

Tomorrow's demonstration [*manifestación*] is, principally, a homage to the Virgin of Guadalupe, inspired by her anniversary. . . . It does not intend to influence the government nor the people [*pueblo*] of the United States against the government of Mexico, given that the people and the government of this country, "are completely involved in what happens in Mexico." . . . Catholics are not, as Consular Martinez affirmed: "the eternal enemies of economic, social and cultural Mexican progress," but instead it is the opposite, "they are the only ones who have always defended national integrity." And, in conclusion . . . as Mexicans, Catholics or not Catholics, they have the right to protest, wherever, against the acts of a government "that has not come from the popular will."[19]

The conflicts felt by Mexicans living in America and by Mexican-Americans regarding ultimate allegiances are reflected in the ambiguity of these statements: "ambivalent Americanism." And yet, while national identity was equivocal, one thing was clear: the Virgin of Guadalupe reigned supreme in their collective imaginations. Their corporate identity as *guadalupanos* surpassed and thus resolved the identity crisis they underwent as ethnic Mexicans in the United States. Guadalupe became the reference point for figuring corporate identity. Through her movements back and forth across the border, Guadalupe created, in effect, a virtual Virgin nation, one based on the principle of continuous *return* to sustaining sacred ideas, while adapting and transforming them.

"Mexico," Tepeyac, and La Guadalupe advanced north, to East Los Angeles. "By 1899," according to Engh, "a Society of Our Lady of Guadalupe existed in Los Angeles at the church of Our Lady of the Angels, the parish known as La Placita."[20] This move is documented in various newspapers published by the Guadalupe Basilica at Tepeyac beginning around 1928. Take, for example, the first edition of *La Voz Guadalupana,* published in December 1936, which accompanied the establishment of an official Guadalupe center at the basilica, the location of the offices of the Holy Mary Guadalupe Mexican Academy. The purpose of the office and the newspaper was to promote the devotion within the eye of a storm of political pressure.

Promotion involved, of course, selling Guadalupe devotional paraphernalia. The paper encouraged visitors to the basilica to not forget to "buy your 'souvenirs' [*recuerdos*] in this, your house, where you will find a magnificent assortment of Guadalupe articles, rosaries, medallions, little necklaces, crucifixes, candles . . . and other articles appropriate for souvenirs and gifts for your family and friends." If pilgrims could not make it to the center, it would be sent to them: "If you cannot come, we will send what you desire by mail, and we will charge you or ship it COD. Everything is perfectly packed."[21] Through mail-order devotion, the Mexico City center was disseminated throughout the peripheries via images and signs by way of market exchange.

In a virtual nation, the center can be and is everywhere and nowhere at once. "This act of inscription had many of the features of ritual," ar-

gues Robert Orsi about Catholic mail-order devotions in the early twentieth century:

> The devout had to gather the writing materials (not an insignificant under-
> taking for people who do not live with pens in their hands), plan the letter,
> and sit down and write. When the writing was finished, they had to bring
> the letter to the mailbox (or ask someone else to do it for them), and then
> they waited for a reply from the shrine, which would begin the process all
> over again. Religious ritual represents a reconfiguration of ordinary space
> and time. Through this process of writing, mailing and waiting, the devout
> opened up the closed experience of crisis with reference to another place.[22]

Receiving the mail, as Orsi notes, brings the center home.

But exactly pinpointing home was increasingly complicated for this
"immigrant generation." During the 1930s, the Mexican government attempted to enlist the support of *mexicanos* in Los Angeles for various
causes, referring to them as *mexicanos de afuera,* or Mexicans of the outside.[23] But Mexicans were becoming increasingly North American, and
East Los Angeles had become a home away from home, a *home,* another
exterior ring to the concentricity of the meaning, a *sacred* center in the
Mexico City periphery. And, of course, Guadalupe was following her
children across the border.

In 1937, *La Voz Guadalupana* proudly reported on Guadalupe's
movement to the Philippines, Japan, and throughout Latin America.
However, it becomes clear, in an article entitled "The United States
Unites with Latin America in Its Love for the Holy Virgin of Guadalupe,"
that the Guadalupe devotion was intended foremost to reach Los Angeles and the diasporic Mexican community there. The article begins as follows: "Cause for true and legitimate satisfaction, it is for the genuine
Mexican heart, that the love and devotion to the Virgin of Guadalupe
does not confine itself within the national limits of Mexico; instead *it
crosses Mexican borders,* and spreads like a heavenly blessing to many
nations."[24] Most of the second and final page of the article is devoted to
a discussion of the upcoming coronation of Guadalupe in Los Angeles,
commemorating the "second centenary of the first Guadalupe patronage
in our continent."

This event was, as noted earlier in this chapter, organized by the archbishop of Los Angeles, John Cantwell. Cantwell made painstaking efforts to reach Mexican Catholics in Los Angeles (often referring to Mexicans as the "the simple people of God"). None of his actions were more
appreciated, however, than the institutionalization of Guadalupe in East
Los Angeles and his establishment of official spiritual relations between

East Los Angeles and Mexico City, forged in the transnational movements of Guadalupe. He was the first American bishop to embark on the
pilgrimage to Tepeyac, and he was honored by the Mexican Catholic
Church with the Golden Rose of Tepeyac in 1941. Somewhat surprisingly, he was at odds with the community's Mexican patriotism and progressive politics. Still, he gave sanctuary to exiled Mexican clerics, made
the Guadalupe parade in East Los Angeles an annual event, and established fifty new parishes for Mexicans, including the shrine to Guadalupe
in East Los Angeles. The shrine was originally planned as a replica of the
original basilica at Tepeyac, with all the grandeur of the baroque carved-
stone facade.[25] *La Voz* spoke often and triumphantly of the shrine that
was to be built in honor of Guadalupe in East Los Angeles.

In the second issue of *La Voz* appeared two brief articles, both by
Miguel de Zarraga. The first, "Mexico outside of Mexico," discusses the
California mission movement, emphasizing that California once was
part of Mexico. More significantly, the second, "Offering to California,"
describes the beauty and mystique of California, inscribing Los Angeles
with a magical, mystical quality. "This earthly paradise," he states of Los
Angeles, "pride of North America, has three fundamental enchant-
ments: its sun, its flowers, and its fruits." These, he claims, are Mexico's
legacy in California. "What doesn't California owe to Mexico?" he asks
rhetorically, and proceeds to write glowingly about the wonders of Hollywood.[26] Mexico's "legacy" in California is a manipulation of memory
as a social tactic. That the articles are set in Hollywood bespeaks the
mythological symbolism of Hollywood (glamour, beauty, transformation) that increased Los Angeles's appeal for Mexicans, in that when they
flocked to Los Angeles they were becoming a part of a magical, enchanted place. *La Voz* is filled with reports from Los Angeles, each more
effusive than the last, describing that "beautiful City of Angels," focusing especially the *guadalupano/mexicano* community in place there.

In a March–May 1937 article entitled "The Mexicans in Los Angeles" the memory of one of the earliest Christianizers is evoked: "It's as if
due to the air that is purified because of the palms and trees that are common to all the California heavens, that the spirit of P. Francisco Kino still
floats, infiltrated in the souls yearning for fraternal union between Mexico and Mexicans." In this way, Kino is kept alive as a mythical, ghostly
presence in Mexican Catholic memory.[27] Mexicans insist that Eusebio
Francisco Kino, a Jesuit, brought *guadalupanismo* to Los Angeles in
1681, and is thus called the "First Guadalupe Apostle to the Californias."
According to the mythology about him, he was trained at Tepeyac and

"evangelized and civilized those [California] regions, under the direction of Holy Mary of Guadalupe of Mexico, to whom he was very devoted."[28]

In this narrative, *guadalupanos* stake a primordial claim to California, and especially to Los Angeles:

> Los Angelinos are demonstrably proud to say that after the capital of the Republic of Mexico [Mexico City], it is the city of the Angels that houses the most Mexicans in the world. . . . They demonstrate memory and love to the ancestral home . . . with their special predilection for what, in reality, signifies the symbol most characteristic of their homeland of their people; The Virgin of Guadalupe.[29]

In addition to the reports from and about *guadalupanos* in Los Angeles, earliest issues of the paper vigorously promoted the upcoming festival in Los Angeles: the commemoration of the two-hundred-year anniversary of the Vatican's recognition and coronation of La Virgen de Guadalupe as Patroness of Mexico and Empress of the Americas, 3–7 June 1937. In none of its articles, including the promotion of the celebration in Los Angeles, does *La Voz* mention government repression of the Church in Mexico—a telling absence. Instead, the paper writes around it by articulating the reasons why Los Angeles is the appropriate ceremonial place for the anniversary: "There are many reasons to crown the Image of Our Lady of Guadalupe venerated in Los Angeles, under auspices [of] *guadalupanos;* the Faith penetrated California. . . . It is the principal nucleus of the Mexican residents in the United States, and the city is called THE QUEEN OF THE ANGELS."[30] Carefully, the northward turn of La Virgen is disclosed.

Issues of *La Voz* following the coronation were devoted almost entirely to comprehensive and various accounts of the events: coverage of every detail of the festival, replete with photographs and continuously replayed, filled the pages of the next few issues of the review, referring to the festivities as the "apotheosis" of Guadalupe in Los Angeles. One declared Mexicans "imperialists" under the auspices of Guadalupe in Los Angeles: "Los Angeles glorifies the Queen of Mexico. This way we exercise, inversely, an uncommon imperialism."[31] Again, conquest is replayed—this time the U.S. conquest of Mexico—and in this version Guadalupe is strategically recast, reversing the historical outcome.

The article hardly makes mention of similar commemorations held in Argentina and other Latin-American countries. The prestige was greater in Los Angeles; that the grandiose capital of modern popular culture, avant-garde, beauty, fantasy, sexuality, and American prosperity, Los

Angeles, would prostrate before *the* Mexican Virgin, symbol of *mestizaje*, was an event not to be taken lightly—it had to be elaborated and reiterated. It was precisely because Los Angeles in the 1930s enjoyed an unsurpassed reputation, owing to the film industry, that it was all the more desirable as a sacred center for Mexicans, who affirmed the uniqueness of the place by lending it their most sacred and enduring symbol, Guadalupe. The eternal mother of the Mexicans had moved, adding perhaps a second residence, following her children to the land of the lotus and of the surreal.

La Voz also advertised a pilgrimage package to the coronation—*from* Mexico City *to* Los Angeles! It afforded pilgrims the opportunity to visit famous tourist sights. Until this point, each issue of *La Voz*, from its beginning until the end of its publication run in the early 1980s, reported on pilgrimage groups from Los Angeles, *mexicanos de afuera*, arriving at Guadalupe's shrine at Tepeyac. This back-and-forth movement of ethnic Mexicans across the border toward distinctively devotional ends adds another path to transnational exchanges (even well before the Internet and its virtual pilgrimages, or before efficient and well-built cars, trains, buses, and inexpensive air fares enabled pilgrims to travel). But most importantly, Guadalupe herself, her soul, was immigrating to Los Angeles. One article in *La Voz* put it frankly: "Los Angeles [is] the new and powerful focus of the desired spiritual union of the continent, under the celestial leadership of the Immaculate One of Tepeyac."[32]

The *Los Angeles Times* also covered the events of the coronation with photographs and narrative accounts. On 4 June 1937, the *Times* ran a column under the heading "Our Lady Fete Opens." It reported: "With the arrival here yesterday of hundreds of visitors from Latin-American countries and with a colorful program at the Philharmonic Auditorium, began the festivities in honor of Our Lady of Guadalupe which will be featured by the solemn coronation of an image of our Lady." A string of events led up to the coronation, at which Guadalupe was crowned "symbolic Queen of all the Americas" at Calvary Cemetery Museum, and then enshrined at the tiny Guadalupe sanctuary in East Los Angeles. The next day, Saturday morning, 5 June, a special pontifical mass was held, officiated by Archbishop Cantwell. Under flags representing twenty-one Latin-American nations, Monsignor Augustín de la Cueva, from the basilica in Mexico City, presented Cantwell with a "solid gold crown, studded with emeralds, pearls, and other gems" for the Church of Our Lady of Guadalupe, "as a gift of international friendship and good will." The *Times* counted forty thousand people at "the ceremonial climax the following day—the crowning of the Guadalupe image and the proclamation that she was 'Queen of all of the Americas.'"[33]

At the time, the L.A. Guadalupe shrine was little more than a one-room wooden shack. According to an article in *La Voz,* a goal of the coronation ceremonies was to raise funds to build a new, appropriate Guadalupe shrine in place of the extant shrine. *La Voz* went so far as to render conceptions of what the new shrine would look like—it was to be an exact replica of the original basilica in Mexico City. Additionally, the article reported that a new head office of Guadalupe affairs, like the one at Tepeyac, would be attached to the L.A. shrine and was to enjoy all the prerogatives of the Mexico City office. In fact, the article stated that "very soon this splendid city of the Angels will be the center of Guadalupe activities for the entire union of the Americas."[34]

In the pages of *La Voz,* excitement over the new Guadalupe shrine in East Los Angeles was palpable. Articles compared the space of the L.A. shrine to that of Tepeyac, pointing out that East Los Angeles was just about the same distance from downtown Los Angeles as Tepeyac was from the center of Mexico City, and that the L.A. shrine was situated on a small hill, and thus a strenuous walk was required to reach it—just like at Tepeyac. The flowers and shrubbery at the shrine were Mexican-derived and the same types as those at Tepeyac. Furthermore, miracle stories associated with the construction of the shrine began to appear in *La Voz,* narrating the experiences of poor ethnic Mexicans in Los Angeles who had donated their only pittances for the construction of the L.A. shrine and were as a result miraculously blessed with financial gain several times the amount they had given to La Virgen.

In 1938, *guadalupanismo* in Los Angeles reached a peak. For the 12 December commemoration, Archbishop Cantwell led a procession of fifty thousand from La Placita Church into Cathedral Field. *La Voz Guadalupana* and *La Opinión* devoted extensive coverage to the event. In a front-page article, the *Los Angeles Times* reported that the marchers were "rededicating" themselves to the ideas of "peace, amity, and tolerance." Indeed, while the procession was based directly in ethnic Mexican urban space, it was populated by Catholics of all varieties, and all of the approximately one hundred Catholic churches in Los Angeles were purportedly represented. The archdiocesan director of the Holy Name Union, Michael O'Gorman, contrasted the Guadalupe devotion to contemporaneous world events: "There are places in the world where we would not dare to meet in a similar fashion. There are places where human liberty is a forgotten thing, where puny silly men shake their fists in the face of God." He was referring, of course, to Mexico, but he also raised the specter of European totalitarianism: "We now have over us the tremendous atheistic menace of communism and Nazism, which, like a gigantic avalanche, threaten to destroy the very foundations of society and wipe out the name of God."[35]

Via Los Angeles, Guadalupe was cast onto a larger, world-wide stage, constituting an international devotion. Although Guadalupe was wildly popular at home and in Latin America, she truly hit the big time in Los Angeles. Ironically, as the City of Angels embraced Guadalupe, it was forcibly deporting ethnic Mexicans en masse. That the 1938 Guadalupe devotion espoused the noble ideas of "tolerance and amity" is laudable, but the absence of explicit condemnation of the deportation actions raises questions about the authenticity of the rhetoric.

As the country's attentions turned to war preparations, the waning of the Great Depression, and the *modus vivendi* reached between the Mexican government and the Catholic Church, Guadalupe passion seemed to ebb a bit in Los Angeles, although the 12 December procession remains today a central temporal ritual for the East L.A. Catholic community. When the excitement of the 1937 commemoration had subsided, *La Voz* focused on the construction taking place at the new shrine in East Los Angeles, again revealing an architectural schema for it, images that pictured stunning and grandiose models of Mexico's basilica. The paper mentioned that Guadalupe's shrine in Los Angeles would be larger than the L.A. temple dedicated to Lourdes.

However, when the temple was dedicated on 13 October 1946, it fell far short of the exterior designs and dimensions of the original plans. The report in *La Voz* called it "beautiful" but "modest." The article gave no explanation for the church's humble design. No longer was the church compared to the Mexico City basilica, but was likened instead to the Guadalupe shrine in Morelia, though it was "smaller," the paper reported. *La Voz* did not display the shrine's exterior, opting instead for several interior photographs. Inside, the shrine is baroque in design and Guadalupe is at the head of the altar, framed in gold. There are elaborate stained-glass windows, and interspersed are smaller shrines for Mexican saints. The sanctuary itself seats only about two hundred people, although benches in the rear courtyard and the covered side annex together seat an additional four hundred. The facade of the church is not the elegant carved stone adorning the Guadalupe shrine in Mexico City but is instead covered in plain stucco.

The church is perhaps a product of economic concerns and of the

emergent postwar "Protestantized" church architecture. Also, it is a symbol of disappointment. The Mexican reportage on the shrine was
somber, even while trying to exhibit an upbeat tone. Certainly the shrine,
though popular, did not become the center of the East L.A. community
as was hoped, although today it does function as a center of pilgrimage
and devotion to Guadalupe. By 1947, *La Voz* no longer dedicated coverage to Guadalupe in Los Angeles.

Instead, the popular image in the review, and others from the basilica,
became one of Juan Diego situated on a map of the Americas, rising up
from its center, Mexico City, holding an open cape displaying a representation of Guadalupe (see figure 4). The image of Juan Diego and
Guadalupe were larger than the entire continents of the Americas. The
caption read, "1747–1947 America United in Guadalupe Patronage."
One article appearing in 1947 claimed that redemption would issue from
Mexico City: "The civilized world is struggling in the midst of problems
that seem to have no solution, but human kind perceives that salvation
may come forth from America where a glimmering light is pointing out
that the spiritual assets of the New World may be fused in the crucible
of Tepeyac."[36] This resonates with the poetics of José Vasconcelos, which
were discussed in chapter 1. Moreover, the *La Voz* article cites a formal
letter issued by Mathias Faust, delegate general of the Franciscan Order
in North and Central America, which discloses Mexico City's renewed
consciousness of itself: "Mexico lies in the very centre [*sic*] of this Western Hemisphere where both South and North may join hands of true and
genuine friendship in her [Guadalupe's] hallowed Shrine."[37]

By the close of the 1940s, Mexico City was reclaiming the mantle of
Catholicism, indeed of being the sacred center in the Americas. However,
the door had already been opened to East Los Angeles, where the Chicano community was recreating its space as a center of sacrality, memory, and power. The virtual Virgin nation had gained a new suburb.

IN, OUT, AND IN BETWEEN:
CHICANA/OS AND THE CATHOLIC CHURCH

The postwar years witnessed a great deal of change for Chicanos in Los
Angeles and across the country as Mexicans became predominantly ur-
banized—and concomitantly suburbanized.[38] Moreover, the ethnic Mexican community was increasingly U.S.-born.[39] By 1950, ethnic Mexicans
numbered some 280,000 in Los Angeles County alone, which amounted
to 7 percent of the total population—the largest minority group in the

county. These people were overwhelmingly young, 62 percent of them under thirty years old. Demographic changes profoundly impacted the religious and cultural expressions of Chicanos, and also changed their collective expectations. Prosperity defined American life, and increasingly Americans of Mexican descent wanted their share—especially those who had risked their lives overseas, fighting a war inspired by the lofty rhetoric of democracy and equality for all. The mutual-aid societies, radical labor organizations, and social and legal clubs prevalent in *mexicano* Los Angeles prior to the war gave way to a more militant brand of activism. Ethnic Mexicans no longer looked to Mexico exclusively for signs to direct cultural identity formation but adapted Mexican culture to the American context and vice versa. A century had passed since the U.S. border crossed illegally into Mexico, and the new generation of Mexican-Americans fostered a consciousness that was distinctively Mexican-American *qua* American.

A field study conducted in Mexican Los Angeles in the 1950s revealed that parishes in East Los Angeles were "characterized by irregular mass attendance and reception of the sacraments. . . . Participation in parish organizations was reported small, and clubs and societies are 'attended by a few old faithfuls.' 'Some of the older families still have the *altarcitos* [little altars] at home, but this is dying out among the younger ones.'" One parish priest explained, "The old families will light candles before their Guadalupe statue at home, but you'll never see them at Mass on Sunday."[40]

If the older generation, including recently arrived immigrants, were caught up in their home devotional practices to Guadalupe—especially the home altar—and mass attendance was low, what was the religious expression of young Chicanos? Mexican-Americans, by the 1960s, took their religious cues from the Mexican anticlerical tradition and Mexican devotion to La Virgen—especially as a sign and symbol of political struggle. They also revived ancient Mexican traditions. Chicanos were influenced also by the general social unrest of the times, and especially by changes within the Catholic Church itself following the Second Vatican Council (1962–65).[41] César Chávez (1927–93) crystallized the sentiments of Chicanos, and in his advocacy of labor rights for Mexican-Americans based on spiritual values, he became, in the words of Gary Soto, "a spiritual leader for all Chicanos." He catalyzed the Chicano movement and unionized the Chicano Farm Workers.[42]

In 1968, Chávez presented a lecture, published under the title "The Mexican American and the Catholic Church," that he said he had received while on a "spiritual fast." The Church, he wrote, "is a powerful moral and spiritual force which cannot be ignored by any movement. Furthermore, it is an organization with tremendous wealth. Since the church is to be servant of the poor, it is our fault if that wealth is not channeled to help the poor in the world." He summarized his position with regard to the Church in the conclusion of his essay, influential words that deserve lengthy citation:

> The Catholic Charities agencies of the Catholic Church [have] millions of dollars earmarked for the poor. But often the money is spent for food baskets for the needy instead of for effective action to eradicate the causes of poverty. The men and women who administer this money sincerely want to help their brothers. It should be our duty to help direct the attention to the basic needs of the Mexican-Americans in our society . . . needs which cannot be satisfied with baskets of food, but rather with effective organizing at the grass roots level. Therefore, I am calling for Mexican-American groups to stop ignoring this source of power. It is not just our right to appeal to the Church to use its power effectively for the poor, it is our duty to do so. . . . Finally, in a nutshell, what do we want the Church to do? We don't ask for more cathedrals. We don't ask for bigger churches or fine gifts. We ask for its presence with us, beside us, as Christ among us.[43]

Chávez's words bore directly on at least one Mexican-American group, who called themselves Católicos por la Raza (Catholics for the Race; hereafter CPLR). Ricardo Cruz, founder of CPLR, had met Chávez and without much delay committed to organizing Chicanos in Los Angeles to enlist the support of the Church.[44]

In November 1969, Chávez's words from this article appeared on the cover of a Chicano political newsletter, *La Raza*, that was distributed throughout Los Angeles: "We do not want more Cathedrals, but ask the Catholic Church to sacrifice with the people for social change."[45] CPLR was headed by Cruz and a number of Chicano—and purportedly Catholic—law students. The group made several formal attempts to meet with Cardinal James Francis McIntyre, but these efforts were unavailing. In the November issue of *La Raza*, CPLR published a letter addressed to their "spiritual leader": "We are confused, our dear Cardinal," the letter reads, "because while our mothers and fathers, brothers and sisters continue to light candles and pray to la Virgen de Guadalupe and give truly sacrificial donations to our Catholic Church, we continue to live in substandard housing as far as our nation is concerned." Additionally, CPLR wanted answers for the injustices Chicanos faced in the Vietnam War: "You see there is one aspect of America wherein Chicanos are apparently considered extremely important. Our people constitute the highest ethnic proportion of those dying in Vietnam."

In what can only be described as a brilliant political maneuver, CPLR uncovered the net property holdings of the Catholic Church in Los Angeles—worth over one billion dollars. The group published these findings in the same issue of *La Raza*. In fact, the Catholic Church owned much of the East L.A. slum property in which many Chicanos lived. How is it possible, they asked, that McIntyre lived in opulence, while Chicanos who lived in Church-owned property faced unimaginable horrors in their places of residence? How could he preach that the poor were blessed with Christ's presence among them while their material conditions belied that teaching?

In the December 1969 issue of *La Raza*, CPLR published several narratives with powerful accompanying images devoted to exposing what they saw as the hypocrisy of the Catholic Church in Los Angeles. In an article entitled "The Church and La Raza," CPLR outlined the problem and drew extensively from the César Chávez movement, and directly from Chávez himself. CPLR concluded the article on a tone resonating with the words of Chávez, explaining that even while they themselves might not need the Church, "THERE ARE HUNDREDS OF THOUSANDS OF OUR PEOPLE WHO DESPERATELY NEED SOME HELP FROM THAT POWERFUL INSTITUTION, THE CHURCH, AND WE ARE FOOLISH NOT TO HELP THEM GET IT" (emphasis original).

In their revised open letter to the cardinal, appearing in the December *La Raza*, they reiterated: "We know of this wealth [of the Church]," they wrote, "yet Chicanitos are praying to La Virgen de Guadalupe as they go to bed hungry and will not be able to afford decent educations." Their list of four areas of demands placed education first, demanding that Catholic education be free for Chicanos at all levels. The other three areas were, respectively, housing, community involvement, and public commitments.

When no acceptable response came from the cardinal, CPLR organized to protest. On Christmas Eve 1969, a group of three hundred Chicanos congregated under the banner of the Virgin of Guadalupe for a prayer vigil/protest during midnight mass at St. Basil's Catholic Church on fashionable Wilshire Boulevard in Los Angeles. Ultimately, according to the *Los Angeles Times,* the protesters "gathered on the steps outside the church and began pounding on the doors for admittance." Inside the freshly built four-million-dollar, postmodern-design temple—a spectacle intended to cement Catholic prominence in Los Angeles—Cardinal

McIntyre led elite Angelenos in a rousing chorus of "O Come All Ye Faithful," intended to drown out the cries of the people who were on the outside. At about a quarter past midnight, the "chanting, club-swinging mob of demonstrators burst into St. Basil's Catholic Church."[46] "Oscar Acosta, a Mexican-American lawyer and spokesman for the Catholics [sic] por la Raza, blamed the sheriff's deputies and police for provoking the disturbance," the Times recounted. "He charged the demonstrators were told they could enter the church 'so long as we did not bring our banners and candles in. When we went through a side door and tried to open the front doors, the police started hitting us with their clubs,' Acosta charged."[47] In his novel on the Chicano movement, Acosta offers an account of the incident that is confirmed by the Los Angeles Times's narration of the events. Acosta describes the climactic moment when two women burst into the mass, making it to the front of the sanctuary, one shouting, "People of St. Basil's, please, come and help us. They're killing the poor people out in the lobby. Please. Come and help!" The other, upon reaching the altar shouted: "'Viva La Raza!'" and "Swoosh, swoosh, swoosh! With three deft strokes [she] clears off the Holy of Holies from the altar of red and gold. . . . The Body of Christ is on the red carpet."[48]

In February 1970, nearly the entire issue of La Raza was devoted to reports and photographs of the CPLR action at St. Basil's Church. The cover was a powerful image divided into a structural binary. On the left were two L.A. policemen holding clubs. On the right was a sole Chicano with long hair, resembling Juan Diego, holding a large painting of Guadalupe close to his torso. The poetic message it conveyed was clear: Guadalupe stood with the poor and oppressed, blessing righteous outrage, while the wealth of the Church was protected by aggressive police. The articles contained in the issue written by CPLR are akin to theological statements, deftly emphasizing the poverty of Christ, his rebuke of the temple money changers, and so forth. In this way, CPLR appropriated the symbolism of Christ and the Church while reflecting it back in critical, rebellious, and even subversive ways. Quoting the words of one elder: "'I love going to Church,' the viejita [little elder woman] said, 'It's so beautiful there, and my house is so ugly.'" CPLR assiduously exploited the "contrast between the grandeur of the church and the squalor of the home," asking why the churches should be the only nice buildings on the East Side.

Significantly, the February issue of La Raza listed thirty-five community-based organizations that supported their cause. These included

"Belvedere Mother's Club, Belvedere Father's Club, Roosevelt High, Garfield High, and Lincoln High Parents, Eastman Block Mothers," and others, thus demonstrating wide support from all sectors and generations of the Mexican-American community. Overall, the discourse of CPLR stressed that they, like other Chicanos, were Catholics and ultimately sought reforms within the Catholic Church. Their position was summed up in their mantra: "The church will become relevant, so be it." The pioneering work of CPLR, although unfolding within less than six months, drew national attention to the plight of Chicanos in Los Angeles and inspired and intersected with other Chicano Catholic movements for social justice.

Perhaps two of the most significant of these movements were PADRES (Fathers), an organization of Chicano priests, and Las Hermanas (The sisters), an organization of Chicana nuns. Both of these groups were national but made significant and lasting contributions to Chicano Catholicism in Los Angeles. PADRES is an acronym for Padres Asociados para los Derechos Religiosos, Educativos, y Sociales (Fathers associated for religious, educational, and social rights); it was founded in 1970 at its first national conference in Tucson, Arizona, with delegates from twelve states. Foremost on PADRES's agenda was the call for the first Chicano bishop and other issues concerning grassroots political and social activism. Las Hermanas was a parallel group of Chicana nuns, founded in 1971, which, in the words of Lara Medina, "brought the Chicano political movement into the Catholic church."[49] In August 1973, Las Hermanas met in Los Angeles, and the meeting deteriorated when most of the sisters drove to Delano to officiate a mass for the striking farm workers. Through their individual work, Las Hermanas wrought changes in parishes in East Los Angeles, most notably through the work of Rosa Marta Zarate, Lucy Barron, and Teresita Basso. Today, Las Hermanas continues their activism.

Father Juan Romero, an East L.A. parish priest and formerly an active member of the now defunct PADRES, explains that in addition to their social and political work, "PADRES promoted a liberation theology and its scriptural hermeneutic which promoted getting involved with the poor and oppressed who have greater need. The PADRES organization raised questions and gave challenges about freedom from one's own selfishness and Christ's preference for the poor."[50] Romero and other L.A. Catholics preached and practiced liberation theology in their Chicano parishes and thus laid the groundwork for the liberation theology that defined Chicano Catholic activism in Los Angeles during the 1980s and can still be found in some parishes today.

The 1970s were a pivotal time for Latino Catholicism in Los Angeles and beyond. The Church responded with special programs for them, including the Cursillo movement, which brought together small groups of Latino and other Catholics for prayer and reflection; and the national and international *encuentros,* which were large-scale stadium meetings and often charismatic masses by and for Latino laity and clerics.[51] The charismatic renewal movement in the Catholic Church was brought directly into Los Angeles in 1972 with the founding of Carisma en Misiones by Marilyn Kramar. Also in 1972, Sister Karen Boccalero of the Franciscan Order founded Self-Help Graphics, a Chicano art collective in East Los Angeles (see figure 6). The center was inaugurated with the erection of a giant and tastefully crafted image and shrine of La Virgen de Guadalupe in the back of the space, and it affords full public access. The center institutionalized the relation between Mexican Catholic aesthetics and Chicano art.

Additionally, the founding of PADRES and Las Hermanas directly preceded the formation of a parish-based East L.A. populist group called the United Neighborhood Organization, referred to as UNO. It coalesced in 1977, patterning itself after the San Antonio group Communities Organized for Public Service (COPS). UNO's first victory was a dramatic public spectacle at the expense of the California automobile insurance industry, which was charging East L.A. residents inflated rates based on discriminatory practices. UNO has been criticized by Mike Davis for their singularly "pro-family" agenda and for taking on only winnable issues.[52] Nonetheless, the group made its presence felt in the community and spawned various leaders.

Perhaps most notable among the leaders UNO spawned is Father Luis Olivares (1934–92), Chicano priest, liberation theologian, leader in the immigrant sanctuary movement, and pastor of La Placita Church for ten years, beginning in 1981. Before taking La Placita, Olivares advanced to the presidency of PADRES in 1979. Olivares could not have been more appropriate for the historic parish, as it had a tradition of civil disobedience: La Placita had been a sanctuary for Mexicans who were in danger of compulsory deportation in the 1930s. From his downtown pulpit, Olivares preached Christ's preference for the poor, resistance to unjust authorities, and home-grown revolution: "The authorities would have us or force us to do something against the will of God," Olivares is reported to have said, "and when we don't do as they wish, they punish us or murder us, all because of our fidelity to the law of God."[53] This message to resist unjust authorities resonated with the twelve thousand parishioners who congregated at La Placita each Sunday from places as far away as Mexico and Central America, many entering the United States without official sanction from the government; most of them had encountered the mythology of Olivares back in their homelands. For them, Olivares's poetic interpretations of scripture articulated and sanctioned in eloquent theological language what millions of Latin-American immigrants had already intuited and practiced for years. In the words of Rubén Martinez, La Placita was "a mythic haven on the well-trodden, obstacle-strewn path to the American Dream."[54]

Olivares adorned the walls of the historic chapel with an immense image of La Virgen de Guadalupe, supported by a cast of renegade saints, including Guatemala's and New Mexico's Black Christ of Esquipulas and the would-be saint Archbishop Oscar Arnulfo Romero, martyr for the cause of justice in El Salvador. Olivares moved the theology of liberation around the full hermeneutic circle in praxis, transforming the once "traditional" Mexican parish into a sanctuary for L.A. rejects—as many as two hundred homeless people slept in the basement of La Placita every night. In conjunction with other L.A. agencies, La Placita offered free medical and dental services, English classes, and legal services—especially for immigration law. Olivares's charismatic leadership reached its self-proclaimed climax on 12 December 1985, when he announced to Los Angeles and indeed to the world that La Placita was a public sanctuary for political refugees—even if the U.S. government did not recognize them as such.

Later, Olivares's life took a tragic turn. In 1990 he was hospitalized for meningitis and was almost completely incapacitated. Martinez describes one of his final sermons to La Placita as follows:

> "But I do not fear death, my brothers and sisters. One must accept the will of God. If he wants me [to] stay on in this," he summons a weak, somewhat ironic smile before going on, "vale of tears, then I will stay. If He wishes me to leave, I will leave." Father Luis Olivares bids La Placita farewell with these words: "Like John the Baptist was called . . . so each of us, upon being baptized, is called to be a prophet of love and justice. I ask the Lord for a special blessing for this community that has fought so hard for justice, not only here and in Central America, but all over the world. May it continue to do so, to live out the true meaning of the Gospel." He sinks back into the wheelchair, exhausted.[55]

Olivares retained his magnetic charisma with the people up to the last moments of his life. Martinez describes a scene reminiscent of the Passion of Christ: "After the recitation of the Lord's Prayer, during the offering of peace, an old Mexicana painfully canes her way up to the altar to touch Olivares. Next, a communion-aged boy does the same. Soon, a crowd of parishioners is tearfully laying hands on him."[56] The Mexican faithful needed to touch Olivares's body in order for their experience of him to be real, to be rewarding.

In June 1990, Olivares announced that he was dying of AIDS. The accepted explanation for his contraction of the virus attributes the cause to medical care he received in El Salvador. Conspiracy theorists add a design by officials of the Salvadoran government, who bitterly resented Olivares's incessant condemnation of them. With the death of Olivares, a tradition of political radicalism and civil disobedience at La Placita died also, and it is yet to be resurrected like the radical Christ the Church professes to manifest. Yet the tradition of liberation theology and praxis lives on in East Los Angeles.

ALTARED CATHOLICISM: MAPPING THE SACRED IN EAST L.A. AND BEYOND

The legacy of Chicano Catholic political activism—spawned largely by CPLR, Luis Olivares, and others—is still operative throughout East Los Angeles, as observed in the work of Father Greg Boyle (who is discussed later in this chapter). Today, Catholicism in East Los Angeles is delimited by a series of movements and exchanges, an uneven matrix of dialectics formed between home devotional practices, the Catholic institution, and a populist politics of social justice—with women at the center "altaring" religious expression.[57] Chicana religious movement challenges static modes of religion that act as a conservative force in the community. Adversity often occasions and guides religious devotionalism, unfolding into creative social activism and change.

Mothers of East Los Angeles (Madres de Este de Los Angeles, or MELA) epitomizes the comfortable blending of authentic faith and activist politics of the left that inspire home-based social justice. They combine Guadalupe devotional practice with a populist politics to struggle within the L.A. community and the state. MELA united in 1985 to prevent the building of a state prison less than a mile from the Boyle Heights community. Since then, the group has achieved national recognition for their continuing struggles throughout East Los Angeles and beyond.[58] Mary Pardo, who worked with and documented the activities of MELA for five years, argues that MELA's activism flies in the face of accepted social theories that claim political involvement is the exclusive domain

of the educated and middle class. In contrast, she describes MELA as follows: "They identify themselves as active and committed participants in
the Catholic church; they claim an ethnic identity—Mexican American;
their ages range from forty to sixty; and they have attained at most high
school educations."[59]

MELA is organized throughout East Los Angeles in Catholic
parishes but is not reliant upon the direction or approval of the
priests. Señora Inés de la Cruz, one of the founding members of the
group, spoke for them regarding the Church; her remarks are instructive for understanding Chicana Catholicism generally. For Señora de la
Cruz and the rest of the group, Guadalupe and other popular Mexican saints are important models of faith and struggle. Señora de la
Cruz particularly resonates with Guadalupe because of her bronze-col-
ored skin; "She looks like me," she notes.[60] Señora de la Cruz has a
large altar in the vestibule of her home, with a gigantic picture of
Guadalupe over it. Images of saints and pictures of family members,
arranged bricolage-style, are displayed prominently atop the altar
proper.

Folklorist Kay Turner reports that altar-making for Chicanas builds
distinct feminine relationships that model broader social relationships.
Significantly, these discourses on relating poetically unfold with their
own authority, or with an authority conferred by the saints. One Chicana
altar-maker in Turner's study declared, "We are our own priests at
home."[61] Turner probed the ways "women interpret and control the
image of the Virgin for themselves and thereby modify and subvert received canonical views on the Virgin."[62] Her feminist reading of altar
practices leads her to contrast the official church altar to the women's
home altar, concluding that when located "at the home altar the Virgin
is freed from the canonical bonds that subsume Her under the authority
of God and Christ. Her maternal authority and hence her relational capacity is forwarded by women in a visual rendering of power, that is, of
how to effectively accomplish the continuing regeneration of family and
social life."[63]

Chicana artist and altar-maker Amalia Mesa-Bains describes her own
experience as follows:

The spaces of home altar and yard shrine [nichos] provided for the practice
of spirituality. In these spaces faithful prayer and devotion to patron saints
and deities extended the relationship of the personal and divine. States of
mentality are reached through supplication for divine intervention which
produce the traditional ex-voto paintings (religious narratives painted on

tin) and *milagros* or amulets. The significance of religious imagery in the development of Chicano popular experience cannot be underestimated. Throughout regions of the Southwest, the everyday practices associated with home altars and the Catholic Church include images of saints, uses of *milagros*, amulets, plaster statuary and front yard shrines of the *Virgin de Guadalupe, Virgin de San Juan de Los Lagos, Santo Niño de Atoche,* and the *Sacred Heart of Jesus.*[64]

As Mesa-Bains notes, the home space is for many Mexican-Americans the place where religion is articulated through mnemonic visual discourse. Mesa-Bains concludes that religious or ceremonial spaces function as "transformative elements in a spiritual geography that invoke the sacred and link private and public memories and practices."[65]

Another community of organic intellectuals and poets, the Latina Catholic activists, base themselves in the Pico-Aliso housing projects just east of downtown Los Angeles—reportedly the largest projects in the United States and among the most dangerous. These women call themselves the Comité pro Paz (Committee in favor of peace) and are involved in numerous grass-roots projects, including feeding the homeless and engaging in educational efforts and job training for youth, but above all aiming to stop gang violence. They've wrenched the gospel out of its rarified centers of interpretation and meet regularly to reflect on it, to make it meaningful to their lives and to the lives of their children and their neighbors. They operate on the Latin-American model of liberation theology, *communidades de base,* or base communities, which are founded on three main tenets:

1. *Ver*: See. See your reality. Look at what's going on around you. Are the neighborhood kids shooting at each other every night? Are the local cops behaving badly? Is one of the neighbors beating his wife and children?

2. *Analizar*: Analyze. Analyze the situation in terms of the gospel. What does the gospel say about such problems? Would the Bible suggest hating the gang members or regarding them as kids in need of help?

3. *Actuar*: Act. What action should we take? *Qué haría Jesús?* What would Jesus do in this situation?[66]

The Comité puts the gospel, and the gift of *conocimiento*, awareness or knowledge, into motion each night by embarking on "love walks," conveying to gang members by deeds and words, "You are all our sons. We love you. We don't want you to kill each other."[67] Thus the ecology of deprivation and poverty is transformed into one of love and nurture.

This group was spawned by Father Greg Boyle, who, perhaps more

than anyone else currently on the East Side, is directly involved not only
in Catholic social activism but in the greater East L.A. community. Boyle,
an Irish-American Jesuit, is an unlikely candidate to head the tiny Dolores Mission Church in the massive Pico-Aliso housing project in Boyle
Heights. Known now as the "Gang Priest," he took the parish in 1986 at
age thirty-two.[68] Since then, he has attained national fame for his unsurpassed and tireless work among the Chicano gang members there. Boyle
regularly patrols the streets of the projects in efforts to prevent gang warfare, and it is not uncommon for him to stand in the line of gunfire.

The gang members adore Father Greg, a surrogate father, and compete for his attention. In an article published in the *Los Angeles Times,*
Boyle writes:

> The week before Christmas I had to bury the 40th young person killed in
> my Eastside community. I've grown weary of saying that gangbanging is the
> urban poor's version of teen-age suicide. The violence that has us in its grip
> has always indicated larger problems: poverty, unemployment, racism, the
> great disparity between the haves and have-nots, dysfunctional families and
> above all despair. And for our neglect in addressing these problems as we
> ought, it shouldn't surprise us that their symptomatic manifestations have
> only worsened.[69]

Boyle *materializes* the gospel through confronting social problems in
East Los Angeles, founding job and education programs for the youth
and personally guiding myriad gang members out of destructive
lifestyles.[70] He attempts to give them positive foresight—the ability to
imagine for themselves a different future.

When I asked Father Boyle about the Church's role in the East L.A.
gang communities, he waxed poetic: "The Church has to make gang
members welcome; welcome the rejected and marginalized, accompany
them and walk with them and advocate for them. They must also un-
derscore the issues—especially the great disparity between what our
community has to suffer with, and the privilege on the other side of
town."[71] Boyle explained that kids join gangs due to the poverty and lack
of opportunity in the community; he cited a common expression the
gang members use when they are on the streets trying to make money:
"You've got to buy Pampers." Boyle explained that East L.A. youth "either join gangs or evangelical churches."

Boyle is critical of evangelicals, attributing to their teachings a "silly
moral overlay" on social problems, offering immediate but superficial
solutions that set people up for repeated failure. "The woman who is addicted to crack and comes to me and says, 'Jesus is the answer and that's

all I need to know,' I just look at my watch and she is back smoking crack again. It's not enough to do Jesus talk; the root causes of gangs don't go away once you stick your nose in the Bible." Boyle summarized: "I believe in the dignity of work; I believe that giving people training, education, and jobs is like an ambulance for the state of emergency in which we live."

The office of priest carries with it great respect in Chicana/o communities—and when one is respected one is invited to hold a formative place in the poetic conversation that constitutes community and family—the *sacred*. Indeed, *el respeto*, or respect, carries with it highest importance and has become a sacred value in Latina/o communities, the attainment of it an end in itself. For men, this involves becoming a *don*, or receiving the title *don* before one's name when one has reached late maturity and enjoys high regard. The noun *don* means "gift." But more importantly, it conveys respect. The equivalent for women is *doña*.[72]

Respeto is earned, but it also thought of as a gift bestowed by those around one, noticeable especially when an elder is being addressed. Earning *respeto*, and establishing ritual modes of gifting, provide avenues for women to exercise social authority and for men to express and explore their masculinities, femininities, and passionate devotion to God and to other men and family. Take, for example, the shepherd's play known as *Los Pastores*, in which Catholic-identified *mexicano* men reenact a gospel account of a shepherd's visit to the baby Jesus, bringing gifts to the savior. The baby Jesus, in various forms—El Santo Niño de Atocha, for example—is a popular devotion for *mexicanos*. *Los Pastores* is still performed every evening for two weeks during the Advent season at La Placita Church and on Olvera Street in Los Angeles. Focusing on San Antonio, Richard Flores has emphasized aspects of "gift" and "play" in the shepherds' performances, which function to delimit new codes and terms of value, critiquing capitalist society and bestowing virtue on *mexicano* forms of relationality, place, and time.[73]

The *compradrazgo* system, a network of godchildren and godparents (the latter are those who sponsor the former in the baptism ritual), is another mechanism by means of which men, those whom Lawrence Mosqueda calls "cultural Catholics," achieve spiritual stimulation and union with others. According to Mosqueda, while the majority of Chicanos are baptized Catholics, only a small percentage actually attend church and accept the sacraments with any regularity. Baptism is the basis for the *compadrazgo* system, which, as noted above, results in godparentage, with the godparents known as a *comadre* or *madrina* for women, and as *compadre* or *padrino* for men. "To become a compadre imposes religious and social obligations on the accepting party," Mosqueda argues. Of the men he surveyed, none really felt the religious/institutional aspects of the commitment were important. "To those who felt an obligation in conjunction with the relationship," he states, "the obligation entailed a social focus—primarily between the adults involved, the natural parents and the Godparents—and only secondarily a religious bond between the adult Godparent and the child."[74] *Compadrazgo* draws unchurched men into distinctively sacred-cultural acts.

Mexicano Catholic traditions are highly gendered, with women typically—but not exclusively—bearing the cross for religious instruction. In addition to the mother-son devotion to Guadalupe, the more pious *mexicano* male Catholics have nurtured devotions to the passionate Christ. During Holy Week, and especially on Good Friday, throughout the Mexican Americas (and in Spain) men embark upon a special *manda* to walk like Christ by carrying a large wooden cross. In spring, death (and rebirth) processions are ubiquitous throughout the borderlands. Marta Weigle argues that in the procession the penitents are accompanied by the spirits of their beloved deceased ancestors; this is the period of death that precedes new life, the darkness, or *tinieblas*.[75] The *tinieblas* resounds throughout *curanderismo*—and *evangelico*/born-again traditions—as people narrate their lives in terms of darkness and rebirth. The origins of the tradition are in the pre-Tridentine Catholicism imported to Mesoamerica.[76] The ideas of male blood sacrifice resonated with the corporeal spirituality of the Mesoamericans, and a fresh tradition was created. In the borderlands, historic San Fernando Cathedral, the "heart of San Antonio," beautifully reenacts the Passion of Christ each year, as do many churches and lay associations. One male Chicano observed the importance of the tradition especially for the boys involved in the drama.[77]

Easter Sunday itself, however, is not as significant as the Crucifixion and the events leading up to it. The key association is with Christ, the colonial god, crucified. Again, the sense is of the inevitable tragic dimension of life that must be managed and incorporated. Alberto Pulido argues of the *respeto* basis of the *penitente* (penitents) brotherhood in New Mexico:

> Over the centuries the New Mexican Hispano community has taught, and lived by, the values of mutuality, reciprocity, and self-determination, historically rooted in the sacred teachings of the penitente brotherhood. These sacred expressions are acts of charity achieved through prayer, and the good

example, reflective of a resilient people with localized and practical faith
that is both communal and devout. These penitente teachings and beliefs
emerge from a historical context in which, under both the Spanish and
Mexican Catholic church, the imprint of institutional Roman Catholicism
and official Catholic sacraments were absent from the daily experiences and
expressions of the people. What we have in its place is a practical religion
based on personal access to God . . . impossible to contain within the
boundaries of Roman Catholicism.[78]

In the *penitente* tradition, the idea of poetics, *to make,* is central, especially in religion, in acts of charity that are not only "the good example"
but also and especially "prayer." Acts of prayer for the penitents occur
during a male initiation that takes place in the sacred and private space
of the *moradas*—community-built *de facto* churches.

The *mexicana* Catholic girls' initiation ceremony is celebrated in
Catholic (and Protestant) churches throughout Mexico and the borderlands: the *quinceañera,* or the fifteenth birthday, which has been likened
to a debutante ball. The *quinceañera* is an elaborate party where a girl,
or *niña,* becomes an unmarried woman, *señorita.* The ceremony is typically an elaborate and costly affair, with the young woman sporting a
white wedding gown and accompanied by fifteen young women in formal matching gowns and young men in tuxedos. The *quinceañera* is held
in church, and the dinner party later is held in a large hall, with a live
band and dancing. Guests typically number in the hundreds. Though its
exact origins are unclear, and there has been lamentably little scholarly
attention devoted to the topic, the observance is commonly thought to
have begun in the ubiquitous puberty rites of young women in pre-Hispanic Mesoamerica and to have been incorporated by the Church—as
perhaps another pocket of resistance, accommodation, and change.

Karen Mary Davalos has brought attention to the competing meanings ascribed to the ceremony. Parents and clergy value its didactic quality, teaching "tradition," religious devotion, and commitment. "The girl
is encouraged to be subservient and to subordinate her wants and needs
to those of her family and the church. . . . A selfless mother/daughter is
the codification of Catholicism's heterosexuality—delayed until marriage
but nonetheless compulsory." One young woman described how, for her,
"the event is experienced through physical placement of one's body and
begins the process of sexual awareness."[79] Davalos concludes that, in
spite of its (hetero)sexist intent, young women involved in the
quinceañera can and have used it as a religious vehicle to resist cultural

assimilation, to make connections to Mexico, and to determine and publicly declare their identity as self-determined women. These religious practices and others enable women and men to "presence" themselves in a land that is familiar yet often hostile.

BORN IN EAST L.A.: *EL BARRIO* AS SACRED CITY

In the decades preceding the Mexican Revolution, in the words of Michael Engh, "religious beliefs aided . . . [Mexican] exiles in Los Angeles to produce dynamic local leaders, to organize challenges to their host society, and to engage in a variety of creative religious expressions. . . . They manifested their faith domestically in their devotions in the home, and publicly, as in the popular Guadalupe procession. . . . The achievements of these immigrants in a land of exile appear all the more dramatic when set in the context of the poverty and prejudice they endured in Los Angeles."[80] When religious belief and practice are transferred from Mexico to Los Angeles and other places throughout the borderlands, not only are the religious codes, as well as the people, changed, but so too is the place transformed. In the case of Los Angeles, the city has attained a mythological status for *mexicana/os:* it has become a home, familiar, a *sacred* center in the Mexico City periphery.[81]

Chicano historian and L.A.-based activist Rodolfo Acuña makes memory and place formative to political power: "Key to that Chicano/Mexicano struggle is reconstructing a historical memory of Los Angeles that has been diluted or denied by Euroamerican forces." As Acuña sees it, "At stake is culture: how to define US culture, and whose definition shall be dominant?"[82] Mexicans have long staked a claim to Los Angeles based on the religious history and symbolism of Guadalupe. And, with the emergence of the distinctively Chicano *qua* Chicano identity in the late 1960s, new narratives of place emerged in poetic constructions such as Aztlán. Other narratives from the Chicano movement shifted sacred place more specifically to the East L.A. *barrio,* such as Javier Alva's "Los Angeles: The Sacred Spot."[83]

More recently, Chicana and Chicano artists have eulogized the mythological place of East Los Angeles in Chicano consciousness. Take, for example, performance artist El Vez, a parody of Elvis Presley, who has poetically inscribed the following anthem to the tune of "Dixie," calling it "Mexican-American Trilogy":

I wish I was in East Los away away
In East Los land I'll make my stand
to live or die in East Los

Porque East L.A. where I was born
One hot and smoggy Summer morn
Look away, look away, look away
East L.A.

While intended as comedy, the verse illumines the place of East Los Angeles in Chicano consciousness. East Los Angeles as sacred center could not be conceptualized, either in the past or today, without its relationship to the archetypal sacred center that is Mexico City. The path between Mexico City and Los Angeles has been well traveled by symbols and narratives, such as Guadalupe herself, but also by people such as journalist Ruben Salazar, whose beat for the *Los Angeles Times* between the years 1965 and 1968 extended the boundaries of East Los Angeles into Mexico City, and vice versa.[84] More recently, the work of journalist, poet, and essayist Rubén Martinez spans the Mexico City–Los Angeles continuum, creating a massive sacred center that is unified in its Guadalupe rituals.[85] Chicana/o sacred cartography is multiply centered, but there is at least one main transnational current running between Mexico City and East Los Angeles. North of the border, traditions are repeated, but they are also transformed in ongoing dialectics between Mexico City and East Los Angeles. More intimately, as Mesa-Bains notes of her own Catholic nurture, there is a dialectic between the home altar and Catholic Church that transforms Catholicism.[86]

CONCLUSION: MATERIALIZING THE SACRED, SPIRITUALIZING THE PROFANE

In the border transformations wrought as sources of spiritual strength in the material world, the composition of religious essences is elaborated, extended, and perhaps overdeveloped to include the material world in one continuous loop, rather than as a discrete realm completely distinct from the spiritual, each with its characteristic rhythms, textures, and rules. A questionnaire-and-ethnography study conducted by a Catholic lay worker in southern California, Jeffery Thies, determined that Chicana/o Catholicism "is often focused on a specific need" and is accordingly organized around devotion to Our Lady of Guadalupe and saints who represent various days on the Mexican Catholic calendar and different parts of Mexico. This study emphasized the importance of material culture, concluding: "The Mexican Catholic seeks to express his/her spirituality in concrete, often visible ways."[87] Thies's survey recorded saints and the common issues that help define them: "St. Anthony of Padua—for marriage to find a spouse. St. Jude of Thaddeus—as he does many miracles. St. Ignatius of Loyola—that he take away bad people. . . . To the White Virgin of the Remedies—when we give birth, we pray a rosary to her every Monday. St. Ignatius of Loyola—like St. Cyprian—that the devil goes away, or that bad neighbors go away one puts his image near the door. St. Jude Thaddeus—when a neighbor is annoying you, you pray to him outside of your house . . . that the neighbor go away, that the people who are envious of one will be quiet, that he will help you find work and have more money."[88]

In her collection of short essays, Sandra Cisneros blurs the boundaries between fact and fiction by inscribing narratives into her work as *retablos* that recount miracle stories. These stories resonate with actual *retablos* found at the Chapel of Our Lord of the Miracles, or El Señor de los Milagros, in San Antonio. One of the narratives in her piece, entitled "Little Miracles, Kept Promises," reads as follows:

> Dear San Antonio de Padua, Can you please help me find a man who isn't a pain in the *nalgas* [butt]. There aren't any in Texas, I swear. . . . Can you do something about all the educated Chicanos who have to go to California to find a job. I would appreciate it very much if you sent me a man who speaks Spanish, who at least can pronounce his own name the way it's supposed to be pronounced. Someone please who never calls himself "Hispanic" unless he's applying for a grant from Washington D.C. I'll turn your statue upside down until you send him to me. I've put up with too much too long, and now I'm just too intelligent, too powerful, too beautiful, too sure of who I am finally to deserve anything less. Ms. Barbara Ybañez, San Antonio, TX[89]

Similarly, an actual ethnographic narrative from south Texas is illustrative of the use and movements of saints:

> Some saints have universal appeal among the Mexican-Americans who call on them for help in a broad range of situations. . . .
>   Graciela remembers the time when St. Isador *(San Isidro Labrador)* was tormented until he brought rain. Her grandfather's farm was dry and brown from drought. Appeals to the saints were unanswered. Thinking that the saint failed to comprehend the gravity of the situation, the grandfather took the image on a tour to view the desolation of the land. When there was no rain several days later, the image was left to bake in the sun. "Soon it became too uncomfortable for him," Graciela related, "and he convinced God to send the rain."[90]

This self-reliant form of Catholicism has developed its own rhythms, places, and a distinct discourse with its own grammar—through *consejos* and *dichos*. Take, for example, a teaching on theodicy that comes from Los Angeles:

> A very poor man who always made sacrifices to provide for his large family decides that just once he would like to know the feeling of a full stomach. He asks his wife to prepare a special lunch for him that he may take off into the countryside and have all to himself. To his dismay he runs into an old man who asks him to share his food. He refuses to do so and feels even more justified when he learns that the old man is God, for God is not just in his dealing with men. He provides some with wealth, while He condemns others to poverty. He is about to settle down once more to his meal, when he is approached by an old woman with whom he likewise refuses to share. When he learns that she is Death, however, he very willingly shares with her, exclaiming that Death does indeed treat all men equally.[91]

God and life often appear unfair, but death is the great equalizer that no one can cheat. Thus, death is the most powerful force in life. The force of death is a theme and symbol that dominates the ethnic Mexican imagination in ways consistent with Nahua philosophy. The devotion to La Santísima Muerte, or Holy Death, is powerfully alive in Mexico and throughout the borderlands. The Chicano and Mexican Catholic ceremonial calendar is marked by days of observance for the dead: Días de Los Muertos. Celebrated during the first days of November, this ceremony falls on and around the Catholic All Souls' Day.

During the ceremony for Días de Los Muertos, special altars are constructed in the home and food is taken to the dead at the cemetery, where families commune with their loved ones, in spirit or materialized, in all-night vigils. According to Davíd Carrasco, "The central idea is that during this period of public and private (family) rituals the living and dead family members and friends are joined together in an atmosphere of communion and spiritual regeneration."[92] Octavio Paz argues that the fiesta of *los muertos* "is a return to a remote and undifferentiated state, prenatal or presocial. It is a return that is also a beginning, in accordance with the dialectic that is inherent in social processes."[93] For Paz, the celebration of the return of the dead belongs to the movement and symbolism of social dialectics, through which Mexicans remap space and time: "Time is transformed to a mythical past or a total present," writes Paz, and "space, the scene of the fiesta, is turned into a gaily decorated world of its own; and the persons taking part cast off all human or social rank and become, for the moment, living images. And everything takes place as if it were not so, as if it were a dream. . . . We throw down our burdens of time and reason."[94] He argues that Mexicans "oscillate between intimacy and withdrawal, between a shout and silence, between a fiesta and a wake, without ever truly surrendering ourselves. Our indifference hides life behind a death mask; our wild shout rips off this mask and shoots it into the sky where it swells, explodes, and falls back in silence and defeat."[95] Paz finds psychoanalytic mystification and delusion in the space of oscillation, of border crossing. The return of the dead, then, provides a means whereby Mexicans accept the limitations of their mortality, of death, which, he argues, is an archetype of the primordial death introduced by colonization. To live with death, as he sees it, is to live with colonization. This, too, informs the poetics of *mexicano* cultural identity.

A Chicana interpreter, Sybil Venegas, describes Días de los Muertos as a "ceremony of memory," in terms of poetic movements. She writes:

> Yet, in its contemporary form, the Day of the Dead in Aztlán can be viewed not only as a transformation of an indigenous past, but as an innovation and a post colonial "border crossing" into the future. Its purpose over the past twenty years has been to define and unite a community divided by a history of oppression, exploitation and domination, and its strength and success as a community event has been its creativity in both performance and the visual arts, a creativity that has since become a foundation of the Chicano aesthetic.[96]

Paz and Venegas agree that border crossings, ceremony, memory, and the resultant transformations are necessary for people who suffer the effects of colonialism or postcolonialism. Both of them point out that space and time are transformed in the ceremony.[97]

Juanita Garciagodoy agrees with Venegas—Días de los Muertos is a resistance and return. Garciagodoy summarizes: "Días de Muertos is interesting in part because it is a popular answer to the dominant Christian mythology of All Souls' and All Saints Days, as well as the dominant mythology about the stereotypical, provincial Mexico and the nationalism it constructs. Whereas pre-Hispanic Mexican cultures seem for the most part to have given in to Spanish Catholicism, some pockets resisted colonization, and this celebration is one of them."[98]

Lara Medina and Gilbert Cadena have documented the Days of the Dead ceremonies in Los Angeles, citing it as a way in which Chicanos and Chicanas empower themselves by reclaiming indigenous traditions.[99]

Similarly, Medina has argued that many Chicanas find fresh stores of energy by rejecting patriarchal forms of Christianity; these women

> (re)turn to an *indígena*-inspired spirituality, learn to trust their own senses and bodies, recreate traditional cultural practices, and look to non-Western philosophies—all of which offers us a (re)connection to our selves, our spirits, and to the ongoing process of creating *nuestra familia*. . . . Chicanas venturing into often undefined spiritual arenas continue a tradition of religious agency as lived by many of our *antepasados . . . consejeras, curanderas, rezadores, espiritualistas,* and even *comadres,* still practicing their healing ways in spite of, in lieu of, or in conjunction with the sacraments and teachings offered by the Christian churches.[100]

In the words of Ana Castillo, the Chicana who acts as a *curandera*

> might associate the fundamental betrayal of the church with her womanhood, with her devout Catholic mother. She, therefore, may be inclined toward her grandmother's beliefs, or the teachings of a community elder. Creating some distance from the last generation, from whom she is unlearning many lessons that have felt harmful to her well-being, allows her to recapture some of her spiritual orientation, and to adapt it to her own needs while still operating within her own culture.[101]

In *curanderismo,* Chicanas powerfully conjure a religious world that is at once individualized and also connected to millions of people and thousands of years. It is to a discussion of this that we now turn.

FIGURE 1. The
original image of
La Virgen de
Guadalupe on the
cape of Juan
Diego, Guadalupe
Basilica, Tepeyac.
(Photo by the
author.)

FIGURE 2. Pilgrims
in the atrium,
Guadalupe
Basilica, Tepeyac.
(Photo by the
author.)

FIGURE 3. Pilgrim at the Guadalupe Basilica, Tepeyac, on 12 December, the feast of La Virgen. (Photo by the author.)

FIGURE 4. La Virgen de Guadalupe and Juan Diego arising from Mexico City, centering Catholicism in the Americas. (From *Tepeyac* magazine.)

1747   1947
AMERICA UNIDA
EN EL
PATRONATO GUADALUPANO

SIMBOLO DE UNIDAD NACIONAL Y CONTINENTAL

FIGURE 5. The Shrine of Juan Soldado, Tijuana, Mexico. (Photo by Richard Hecht; used by permission.)

FIGURE 6. Guadalupe at Self-Help Graphics, East Los Angeles. (Photo by the author.)

FIGURE 7. El Niño Fidencio as La Virgen de Guadalupe. (Photographer unknown.)

FIGURE 8. Sagrado Corazón Botánica, healing center, East Los Angeles. (Photo by the author.)

FIGURE 9. A *limpia*, or spiritual cleansing, is conducted by a laying on of hands, performed by a *curandera*. (Photo by the author.)

FIGURE 10. *Espiritualistas* in *cátedra*, or ceremony, Mexico City. (Photo by the author.)

FIGURE 11. Alcance Victoria, Boyle Heights, Los Angeles. (Photo by the author.)

FIGURE 12. Alcance Victorians in ceremony, Boyle Heights, Los Angeles. (Photo by the author.)

FIGURE 13.
Yolanda M. López,
*Nuestra Madre/
Our Mother,*
acrylic and oil on
masonite, 1986–88.

FIGURE 14. *La
Santissima Muerte*
(Holy Death),
Mexico City.
(Photo by the
author.)

CHAPTER 4

El Don

The Gift of Healing, from Mesoamerica to the Borderlands

Centuries of observing the world and its workings from the
macrocosm to the microcosm of the body itself produced
Nahuatl thought with its distinctive characteristics of duality,
fluidity, and balance.

> Sylvia Marcos, "Sacred Earth: Mesoamerican Perspectives,"
> *Concilium* 261 (October 1995)

From specialized healers to more ordinary women . . . who
labor privately in their homes, it is such *curanderas* who daily
and relatively uncharismatically engage with late capitalism's
baleful effects on the *mexicano* body politic as they continue
a struggle with the devil.

> José E. Limón, *Dancing with the Devil: Society and Cultural Poetics
> in Mexican American South Texas*

During the fall of 1999, "Esperanza Perdida" was in dire straits. Her story unfolds as if it were testimony for canonization: At thirty-eight, she was without a partner, "papers," money, or legal U.S. residency. She was supporting two children. "With my remaining savings, I paid rent, bought food, and visited Caridad, a *curandera.*" The spiritual cleansing, or *limpia,* she received from "Caridad" was enough to strengthen her spirit, and the herbs and *sobadería,* or "massage therapy," she received was enough to strengthen her body.[1] Esperanza survived. Still, Mexican religious healing, *curanderismo,* sometimes increases conventional suffering—as most religions can. *Curanderismo* is a response, typically, to crisis: thus, there is a necessary tragic element to this set of religious practices.[2]

The term *curanderismo* comes from the Spanish verb *curar,* "to heal" or "to cure." In contemporary *mexicano* parlance, *curanderismo* signifies a wide variety of community-based curing traditions organized around charismatic and prophetic healers. People who practice *curanderismo* range from those who occasionally use herbs to matriarchs who administer spiritual cleansing to full-time healers whose rituals are described by Davíd Carrasco and others as shamanistic.[3] Religious healers are both female and male: *curanderismo* seekers demonstrate no preference between genders; they go by reputation alone.

Curanderismo is a collection of religious-based tactics, especially healing with herbs and teas, massage therapy, midwifery, card reading, and divination. Also common are more elaborate symbolic or spiritual "operations," including unclogging arteries, healing cancer, and addressing other physical, social, and personal problems. But the most common procedure is the spiritual cleansing, or *limpia*. A *limpia* releases negative energies while conjuring positive spirit through prayer, recitation, and a laying on of hands. (As we shall see in the next two chapters, spiritual healing ceremonies involving a laying on of hands are central both to *espiritualismo,* Mexican spiritualism, and to *los evangélicos,* or evangelicals/Pentecostals.)

The crux of *curanderismo* is formed in the religious matrix emergent in colonialism: it inscribes ancient Mexican rituals and idioms onto Catholic grammars and symbols, which is why I treat it as a religious tradition. When speaking of the famed *curandero* El Niño Fidencio (1898–1938), Carlos Monsiváis notes: "When he dies, however, he receives the blessings of the Church, which refuses to see him as the founder of a new religion, preferring instead the image of a Catholic saint."[4] Though based in Catholicism, *curanderismo* turns on the traditions of the prophet and of spiritual poetry, and thus it narrates across conventional religious borders into creative and expansive social terrain. Further, it is a distinct persistence of pre-Columbian Mexican religious practice: a borderlands religion.

My thesis in this chapter is that *curanderismo* is an expression of religious poetics that emphasizes the body and restructures the order of the world through gifting, reciprocity, and exchange. In *curandero* practices, individual religious agents contest the borders of institutional religion and healing. As in Guadalupe devotion, *curanderismo* practice obscures the boundary separating indigenous traditions from Catholicism through various movements, particularly a praxis-wavering across the Enlightenment boundary separating the logics of modern "science" and spirit. One anthropological study from south Texas concludes that "many Mexican Americans are caught in the conflict between the scientific theories of modern medicine and the supernatural theories of folk magic."[5] This is the *nepantla* situation.

Statistics have been collected on *curanderismo* in the United States, but the available data are contradictory. One major quantitative study conducted in 1984 concluded that not many Mexican-Americans had consulted a *curandera* or *curandero* within a year of the study.[6] This conclusion was based on the number of respondents to a questionnaire who admitted seeking the aid of a *curandera/o;* as a result, the study admittedly was plagued by lack of truthful responses. A host of other, more qualitative studies, including one on East Los Angeles published in 1995, have argued that "folk healing has historically played an important role in meeting the health care needs of residents." And while participants in this study "relied on modern medicine to treat serious injuries and major health problems, they still considered traditional folk healing a viable alternative in situations in which modern health care was unsatisfactory or ineffective."[7] Another ethnographic study of ethnic Mexicans in Los Angeles during the 1980s emphasized the vitality of traditional healing practices in contemporary Chicano life—while stressing also the diversity among the Mexican-American population there. The study emphasized the characteristic pivoting (border crossing) of *curandera* practitioners, arguing that

> (1) personal experience narratives play a major role in the perpetuation of folk medicine, and (2) that the experience of immigrating or of being a minority person, exposed to different modes of belief and behavior, provokes conscious awareness of beliefs and practices once taken for granted, and thereby leads individuals to analyze and reassess their own health beliefs and practices. Some aspects of traditional medicine are rejected; others are found to be worth preserving. At times individuals waver back and forth, unsure as to whether to try traditional or orthodox treatment—or both.[8]

With this wavering in mind, I characterize *curanderismo* as a border phenomenon—a religion that is poetically interpreted to meet the crises of quotidian life, another set of variations on a poetic religious theme.

HEALING IN CONTACT ZONES

At its most general, *curanderismo* is a synthesis of pre-Tridentine Catholicism and Spanish-Moorish medicine, combined with ancient Mesoamerican medicine and religion. Spanish Renaissance ethnographers documented the presence of Mexican healers, wise medicine women and men, who persisted well into the colonial period. William Taylor reports that in the eighteenth century *curanderismo* thrived in central Mexico, citing an account of a healing in 1761 that combined indigenous and Catholic elements:

> Ground peyote in a cup of water was placed on an altar with lighted candles late at night. The saints on the altar were perfumed with incense while the sick man knelt before it. Those present then said the rosary and sang the *alabado* (a hymn or praise sung as the Host is placed in the tabernacle). The sick man danced with a bow and arrow in his hands. The patient's brother

said that he next saw his brother dead, and cried out. The curer told him to kneel, pass the smoke of the incense over the saints, and say the Apostles' Creed three times. When he turned around he saw his brother sitting up. The witness passed out until morning, when he found his brother somewhat better though not [completely] cured.[9]

The exact origins of the multiplicity of myths, rituals, narratives, practices, and more general symbols commonly referred to as *curanderismo* are a matter of speculation and debate. It was typically thought that the Spanish Moors had contributed all that could be classified as "nonsuperstitious" to *curanderismo*. However, as Bernardo Ortíz de Montellano has shown through an examination of Aztec codices, "Aztecs were much more empirical and scientific in their attitude toward medicine than generally believed, and second, evidence [demonstrates] that there was a high correspondence between native and European beliefs concerning disease." Similarities facilitated combination and synthesis and "should make us cautious in assigning any aspect of folk medicine to one culture or another."[10]

The Aztecs and Spaniards had several points of convergence in "magico-religious" concepts as well, including ideas about the origins of illness, especially illness as divine punishment, and witchcraft. Another point of agreement between Aztec and Spanish medical systems was the belief that prayer was an effective treatment for illness. Ortíz de Montellano points to the example of the "evil eye" as a cause of dysfunction, an idea that is salient in both Aztec and Spanish faiths.[11] He delineates the empirical and careful usage of herbs and plants medicinally and shows how that ancient Mesoamerican knowledge persists in contemporary *curanderismo*. Perhaps most striking in this comparative work is that "the idea of a balance of Hippocratic humors parallels the native philosophy of moderation and a middle way. The fusion of these two cultural streams produced Mexican folk medicine."[12]

By interfacing primary Nahuatl texts with fieldwork, Sylvia Marcos has identified the concepts of "duality, equilibrium, and fluidity" as key to unlocking the mysteries of Mesoamerican healing systems and understanding contemporary Mexican healers. Through highly articulated dualities, "the material and the immaterial, the exterior and the interior interacted constantly. It is in this interaction that pathological categories and therapeutic practices developed."[13] Marcos notes that the concept of duality was embodied in the highest Aztec deity, Ometéotl, who had both male and female avatars:

> Bi-polar duality is ubiquitous in Mesoamerican concepts of the cosmos. Dualities such as life and death, good and evil, female and male, earth and sky structure the Mesoamerican world. Through opposites, these pairs were complementary. The feminine-masculine duality is a typical example. Feminine and masculine fused in one bi-polar principle. This dual unity was fundamental to the creation of the cosmos, its (re)generation, and sustenance. . . . Many Mesoamerican deities were pairs of gods and goddesses, beginning with Ometéotl, the supreme creator whose name means "two-god" or dual divinity.[14]

In ancient Mesoamerican discourse, Ometéotl symbolized the structure of the cosmos, and humanity's charge was to keep both the cosmos and the body in a state of balance.

For *curanderas* today, as then, a healthy body exists in a state of equilibrium with the other forces of life. Balance in the body may be upset for a number of reasons, and imbalance produces illness. *Curanderismo* operates on a conceptual binary: between light and dark, good and evil, wet and dry, up and down, male and female, and especially between hot and cold. These forces are constantly in dynamic tension, fluid and shifting—*in motion*. Marcos characterizes these dynamics in three terms: duality, fluidity, and complementarity. For example, the difference between hot and cold is believed to be manifested in the body, and every individual is thought to have a hot or cold type that delimits the personality one has, the kinds of diseases to which one is prone, and the care one should take to achieve equilibrium. If predisposed toward cold, then balance, or equilibrium, is achieved by eating more hot foods, and vice versa. In this way, the body is at the center of perception and knowledge. Still, these beliefs sometimes obviate regular medical care.

Curanderas posit a number of origins for imbalance or illness—the predicament of being physically *displaced*. Some attribute it to supernatural forces and others to more conventional sources: poor body maintenance, smoking, drinking, and eating excessively are said to bring about imbalance in the body's humoral system, for example. *Curanderas* consider themselves knowledgeable about anatomy and physiology and recognize that viruses and other biological infections can afflict the body. Therefore, *curanderas* also value conventional medicine and will refer patients to doctors. But relationships to doctors are problematic. *Curanderas* are aware of the high cost of medical care and the difficulties that visiting a doctor presents for many ethnic Mexicans—especially for undocumented workers in the United States.[15] *Curanderismo* holds that illnesses exist that doctors cannot cure. In the words of one healer, "*Cu-randeras* remove spells, and that's why [there are diseases that doctors] cannot cure because they don't know how to remove spells."[16] Still, *cu-randerismo* is an oral tradition, and while principles are remarkably similar, there is much variation in belief and practice.

The drama of *curanderismo* is enacted on three fundamental levels: physical or material, mental, and spiritual.[17] "Certain curanderos may choose to emphasize one above or even to the exclusion of the others," notes one *curandero* insider. "These [levels] are the material (the most common, with its emphasis on objects such as candles, oils, herbs), the spiritual (here the curandero is often a medium), and the mental (psychic healers, for example). Rituals—formulaic or patterned ways of treating the various illnesses of those who come to see the curandero—are present on all three levels."[18] In Mexico and throughout the borderlands, the spiritual level of *curanderismo* has joined with spiritualism and formed a fresh tradition, *espiritualismo,* which is the subject of the next chapter. Spiritual and physical healing remain the most popular of all the techniques, while psychic (or mental) healing is the rarest form of *curandismo.*

Curanderas have self-identified specialties. "A *yerbero* will be an herbalist, able to prescribe botanical remedies. A *partera* is a midwife. A *sobador* or *sobadora* will be a masseuse or masseur."[19] Common to all specialties and levels are the ritual tools for healing. Material cultural objects typical of *curanderismo* include eggs, garlic, candles, lemons, Christian symbols such as crosses and saints, and more standard medical fare such as cotton and rubbing alcohol. Herbs used for cleansing purposes and for treating all manner of diseases in hot- and cold-water teas are perhaps the most commonly prescribed cures. Eggs are thought to have absorbing or cleansing properties; they are believed to actually soak up negative energy from the human body and from the environment, as are garlic, cloves, and lemons. *Agua preparada,* or "prepared water"—prepared by prayer and blessing, either by a Catholic priest or another religious specialist—is central to ritual practice. Water, it is postulated, has curative properties and is especially powerful because it functions as the physical connection between the realms of the living and the dead. The symbolism of water is charged with formative properties in Mesoamerican discourse, and also holds (re)generative forces for *curanderas* and *espiritualistas.* I turn now to describe the practice of *curanderas.*

CURANDERA PRAXIS

For *curanderismo* healing practices, the organizing principles of "sympathetic" and "contagious" magic are helpful. The concept of sympathetic magic, or "proximity and similarity," teaches that "like produces like," and hence illnesses are treated based on this principle. Contagious healing, on the other hand, operates on the logic of direct connection, touch, repulsion, and attraction. Although there is a *curanderismo* discourse that is repeatable and mobile, healing narratives are constructed by each healer, depending on the problem.

Traditional healers are sought for every conceivable type of ailment, from childbirth problems to cancer and AIDS, but also to repair social and personal physical, mental, and economic disorders. And while *curanderas* typically are consulted as one alternative in a range of healthcare options, there are maladies that only a *curandera* can heal and that characterize, therefore, *curandera* practice. Such illnesses include *mal de ojo, mal ojo,* or *ojo* (the "bad" or "evil" eye); *susto* (fright or loss of spirit); *caída de mollera* (fallen fontanel); *empacho* (indigestion); *mal aire* (upper respiratory illness and colds); *desasombro* (a more severe grade of *susto,* or spirit loss); *espanto* (the most serious form of spirit loss); *bilis* (excessive bile); *muina* (anger sickness); *latido* (palpitation or throb); and *envidia, mal puesto, salar,* or *maleficio* (a physical disorder caused by envy).

Healing methods vary from curer to curer, but they do follow patterns. Children are the ones most often afflicted with *mal ojo,* or evil eye, for example. *Ojo* can occur when someone or something (a personal possession) is admired too intensely—in this instance, *envidia* results. *Envidia,* or sickness caused by jealousy, is a more severe form of *ojo.* The touch of the unwitting perpetrator can prevent the effects of *ojo* he or she may have caused. In more serious cases, a *limpia* is required. According to one healer,

> *Mal ojo* is treated by having the child lie down and sweeping him three times with an egg. The sweeping is done by forming little crosses [*crusitas*] with the egg, on the child's body, starting at the head and going to the feet. While sweeping, the healer recites the Apostles' Creed three times, making sure that he sweeps both the front and the back. The egg is cracked and dropped into a glass or jar filled with water. The jar may then be placed on the child's back. The jar may then be placed on the child's head, and another Creed recited. The next morning at sunrise the egg may either be burned or cast away in the form of a cross.[20]

Another healer, Dolores Latorre, offers the following remedy to cure *susto,* or spirit loss. Her method also involves an egg, as well as a broom:

> The cure must be done on three consecutive nights: Wednesday, Thursday, and Friday, the last day being the most effective. The patient lies on the bed with arms extended in the form of a cross while his entire body is cleansed with a lemon or a whole egg and he is swept with a bundle or broom of herbs, preferably horehound, rosemary, California peppertree, redbush, or naked-seed weed, tied together or separately. Each evening fresh herbs are used.[21]

The *susto* cure summons the spirit to return to the body. The patient is made to recite an invocation to the fleeting spirit for its return—*aquí vengo* (here I come), *allí voy* (I am coming now), or some variation on these are typical responses. Both are affirmative rituals of call and response suggesting that the spirit is indeed returning.[22] In *curanderismo,* as in other Latin-American postcolonial indigenous traditions, the border between the living and spirit worlds is commonly crossed.

Both of the examples above describe the most common ritual technique, the *limpia,* or cleansing, which consists of sweeping the body with a symbolic object, usually held in the left hand of the healer. An egg, lemon, or a bunch of herbs bound together with a string are the most commonly used ritual tools. Some healers conduct *limpias* by systematically passing a large crucifix over the body of the supplicant. A *limpia* is thought to absorb negative energy from the body, driving evil forces into the ritual object used for the sweeping. Afterward, the object used to perform the cleansing is ceremoniously destroyed, most often by burning it.

In their ethnographic study of *curanderismo,* Robert Trotter and Juan Antonio Chavira provide accounts in which *curanderas* recite biblical narratives while conducting a *limpia.* Doña Juanita describes her remedy for healing *susto,* or fright sickness, as follows:

> First, I dagnosis [*sic*] the case by cleaning the patient's body with an egg. When I crack the shell and drop the raw egg into a glass of water, I can tell whether the affliction is fright or another illness. Some of the disease enters the egg and you can see it is fright by the way the egg white curls in the water. Sometimes, I also feel the patient's pulse. An irregular pulse means that he has *latido,* an exhaustion that often comes from fright. To treat the patient, I must remove the fright from his body. My treatment lasts nine days. You must understand that it is not I, but God, who really cures. I pray constantly and so does my patient. Throughout the treatment, I give the patient purifying and strengthening teas. I sweep his body daily with an herb bundle containing *albahaca* (sweet basil), *poleo* (pennyroyal), and *romero*

(rosemary). The most important part of the cure consists of drawing an outline of his body in dirt three times a day. The patient lies on a dirt floor
while I use a knife to cut an outline of his body in the ground. When he
rises, I take dirt from the lines cut in the ground and mix it with water for
him to drink. This I do three times a day for nine days. During each treatment, I say nine Lord's Prayers and nine Hail Marys. On the final day of the
cure, the last thing I do is recite the Twelve Truths of the World forward
and backward. Then, if it is God's will, the patient is well.[23]

Note especially the use of the number nine, as in a novena. But even
these individualized poetics of healing share the religious fact of the gift,
or *don.*

THE GIFT

Each healer believes that his or her curing power is a "gift" that comes
directly from God; in some cases, this gift is brokered through a helper
spirit who acts, in effect, as the familiar of the healer. If a person is endowed with the gift of healing, she or he will ultimately need to employ
that gift in the service of others or else suffer dissatisfaction, unhappi-
ness, and in some cases more severe types of penalties. The original gift
of healing imparted to the *curandera* sets into motion a distinct symbolic
chain of gifting organized around three fundamental obligations: to receive, to reciprocate, and to gift.[24]

In the following account, from south Texas in the 1950s, a woman's
husband has left her and she imagines his absence as an opportunity to
use her gift:

A voice that I felt but did not hear said, "I have done this to free you so you
can use my gift. It is not a punishment and your husband is in peace. I have
sent you no children because I want you to use this gift. You have not used
it freely before because of other obligations. Now you are free to cure and
remove evil from the world. Share your blessings with others. Through you,
I will cure."[25]

The "gift" obligates; a gift without responsibility belongs to the realm of
the impossible.[26] Instead, the gift of healing emerges as Max Weber's primary endowment of charisma—it is innate, it comes directly from God—
rather than the gift received as conferred by a charismatic office such as
"priest."[27]

The gift that is truly charismatic is *revealed,* not conferred. William
Madsen explains, "The gift of curing may be revealed through a dream,
a vision, a voice, or merely a deep understanding of the sick. The reve-

lation is frequently associated with a grave illness suffered by the gifted individual or a member of his family."[28] Revelation of the gift subverts official institutional forms of submission and reward and democratizes access to religious discourse by engendering the prophet, prophecy, and shamanism. In *curanderismo,* healers act as shamans, spiritual mediums and healers, and prophets, and they are both female and male. Madsen observes:

> A male curer received his gift during a pilgrimage to a distant shrine where he gave thanks for his daughter's recovery from a critical illness. As he looked up to the altar, he felt pain and great weariness from the long trip. He looked up at the altar and said, "But, I would suffer anything to repay your blessedness in curing my daughter." At that moment, his pain and fatigue vanished. "My body was suddenly filled with strength and joy," the curer recalled. "I saw an added brightness around the altar and felt a cool, loving pressure on my head. And I heard a voice say, 'It is through you that I cured your daughter. You have my power within you. If you wish to truly repay me, use this gift to help the sick and suffering.' "[29]

Personal tragedy, followed by healing, typically catalyzes the awakening to consciousness of the gift. As Carrasco sees it, in *curanderismo* "the pattern of initiation involves a great ordeal, sometimes experienced during a sickness which takes the novice close to death, and introduces him or her to the terrors of finitude and spiritual forces. During this ordeal, which often includes ecstatic dreams, the hero is tested. He is symbolically killed and reborn into the vocation of singer, healer, and poet."[30] The healer gains a new understanding of himself, others, and the spiritual realm—*conocimientos*—and also gains the disposition to manifest the gift. This pattern is instantiated in *curanderismo,* and it is ubiquitous throughout the borderlands, as we shall see.

In a personal healing, or the overcoming of another obstacle, the individual discovers she possesses the gift, and that fact determines her destiny. The healer is gifted by God, and she must in turn gift others, who then must reciprocate and return the gift to the healer, to God, and to others. In healing bodies, new modes of exchange are delimited. Concomitantly, knowledges are assessed, advanced, and rejected. In healing the body one acquires intimate familiarity with God, the body, the spirits, self, and others, rearranging the norms of capitalist accumulation and consumption. This is done via the *conocimientos,* new gnosis, new epistemology. A charismatic healer is capable of galvanizing mass sentiments; in fact, utopian communities of tens of thousands sprang up around three borderlands healers: don Pedrito Jaramillo (1829–1907), Santa Teresa Urrea (1873–1906), and El Niño Fidencio.

DON PEDRITO JARAMILLO

Don Pedrito Jaramillo earned fame as a healer in the Texas border region at the turn of the century.[31] The healer, born Pedro Jaramillo, is referred to with the ultimate title of respect, *don*, combined with the diminutive suffix *-ito*, as a term of endearment. Octavio Romano notes that *don* in the healer's appellation is a double entendre, signifying both gift and respect.[32] Hence, "don" Pedrito was respected by the terms and conditions of Romano's ideal type of man. He is also called "the Benefactor of Humanity," which appears on his tombstone in the Corpus Christi area of Texas (during don Pedrito's time it was known as Starr County), close to the Mexican border.

Texas was the locus of don Pedrito's healing ministry after he crossed the border in 1881. As the mythology goes, he was born in Guadalajara, Mexico, and first visited Texas as a laborer delivering bootleg whiskey to a wealthy "Mexican" ranch for the feast of Saint John the Baptist, celebrated on 24 June. He later returned to Texas to make his home there. Before this, there is no record of his life. Don Pedrito migrated to Texas after he realized his healing gift at the age of fifty-two. According to one hagiographer,

> He had modest beginnings and all his life he remained humble and unpretentious. His fame and the thousands of people seeking him from all over the United States and Mexico did not change him. He was born from poor parents, on a small ranch, close to Guadalajara, Mexico. He had no formal schooling but managed to learn to read and write on his own. All we know of him till age fifty is that he was a shepherd. As far as he knew, he was going to be a shepherd until death. But, one day, while riding a horse, he was hit by a branch. He fell off the horse and remained unconscious for a long time.[33]

Upon awakening, he felt intense pain and discovered that he had broken his nose. A strange force compelled him to go to a lagoon, gather mud in his palms, and rub it onto his face. Miraculously the pain disappeared. While sleeping that same evening, he heard a voice say to him: "you will cure IN MY NAME. Always give as a prescription the first thing that comes to your mind. It will always be the right one."[34] Thus, he experienced death and rebirth—his mystical, shamanic transformation.

At this point don Pedrito embarked upon his journey north, settling finally at Los Olmos Creek, situated between the Nueces River and the Rio Grande in south Texas. There he built a small shed and publicly announced his calling as spiritual healer. Romano writes that it wasn't until five years after establishing Texas residence that don Pedrito announced his occupation as a healer, making a public declaration at a wedding. Don Pedrito traveled on horseback for many days to cure thousands who could not make it to visit him in Los Olmos. His sphere of "healing influence," according to Romano, stretched as far south as Mexico City. In 1894, a San Antonio newspaper reported Jaramillo's month-long visit:

> Don Pedrito, the queer old man who performs such wonderful cures in such mysterious ways, continues to be a source of wonder and interest to the people of San Antonio and the surrounding country. . . . As fast as the patients are disposed of at the other end there are many to take their places. The crowd surges forward. Some are on crutches, others supported on either side by friends. Rheumatics, consumptives, paralytics, all are there. It is a wonderful and piteous sight. As soon as it is dark Don Pedrito and Blas Vela climb into a two-seated wagon and another old Mexican drives them about the city. They call at places from where requests have been sent for assistance. The old man keeps traveling until nearly daybreak. He then goes back to his cabin, sleeps about two hours, and as the first sign of day appears in the east comes out to where 200 or 300 people are already in line waiting to speak to him. He works twenty hours out of the twenty four.[35]

Eventually, don Pedrito's fame grew and people traveled to see him. Thus his hut evolved into a healing center. As many as five hundred would congregate there on any given day, and he accepted a small plot of land as a gift from a widow of considerable financial means. There he developed a larger healing operation and started a farm to grow food to feed people who came to Los Olmos to be cured. He led by the charisma of the prophet.

A key part of don Pedrito's approach was that he did not charge for cures. Typically, however, he accepted donations. If the patient "cares to," reported the *San Antonio Express,* he or she could "donate a half dollar or 25 cents," but "it is not asked or expected. The patient goes away, looking shamefaced perhaps and generally doubtful, but hundreds of cases are on record where the ailment has entirely disappeared by the time the treatment is completed."[36] Patients would leave money, animals, and other offerings for don Pedrito. Normally he refused the gifts if he believed them to exceed the donor's means. Any money collected went to his commune. It was often said that "don Pedrito would give back with one hand what he would take with the other." Don Pedrito challenged the faith of each believer. He would thus prescribe healing tasks that seemed absurd. Most of the tasks involved water: for example, drinking water and whisky at regular intervals; mixing water with mud and spreading it on the body; or he would ask men to bathe nude in public springs. Additionally, don Pedrito is said to have read minds, and one of the most popular stories about him involves his caution to a rich man. The man did not heed don Pedrito's prophecies and as a result he lost his fortune.[37] Don Pedrito's "prescriptions did not follow any logic. Indeed, they often defied logic as if he were testing the faith of the patient. If a person came to him with a sore leg, he would often recommend that the right leg be soaked in cold water. The 'prescriptions' always called for simple inexpensive ingredients like water, cumin tea, beer, and even a cheap whiskey (0.25 a quart)."[38]

Don Pedrito's methods were a form of religious poetics. The *San Antonio Express* reported:

> As to his method and his prescriptions, his medicines are water in the form of baths and drinks, hot or cold as the case may be, and the common fruits of the earth, such as oranges, lemons, potatoes, and tomatoes. No two cases are treated alike, even of the same disease. The patient in search of relief stands before the don, who is apparently oblivious of all surroundings. . . . Don Pedrito then writes on a slip of paper in Spanish some such prescription as this: "Drink seven cups of cold water on Monday, Wednesday, and Friday mornings until seven are taken."[39]

Don Pedrito achieved fame throughout the borderlands. In addition to the farm he built to feed pilgrims, he spent four hundred dollars weekly on groceries to feed his *de facto* commune. His fame spread and the crowds grew as the lame, the blind, the deaf, and other broken pilgrims returned from Los Olmos restored. He was transformed into a public symbol. His healing crossed national borders via the mail. More than two hundred letters arrived for him each week from all over the continent, asking him to prescribe cures. He was investigated by the federal post office department in Washington, since the amount of mail he sent out far exceeded the amount of stamps he bought from his local newly established post office. But most of don Pedrito's petitioners included self-addressed stamped return envelopes and other gifts. In one story, the post office approached don Pedrito to buy stamps from him!

The period following the United States' conquest of Mexico and the subsequent annexation of several northern Mexican states, including Texas, was wracked with strife and anomie as old institutions and social structures were dismantled and replaced with new systems of governance. In short, there was chaos for many. Texas Rangers were particularly ferocious in their violent and racially motivated attacks against Mexicans, and Mexicans were systematically disenfranchised from their lands and lynched in greater numbers than were African-Americans in the South during the same period.[40] In the act of writing to and receiving letters from don Pedrito, of exchanging sacred narrative through the mail, the boundaries erected by colonization were ignored, and distance and time were reconciled by memory; fresh transnational and transcontinental networks were created by the universality of body and suffering and spiritual healing, which, in a grand sense, stand outside of historical time and place. Healing the body, then, served as a microcosm for repairing the nation that was dismembered in colonization—and the commune of don Pedrito was the locus of sacred, symbolic repair, another nodal point on the border between Mexico and the United States.

The shift from individualized personal healer to public spectacle added an element of urgency and performativity to his movement. With the crowds came fame, and as a result healing practices became public drama—powerfully unhidden transcripts. Consequently, don Pedrito was inscribed onto the emergent Texas memory. He occupied several distinct identities: Texan, Mexican, Mexican-American, healer, elder, and more: shaman and prophet. He sacralized *mexicano* identity by appearing among them, as one of them. Disoriented by exile—which, paradoxically, was an exile *within* the homeland—the poetic religious movement of don Pedrito centered and thus ordered the anomie of ethnic Mexicans. Healing the brokenness of their individual bodies functioned as a public allegory for healing the broken Mexican national body; his work assumed cosmic, national, and individual meaning.

SANTA TERESA

Teresa Urrea, or "Teresita" (note the diminutive suffix *-ita*), was born in Sinaloa, Mexico, the child of a wealthy *hacendado* (landowner) of "Spanish" heritage, don Tomás Urrea, and a "humble" Yaqui Indian woman, Cayetana Chávez. Cayetana was one of don Tomás's many employees (or rather, serfs) with whom don Tomás enjoyed sexual relations and fathered children.[41] "I am not a legitimate child," Teresa explained in an interview for the *San Francisco Chronicle* conducted in San Jose, California, during the summer of 1900. She continued:

My mother was only fourteen when I was born. My father has eighteen children and my mother four, and not one of them is my own brother or sister. I went to school when I was nine years old, but I did not want to study; but later I felt I wanted to know how to read, and I learned my alphabet from a very, very old lady. My writing came to me of itself. I wanted to write, and I wrote, but how I learned I don't know, for I was not taught. On the floor of my mother's house I first wrote with my little finger in the dust.[42]

According to Teresa, she was sixteen when her father sent for her, and she went to live with him on his hacienda in Cabora, Sonora.

Like that of don Pedrito, Teresa Urrea's movement is very much a product of its historical moment and place. Urrea became a high desert shaman, a symbol of indigenous agrarian resistance to the Americanizing forces of General Porfirio Díaz, who attempted to eliminate the Sonoran Indians through his *scientífico* programs, which allowed North Americans to mine Mexican land. Reluctantly, she became a prophet.

In 1876, Teresa Urrea's father backed the liberal candidate Sebastián Lerdo de Tejada in Tejada's presidential reelection bid against the conservative opposition represented by General Porfirio Díaz. Díaz seized power via a military coup and began to eliminate his enemies. Fearing reprisal for his political views, don Tomás moved to Sonora. He installed his wife (also his first cousin), doña Loreto Eceberri, in a palatial home aptly called La Capilla (the chapel) for its cathedral ceilings and ornate decor. At the Cabora ranch, where he himself lived most of the time, he eventually instated his teenage mistress, Cayetana Chávez, Teresa Urrea's mother. According to several of the sources, it was at the Cabora hacienda that Teresa met María Sonora. María Sonora has been described as a very old woman with only one tooth in her mouth—a common caricature of a *curandera*. María was the practicing *curandera* for the hacienda, making daily rounds to treat the ill, and Teresa soon became her apprentice. "From Maria she [Teresa] learned the names of more than a hundred herbs and what maladies they were supposed to cure. Maria was pleased with the girl's aptitude and began thinking of her as a curandera who would succeed the old one at Cabora."[43]

The next movement in Teresa's life narrative is the most significant of all, what I call her first mystical death and rebirth. At Cabora, Teresa fell into a deep cataleptic coma, lying unconscious for two weeks. Her heart grew progressively weaker, and a coffin was built for her burial; some sources say it was placed expectantly at the foot of the bed where she lay.

On the evening of the fourteenth night of the coma, Teresa's room was crowded with women dressed in black mourning veils, holding a candlelight prayer vigil for her. Suddenly, Teresa awoke, sat up, and in a stupor asked for an explanation, startling the praying women who had surrounded her in anticipation of her death. Don Tomás was summoned, and Teresa informed him of voices audible only to her, instructing her to help people. These same voices unfolded the future. She prophesied that the coffin built for her should be used for María Sonora, who would die in three days. Three days hence, María Sonora died and was buried in the casket built for Teresa.[44] In another version of the Urrea biography, written by Mexican historian Mario Gill, beginning at age twelve Teresita suffered from nervous seizures resembling cataleptic states.[45] In yet another account, Urrea awoke in the middle of the night screaming, and her father "found her in the throes of terrible nervous convulsions and unable to speak. Toward dawn she calmed down, and in a state of fatigue was able to say only that she had a 'very deep grief in her soul.'"[46] According to an "eyewitness," these attacks lasted thirteen days.

Teresa herself recounted her first death and rebirth as follows:

> For three months and eighteen days I was in a trance. I knew nothing of what I did in that time. They tell me, those who saw, that I could move about but that they had to feed me; that I talked strange things about God and religion, and that the people came to me from all the country and around, and if they were sick and crippled and I put my hands on them they got well.

When she emerged, she was a new being, a prophet, speaking a poetics of religion:

> Then when I could remember again, after those three months and eighteen days, I felt a change in me. I could still if I touched people or rubbed them make them well. I felt in me only the wish to do good in the world. I spoke much to the people about God. I told them what I believe: that God is the spirit of love; that we who are in the world must love one another and live in peace; otherwise we offend God. When I offend I say to the one whom I have pained: "Sister or brother, I have offended you. I ask forgiveness." When I cured people they began to call me Santa Teresa. I didn't like it at first, but now I am used to it.[47]

Thus is Teresa's conversion: a mystical union with "God." In it, she becomes a religious shaman and prophet who speaks for the poor and the oppressed and delineates fresh modes of exchange—or, better, reiterates and revives classical ethical norms. Her healing techniques involved mix-

ing her own saliva with "earth" and massaging the paste into her patients. Additionally, she began accurately predicting natural disasters and
other international events. Eventually she gained control over her mystical endowment and delighted in its expression, taking special pleasure
in magical flight to other places and times, often accompanied by her
childhood friend Josefina. On one particularly formidable occasion,
Teresa and Josefina traveled to Mexico City:

> Josefina later described to her family her strange experience. No doubt
> Teresita cast a hypnotic spell, but, as Josefina told it, everything she experi-
> enced was real. They went flying through the air over mountains, forests
> and deserts to Mexico City, where they descended and strolled along the
> streets and through leafy parks. . . . Next, they flew over Xochilmilco and
> saw the "Floating Gardens." Finally they took a swoop over the Pyramids
> of the Sun and Moon at Tenochtitlán.[48]

Teresa's mystical raptures bear some resemblance to those of her sixteenth-century namesake, Santa Teresa de Ávila. Like Santa Teresa de
Ávila, Santa Teresa de Cabora, according to the popular mythology, es-
chewed material gains. "The power to do good makes me happy," Teresa
de Cabora explained. "I have no wish to be paid. I do not care for fine
things or fine houses or money. I will refuse no one to help him."[49] Teresa
de Cabora, however, was excommunicated from the Church.[50] She was
not Catholic, but something beyond: *curanderismo* and *espiritualismo*.[51]

Between the years 1890 and 1892, subsequent to her mystical conversion phase, word of Teresa's healing power spread and people descended on Cabora en masse. Eventually the crowds "grew larger with
pilgrims coming by the hundreds, and finally by 1891 the stream [of
seekers] swelled to a flood. Pilgrims numbering in the thousands con-
verged on the ranch at one time. A newspaper reporter from Las Cruces,
New Mexico, estimated the crowd at five thousand the day he was there
in November 1891."[52] In May 1892, a reporter hailing from Mexico City
estimated the crowd at ten thousand.

At first, don Tomás condemned Teresa's role as healer and denounced
especially the unruly mobs who appeared at his hacienda seeking healing. Nonetheless, he felt obligated to feed the seekers, and after witnessing the magic of Teresa's work with the people, he gave Teresa her own
space on the ranch as a base for her operations. Teresa never asked to be
compensated. Don Tomás established a *de facto* collective/commune that
fed the masses hungry for material food, and he asked payment from
those who could afford it. Another course of exchange was situated be-

tween Teresa and her seekers: Teresa's devotees were compelled to receive, reciprocate, and to gift. In fact, Cabora developed into an elaborate marketplace, replete with food and beverages, crafts, games, dancers, devotional objects bearing Teresa's likeness, and even thieves—another manifestation of the carnivalesque developing around the cult of the healer but with many of the freedoms and restrictions of the pilgrimages throughout the borderlands.

Typically, upon receiving their healing, Teresa's devotees would leave animals, religious articles, money, or sundry material goods. They would also volunteer service. One woman who received the ability to use her legs made a vow of commitment to Teresa. "Blessed Teresa," she sobbed, "you have made me well again. We are now your servants. My husband and I will serve you all the days of our lives. We made this promise to each other before we left our home."[53] Hence, the *promesa* tradition was reiterated and recast, reshaped yet again, and Urrea gained a full-time staff of helpers.

Yaqui Indians had participated in Teresita's healing center from the beginning. On 26 December 1891, twenty-eight Indians arrived at Cabora from the village of Tomochic in western Chihuahua. These men wanted to test Teresa's powers for themselves. After four days they returned to their village and adopted her as their own "living saint." They named her La Niña de Cabora. Concomitant to their adaptation of Teresa as their patron saint was the Tomochitecos' armed resistance to the forces of Porfirio Díaz, who were appropriating Indian lands and distributing them to wealthy Mexicans and Americans. In fact, "the battle cry of the Tomochitecos and Mayo tribes was *'Viva la Santa de Cabora.'*"[54] Efforts to hold Teresa responsible for the Yaqui and Mayo revolts were futile. Nonetheless, the Mexican government identified her as a threat and imprisoned her for a brief period in 1892. Of her arrest, Teresa was later to say, "The government sent five hundred soldiers to arrest one nineteen-year-old girl."[55] On 19 May 1892, don Tomás and Teresa were forced onto a train by the Mexican army, sent across the border to Arizona, and told never to return to Mexico.

Soon the *New York Times* began reporting stories of the Indian rebellion in Sonora, with special attention to Urrea. On 13 May 1896, the *New York Times* reported that seven Yaquis who died in an attack on the Mexican side of Nogales (executed from the American side) were carrying a newsprint photograph of Teresa, and that the Yaqui revolutionaries called themselves the "Teresitas." On 14 August 1896, the paper reported, "The Indians seem to be crazed with their fanatical ideas and their worship of Santa Teresa."

These events mark not only Urrea's American exile but also the beginning of her decline, spiritually, morally, and physically. She nonetheless retained a devoted following. According to one source, "Teresita's
fame preceded her in her sojourn, and the citizens of Nogales, Arizona,
turned out to welcome her and Don Tomás. . . . On July 5, the Mexican
Consul in Nogales reported to the Department of Foreign relations in
Mexico that Indians from Sonora and Arizona were flocking to her in
large numbers."[56] In 1896, Teresa and don Tomás moved to El Paso, and
on 18 June of that same year the *El Paso Daily Times* reported:

> At first El Paso was inclined to pay only a passing attention to the presence
> in this city of the famous Santa Teresa Urrea, but yesterday morning hun-
> dreds of people from the valley and mountains and from Mexico began to
> swarm into the city in wagons and on burros, all headed . . . where the
> wonderful Mexican maiden is stopping. All day long the crowd was being
> augmented by new arrivals. Wagons would drive up, invalids, the lame, the
> halt and the blind would be lifted from them and deposited as near the
> house as possible. . . . There were no less than 3000 people who visited
> [Teresa's] house yesterday.

While in El Paso, Teresa published a statement dissociating herself
from the Teresita revolutionary movements. She wrote:

> I am not one who encourages such uprisings, nor one who in any way
> mixes up with them, and I protest once, and as many times as may be nec-
> essary, against the imputations of my enemies. . . . In conclusion I will state
> that if in the future more uprisings follow in the Republic of Mexico, and
> as, even now, it has been said by my enemies that I am the kind of a person
> to start these movements, I will say once more that I am taking no part in
> them. Am I to blame because my offending compatriots demand justice for
> me? I think not, and appeal to the judgment of every sensible person.[57]

The Mexican government pressured the U.S. government to move
Teresa farther from the international border. There were several threats
on her life. In 1897 or 1898 don Tomás moved her to Clifton, Texas—
an obscure location but close enough to Mexico that he could monitor
his Mexican properties and begin some new business ventures. Teresa
had many famous visitors in Clifton who arrived from places as far away
as Mexico City and New York.

Teresa had always indicated that she would marry—declaring repeatedly that she would not remain a virgin—and over the years several
men expressed their desire to marry her. Against don Tomás's wishes, on
22 June 1900 she married Guadalupe Rodríguez, a Mexican copper
miner. Rodríguez brought a rifle and a priest with him to the Urrea res-

idence to ensure that don Tomás would not interfere with the marriage. Before leaving Mexico, Teresa had predicted her marriage, claiming that her husband would hurt her and try to kill her. Again, her prophecy proved correct, as the day after her marriage her husband began firing his gun randomly after a series of other unexplainable actions. He was incarcerated and declared legally insane.

Teresa returned to the home of don Tomás, but the bond between them had been torn asunder by Teresa's defiance of her father's marriage proscription, which indicated that she would not be subject to his patriarchy. She accepted an invitation to travel to San Jose, California, to work with a terminally ill patient. While in San Jose she was approached by an American medical company who offered to take her on an international healing tour. She was offered ten thousand dollars for a five-year contract. Urrea believed this to be a philanthropic enterprise funded by private donations. She had always been financially reliant on don Tomás, and the idea of achieving economic independence appealed to her. In August 1900, she signed the contract after stipulating to the company that she would never charge any patient for her services. The medical company perpetuated a subterfuge: they exploited the fact that nothing in the contract prevented the company itself from charging for Teresa's services, against Teresa's intentions.

On Sunday morning, 9 September 1900, the *San Francisco Examiner* published a story complete with photographs called "Santa Teresa, the Yaqui Idol, *a Cause of Fierce Indian Uprisings*, Has Come to Heal Diseases" (emphasis original). In San Francisco, Teresa was put into a large auditorium and promoted with music, lights, and emcee. The *San Francisco Examiner* described a "whisky drummer" complaining of spinal paralysis:

> He couldn't walk very well. The young lady held his hands for five minutes and looked into his eyes with a trance-like far-away expression. The drummer liked it. She placed her hands upon his cheeks, and he liked that. The back of his head she manipulated with gentle touches. The drummer smiled joyously. He was directed to sit down and take off his shoes. With no little difficulty he extracted his feet from their coverings; then Teresa of Sinaloa imparted to them the gentle magnetic current. That was followed by further grasping of the hands and after fifteen minutes or so the manipulations were ended.

In January 1901, the medical company moved temporarily to St. Louis. Because of her problems with English, Teresa asked her longtime friend Juana Van Order to send one of her children from Arizona to act as a translator for her. Van Order sent her son, John Van Order. Soon thereafter, John and Teresa were "married," although her divorce from her first marriage was not final until 2 February 1905. Thus her second marriage could have been only common-law. From there, the medical company moved Teresa to New York, where Teresa's first daughter, Laura, was born in 1902 in either September or February (conflicting information exists on the exact birth date). On 25 September 1902, don Tomás died in Texas at age sixty-three, while Teresa was still in New York.

After her father's death, Teresa moved to East Los Angeles, into the center of Boyle Heights. On 15 December 1902, the *Los Angeles Times* recorded her presence in an article called "Flocking to See Mystic Santa Teresa":

> Santa Teresa, the famous Mexican girl from the land of the Yaqui, in Sonora, who is implicitly believed in by the majority of Mexicans of the Southwest as a healer, who exercises supernatural powers, has settled in Los Angeles permanently, her followers say, and is daily besieged by a pitiful throng of Mexican 'enfermos' [the sick]. The halt, the blind, the inwardly diseased, paralytics almost helpless and others with bodies ravaged by consumption, are helped to her doors each day by friends and relatives: and none go there without the belief that by the laying on of her magic hands they will be cured. . . . No distance seems too great for the Mexicans who believe in the magnetic young woman from the South, and behind her house are drawn up wagons that have borne cripples from points in Sonora, and other districts along the Mexican line.

Espiritualistas, or Mexican spiritualists, are reported to have visited Teresa Urrea, and it is likely her home was an *espiritualista* center.[58]

While in Boyle Heights, Teresa reportedly spoke as a prophet, speaking for the poor and the oppressed and claiming a religious poetics as if she brought a new message from God—as *espiritualistas* do: "In Los Angeles she became actively interested in the social and economic plight of the Mexican population of that city. Her concern for the paid and underpaid workers and their families caused considerable apprehension among the less sympathetic members of the Anglo-controlled economy and political system."[59] On 25 August 1903, Teresa's Boyle Heights "cottage" mysteriously burned down to ashes. She moved in with friends nearby.

During the spring of 1904, Teresa found justifiable legal grounds for breaking her contract with the medical company (although the payments on her contract had been met). With the money she had earned, she returned to Texas to erect a house in Clifton. She gave birth to her second daughter, Magdalena (Naida), on 29 June 1904. On 12 January 1906, Teresa died of a bronchial condition contracted while rescuing people from a flood in Clifton in December 1905. She was thirty-three years old. This parallel to the death of Christ was not overlooked; Teresa had often likened herself to Christ and had predicted that she would die at age thirty-three. Expecting her final demise, she organized her own funeral. As her last act, she sent for her mother, Cayetana. On the morning of the third day after Cayetana had arrived from Nogales, Sonora, Teresa announced that it was her last day of life. Cheerful throughout the day, she died that afternoon.

In an article published during the Chicano movement of the 1960s and 1970s, "Santa Teresa: A Chicana Mystic," by Carlos Larralde, Teresa emerged as an ancestor, a psychedelic revolutionary. The work's citations of its sources are thin and sketchy, although they could be recorded oral tradition. Perhaps the most strikingly original episode of her life as imagined in this work is a six-year period she spent with her mentor, María Sonora, who, according to Larralde, "looked like a toothless witch." Sonora took Teresa into the desert and taught her the secrets of curing— particularly the use of plants: "As a religious ritual, Teresa learned about magic mushrooms causing hallucinations.[60] Indians ate them during sacred ceremony, followed by a night of penance with special prayers."[61] Larralde paints Teresa as a character not unlike Carlos Castañeda's Don Juan: the mythical Don Juan was a Yaqui Indian, and Teresa was half Yaqui.[62] Larralde writes: "Maria taught her about mescaline, a sacred herb used for transcendent experiences, such as the dramatic alternations of consciousness and perceptions. Teresa realized the value of this drug to probe the inner mind. . . . But Maria cautioned Teresa about these potent drug effects and told her to use them with great care. Teresa experimented with herself in order to induce sensations and visions."[63]

Larralde attributes the burning of Teresa's house to political adversaries:

Teresa went throughout Los Angeles County into the Chicano sections seeking those in distress. Again, she applied her ideas of stern self-sacrifice and rigid discipline, along with practical humanitarianism. The *spiritualist* simply believed that hungry people couldn't wait for justice. She had no patience with red tape and bureaucratic procrastination. In her rush to get things done, she offended numerous politicians. City and county administrators were jarred by her constant demands for action. They resented her "unprofessional" approach to relief [*sic*] problems.[64]

William Curry Holden rewrote Teresa's life with another cause in mind. Published in 1978 (as was Larralde's article), Holden's *Teresita* is a mix of myth, history, and biography. The text is written as a historical novel, replete with dialogues between Teresa and others, though Holden, a Texan of Anglo descent, maintains that it is a factual story. His reconstruction of Teresa's life is allegorical, signifying processes of conquest, *mestizaje,* colonization/civilization, and Protestantization. As Holden represents her, Teresa is a microcosm of the possibilities that *mestizos* can bring to Protestant society. In Holden's narrative, Teresa is transformed into a Protestant saint who, as an Indian/"primitive," embodies "nature" and therefore enjoys a closer relationship to "God." Teresa emerges in the tension between "civilization" or "culture," as propagated by European men and their descendants in the Americas, on the one hand, and nature, represented by women and Indian non-Christians, on the other. In this way, Holden romanticizes and attempts to justify don Tomás's rape of Indian women on his hacienda.

In Holden's narrative, don Tomás is of "noble" Spanish heritage ("a grandee of distinguished lineage"); he represents science, civilization, and culture, the *científico* attitude characterizing this period of Mexican nationalism. His sexual violation of the Indian girls and women is simply his method of advancing civilization through internal colonization. Teresita's incorporation into the hacienda life of her father is an allegory for the Christianization and civilization of *mestizos.* In Holden's account, at the hacienda Teresa first learns to wear shoes and to dress properly; she must not laugh too robustly; she must learn to eat properly. In short, she must observe the customs of the Spanish-Mexican aristocracy, the *hacendados,* by aligning her body to the registers of a courtly class. Social transformation, in this case the "civilizing process," involves mastery over the body.[65] Holden's progressive Protestantization of Teresa is completed toward the conclusion, when he claims that she "objected to the prayers of priests—empty, external, impersonal, without feeling; memorized passages, alike for all persons and all occasions. A parrot could perform as well." Ultimately, "by this time Teresita's religious concepts had developed past the point of considering necessary the adoration of saints or the intercession of priests."[66]

Hagiographies of Santa Teresa Urrea evince her power as cultural symbol, trying to locate her in a life context that makes sense—even though during her life she was, in a sense, out of place and time and therefore not so simply categorized.

EL NIÑO FIDENCIO

The best-known Mexican curer is without question Fidencio Síntora Constantino, known as El Niño Fidencio.[67] José Fidencio de Jesús Constantino Síntora was born in the state of Guanajuato, on 13 November 1898 or 1900 (although his birthday is celebrated on 17 October). The reports of his childhood conflict. He likely had twenty-four siblings. His parents died when Niño was only ten, or possibly younger. Niño and his younger brother Joaquín were paired off and left to fend for themselves, Niño accepting responsibility for his younger charge. During this period, Joaquín took ill and Niño cared for him. It was then, during his brother's illness, that Niño experienced his first "calling." According to the mythology, suddenly the door to their shack opened and a man came in and handed Niño a book. The man told Niño that the book contained many curing remedies from plants and herbs that he was to use to cure his brother. Niño followed the instructions and healed his brother. Later, it occurred to Niño that the man who appeared to him was Jesus Christ, posed in the Sacred Heart position. This stance became one of Ninõ's most famous poses. Niño referred to the man who gave him the gift as "the stranger."

After receiving the visit from the stranger, Niño was hired by the López de la Fuente family to work as a *criado,* that is, as a live-in servant who is raised by the employer. Niño enjoyed cooking and washing clothes. By the time he was twenty, he had transferred with the family to work on a hacienda in an obscure and "dusty" northern Mexican town, Espinazo, in Nuevo León. While employed as a cook, Niño turned to working as a healer as relief from his monotonous responsibilities, and he practiced healing on animals, perfecting his signature technique, the removal of tumors. Fidencio had a complex and dysfunctional relationship with the *hacendado,* don Enrique López de la Fuente. Mexican historian Fernando Garza Quiros reports that "with the passage of time Fidencio started to call don Enrique 'papa' and continued treating him this way until his death, and he would kiss his [don Enrique's] hand in a show of respect."[68] Yet Enrique physically and verbally abused Niño, beating and degrading him.

After a beating, Fidencio would tearfully seek refuge in a nearby *pirúl,* or pepper tree. It was at this tree that Fidencio received his second and decisive calling, as recalled in his own words:

> [I was filled] with sadness, thinking that I would die of hunger without a guardian, without a friend, absolutely alone in life. Precisely the day on which they ran me off, I had a hallucination. A tall, bearded man with a luminous halo around his venerable head appeared to me and said: "Fidencio, you are called to a very high destiny. I put in your eyes a marvelous curative power which will serve to alleviate the suffering of those with pain; I

give you this divine power only for the good of humanity only in order that you will cure those who are deserving, never for you to enrich yourself with it, nor to benefit those who do not deserve such good things." The venerable old man disappeared, and I am sure that from the moment of his leaving, curative power remained in my hands, of which I have given so much authentic proof.[69]

Niño was convinced of his calling, and his fame grew, beginning especially when he was twenty-seven years old. Niño was also associated with spiritism and spiritualism, especially while he was employed, from 1925 to 1927, by a German and former Villista named Teodoro von Wernich. Niño cured von Wernich of an ulcer, and, in turn, von Wernich shared with Niño the more formal esoteric European traditions of spiritism.

Certainly the most remarkable event for the Fidencio movement was the visit of General Plutarco Calles, who was then president of Mexico, in February 1928. Calles's visit is all the more intriguing in light of the fact that in the midst of his visit he was engaged in post-Revolutionary persecution of the Catholic Church. Accounts conflict as to how Calles was treated by Niño. Some have him ignoring Calles, preferring instead the company of the poor, while others have Niño treating Calles with great care. In either case, Fidencio emerges as a champion of the poor. Furthermore, Niño cured Calles of back pain and his daughter suffering from flu. In fact, Calles reportedly put on one of Niño's gowns and submitted obsequiously to the healer's odd prescriptions. One verse from a *corrido* about the visit goes as follows: "Kneeled in front of his presence he lifted his arms high and gave his excellency three hard slaps."[70] Indeed, there is an unmistakably erotic aura, perhaps masochistic, in the imagery and sexualized play of Calles's healing: Niño has utter control over Calles's naked body, which he rubs completely with honey (itself an aphrodisiac), cleans off, and rubs down again with "virgin" honey. Finally, he pounds Calles's back with a small squirrel three consecutive times; afterward, Calles experiences blissful relief.

El Niño's popularity grew; seven thousand persons visited Espinazo that February, and the crowds increased to thirty thousand in March.[71] This is all the more remarkable given that there are no roads into the high-desert town of Espinazo; the only way to reach it is by train. An official from the health department in Mexico City visited Espinazo in 1930 and subsequently wrote a series of condemning reports on Niño, claiming that two thousand people died there each day. But he also wrote that

Fidencio is innocent, and without knowing it suffers from a mental condition which consists in thinking he has been blessed with the task of curing the sick. Those around him, however, are not innocent children, and have taken advantage of the credulity of the ignorant masses, including some who are not so ignorant. Espinazo has been and still is an embarrassment to Nuevo León and the Nation as a whole. When will it all end?[72]

Monsiváis stresses the tragic aspects of El Niño's movement. Citing the documentary film by Nicolás Echevarria, *El Niño Fidencio,* he argues: "The camera registers the details of faith in this film: damaged bodies burdened with pain; faces on which is registered only one emotion; the stubborn, recalcitrant expressions, hardened by monomania; immersions in mud; songs, prayers, prematurely aged women; invalids, people suffering from polio, cancer; the Boy's 'slaves' and priests. And in fact, all this is irrecoverable."[73]

Niño did not charge for his cures; he did, however, accept offerings to support his work. A hospital was established in Espinazo, staffed by those who dedicated themselves to Niño's movement, who called themselves "slaves" of Niño. A community grew in Espinazo around Niño, delimited by the *manda/promesa* system of exchange. Above the entrance to the hospital, the following sign was placed:

The Poor Are Not Poor
The Rich Are Not Rich
Only Those Who Suffer Pain
Are Poor[74]

Niño's prophecy and power began to conflict with Church authority when the seekers began asking him to perform ecclesiastical functions. "It is totally understandable," writes Quiros, "that mothers grateful for the healing of their small ones, wanted them to be baptized by the one who cured them in the name of God, or that the sick wanted to confess before they were cured (or before they died) and of course the administration of sacraments of marriage and extreme unction were also sought of Niño."[75] Monsiváis claims that the Church preferred to ignore Niño, while Quiros reports that in 1936 representatives of the archdiocese of Monterrey, which included the jurisdiction of Espinazo, visited Niño to "prevent the continuation of the administration of sacraments that according to Catholic orthodoxy were the exclusive faculty of people who had received powers for them."[76] Niño received the officials warmly and is said to have cooked a very good meal for them. Without protest, Niño agreed to stop administering Catholic sacraments and explained that he only did it when people forced him.

In yet another story of religious persecution, the government *(el Gobierno)* of Nuevo León ordered a covert investigation of Niño's movement by a group of medical professionals, who reported that Niño was not doing any harm and that most of his patients seemed to be much improved. Nonetheless, following this investigation a group of doctors calling themselves the Sons of Hippocrates filed a lawsuit against Niño, charging him with "usurping the profession." They accused Niño of witchcraft and asked for five thousand pesos in damages; the case went to court and the decision was in favor of Niño. To celebrate, Niño hosted a banquet in honor of his lawyer. When asked why there were no women at the party, Niño reportedly told his lawyer that women "should only assist men."[77]

Niño is said to have paid his lawyer by assuring him, "My spirit will always be with you." Quiros claims that at this point Niño became an "idiot" *(se idiotizó)*; the moment was at once "in bipartite form the climax of the apotheosis of Fidencio, and the initiation of his decline [*decadencia*]."[78] By 1935 Niño began to experience ill health and therefore to cure people from his bed. In 1938 he died, some say of cirrhosis of the liver. The exact cause of death is uncertain, but certainly exhaustion was a cause; he hardly slept during his lifetime, often curing for ninety-six hours straight without rest.

A widely circulated story holds that Niño told his followers that he would resurrect himself three days after he died; this plan, however, was thwarted by don Enrique López de la Fuente, who gained control over Niño's body. Central to the Niño mythology is the conspiracy theory related to this control; Niño's body in itself became a site of intense symbolization and contestation. Nowhere is this clearer than in the myth of Niño inscribed by Manuel Terán Lira in a hagiography of Niño. Lira claims to have been an eyewitness to many of the events he writes about, and the text is replete with photographs of Niño and his movement. Lira narrates the life of Niño so that it mimics the life of Christ: Niño's mother appears at the end of Lira's gospel as one of Niño's followers and as one of the faithful who buries him. Furthermore, this version refers to Niño as "Fidencio de Jesús." The photograph most prominent in the text depicts Niño carrying a wooden cross over his shoulder while sporting a white linen floor-length gown—in emulation of the passion of Christ—a penitent male characterizing the devotion of pious *mexicano* Catholics. In another attempt to liken Fidencio to Christ, Lira portrays Niño frequently visiting and doing healing at a colony of lepers that was supposedly located in Espinazo.[79] In Lira's myth, El Niño predicted his own death, telling his devotees, "I now have to die; after my death there will come many Fidencios, but remember that there was only one and that is me; soon I will go to delight in the goodness of God."[80] This was not to say that Niño would return in other bodies. Niño may "come back to life, in [his] own way," as Tomás Eloy Martínez writes of Evita Perón, "by not dying; and Evita had done so too: by multiplying herself."[81]

Niño's body was viewed for three days, the number followed also for his memorial: three days in October, beginning on his birthday, and three days in March, marking the anniversary of his death. "Espinazo is a sacred place for us," claims one Niño devotee in the documentary *We Believe in El Niño Fidencio,* made by an anthropological team from California State University, Los Angeles, in 1972.[82] This film follows Niño's two annual festivals over their respective three-day periods and claims that up to fifty thousand attend. Within the sacred place of Espinazo there are four holy sites: Niño's grave, the pepper tree, the chapel where Niño sometimes prayed, and especially the pond where believers bathe in mud, hoping to receive the healing it offered when Niño walked the earth.

Today, healing collectives dedicated to El Niño exist throughout the Mexican Americas, and women constitute the majority of his followers. The mediums for Niño are called *materias, cajitas,* or *cajones*—literally, "little boxes." Mediums/spiritualists/spiritists channel the spirit of Niño. Suffering and transformation are the grand symbols for the movement. As one Niño devotee explained, "The path of Niño is very hard, very hard. El Niño suffered and all those who want to follow him must also suffer."[83] In 1990, Francisca Aguirre, "Panchita," a *materia* from Texas, explained her Niño devotions as follows:

> Two times I had a dream recently that my body was over there with Niñito. You know he tells *materias* when they will die. . . . My spirit is beginning to go up an elevation to God's. . . . Niñito is a doctor, a lawyer, a father, a protector of blessing. He is medicine. He is nothing but for natural. When the sick come to the *materia,* she has got to be prepared because Niñito will be all these things to the person who comes. . . . As a *materia* myself, whenever or wherever they call me, I am there. . . . Niño is also a speaker. He says, "I am the *peregrino misionero* [missionary pilgrim] in your heart," because he sends me everywhere. He is always with us.[84]

The designation "Niño" is notably distinct from the appellation *don,* in that it suggests innocence and purity. The young man who came to be known as El Niño Fidencio died at thirty-nine or forty, and yet he was remarkably childlike and innocent.[85] He spoke then, as now, through devotees, in a high and staccato voice. He is distinctively androgynous and most often depicted through a famous photograph in which he is dressed as La Virgen de Guadalupe. Most likely, Niño died a virgin. (I will treat the sexuality of the Fidencio movement in greater detail in future writings, devoting greater time and space to the erotics of Latino male devotion.) Let's turn now to a discussion of what I call "spiritual convenience stores."

HEALING AND PLACE

Niño Fidencio, Santa Teresa Urrea, and don Pedrito Jaramillo continue to appear and are *sited* throughout the borderlands and beyond. The souls of these healers and more abound at *botánicas*—urban storefront healing centers. Latina/os have long been adept at transforming the architecture of U.S. urban space—designed to subjugate working populations and privilege the benefactors of neocolonization—rendering it as familiar, domestic, sacred space by inscribing it with distinct religious grammars in religious processions and other activities that shake the borders between public and private space.[86]

Curanderas have delineated Latina/o urban neighborhoods with multiple-use storefront religious and spiritual centers. *Botánicas* bring the sacred into the realm of everyday capitalist exchange, again blurring the boundaries between sacred and profane. Guadalupe, the saints, the Buddha, the *orishas*, Shiva, and more can be found there on candles, perfumes, teas, sculpture, and paint, in and on aerosol spray cans. It's all for sale. Here is where contemporary *curanderas* do their work; these places function as churches, clinics, spiritual convenience stores, and more: they are postmodern sacred centers.

Sagrado Corazón ("Sacred Heart") Botánica, one such center in East Los Angeles, is a small stucco niche in an urban row of continuous structures covered with faded light-blue paint; it is flanked by a barber shop and a restaurant.[87] The facade of the building consists of a display window, and a glass door, exhibiting products for sale: images of Catholic saints, sprays, powders, herbs, potions, spices, special soaps for baths, candles, incense, and *aguas,* or various types of prepared waters. A large, hand-painted sign placed directly outside the entrance reads "LOVE, HEALTH, MONEY." The sign offers card readings, spiritual consultations, and fast, effective weight loss without diet or exercise. Throughout the shop are several sculptures and images of La Virgen de Guadalupe, and there is a large depiction of Jesus Christ in a Sacred Heart pose.

The *curandera* at Sagrado Corazón, Caridad, keeps extended business hours between Monday and Saturday. On Tuesdays and Fridays—days, she explains, that possess the most powerful energies—she accepts walk-in clients on a first-come, first-served basis. Caridad's private chambers are partitioned off from the main space by drywall. Two discrete rooms in the rear of the space function as Caridad's work rooms. In one she has a desk, chairs, and a large table serving as an altar, on which is placed La Virgen de Guadalupe and a Sacred Heart of Jesus. Candles and incense burn in her office. Prepared waters line the walls. In the second room is a padded massage table covered with clean white sheets. This is where Caridad performs her work as a *sobadora,* or masseuse.

Many saints are sold at the *botánica,* including especially Saint Francis, Santo Niño de Atoche, San Martín de Porres, and Santa Bárbara. Included among the small images of saints are also replicas of the Buddha, Shangó and Elegua from Santería, and numerous Hindu deities. There are also various Latin-American manifestations of the Virgin Mary, including Los Lagos, Cobra, Caridad, Zapopan, and especially Guadalupe. Perhaps the most striking and even prominent saints are those not officially recognized by the Catholic Church, including San Simón and Juan Soldado. At Sagrado Corazón, these saints share equal space and authority with the official Catholic saints.

The candles are the dominant item on the shelves of the vestibule. There are candles for just about every conceivable type of problem; they are encased in colorful glass, painted with images and text. One candle reads (in Spanish), "Do as I say, now." This candle is adorned by two images, on one side a man submitting to a woman, on the other side a woman submitting to a man. There are candles representing each sign of the zodiac, many of the saints and manifestations of the Virgin Mary, Jesus, popular saints, and various wishes, including "Instant money," "Shut your mouth," "Go away," "Protect me from evil," "Work," "Love," "Romance," "Seduction," "Instant luck," "Big money," "Lottery," "Health," and "Power." In this space, religious poetics thrive.

INTERVIEW WITH A *CURANDERA*

Not only Catholics but evangelicals and other Protestants visit "Caridad," who was thirty-eight and the mother of three at the time of our interview.[88] She was born in Mexico and attends mass at her local parish about twice a month. "The only difference between the Catholics and evangelicals," she said, "is that when they get here the evangelicals are more secretive; they visit me with a bad conscience." For Caridad, conscience is the key to ethical religious practice. Conscience is also her guide in her relationship to the Catholic Church. Caridad says of Catholics and evangelicals:

They believe it's bad. Because they themselves [the Church] believe that no one can do anything but God. And you yourself know that this is against the Catholic religion from whatever aspect you view it. This is against it. But if you yourself are content [*tranquilo*] that you are not harming anyone, then it's good, and for that reason I go to mass. I am satisfied [*tranquila*] with myself. I'm not going to honor God if I know that I am sinning against him—it's one or the other thing—either you are with God or you are against him. But I am content because I am trying to do good. I try to do only good. I have to maintain my good conscience.

Any priest will tell you [that *curanderismo* is wrong]. My priest back in my village [*pueblo*] in Mexico would tell me all the time, "Caridad, you [*tú*]"—excuse my use of the informal, but that is how he would address me—"you need to change your ways because if you continue lying to people, you are going to die." He himself saw that I could help people. But I *never* myself said that it was I who was helping people. No one can help people without God. I'm not going to go around saying that I am the greatest *curandera* in the world. I do what I can do to help the people [*la gente*]. And, well, perhaps that is why God, he helps me, because he sees my desire to do the good.

There are people who sometimes come here and say, "I would like this to happen to such and such person." I'm not here for that. If you need to resolve a problem with someone, you know what, just go and have it out with him and that's it; your anger will pass. Why would you want to do harm to the people? That will only work against you yourself. What I do here is try and help people.

People come to me with all sorts of problems. Mostly, people have money problems; they don't have enough money for their families [*casa*]. So, for example, if someone comes to me and says they don't have enough money, I tell them to take a [special herb], a one-dollar bill, a [special] small rock, and a red pepper. Take a glass of water, and in that water you will put that rock, and that red pepper and then the dollar. Do you know what a dollar means? Do you have a one-dollar bill?—and I'll show you. No? [She moves to the window that opens into the vestibule and calls for Daisy, the receptionist, to bring her a one-dollar bill.] Do you know what religion the dollar bill comes from? Now we are really talking about religion. It comes from the Masons. And why do you think it was the Masons? Because they wanted to make this the strongest country of all. [She takes the dollar bill, pointing.] This pyramid signifies positive energy. The eye is the eye of the Holy Spirit that you see there. Are you Catholic? I'm Catholic, as I told you, and when you go to mass you will see the same Holy Spirit symbolized. These are things I'm telling you so that you will learn how things work. Take water, for example. Water is a material [*materia*]. Water is made by God. *Man didn't make water.*

Everything has a mystery. Just like the recitation I was telling you [earlier]. Pepper, I was telling you, that is a plant that comes from the earth [*la tierra*] that is made by God, not by man. Just like the rocks. The rocks are a *materia* because they are not made by man but are made from nature [*la naturaleza*]. Okay? When you have four of those stones, it signifies harmony for all. People who know a lot about stones will tell you that the [*cuatro rosados*] are to create harmony, to bring happiness to your house [*casa*], and to bring peace. So, you take a piece of foundation from your house, with your pepper, and put it in your water with the dollar bill. These are three things that symbolize the earth. It doesn't have to be there more than seventy-two hours. You then put it in the doorway of your house, or in the doorway of your business. After three days you take the dollar from your water and let it dry in the sun. After it is dry you put it in your wallet; and that is one way to bring prosperity. Because it is made from things that are purely natural. People don't have to pay in order to be helped. That is one way to help people who come with need. Here I do works [*trabajos*] or offerings that you give for your prosperity.

I can't tell you that I learned anything. I had premonitions. How do I explain to you? These are things that Diosito can give you. It's like a sixth sense. When I want to clean [*limpiar*] a person to bring prosperity, I do it with apple and honey because that will create abundance, and honey will bring good luck. Cinnamon [too] will bring good luck. These are things that come from times long past, ancient times, you know. One doesn't know how one knows these things. I can't explain. I can tell you that my spiritual child [*niño espiritual*] guides me: he tells me what to say, he whispers in my ear.

I was seven years old when I first discovered my gift. It is something unexplainable. I can tell you that I wouldn't wish it on anyone. Let me tell you that, in the first place, where I come from is a very small village, and people would say that I had the Devil inside of me. Why? Because of the reactions my body would bring. Things would fall when I got a little aggressive—I'm not very aggressive but a little. My mom would say, "Don't ever tell your brothers [*hermanos*] anything, because it could happen." If I would say to my sister, "I hope you get hit in your mouth," well, in a little while, she would come with her mouth broken. These are things I cannot explain.

I identify myself as a *curandera*, but I don't describe my work with people as curing them but as helping them. Because there are many things that you can't cure, and you won't fool anyone. If someone comes to me and says, "I have a pain in my chest," the first thing I say to them is, "Go and see your doctor." It's like the plants, my son [*mi hijo*]. The plants can help you, but over a long period of time. If someone has high blood pressure, I can say, "Drink this tea," but if that person has high blood pressure, he can have a stroke—he needs to go the doctor. There are many ways to help people, but a person shouldn't get involved with something in which they don't belong. This is to say that when you come to me to have your cards read, I can do that for you because that is what I can do; look a bit at your future, look a bit at your problems to understand what you can do to help yourself, or what I can do to help you resolve your problems. But I won't get involved with things that I have no business in.

There are people who have that great gift, but there are people who are charlatans, and they take advantage of people. I can tell you about many people who come here complaining about how they went to such and such a place and how they got tricked into spending a lot of money. That is not helping someone. When you want to help someone, if you can't help, you tell him that you can't. "Go with your doctor, he will help you." In those cases based on bad luck [*mala suerte*] I can help, and I say, "Yes, I can help"; cleaning your aura or cleaning your spirit—those are things I can do. But to get involved in things I can't do, that would work against me and the people who are trusting in me. I do my work to help people.

CONCLUSION: HEALING ACROSS BORDERS

Ser tranquila, that is, to be at ease, is the grammar of Caridad's religious ethics—a poetics of the good and the beautiful. This appeal to conscience is a triumph of Gloria Anzaldúa's *mestiza* consciousness. Anzaldúa argues that the definitive characteristic of *mestiza* consciousness is "a tolerance for ambiguity, a tolerance for contradiction."[89] This consciousness, a *mestiza* soul, is the impulse for (meta)physical, geopolitical, and symbolic boundary transgression: border crossings. As Caridad and other practitioners of *curanderismo* confess, they believe the practice of *curanderismo* to be contrary to the teachings of the Catholic Church.[90] They profess a Catholic identity while concomitantly defying the Catholic Church. For them, only a "tolerance for contradiction," a pragmatics of truth, works to produce good in the world.

But toward what ends does *curanderismo* work in the world? As Monsiváis has wryly remarked, "The history of the Boy Fidencio is a question of that extreme vision of the vanquished whose sickness is poverty."[91] The dis-ease of poverty is also directly addressed in *curanderismo* practices, and the root causes of poverty are identified, named, isolated, and discursively deconstructed as well—if nothing else, this narrative foregrounds social change by forging a distinct consciousness of defiance and change. In many respects, *curanderismo* creates a shamanistic and often prophetic consciousness.

Carrasco has uncovered the remarkable parallels between *curanderismo* and shamanism by interpreting a seminal Chicano novel, a sacred text for Chicanos, Rudolfo Anaya's *Bless Me, Ultima.*[92] The myth tells the story of Ultima, a wise Mexican-American female elder who functions as a *curandera* on the sacred lands of New Mexico. Carrasco describes Ultima as a "religious virtuoso" or "religious specialist." Ultima teaches a seven-year-old boy, Antonio, the secrets of *curanderismo*. Carrasco suggests that the relationship between Ultima and her initiate, Antonio, "reflects some characteristics of the initiation scenario typical of shamanic ecstasy." For Carrasco, *Bless Me, Ultima* is the story of a young boy's rite of passage. In his transformation into a "new person, he acquires new and special knowledge of not only Ultima and the forces of his world, but of himself. This new knowledge . . . emerges through powerful personal experiences highlighted by religious ecstasies. As in shamanic or archaic mystical initiations, Antonio is taught wisdom." Carrasco does not suggest that the characters in the novel, Ultima and Antonio, are shamans. Rather, he argues that "we are witnessing in Anaya's novel a Chicano variation of an archaic pattern of spiritual creativity; what I would call the lyrics of Chicano spirituality."[93]

In deploying this new knowledge, *curanderas* often function as prophetic figures, as outlined by Max Weber. Weber's prophet possesses "charisma," or the "endowment in humans of extraordinary powers." For Nietzsche and Weber, the formation of a new religion is based on various returns to the old. As Monsiváis describes it, El Niño is illustrative of a "religion that is both innovative and heterodox, and fuses Aztec gods and Christian saints, spiritualism and Marianism, revolutionary messianism and Father Rispalda's catechism, [with] the Saint of Cabora [Teresa Urrea]. . . . Nothing is foreign to this endless mix."[94] This poetic religious tradition embodies the irony of empire—representing, as it does, inchoate colonialism, colonization failed, empires lost, traditions forgotten, but spirit persisting. *Curanderismo* is both the failure and triumph of Christianity. Certainly in its *espiritualista* form it represents exactly this. Let's turn now to a fragmented genealogy of *espiritualismo*.

CHAPTER 5

Diaspora Spirits

From the Virgin City to the City of Angels

In the ancient Meso-American cosmos and in popular healing practices where its influence still pervades, medicine is the art of exchange with the divine.

Sylvia Marcos, "Women, Healing Rituals, and Popular Medicine in Mexico," in *Concilium: International Review of Theology* 2

The gift gives, demands, and takes time.

Jacques Derrida, *Given Time: 1. Counterfeit Money,* trans. Peggy Kamuf

What one cannot see is shown in the distance from what one *must not* see.

Michel Foucault, *The Birth of the Clinic: An Archaeology of Medical Perception*

The first woman who descended to the planet earth in order to make the light of the Lord known was Damiana Oviedo. From the moment Damiana Oviedo was born she said many things that the Lord had indicated to her; she lived three days and died, and in twenty-four hours she resuscitated and lived a normal life. She died . . . [again] when she was ninety years old. Since she was seven years old, her parents, who were Christians, would ask her why she didn't like to go to church; and she would answer them: "Instead of going to church, where I don't learn anything, it would be better for me to go to school." . . . The Lord arrived and talked to her and told her that she had to go and plant the light in Mexico City, and she went there and she founded it and the multitudes followed her.[1]

This narrative was told to Silvia Echániz during the 1970s in the state of Veracruz, Mexico. It was authored by a member of a Mexican spiritualist temple known as *espiritualismo*. And even while it is not the "standard" foundational narrative, it demonstrates several formative characteristics of Mexican spiritualism. First, though texts exist for its basis, it is mostly an oral tradition filled with contradictions and inconsistencies. Second, it is based in Mexico City, though it has spread throughout the borderlands. Third, and perhaps most importantly, while men are also devotees of the tradition, it is primarily in the hands of women.

Mexican anthropologist Isabel Attias describes *espiritualismo* as follows: "The Espiritualistas Trinitarios Marianos are members of a theosophical society [in a general sense] dedicated, with the intercession of the spirits, to curing their peers physically, or by spiritual consultation. Generally, they manifest their gifts in local temples specifically dedicated for this purpose."[2] *Espiritualismo* is institutionalized *curanderismo* that emphasizes the spiritual level of healing and mediumship. It is both "popular" medicine and a distinctly Mexican religious protest—protestantism: a modernist impulse in Mexican religion stubbornly tied to ancient traditions. *Espiritualismo* began as a protest movement against Mexican Catholicism; as such, it shares narratives and sensibilities with Catholicism and cohabits the same spaces.

Espiritistas (Mexican spiritists) share beliefs with *espiritualistas* regarding communication with spirits, clairvoyance, and divine healing. The two traditions developed simultaneously during the nineteenth century throughout Europe and the Americas. Distinctive to *espiritualismo*, however, are its prophetic founders, particularly Roque Rojas Esparza (1812–79), also known as Father Elías, and Damiana Oviedo, one of his first followers, who died in 1920 and about whom less is known. *Espiritistas* trace their origins to the French medium and teacher Leon Denizarth Hippolyte Rivail, who published under the name Allen Kardec (1804–69).[3] Though both are mediumship-based traditions organized into churches, the two movements also differ for their teaching on reincarnation. Rojas condemned reincarnation—and denounced *espiritistas* for teaching it. However, continuing revelation and religious poetics have amended that proscription in some *espiritualista* denominations, which now teach reincarnation. Mexican spiritualism differs also from American spiritualism, in that the former is hierarchical and resembles the structure of the Catholic Church, whereas American spiritualism is congregational and based on the Protestant model of local control.[4]

In 1977, there were an estimated eight million followers of *espiritualismo*, which does not include devotees in the United States. In 1981, one ethnographer reported that there were over one thousand *espiritualista* temples in Mexico and throughout Mexican-American communities.[5] Subsequent reports consistently indicate that the movement is growing, although, like for *curanderismo*, exact numbers are unavailable.[6] A 1996 documentary series on religion in Mexico, produced for Mexican television, claimed that there are "thousands" of temples in Mexico—at least one temple in every *pueblo* throughout the nation, and at least one in every *colonia* in Mexico City.[7] However, it is impossible to calculate the number precisely because the temples are largely hidden. There are at least three highly public *espiritualista* temples—each with several hundred members and many more "visitors"—in East Los An-

geles alone, and numerous temples in Southern California and in Mexican-American communities throughout the Southwest. While the majority of Mexican spiritualists hail from the working classes, middle- and
even upper-class individuals can be counted too among *espiritualista*
devotees. And Francisco I. Madero, president of Mexico (1911–13), was
an avowed *espiritista*.[8]

Silvia Echániz estimates that in Mexico City nearly 80 percent of *espiritualistas* are women.[9] While a survey of the foundational *espiritualista* texts reveals considerable linguistic patriarchy, women are the primary *espiritualista* agents, who adopt its flexible spiritual revelations to
serve their own needs. The Mexican scholarly literature, published
mostly in Spanish, agrees that *espiritualismo* developed to empower
women: "Thus, women joined the ecclesiastical structure of this new denomination, with the objective of democratizing a Catholic church characterized by its rigidity, and arguing that both genders are spiritually
equal." And yet, Mexican anthropology, unfortunately, too frequently re-
sorts to socioeconomic theories of deprivation for explaining the creation and persistence of *espiritualismo,* "a compensation for the real
problems of social marginality."[10] Echániz claims that *espiritistas* come
from higher classes than do the *espiritualistas,* who draw from the most
degraded social population: "Thus, spiritualist temples tend to recruit individuals with frequent symptoms of depersonalization, amnesiac psychosomatic states—including somnambulism, certain forms of split personality and several forms of epilepsy—as well as hysterical states,
which are frequently found among the female population."[11] My research and interpretations are mindful of these theories, though I avoid
reductionist models.

The following is a fragmented genealogy of *espiritualismo*—it is not a
history qua chronological narrative. A history of *espiritualismo* would
document a single movement or founder. Instead, this discussion traces
myths and rituals that overlap and intersect in an attempt to introduce *espiritualismo* and figure it within the context of borderlands religions. My
thesis in this chapter is that *espiritualismo* is another prophetic expression
of religious poetics. Following this proposition out, I've read foundational primary Spanish sources and studied the Spanish and English literatures. I've also documented temple practices in the Boyle Heights district
of East Los Angeles. There, I spoke with and interviewed practitioners.
Based on these texts and interviews, this chapter first describes beliefs *espiritualistas* hold in common before delineating beliefs and practices
among three temples: two in Mexico City and one in East Los Angeles.

WHEN ASKED: "WHO ARE THE *ESPIRITUALISTAS*?"

The largest *espiritualista* denomination is called Mediodía. Its main
church in Mexico City boasts ten thousand members alone; however,
based on my field work, this number seems exaggerated. On any typical
Sunday, there are nearly two thousand members attending the ceremony.
Mediodía's leader is a woman. Mediodía has produced its own liturgy
and texts, and all *espiritualista* movements adhere to Mediodía's Bible:
*The Final Testament: Given by God to his Divine Chosen One the True
Mexican Messiah Roque Rojas.*[12]

Rojas's *Final Testament* claims to have been revealed during the years
1861–69, in Mexico City—the city that *espiritualistas* expressly hold as
their sacred center. The text contains Rojas's foundational teachings on
the organization of temples, hierarchical structures, and eschatological
teachings. It also contains the Twenty-Two Precepts of Rojas, which constitute the basis of *espiritualista* theology. The precepts, including the
preamble, read as follows:

> IN MEXICO, SINCE THE FIRST OF SEPTEMBER OF 1866, THE WORD OF THE DI-
> VINE LORD "JESUS OF NAZARETH" IS MANIFESTING BY WAY OF HUMAN
> BRAINS/INTELLIGENCE [*CEREBRO*], AS THE HOLY SPIRIT AND HE HAS ORDERED
> THAT WE MUST KNOW ALL OF THE COUNTRY'S VISITORS: THE LAW OF GOD
> AMPLIFIED IN THE 22 PRECEPTS AND PRACTICING THEM WILL BE AS AN ANTI-
> DOTE TO THE TIMES THAT ARE GETTING CLOSER, THAT WILL BE A SCOURGE
> FOR HUMANITY, IN THE FORM OF GREAT WARS, PLAGUES, DROUGHTS, AND EPI-
> DEMICS. FOR THE TIME OF COMPLIANCE TO THE PROPHECIES OF SAINT JOHN,
> OF HIS BOOK OF REVELATIONS, THAT MARKS THIS ERA, HAS ARRIVED.
>   THE LAW IS THE FOLLOWING:

> THE PRECEPTS OF MOSES, OF JESUS, AND OF THE SON OF MAN
> 1 SEPTEMBER 1866

> 1. Love God above everything created.
> 2. Do not judge your brother but ask him for justice.
> 3. Do not belong to, or love, a religion that does not practice love for
>   God, charity for His sons, and the purity of Mary.
> 4. Love your parents next to God and your sons in the same manner; for
>   the first, veneration and respect, and for the second, love and a good
>   example, above all. If you do the contrary, you will be judged with
>   vigor as authors of evil.
> 5. Do not judge or criticize anyone or testify falsely; if you do the Holy
>   Spirit will judge you, because He will defend your cause only if it is just.
> 6. Do not work for money on Sunday; should you do so, repent, for this
>   day belongs to God.

7. Do not possess the wife of another as your wife, or harm anyone.

8. Do not take what does not belong to you without permission of the owner, or practice usury. You are only permitted to gain an honest and legal interest on loans.

9. Do not drink intoxicating liquors.

10. Do not follow an occupation that will ruin you, or lower your morality and lead you into vice.

11. Do not enlist in a civil war dividing your brothers. You are only permitted to enlist in a foreign war when your government demands, and then you will act with the best of good will, because we are all brothers, sons of God.

12. Do not commit infanticide. If you do, you will be punished by God's law.

13. Do not abuse the poor or overwork them.

14. Do not curse anything created.

15. Do not treat with repulsion anyone suffering from a repugnant disease.

16. Do not judge or criticize any human being in public or private, which would cause their dishonor.

17. Do not leave your sons in strange hands, or do this only of necessity, and be sure the benefactors are well known for moral conduct and will take good care of the children.

18. Do not force children to work in places where they may learn of vices.

19. Do not relate to anyone any history or story of the following nature: devils; the condemned; witches; gnomes; evil spirits; miracles which are merely phenomena, astral occurrences which are not real, appearances of images that have no truth; false punishment; materialization; all of which is superficial and bad.

20. Do not rob, or keep stolen goods in your power.

21. Visit and console the sick whenever you can.

22. Do not kill your brother in thought, word, deed, or in civil war, or take his life in any manner.

Our guide Elías and spiritual Pastor Elías said: "My children, fulfill these 22 precepts and see my Father in all His splendor. Have charity and more charity for your brother, and give testimony of my Father."

The precepts are supplemented by Mediodía with the following narrative, written onto a pamphlet and distributed free of cost and without specific publication information:

WHEN ASKED: WHO ARE THE ESPIRITUALISTAS: WE ARE TRINITARIAN BE-CAUSE WE BELIEVE IN THE HOLY TRINITY: GOD THE FATHER, GOD THE SON, AND GOD THE HOLY SPIRIT. . . . WE ARE MARIAN [MARIANOS] BECAUSE WE BELIEVE IN THE PURITY OF HOLY MARIA, MOTHER OF GOD, AND OUR

MOTHER. . . . SPIRITUALISM MEANS THAT WE OPPOSE MATERIALISM AND
THAT WITH OUR ACTS AND THOUGHTS WE ARE PREPARING THE PATH
WHEREBY THOSE WHO WILL COMMUNICATE SPIRIT TO SPIRIT WITH GOD
OUR FATHER MUST PASS. . . . GOD OUR FATHER IS INDOCTRINATING US BY
WAY OF HUMAN UNDERSTANDING.

Additionally, when asked: "Who is God?" *espiritualistas* are instructed to respond that "GOD IS REASON, LOVE, CHARITY, AND FORGIVENESS." And finally, when asked what is the purpose of *espiritualismo,* the answer is: "TO BENEFIT HUMAN KIND, STOP PRIDE, AND REJECT FANATICISM."[13]

These explanatory narratives do not appear in *The Final Testament.* However, *espiritualista* leaders I spoke to agreed on these broad prescriptions—with the exception that some non-Mediodía temples (hereafter referred to as "independent" churches) place greater importance on the Virgin of Guadalupe. One anthropologist surmises that Guadalupe is not named by Mediodía specifically because the Catholic Church claims ownership of her.[14] The female leader of an independent Mexico City congregation maintained that "Trinitarian Marian" refers to God, the Holy Spirit, and the Virgin of Guadalupe.[15]

The precepts of Rojas, like the *espiritualismo* movement itself, are intimately tied to Mexican statehood and respond directly to national traumas as experienced by individual citizens. For example, precept 11, proscribing participation in civil war, points directly to the nationalist impulse. Notably, *espiritualistas* mark and commemorate Mexican Independence, 16 September, with religious ceremony. *Espiritualismo* arose to stem the tide of the Mexican national identity crisis that emerged during the late nineteenth century and was brought fully to bear during the Porfiriato. But it also addresses industrialization and urbanization by stressing fraternity, honest work, and sobriety. At its origin, *espiritualismo* intended to empower the individual and redeem the nation.

THE RETURNS OF THE MEXICAN MESSIAH

Rojas is said to be of Otomi Yaqui Indian heritage on his mother's side and descended from Spanish Jews on his father's side. In his autobiography, Rojas identifies his parents by full name and identifies himself as a "legitimate son." He boasts that he was born in the "noble" and "faithful" city of Mexico, on 16 August 1812. He was also baptized a Catholic in Mexico City. When he was between the ages of eleven and twelve his mother died, and he was placed in the care of the Mexico City Seminary, where for three years he studied to become a priest. Rojas offers no direct explanation for his leaving the seminary; he says only that God had "illuminated" him, that he had learned twenty-two offices, and that he was "much later" married to "doña Guadalupe Arias Malanco." He reports having two children, a boy and a girl. The boy, he tells us, died while an infant, and he provides no further information on the girl. Rojas creates nonetheless a genealogy, much like those found in the Bible. There is no question that the texts attributed to Rojas and collected and published as *The Final Testament* are meant to reproduce or mimic Jewish and Christian scriptures. In this case, text is mimetic, it is performative.

After he was married, Rojas very likely worked as a low-level civil servant until the economy worsened and he lost his job. As a result, he and Guadalupe moved in with her parents—her father was a medical doctor—in the *colonia* of Ixtapalapa, on the edge of Mexico City. Ixtapalapa is famous for its spectacular annual re-enactment of Christ's passion. While living there, Rojas landed a job as a civil magistrate miraculously; the opportunity came as a result of a chance meeting one 12 December while on pilgrimage to Guadalupe's shrine; Rojas claims to have become the judge of the Civil Registry of Ixtapalapa. It was in Ixtapalapa on the night of St. John, 23 June 1861 that, according to Rojas, God began to reveal to him that he was the Promised Elías of the Third Age. The revelations continued until "Resurrection Sunday," 1869. The "mystery" of his "church" was revealed as the central structure for the spiritual architecture of this new Third Age.

I, Roque Rojas, chosen son of the Highest, and inheritor of your Eternal Glory, have come from the Sacred and Glorified seventh seal or sign of Abraham, to found in the blessed Mexican nation THE HOLY AND TRUE CHURCH of the Third Era and Sixth Seal of the reign of God on the earth, that church who is responsible to give THE TRUE INTERPRETATION [*sentido*] TO THE HOLY SCRIPTURES, the church of whom, for all of the ages, will be called PATRIARCHAL MEXICAN CHURCH OF ELÍAS, and it will also be called and titled by other names which are: *The Beautiful Woman Dressed in the Radiant Sun, adorned with the Royal Mantle Scarlet of Elías, who has at her feet the Moon, and around whose head border the crown of twelve stars; the New People of Spiritual Israel of the Third Era, the New Israelites regenerated in the Sixth Seal of the Reign of God on the Earth, the New Zion of the Mexican Pearl.*

I, *Roque Rojas, who is the same Elías Thisbita, who came from a commandment of God to restore and regenerate the world, as to pay my tribute I owe to death, I've come to form anew the twelve tribes of Spiritual Israel,* formed from the one hundred and forty-four thousand marked with the

blood of the lamb sacrificed before the Holy Lamb, in the new Mexican Patriarchal Easter [Pascua], during the Summer equinox, placing in front of
the faces the seal of the Lord God and the Marian Trinitarian Triangle, in
order to put in the twelve tribes the indelible seal of the Lion, victor and
dominator of the key to knowledge.

I, Roque Rojas, open the mystery of the divine screens, and I say to you:
THIS IS THE MYSTERY OF MY CHURCH, I am the fulfillment of the third person of the Holy Trinity, the representative of the Holy Spirit in the world,
and I've come to show the true doctrine of the Third Era that is no longer
the doctrine of Moses nor that of Jesus, but my own doctrine, genuinely
and purely original so that you may know the true law of God, in his reign
of the Sixth Seal; my universal law, which is the Divine law of God are: *The
Twenty-Two Precepts of Elías, the True Son of the Sun [Sol] and Mexican
Messiah of the Third Era, called the Son of Man.*

I, Roque Rojas, leave you the theological mystery of my revealed church,
listen to it, analyze and understand it. *My church is neither Mosaic nor
Christian, but instead Mexicana Patriarchal Elías,* in which it was revealed
that the Final Testament of the last times closes with a golden hook the Sacred Scriptures.

I, Roque Rojas, the true Mexican Messiah, come to you, to found seven
churches that show as your shields, seven seals, each one ranked as one
level in the hierarchy, each one having been invested as revealed churches of
the Holy Spirit, each one with its message, in the Divine Mystery of the
Church.[16]

In addition to drawing on Victorian celestial imagery, Rojas reclaimed
the spiritual heritage of the Aztecs, reviving discourses that percolated in
the culture since the messianic attitudes of the Franciscans, who thought
of Mexico City as the new Jerusalem. During the conquest, Spanish
monk Diego Durán speculated that the origins of the people who inhabited the Americas were the twelve lost tribes of Israel.[17] Additionally,
Rojas was influenced by Judaism, Catholicism, and nineteenth-century
holiness movements preaching primitive restoration and physical purity,
and rejecting modernity. Mediodía, as we shall see, manifests Masonic
astral imagery. For example, the head of all the churches is called the
Great Son of the Sun (El Gran Hijo del Sol).

In addition, Rojas created a genealogy that traced the churches, and
the Mexican people, to the twelve tribes of Israel, who he names as follows: "Gad, Aser, Manasés, Neftalí, Simón, Leví, Issachar, Zabulón,
Benjamín, José, Rubén, and Judá and designated that they were 'the
144,000 marked and appointed [in Spanish *señalados*—or signed]' those
who formed the new people of Israel regenerated and restored in 'the
Land of the Eagle, the New Zion of the Mexican Pearl' will guide the

multitudes of the world on the path of the truth and repentance."[18] In this biblical allegory, one hundred and forty-four thousand people of the new era will be "marked," or given the gift of light.

The revelation of Rojas delimited seven churches—undoubtedly taken from the New Testament—each with a distinctive gift:

> Church of Efeso, Head: Leader of the Church, Seal I; Church of Esmirna, Head: Rabbi, teacher of theological grade, Seal II; Church of Pérgamo, Head: Supreme Priest, faithful conservator of the liturgies, rituals, and canons of the I.M.P.E., Seal III; Church of the Tiarira, Head: The Leví, part teacher of esoterica and symbolic knowledge of the church, Seal IV; Church of the Sardis, Head: The Prophet, the greatest seer or visionary[,] one [leader in the church] should have the gift of Prophecy, Seal V; Church of Filadelfia, Head: The Guide, responsible for discerning the spiritual element of the church, Seal VI; Laodicea Church, Head: The Patriarch, care of the patriarchy of each of the churches, Seal VII.[19]

As curators of each church Rojas appointed twelve women and twelve men whom he called *guías,* or guides.

Padre Elías's revelation, and the founding of the temples, are said to have initiated a new age, a Third Era, that unfolds a millennial prophecy. Padre Elías taught that the history of the world is divided into three dispensations: The First Age *(tiempo),* the Mosaic Era, began with the Mosaic covenant, when Moses was harbinger of the divine word as established in the Old Testament. The Second Age began when Jesus Christ, Divine Teacher, accepted a covenant with his Father to redeem humanity, as described in the New Testament. The Third Age began with the full revelation of Roque Rojas in 1861, and it marks the arrival of God among humanity to "destroy idolatry, fanaticism, mysticism, and materialism."[20] This age is called the Mexican Patriarchal Age of Elías, or the Age of Elías.

The Third Era will last two thousand years. Its end will mark the arrival of the New Era, or Age, and with it, a complete transformation of the world. This fourth and final era will begin in 3861, with Mexico City restored as the sacred center of the world. The social and economic order attendant to that global configuration will likewise be "restored." The world's population will congregate in Mexico City, and Roque Rojas will sit in judgment and governance over the totality. *Espiritualista* devotees are thought to be the chosen people destined to be resurrected at the dawn of the new times. Natural disasters and the slaughter of masses of people will announce the "special mission of the Mexican nation in the restoration of humanity."[21]

Adapting biblical mythology to its own circumstances, Mexican *es-piritualismo* teaches that Mexicans are the chosen people of the Third Era. Mexicans are the New Israelites, and Mexico is the chosen nation—the "New Israel," and Mexico City the New Jerusalem.

THE THIRD ERA

The Third Era, or Third Age, is distinguished by God's continued revelation in the world by means of human *entendimiento,* which translates as "intelligence" or "understanding" but in *espiritualista* vernacular signifies the ability to communicate with the spirits. Thus, in the present era God's mind is revealed through the mediumship of those who have been gifted with "intelligence." The hierarchy at any given temple is comprised of people who have been "marked"—or identified as "gifted"—and have begun the arduous process of preparing to become *materias,* or mediums. Spiritual gifts manifest as *conocimiento,* spiritual intelligence that enables powerful acts. Temple curators perform various liturgical and healing jobs. Indeed, tasks performed in temple service are referred to as "work" and credit one's spiritual path toward full membership and one's position in the next era. Generally, only at the very largest temples do full-time curates receive a regular salary; mostly, *guías* in training either live at the church or work full-time to contribute to and take from the small financial budget.

Espiritualista temples divide their time between healing ceremonies, *curación,* masses called *cátedras,* and study, or preparation *(preparación).* The majority of temple visitors come seeking healing. Healing ceremonies are scheduled during normal business days and hours and, typically, on one night a week. Days of healing can also fall on Sundays. Mass, or *cátedra,* is held nearly every Sunday, unless it is a healing day, and one other day during the week, depending on the church's calendar. On the *espiritualista* calendar it is the day of the month, rather than the day of the week, that prioritizes which events will occur at what times. Preparation or study for the trainees must also be scheduled; it usually occurs at least once a week, sometimes twice, and can last many hours. Each movement decides, however, which dates and ritual commemorations it considers most meaningful.

Days of preparation are reserved for teaching *espiritualista* theology. Key to the *espiritualista* discourse of God and the drama of healing are the doctrines of *esciencias,* or "essences," and *seres,* or "beings." *Espiritualistas* believe that the phenomenal world turns on the divide between the spiritual realm and the material realm and that the spiritual realm is organized into a tripartite hierarchy. The most powerful spirits belong to the *alta luz,* or high light, or the *media luz,* or medium light; bad or evil spirits are of the *luz obscura,* or dark light. It is believed that Jesus was an *espiritualista* ancestor and wise teacher who is now a being of *alta luz,* as are the Virgin of Guadalupe, Roque Rojas, various Aztec deities, and ancestral healers such as Teresa Urrea and Niño Fidencio. Beings belonging to this highest category materialize in the bodies of *espiritualista* devotees during ceremonies to bring words of consolation, teaching, chastisement, prophecy, and other gifts from the great beyond.

Orthodox Rojas teaching holds that regeneration will occur at the Resurrection, during the Third Age. In some movements, against the expressed condemnation of Rojas, regeneration translates into reincarnation. Unorthodox *espiritualista* teachings on regeneration hold that depending on one's spiritual preparation and resulting condition, a believer chooses his or her postmortem destiny. But all believe that a highly prepared or "advanced" soul can incarnate after death in living believers, who then act as agents of the divine. Additionally, a doctrine of hell, or Gehena, was revealed to Rojas, and he describes hell as a lake of fire where evildoers will suffer. Thus, preparation is of utmost importance and is symbolized on the altar itself. Each temple's main altar is adorned with an Altar Jeremias, a free-standing staircase consisting of seven steps. Above the steps hangs a triangle encasing the Eye of God. The steps symbolize the goals of *preparation.*

Rojas's teachings are left without official interpretation, and thus invite study, discussion, debate, and evolving understanding. In a section of *The Final Testament* entitled "The One Hundred and Forty-Four Symbols of the Mexican Patriarchal Church of Elías," Rojas lists Altar Elíasista as the first symbol. This is the stepped altar that *espiritualistas* place at the front of their temples, and it likely represents the first seven churches founded by Father Elías. The steps are meant to be read both up and down, in cycles of regeneration *(regeneración),* each symbolizing the steps to advanced *luz,* or light, bliss, union with God.

The altar is where the most important rituals take place—the steps representing the center of the world, the *axis mundi,* or world pole, the center from which all power flows. The most important rituals are, respectively, the work of mediumship, or *desarrollo,* interpretation; the work of "giving light"; the work of spiritual healing; the work of spiritual counseling; and the work of *cátedra,* or mass, on various days.[22]

To receive visitations and gifts from the spirits, a devotee must prepare himself or herself. In fact, *preparación,* bound to sacrifice and discipline, is a central trope in *espiritualista* discourse and practice. If an individual is "marked," she must prepare herself for elevation to the next stage in the hierarchy, to the next pedestal. The *materias* need to prepare themselves to receive the beings of high light, to hear and interpret messages from the spirit world. And more, each individual lives in perpetual preparation for the determining of his fate at the end of this physical incarnation—all hinging on the quality and extent of one's preparation, for preparation opens doors. The overall goal of preparation is to attain the spiritual apex, to reach a state of perfection, to become a being of high light.

It is believed that spirits manifest gifts in the devotees. Such gifts include: sight *(ver);* clairvoyance, or "understanding" *(entendimiento);* hearing *(oir);* prophecy, or "voice" *(voz);* and healing *(curar).* A seer has the ability to see the spiritual world, to envision the ghosts, and to see into the future. The gift of clairvoyance entails psychic abilities—the *materia* can picture unseen events. The gift of hearing enables the medium to discern messages from the spirits. The gift of voice, or prophecy, enables the medium to convey those messages. An acolyte may possess all of these gifts at once, but each *materia* must pass through successive stages of preparation before his or her gifts can be effectively manifested.

Upon Padre Elías's death in 1879, he was succeeded by his wife, and the movement underwent tremendous division and thus dispersion and growth. The most enduring of the original offshoots is the Sixth Seal, a movement credited to Damiana Oviedo, who was one of the original *guías* installed by Rojas. Today most temples are of the Sixth Seal, which, as outlined by Padre Elías, is centrally concerned with "the Guide" and with "discerning the spiritual element of the church." One *espiritualista guía* and temple elder from Mexico City told me that all the *espiritualista* temples she knew of were aligned with the sixth seal except for two of the second seal; she knew of none from the other seals.[23] Without doubt, the Sixth Seal, in the lineage of Oviedo, is the main division—which may explain why, despite usage of the term "patriarchy," women are the dominant force within *espiritualismo.* The sixth seal emphasizes spirituality and the spiritual guide without gender distinction. In contrast, the second seal as outlined by Roque Rojas is headed by the "Rabbi," and concerns a "teacher of theological grade." In the Orthodox Jewish tradition, rabbis are male, and thus the term "rabbi" is associated with a patriarch. In contrast, the word *guía* has feminine gender. The two extant churches belonging to the second seal that my research uncovered are headed by men—the only male-headed churches to emerge through these bibliographic and field investigations. Thus, through the heritage of Oviedo and the tradition of the Sixth Seal, women have kept the *espiritualista* movement alive and growing.

MEDIODÍA, MEXICO CITY

The "mother" temple for Mediodía is located about two miles from the center of Mexico City. Reunions of the Mediodía membership occur each 1 September at the main church, commemorating the revelation of Rojas, and re-establishing the temple's authority. The temple is situated in a working-class neighborhood and is surrounded by a large wrought-iron gate. Just inside the gate are small courts that contain sinks and water faucets, "fountains of gold." Visitors to the temple bring containers to be filled there, believing the water possesses curative properties.

Erected in the architecturally decisive 1970s, the edifice is a triumph of Mexican postmodern design and a tangible expression of *espiritualista* principles. The building's facade is painted white and shaped as a triangle. The ceilings and floor plan are triangular as well and thus form a pyramid. The interior is grand and mysterious—divided into three distinct seating levels and many platforms at various heights exclusively for ritual objects. The seating capacity is two thousand. The floors are marble. Entrances are at the second floor rear and on the sides, which open to the first floor. The sanctuary represents the theology of *espiritualismo:* the spaces hidden from public view are accessible only to those who have advanced spirituality. The top, or third, level of the sanctuary is where the rituals take place and where the approximately five hundred *materias* sit.

Women and men sit on separate sides of the temple. The dozens of ushers—women and men who are in various levels of *preparación*—wear white smocks and guide people to their seats. They additionally monitor the flock to prevent parishioners from crossing their arms or legs, as such blocks the flow of energy. The *materias* wear long white lab coats and sit with their backs to the audience. The pulpit contains the seven-step staircase, flowers, and candles. Directly above it is the Eye of God, framed in a golden triangle.

The hierarchy at *espiritualista* temples generally places the *guía* at the top and the acolytes arranged in descending order according to their preparation. For Mediodía, the hierarchy is as follows: Guide; Novice; Peter the Fundamental Rock; Pedestals; and Faculties, divided into speakers, seers, clairvoyants, and healers. There is also the Pen of Gold, which distinguishes Mediodía from other *espiritualista* movements. The Pen of Gold is responsible for recording the revelations spoken during ceremony, to be kept in the Book of Gold.[24]

Following the numerological patterns established by Damiana Oviedo, *cátedras* at the main Mediodía temple occur on the first, ninth, thirteenth, and twenty-first of each month, and on Sundays at 10 A.M. and again at 6 P.M. *Cátedras* begin with singing from the Mediodía song-book and readings from Mediodía's standard liturgy. Prayers are offered. *Materias* have an opportunity to share their revelations with the congregation in the form of call and response. Messages from the spirits are localized—as they are at the Mediodía temple in East Los Angeles—speaking to struggles of poverty, of spiritual yearning, while offering eschatological hope to those who can submit to and flourish in spiritual and physical discipline.

At the Mexico City temple the *cátedras* include baptismals. When one feels prepared for adult baptism, or spiritual initiation, a person places her name on a list prior to the beginning of *cátedra* and is seated in a discrete temple section. Baptism involves sprinkling the believer's body with roses wetted in *bálsamo* (balsam), a holy water that is blessed prior to ceremony. Baptisms occur in the name of God, the Holy Spirit, and Padre Elías.

Finally, there is a prophetic message from the main *guía*. She proclaims the words of the spirit who manifests through her on that particular occasion. Messages in Mexico City are brief and formal, declaring the divinity of Rojas and exhorting congregants to remain faithful, for the time of Elías is at hand. One young temple guardian explained to me that "The spirit is always speaking. Revelation continues, changes, advances."[25] One constancy, however, is the place of Mexico City. While awaiting the opening of the main Mediodía temple in Mexico City, seeking shelter from a thundering rain, I interviewed two *espiritualista* women in their twenties who boasted of the protection Mexico City provides: "This is a sacred city, a city chosen for Rojas's work. We are blessed and protected to live in this city. Think about all the other places in the world where there is violence and war. Here there is no war. We are safe here."[26]

MEDIODÍA, EAST LOS ANGELES

The rituals of the Mediodía temple in East Los Angeles closely resemble those of the Mexico City temple. Templo Mediodía Trinitario Mariano in Boyle Heights is adjacent to the infamous Pico Aliso housing project. The temple is a store front, located between a Korean-owned grocery store and a plate-glass window company in a residential neighborhood. The entire building is painted beige, and on the facade of the temple appears the following: "Spiritualist Temple, Trinitarian Marian, Revelation of God, Unified with the Mediodía Temple in Mexico City (Mexico, D.F.)."

The main *guía* here is Sister Nati, a small woman who is probably in her eighties. She has long gray hair worn in a tight bun. Her skin is brown and wrinkled. She is alert and strong. She founded her temple twenty years ago upon her arrival from Mexico. She cannot read or write. Sister Nati lives with her daughter in East Los Angeles and is considered a stern *guía* by the devotees.

The entrance to the space is nondescript. The small wooden door is covered on the street side with a heavy iron screen painted white; on the temple side a floor-length white curtain covers the door. Inside, the building is sparse, and everything is painted white, save for the red carpet. The space is rectangular, with seating for 120 people. During *cátedras* there are ten rows of wooden folding chairs, twelve chairs wide, that are painted white and separated into two sections by a narrow aisle. In the very front of the space is a slightly elevated platform decorated with candles and fresh flowers. In the right corner of the stage is an elevated large wooden seat, creating a small third level. The seat, also painted white, has a long, cone-shaped back that stretches the length of the wall. The platform space can be enclosed with an opaque curtain hanging from the ceiling. The corner chair is flanked by two other chairs.

At the center of the pulpit is a white staircase with seven steps that lead up to the Eye of God, encased in a gold frame and trimmed with a few small lights. The steps are trimmed with various types of fresh flowers. At the front of the staircase stand two giant white candles and containers of water. To the left of the pulpit is a narrow aisle that leads to a small changing and storage chamber, opening to a tiny bathroom located directly behind the pulpit. For reasons she refused to disclose Sister Nati sometimes leaves the bathroom water faucet running during particular ceremonies.

This temple boasts about fifty *materias* at various levels of training, of whom about forty are women. At Sunday-morning *cátedras* the space often exceeds its capacity. The leadership here is mostly women, in their fifties and older; most are *guías* themselves. The majority of the devotees are immigrant couples in their thirties and forties with children in tow.

Chicanas bring their gang-member sons who are in need of spiritual and physical support. *Espiritualismo* requires no confession, no act of contrition, no declaration of conversion; all it asks is that you believe. Also typically in attendance are older women alone and single men from Mexico in their twenties, thirties, and forties who come with the desire to have their bodies healed and their spirits renewed. There are also, however, younger Mexican and Chicana *materias* in training, in their twenties and thirties, who attend temple functions regularly, thus assuring that the work here will continue.

During *cátedras*, the men sit to the left of the aisle, the women to the right. The *materias* sit in the very front rows. The female *materias* are dressed in their solid-white gowns, and the male *materias* sport white smocks with dark slacks. The laity are asked to do likewise. During *cátedras* a guardian watches at the door to guide arrivals to their seats. As in *curación*, strict order is maintained during *cátedras*—the devout must not talk, turn their heads, or cross their limbs. The guardians watch carefully and hasten to correct anyone who may be violating a rule.

Cátedras in the Boyle Heights temple average two and a half hours in duration. They begin with prayers and readings from the Mediodía liturgy. Next the offering is collected by the guardians. Then, the main *guía*, Sister Nati, mounts the thronelike chair in the corner of the pulpit to deliver the message. The message she delivers in the *cátedra* is from Jesus Christ; Sister Nati channels Jesus. However, for Mediodía, different spirits visit at select seasons of the year, and hence other *materias* are chosen to deliver their messages at other times; *materias* are able to host multiple spirits, though one at a time. Occasionally, uninvited spirits will possess the body of a *materia* to proclaim a message. Sister Nati discourages this practice vehemently and insists on sticking to the Mediodía ritual calendar. The entrance of an uninvited spirit signals a lack of adequate preparation and bad timing. Like the Holy Trinity temple in Mexico City, Mediodía has produced its own calendar and thus has its own methods for dividing and sacralizing time.

The direct intervention of Jesus Christ into the discourse of the community comes as no surprise to the faithful. They anxiously anticipate his arrival and prepare to enter into dialogue with him. Sister Nati is visibly transformed while in trance, exhibiting mild shaking as Christ takes control of her body and vocal chords. He begins: "I am the Father, the Son, and the Divine Light. I greet you my people, people of Israel, my much beloved people, my people of Israel, follow my teachings and no other; I have given you the gift of grace to fulfill your obligation; now take my blessings." The *guía* continues in similar and repetitive greetings and exordiums for a while before pausing to listen to the "contemplations" of several *guías* in the crowd. The novice *materias* begin with their own greeting, "Blessed Light, you have given me license to contemplate," and then state what they were gifted with to contemplate, either while the message was being delivered or sometime since they last reported. Often these are specific and detailed descriptions: "I was walking in a field and saw seven doves," or "I witnessed the stars coming out of the sky," for example. Without fail, however, the response is rather simple and follows standard tropes: "You have witnessed my Divine Light," "You have contemplated the seven signs of the Third Era," and the like. Nothing specific is offered in response to the contemplation. Nonetheless, the "contemplation" ritual bespeaks the authorization of religious poetics— each *materia* is "licensed"—to use the *espiritualistas'* own words—to reimagine the cosmos in terms that originate from his or her own experience. And, most often, the response from the main *guía* is to allow each to discern the message for herself, to continue in preparation.

After this public interaction, the congregates are allowed a semiprivate audience with the being of high light. Under the direction of the guardian, the supplicants form a line to "arrive at the feet of" the *materia* who is, at least symbolically and even spiritually, performing as Jesus Christ. They tell the *materia* their troubles, and the spirit responds to them with words of comfort: "Don't be sad, seek me in light and spirit, things will change if you have faith, for I am the Father and the Light. I have already resolved your problem. Arise and go in peace." Some people arriving at the feet of the *guía,* who at that moment is Jesus, are baptized—sprinkled with *bálsamo.*

On one Sunday morning in late February 1997, when the seasons were changing in Los Angeles, many of the seekers arriving at the spirit's feet were embarking on trips to Mexico; hence, they sought the aid of the spirit world for their safe—and illegal—return. To these requests, the spirit of Light assured: "I cover you; I guard and watch you in my arms; you will return, return, you will return. I will open your path, and the army of God will be with you; you will return; you will return to tell of my goodness and grace. Once again you will return to the nation to which you correspond and come back again—I don't contemplate races or nations; I only contemplate hearts. Anew you will return to your nation; I will clear your path here. Take what I give—the Divine Light of the Holy Spirit, for I am the Father, the Son, and the Light."[27] Here, again, the return song is performed in religious ritual—perhaps in a different tune than in Catholicism yet set to similar sacred rhythms.

Before the spirit of high light departs, he offers additional words of exhortation and a peroration: "O people of Israel, generation of the Third Era, my sweet love you can find, you are my chosen people, I hear you, I hear you because I am the Divine Light, I will help you in everything you ask me, in pain and suffering you have discerned, even in the spirit of death you have discerned my will, but the spirit will be resurrected do not despair, if you have faith, that faith will be your salvation. Always remember, never forget, we are of the Third Era, your time will come, prepare, take my blessings. Good-bye, my much, much beloved people of Israel."[28] The final congregational song is typically number 21 in the Mediodía songbook, "Marchar, Marchar, Israel" (March, Israel). The Mediodía temple in East Los Angeles stresses the themes of election and a chosen nation experiencing forced dispersion, diaspora: a sacred community of outsiders—the *galut*—spiritual Israel, awaiting its destiny, the people's moment in history when they will be reunited as a nation and the world will prostrate before their sacred capital in Mexico City.

Upon exiting the space, everyone is handed a Styrofoam cup of purified water. This act closes the ceremony.

Curación is held on Tuesday, Thursday, and Friday evenings. On nights of healing ceremonies, the chairs on the right side of the pulpit are removed, so the healers can line up against the wall and receive people. On these nights, Sister Nati arrives at around 5:30. She straightens up and cleans the temple and sprays sacred air fresheners; these include "Water of Florida" and the "Seven Machos," purchased at local *botánicas*.

The ceremony begins at 6 P.M. with about thirty minutes of singing from the Mediodía songbook. There is no accompanying music. The singing affords additional time for people to arrive. There is a male guardian (a position for men who are "unmarked" but serve in the church as ushers of sorts) positioned at the entranceway, guiding people to seats in the order in which they enter. Anyone is welcome at the ceremony, and many who do not attend *cátedras* come for an audience with a healer. Regular members may bring along their friends and relations, many for the first time, to receive a treatment. The arrivals sit and sing while waiting for healing to begin. Anyone seated in the temple is prevented from crossing their arms or legs, or from facing in any direction but forward.

At 7 P.M. Sister Nati gives the signal for the healers to take their places. These women, mostly elders dressed in solid-white ankle-length gowns, line up with their backs against one wall of the room. Each is accompanied by a junior *materia* who functions as an assistant. The women pray and appear to enter trance states of consciousness. The seekers, seated in the order in which they entered, are in turn summoned by one of the junior *materias*. As instructed by the assistant, the ailing seeker stands in front of the healer and says: "Sister, I greet you in the name of the Father, Son, and Holy Spirit." The healer then anoints the person's body with *bálsamo* dispensed from a plastic liquid dishwashing soap bottle. The *materia* waves her hands in circles and performs other elaborate gestures, lays hands on the believer, and rubs and massages his arms, back, and neck. Overall, the healer makes vigorous contact with the follower, spinning and shaking him or her, slapping the seeker's arms and neck while reciting prayers to the spirits. No information from the supplicant is requested. The session lasts approximately five minutes, and when it is over, a "blessing" is put into the palm of the seeker, and he or she is told to meditate at the altar. At that point, the supplicant is free to leave, and, after meditating, most do. The guardian at the door holds a small collection basket, and a donation is expected but not required. Upon leaving, all are handed a small white Styrofoam cup filled with water.

The healing session continues until nearly 11 P.M., when the flow of supplicants ends. At this point, the *curanderas* meditate and pray before gathering together to recount the events of the evening, comparing notes, debriefing, singing, and praying. On one occasion, a woman asked the others to marvel with her at the power of the spirits, for when she entered she had had a cough, but at that point her cough was gone. She asked whether or not she had coughed while in trance, for she would not have been aware of that. The others reported that she did not. I also did not notice her coughing during the ceremony, but she seemed to me to be coughing slightly again before leaving.

The lyrics of *espiritualista* poetics are spelled out in their hymnology. With songs such as "Marchar, Marchar, Israel," the Templo Mediodía songbook illustrates the metaphor of election.[29] The songbook reflects also the pastiche character of *espiritualismo*, for it includes classic Protestant hymns, Mexican Catholic songs dedicated to La Virgen de Guadalupe, along with distinctively *espiritualista* choruses that venerate Roque Rojas, praise the healing agency of *bálsamo*, or sing of the condition of "Mediodía."

There are songs in the collection that refer to the sun; one in particular is called "The Sun Is So Pleasing." The symbolism of the sun figures prominently in the Mediodía movement, "Mediodía" meaning midday, or noon. The sun reaches its zenith at 2 P.M., therefore at noon it is two hours away from its peak. Similarly, the *espiritualistas* who belong to

Mediodía believe they are, in a sense, at the millennial/temporal mid-point—two thousand years from the zenith, the time when Padre Elías will sit in judgment and Mexico will rule the nations. The symbolisms of astral time permeate the Mediodía movement and suggest a Masonic influence, as does the Eye of God framed in a golden triangle that is the centerpiece of most *espiritualista* temples belonging to the Sixth Seal, whether they are Mediodía-affiliated or not.

The Templo Mediodía has published the precepts of Padre Elías in a small twenty-nine-page prayer booklet together with recitations and a credo. The liturgy at *cátedras* is read from this text. The text is called *Prayers Offered to the Sixth Seal,* and in East Los Angeles the booklet sells for three dollars.[30] This text does not represent the whole of *espiritualista* liturgy, just the Mediodía denomination. Other nonaffiliated Mediodía temples use a different liturgy. The Mediodía prayer book draws heavily from Catholic rites but takes poetic license in its interpretation. The first narratives in the booklet are prayers, including an "Act of Contrition," an "Our Father," and an "Ave Maria." The first and one of the most original prayers in the book, "Prayer to the Sixth Seal," emphasizes God's liberation of his people from bondage in Egypt: "He frees us, He protects and defends us from all in as much as we cannot take care of nor watch ourselves, in this day, in this hour, and for the rest of our lives."[31] The allegory of liberation from Egypt and the narrative of God's constant protection resound meaningfully for individuals who undergo daily perils.

The text contains a "Credo," similar to that of Catholicism but modified. In it there appears confessions of faith in God the Father as all-powerful, and he is positioned also as infinite wisdom and true light. The narrative emphasizes the role of the Holy Spirit more than that of Jesus. In fact, Jesus is not mentioned in the Credo until near the end, and he is identified not as the Son of God but as "the man who God chose to save his children from vices."[32] The Holy Spirit is God's messenger. The Credo states: "I believe that He [God] communicates by way of intelligence, as the Holy Spirit."[33] Before the closing prayer of thanks, there appears a prayer called "Invocation for the Descent" ("Invocacion Para el Descendimiento"). The longest prayer of the book, it beseeches the Holy Spirit, as the title announces, to descend so as to give comfort and illuminate and to move the acolytes through. It opens: "Divine Spirit of the Third Person of the Sacred Trinity who is God the Holy Spirit, Descend Divine Light and illuminate our blindness. . . . And that whereby we bad disciples do not want to go through, but with your Divine Light enlightened we are, to begin our march following in your Divine footsteps."

INDEPENDENT: TEMPLO ESPIRITUALISTA TRINITARIO MARIANO

The temple in Mexico City called the Holy Trinity, Spiritualist Temple Marian Trinity (hereafter, Holy Trinity), is a medium-sized edifice constructed in the 1970s specifically for the *espiritualistas*. It is located in a working-class neighborhood not far from the basilica of Guadalupe. Its stucco exterior is cream-colored, with the name of the church and its denomination spelled out in gold letters on the facade. The vestibule contains a large desk, an image of La Virgen de Guadalupe on a stand-up collection box, a signboard announcing the order of the services, and display cases containing rosaries, candles, and other Catholic paraphernalia. The entrance room is separated from the main sanctuary by heavy red velvet curtains that are normally tied back with golden ropes. Here an image of La Virgen de Guadalupe reigns over the vestibule. The space of the sanctuary is delineated by old, dark wooden benches arranged so as to create a center aisle, with enough seating for approximately two hundred. Mexican *espiritualistas* prefer ornate, Victorian styles, while Mexican-American *espiritualistas* opt for less liturgical adornment.

At the front of the shrine is the elaborately decorated altar. In the center of the altar is a white, self-contained staircase about ten feet high and two feet wide, with fifteen steps, each trimmed with seasonal flowers. The staircases at *espiritualista* temples are always elaborately adorned with fresh and beautifully arranged flowers. The ethereality of the flowers symbolizes life stages and (de)evolutionary processes: echoes of pre-Christian times.

While the Eye of God and the altar are common *espiritualista* symbols, the size and adornment of the altar otherwise vary a great deal from temple to temple. In this temple, stage right of the altar sit four red velvet chairs, forming a right angle with three more chairs that sit off to the side of the pulpit. The chairs are for God, the Holy Spirit, Padre Elías, and La Virgen de Guadalupe, who visit—occupying a *materia*'s body—on special days during ceremony. In the right corner there is a podium, and a framed picture of Padre Elías hangs on the wall. At stage left hangs another framed image of La Virgen de Guadalupe. The entire stage is adorned in baroque style with candles and flowers. Images of the crucified Christ and the precepts of Padre Elías hang on the side walls of the sanctuary.

Directly above the rear of the main sanctuary is a loft that contains two double rows of pews and looks out into the main sanctuary. In the right-hand rear corner of the loft is an office, and in the left-hand corner is a bathroom. A curved narrow staircase connects the first and second floors and leads to the third floor; the entrance to the third floor is separated by an iron screen door painted white. The third floor is an ornate flat where the main *guía*, Sister "Luzina López"—or Sister Lucy, as she is called informally—lives with her sister, also a *materia*, and two of the other *guías*, one of them functioning as the *criada*, or live-in servant. The floor plan of the flat is cleverly designed, housing three bedrooms, two bathrooms, a kitchen and dining room, and a patio garden. It is decorated with gaudy Victorian-style furniture upholstered mostly in red velvet, with long wooden tables, gold carpeting, and dark blue Mexican tiles. In the living room sit a pair of twenty-seven-inch Sony television sets on separate stands.

The hierarchy of this temple consists of about sixty people, referred to as *labriegos,* or "workers," who are at various levels of training. The laity who frequent the temple tend to be either young adults or people over forty with their young children in tow. People come to the temple for different reasons, but most people who arrive at the *espiritualistas'* doorstep come for inexpensive healing, and they are asked to return for the *cátedras* as part of their treatment. Some return of their own volition. Upon visiting an *espiritualista* temple, many experience a healing so profound that they become "marked" and enter the leadership pipeline.

Not all people who frequent the *espiritualistas* in Mexico are poor, however. Take, for example, "Juana." A regular at the temple, she is a forty-four-year-old accountant who handles Sister Luzina's finances. She appeared to be educated and middle-class, sporting fashionable clothes and a big car. She told me how the sisters helped her in times of need. "These sisters do miracles with their little brothers," she said. "They've healed me many times." (The spirits of *alta luz* in this particular variety of *espiritualismo,* are referred to as "little brothers," *hermanitos,* regardless of their gender.) One afternoon, Juana brought her teenage son to the temple for healing. He had taken ill from eating bad shrimp. He lay on a blanket on the floor with candles at his feet and a warm towel covering his forehead. Juana sat vigilantly over him. Juana visits the temple for *cátedras* simply because she finds it the most effective and satisfying choice. As an educated, professional women, she made no apologies for participating in *espiritualismo:* "I can go to whatever church I please," she said, "and I choose to come here with the sisters."[34]

A twenty-two-year-old woman, "Sophia," is in the *guía* pipeline, preparing herself in the temple two days a week alongside her studies at the University of Tepeyac, a private college where she is earning a degree in business administration. "I'm here because I'm interested in spiritual evolution, to get closer to God. I don't want to be a great business-woman," she claims, "but I want to understand business, to combine spiritual and material preparation. I want to be prepared in all senses: spiritual, mental, physical. It's integral—it's planning and organization; implementation can be applied to all areas of your life." She was brought to the temple one fateful day by a friend for her back pain. "From the first moment I walked in here I've felt at home," she relates. She received her healing, felt the calling, and has since become marked. She has been a faithful helper for the past two years. "I know that it is difficult for many people to understand. But in time they [her family] too will come to accept it."[35]

There are several stages through which to advance before becoming a full *guía;* each typically takes a year or two. Another devotee, "Dolores," a forty-seven-year-old woman, had been in preparation for twenty years at the time of our conversation. She was working as a telephone opera-tor. Her path had been fraught with trouble, and she had moved in and out of preparation with the *espiritualistas.* She had nearly gotten married on three separate occasions but did not because of her illness. She was unable to sleep for seven full years, she recounted. "I had to take pills." On one occasion her pharmacist recommended that she seek out the *es-piritualistas.* From the first day she arrived she was able to sleep without pills. "I had gone to Catholic churches to seek help, but not until I ar-rived here was I able to sleep." When we talked, she felt that she was solidly grounded in *espiritualismo* and would not fall back into her old ways. "My family had the gifts," she related. "My mother taught me to love Our Lady of Guadalupe, and my aunt was a healer. The gifts run in my family."[36]

People are initiated into *espiritualismo* through the body by seeking healing; concomitantly, they become inundated by the *espiritualista* worldview, especially the gifts of the spirits and the myths of temporal-ity. Conversion occurs by various means and typically involves a num-ber of oscillations between Catholicism and conventional medicine. Only in *cátedras* and preparation does the assumptive worldview of the *espiritualistas* fully unfold; it is kept veiled until a believer is prepared.

Espiritualistas do not proselytize: a believer must be sent by the spirits and must be prepared to be indoctrinated.

Cátedras are observed on Sundays, the first Saturday of the month, the ninth and thirteenth of each month, and special holidays. Holy Trinity, like Mediodía, has printed its own liturgical calendar and has thus given new meaning to time. For example, on 1 January, the temple celebrates the "Solemn Cátedra of the Four Powers," and the first Saturday of each month they celebrate the "Cátedra of the Holy Mother." On 1 September believers make the pilgrimage to Contreras to celebrate the founding of the "Holy Order." They also selectively celebrate Christian-derived observances, such as the Advent season, and perhaps more significantly, the celebration for the commemoration of La Virgen de Guadalupe on 12 December. The *cátedras* held on the first Saturday morning of the month are dedicated to the Holy Mother, and the first Sunday morning of each month for the "Convivencia Mensual," the monthly celebration of collective living. On Thursdays and on the twenty-first of each month *cátedras* are celebrated at 10 A.M. and again at 6 P.M. Each year the cycle varies, as the *espiritualistas* order time according to the way they understand that particular year. On Wednesday evenings they have *desarrollo,* or *preparación,* which is a special session for *materias* in training. During these meditative sessions the *materias* learn to be still; they sit silently for at least half an hour before receiving instruction from the *guía.* The *guía* explains to them the spiritual structure of the world, the poetics of healing, and, perhaps most importantly, the temporal structure of reality, including the divine election of the Mexican nation and its impending triumph.

Although the Mediodía denomination tends to exhibit greater uniformity than the independent congregations, the relationship between the *espiritualistas* and the Catholic Church varies with each temple and with each *guía.* In Mexico City, the boundaries of this relationship are drawn most clearly on 12 December, during the commemoration of La Virgen de Guadalupe's first appearance in Mexico. The Holy Trinity temple in Mexico City celebrates a special *cátedra* to Guadalupe on 12 December, as do other temples. On 12 December 1996, a group of about fifty *espiritualistas* were sporting Aztec-style costumes and dancing in front of the basilica to La Virgen de Guadalupe. This group belonged to the second seal, calling their temple "Spiritualist Temple of the Four Powers of the Lineage of Jacob, Marian Trinity." When asked about their relationship to Catholicism, the *guía,* "Francisco Alvárez," a tall man in his late forties, spoke for them, insisting that they were not Catholics, but they respected the

Catholics and had come to the ceremony to venerate Guadalupe, who is, he stated, an Aztec goddess. He explained further that they practiced all year long to perform the dance there, which was intended to venerate the other Aztec gods because they too are Aztec ancestors.[37]

On 12 December at Holy Trinity temple, the *cátedra* celebrates Marian veneration. In 1996, the *cátedra* began with a reading from the Mexican Catholic liturgy book. It was Patti, the junior *materia,* who solemnly led the liturgy. Prayers were read, followed the official prayer devoted to Guadalupe in the Mexican liturgy. All the *guías* on the pulpit were in deep purple gowns, the *labriegos* in white robes, while Sister Luzina wore a violet robe. A large painting of Guadalupe, framed in gold leaf, was installed on the altar and trimmed with a string of colorful Christmas lights. Choruses were offered to La Virgen, accompanied by Brother Adolfo on the organ. Without much ado, an offering was collected. In many respects the *cátedra* resembled a Catholic mass—except that it was women who were in charge.

The climax of the *cátedra* was a visit from the Virgin herself, in the physicality of Sister Teresa—also called Sister Terry—Sister Luzina's birth sister. During the choruses, Sister Terry, wearing a white gown, mounted the stage and sat in the fourth chair from the center—the place symbolically reserved for La Virgen de Guadalupe. Her face wrinkled in intense concentration, she began to shake slightly, almost as if she were trying to resist. During the choruses, Sister Luzina passed a small incense-burning urn in front of Sister Terry and sprayed her with a blessed fragrance from an aerosol can.

Finally, when the music stopped, the Virgin of Guadalupe began to speak. Her voice was high and melodic, poetic and comforting—though she spoke in Spanish, the meter of her speech was poetically Nahuatl. She told those in attendance that she loved them, that she was their mother, and that she had appeared to tell them to stay firmly on the spiritual path. She told them she realized that things were difficult in Mexico at the moment and that their lives were hard, but if they only believed in her things would get better, for she would help them; she reassured them over and over that she had transcended time—crossed the spiritual and temporal boundary—to be there with them.

Next, one of the male *guías,* the only male on the podium, approached the Virgin and kneeled down before her—this was Juan Diego. Juan Diego thanked La Virgen for choosing Mexico for her revelation. He praised her effusively, loudly, and tearfully. Suddenly he began uttering a language that sounded like Nahuatl. This brought the *cátedra* to a more intense level of effervescence. Following the utterance of Juan Diego, a stream of supplicants lined up on the left-hand aisle of the sanctuary and waited their turn to mount the pulpit and approach the Virgin, "arriving at the feet" of the deity for a semiprivate audience with her. The supplicants bring gifts for the Virgin, mostly flowers and candles for the altar. (Different deities arrive on different occasions, depending on the ritual calendar. Therefore, depending on the nature of the problem, the devotee is required to bring a gift to a particular spirit, arrive at the spirit's feet, and make a petition. Thereafter, the devotee will be able to invoke that spirit in times of need.)

By the close of the *cátedra*, between 150 and 200 people were in attendance, most of whom were incited to a more intense level of passion and emotion with the visit of La Virgen. After the appearance of La Virgen, the crowd was instructed to lift their hands in a charismatic worship style. However, no one spoke in tongues or uttered glossolalia.

Surprisingly, in the closing benediction, small paper cups of water were passed out to the crowd. Concomitantly, one of the senior female *materias* approached the front of the altar and offered communion—a wafer and a cup of water. Some of the faithful brought their own containers to be filled with water. After the service, people milled about in the vestibule, buying candles, rosaries, and other religious articles. Among the most popular devotional items were candles bearing the likeness of Santa Teresa. Other devotees used this time to make appointments for spiritual operations and consultations.

Consultas, consultations or healing ceremonies, are held every Thursday and Friday from 10 A.M. to noon, and then from 4 to 8 P.M. Healing ceremonies begin with a brief service of prayer and liturgical reading. Holy Trinity recites directly but selectively from the Mexican Catholic book of prayers. At the start of the service on weekday mornings there are two or three dozen people in attendance. After the readings and prayers, the faithful line up for a *limpia*—everyone who enters the temple must receive a *limpia*. The *limpias* are performed by one of the youngest and most junior of the *materias,* Patti, a woman in her early twenties. Sister Patti is also the *criada,* or live-in maid, for Sister Luzina and Sister Teresa; she cleans and cooks the meals.

In the vestibule Sister Patti stands adjacent to an urn, standing on newspapers, in which burn sage and Mexican herbs. She wears a white lab coat and greets the devotees one by one, beckoning them over with a wave of her hand and a reassuring nod of her head. She positions the "patient" on the newspaper, lays hands on her and prays fervently for her. Then she proceeds to give her a sweeping from head to toe. She sweeps with either a large bushel of herbs, a steel knife, or an egg, depending on the procedure that the supplicant will undergo in that session. She turns her around several times and may blow on her neck while reciting an invocation and a blessing that are barely audible but have a low, poetic resonance. This takes about five minutes. Last, she removes the newspapers on which the clients have stood, and if cleansing was done with an egg or herbs, she wraps the cleansing tool in the paper and neatly piles the bundle off to one side to be ceremonially burned later. After she has finished cleansing everyone in the temple, she remains perfectly—meditatively—still. With her head bowed and hands folded in front of her, she awaits new arrivals.

Cleansing is meant only as a preliminary procedure. It is predicated on the theory of energies and spirits; the cleansing is meant to banish bad spirits and to extract negative energies, leaving the body decontaminated for healing. Once the devotees have received a *limpia,* they approach the desk where Brother Adolfo sits. Brother Adolfo is himself a *guía* whose familiar or helping spirit is Thomas Aquinas (Tomás Aquino). He once had polio and no longer enjoys full use of his legs; he walks with crutches but insists that his condition has greatly improved through *espiritualismo* ritual. Brother Adolfo wears a white lab coat and works authoritatively with a large appointment book. He listens to each seeker's problems, assigns him to a healer, and hands him a poker chip with a number taped onto it before collecting payment. A seeker may also request a particular *materia.* Payments are based upon the procedure the afflicted will receive. Fees are nominal, from two dollars for a basic consultation to twenty dollars for a full-day operation. He then tells the person which *materia* he or she will see and a little about how that spirit works. Next, the patient is directed to the main sanctuary for a prayerful wait.

Each corner of the temple is sectioned off and occupied by the various healers, who sit to receive the ailing seekers. Services range from a simple consultation to a spiritual operation. A consultation is like a diagnostic session. During healing, the spiritualists wear white lab coats, and their helpers, or temple juniors, wear light blue lab coats. The assistants hold clipboards and pens. Upon a seeker's arrival in one of the healer's areas, the assistant offers instruction: "Is this your first visit? Do you know how to greet the brother [or sister]? Today you will be consulting with Cuitlahuac. It will be about another twenty minutes." When a consultee's number is called, the assistant again briefs the person before she approaches the *curandera,* telling her how to greet the healer.

The healer is greeted with the statement: "In the name of my father, I greet you, Brother [or 'Sister'] ——." This is said three times.

When Sister Luzina, the temple's main *guía*, is healing, her body is occupied by Cuitlahuac, an ancient Aztec deity (her desk actually has two placards; one reads "Her. Cuitlahuac," the other says "Her. Luzina, or Sister Luzina"). The *curandero* returns the seeker's salutation and sits for a minute, meditating and waving his or her hands in front of the seeker's body with eyes closed. The healer appears to be in deep concentration while diagnosing the situation and asking the seeker, "How can I help you?" The supplicant then relates the nature of his illness and/or problem. The *curandero* listens intently, asks probing questions, and talks to the client a little before recommending a solution. While the *curandera* is narrating the healing remedy, the *labriego* is nearby, noting it down on a piece of European-sized letterhead attached to his or her clipboard so the patient can have a record of what was prescribed. Since the healer is in trance, after the spirit leaves her body she cannot recount what was said: she was not speaking, but a spirit was speaking through her.

After the consultation, the patient is handed the prescription, a standardized typed form. On it is a line to write in who the attending healer was; this is filled in with the name of the spirit. There are also ten typewritten remedies, some of which are checked if the spirit recommended them. These include reciting prayers and rosaries, attending *cátedras*, washing with *bálsamo* daily, bathing with herbs, invoking one's particular helping spirit three times daily, practicing certain rituals during *cátedras*, and taking certain herbs. The bottom half of the prescription is a section for "other recommendations." The lab coats, the prescriptions, and the general organization of the healing session illustrate the mimetic faculty characteristic in the poetic performance of borderland religions. In mimicry there is appropriation, subversion, and power.

If a seeker has an extremely serious problem, the *espiritualistas* will ask him to come back for a series of preparations and treatments leading up to an operation. Illnesses that require operations are typically heart and lung disease, cancer, and other major sicknesses. During treatment, patients are asked to remove their shoes, loosen their clothes, and lie still on one of the pews in the temple. Three candles are placed on a chair at the patient's head. The patient lies still in prayer and meditation, awaiting the *curandera*. When the healer arrives, she anoints the seeker with *bálsamo*, wraps cotton around the afflicted area—usually the chest—and places eggs strategically on the patient's body. The patient is then prayed over, wrapped in a blanket, and made to lie completely still for several hours. Sometimes this lasts all day. This is meant to bring heat, life energy, back to the body.

Patients are asked to bring bottles of water with them. When the healer treats them, she takes their bottles and prays over them and thus transforms them into medicine. She then prescribes the dosage while the *labriego* records it. An operation is similar, only it culminates with the healer mimicking a physical medical procedure. For example, in one case when operating on a heart, the healer symbolically held an invisible knife in her hand, made an incision, removed the cause of disease, placed the contaminants on a plate, and sewed the patient up when it was over. All of this was done without anything actually in the healer's hands. Many have testified that during an *espiritualista* operation they opened their eyes and actually witnessed blood and openings in the body. This is something only the healing spirit is supposed to see, and thus patients are instructed to maintain their eyes closed in silent prayer. Once the operation is complete, the patient is ordered to recuperate in bed for several weeks.

ESPIRITUALISTAS SPEAK

Hermana Luzina, a.k.a Cuitlahuac

The main *guía* at the Holy Trinity temple, Luzina López, is a woman in her early seventies who appears to be much younger. She stands about five feet six inches high and has a medium build and dark hair and eyes. She was born to a middle-class Mexican family in Morelia, where she studied to be a public accountant. She recounts how difficult it was for her to study at the university against her father's will; she had to sneak around, she says. While practicing as a licensed public accountant in her early twenties, she began attending medical school and ultimately became a nurse specializing in pediatrics. At age twenty-three she was awarded a scholarship to study in the United States, but instead she entered a convent, to which she remained yoked for twenty years. While a nurse and a nun she left Mexico to study at the Regina Mundi University of Rome, where she earned a degree in theology. Together with her younger sister, Teresa, who worked previously as a secondary school teacher, Sister Luzina runs this main temple in Mexico City. Additionally, she has founded five others: in Guadalajara, Yucatán, Chiapas, Michoacán, and Hidalgo.

Sister Luzina's conversion to *espiritualismo* came later in her extraordinary life. She was fifty-three years old when she began to experience serious illnesses; she had heart and lung problems and pains in her stomach. She claims that she died three times; thus she underwent the mystical transformative experience the number of times that directly parallels the tripartite division of the Godhead. Medical doctors could not cure her. Then, one day, her sister discovered a spiritualist temple that offered religious healing. Armed with only this information, she took her Luzina there to be healed. As she tells it, Sister Luzina's healing was complete and dramatic. Like most others who commit to a life of *espiritualista* healing, Sister Luzina began her commitment with a powerful conversion experience concomitant to a physical healing—body and spirit coalesced in a mystical moment of healing. It was only after she was cured that she was inculcated into the *espiritualista* millennial myth. Thus—factoring in the myth of Elías and the prophecy of Mexican world domination around which Sister Luzina is oriented—body, spirit, and nation were melded together in a ritual drama of shamanic healing.

In 1965, after having been in the movement for nine years, Sister Luzina was instructed by the spirits to found her own temple, together with her younger sister, Teresa, with very little money and a lot of faith. The narrative of the temple's founding is itself a myth of beginnings. While searching for a space to build a church, one of the "spiritual brothers" materialized, physically directed them to the property site, and then instantly disappeared. In addition, nearly every person who was contacted to help build the temple had either been healed by an *espiritualista* or knew someone close to them who had been cured. Hence, favors were proffered, fees were waived, and building permits were hastened along—a miracle of grand proportions in Mexico's overwhelming bureaucracy. Today, the temple is in constant use for either religious purposes or the personal use of Sister Luzina, who lives on the third floor of the temple.

When asked about the relationship between her movement and the Catholic Church, in light of the obvious Catholic overtones, Sister Luzina claimed that she teaches belief in Christ and especially La Virgen de Guadalupe as beings of higher light but that there are other spirits who incarnate to heal and to help. She spoke knowledgeably and critically about the corruption of the Catholic Church, explaining that the Vatican demands a lot of money from each parish in the form of tithes. "No matter how poor, each parish must somehow get some money together and send it to the Vatican. Why does the Vatican need all of that money? Can you imagine how rich they must be from collecting tithes from every single parish around the world? And each day they get richer."[38] She also criticized the Catholic Church for its treatment of the poor and of women. She explained that the *espiritualistas* ordain women, unlike the Catholic Church, which, as she expressed it, is "sexist." Additionally, she lamented the fact that Juan Diego had not been made an official saint. She was outraged that a person like Juan Diego, who had done more than enough for sainthood, should be consistently overlooked. She attributed this travesty to the Pope, who, she believed, would only canonize individuals from rich countries. "Every time he goes to France or Spain he makes twelve saints at a time, but Latin America is largely without saints because we are poor." She added that ultimately it did not matter whether or not the Catholic Church recognizes Juan Diego, for Mexicans recognize him as a saint—regardless of what the Church says.

Sister Luzina explained that just as there are good spirits, there are also bad spirits, and the *limpias* and *bálsamo* serve to "chase the bad spirits way." Doctors, according to Sister Luzina, lack the ability to heal people who are tortured by evil spirits; such people have been cursed by a witch. She waxed critical of the medical establishment for its high costs. Even though there is "social medicine" in Mexico, Sister Luzina claimed that any medical procedure performed by a doctor costs at least ten thousand pesos. The *espiritualistas* offer a much more affordable alternative. She did not take her gifts lightly, claiming that for curing "it is not enough to have the gift; you must prepare." Preparation leads to perfected abilities to discern and to effective execution of the gifts of "seeing" and "hearing." These are gifts medical science lacks, and therefore the medical system is deficient. And it is corrupt because it charges too much money.

Sister Luzina related countless stories of individuals and families who were turned away by the medical establishment because they could not afford to pay for care. Such people continue to turn up on Sister Luzina's doorstep as a last resort; there they receive care at a price they can manage. Because it fails to provide this service, Sister Luzina was critical also of the Templo Mediodía movement, which she spoke of as a hegemonic force. Mediodía, she explained, eschews the practice of spiritual operations, opting instead for simple procedures such as *limpias* and consultations that appeal to a modern sensibility. Conversely, she believes that she runs her operation the way Roque Rojas originally intended for it to be run. She asks: "If we do not perform operations, where are the poor people of Mexico City to go for healing?"

Sister Ester

"Sister Ester," who is marked to succeed Sister Nati as head of the Mediodía temple in East Los Angeles, elected to speak on behalf of that congregation.[39] She is in her forties and migrated from the state of Guanajuato around 1977. Sister Ester lives with her husband, "Jeremias," in a relatively new, spacious condominium in an upper-working-class/lower-middle-class "suburb" just a few miles east of Boyle Heights. Jeremias works in car repair and is a guardian at the temple. At the time of our interview, Sister Ester was unemployed and commented that they were going to lose their home because they could not afford to meet the payments. They have three young teenage daughters who, Sister Ester claims, have their mother's gifts: vision, hearing, and prophecy. She is not going to force them into *espiritualismo*, however. Instead she wants them to make their own decisions. Sister Ester claims that her mother attended an *espiritualista* temple in Mexico but never forced religion of any kind on her.

She and Jeremias were having difficulties in their marriage before coming to *espiritualismo*. He began to drink excessively and smoke marijuana. However, when they both converted to *espiritualismo*, he stopped. They just happened to pass the temple in Boyle Heights one afternoon, and Sister Ester decided to go in. Once there, she felt like she belonged. She added, however, that if the evangelicals had approached her first, she would probably have gone with them. In contrast to most other people involved in *espiritualismo*, Sister Ester was not converted via a physical healing; she came seeking healing for her marriage. Still, she emphasizes somatic healing in the ministry and when asked why Mediodía eschews spiritual operations, she clarifies that they still perform them but only on special occasions.

Sister Ester believes that *espiritualismo* is a persecuted religion because people associate it with *brujería*, or witchcraft. "In my personal opinion, they are two different things. One is white magic, and the other is black magic. When a person has the gift, they can express it in either way." She is careful to distinguish her doctrinal opinions from those of her main *guía*, Sister Nati. Her own concept of sin in particular, she stresses, is directly opposed to that of Sister Nati, who

> believes that God sends us tribulations and trials as punishment for misbehavior. For me, I believe that my father does not punish or hurt or give us tribulations, but, like any other father he is going to give me the option to choose one path or another—it depends on me to choose the one that suits

me best. If I make a mistake, he is not going to hurt me, I have confidence that he is going to love me. . . . God gives us the twenty-two precepts as a guide. In the *cátedras* he tells us that if we follow at least one of the precepts, we have already advanced.[40]

Finances are a source of consternation among the devotees. Certainly the main *guías* of the temple, both in the United States and in Mexico, are able to support themselves in addition to paying temple costs from the revenue of their religious work. In the Mediodía temple in East Los Angeles, the *guía* sometimes opens her temple during the day to sell recycled clothing and other donated household goods, earning money to cover expenses. The extent to which the *guías* can support themselves based on the temple's income is, of course, a function of the temple's success or failure. This amounts to charismatic administration, for none of the trainees receive monetary remuneration for their work. At the time I interviewed her, Sister Ester had stopped attending healing ceremonies at the congregation because the last time she had gone she was not feeling well, yet Sister Nati had forced her to "work" against her will. Brother Jeremias says he often wonders what is done with the offerings of money he collects as a guardian. Sister Nati, however, claims that the offerings are barely enough to pay the expenses, including the flowers, and complains that people give very little. "There are never fives or tens in the offering," she asserts, "only one-dollar bills and change." Sister Ester's complaints have never gone further than wondering out loud what happens to the money and commenting that Sister Nati is the owner of the temple's property.

Ester and Jeremias try to focus on spiritual advancement. Each step on the Altar Jeremias, she explains, symbolizes a higher plane on the *espiritualista* vertical map of the world; each of the seven levels represents a stage one must reach and transcend before advancing to the next one. When asked about the three stages of history and the return of Padre Elías, she responded that it is particularly meaningful for "Mexicans who have had to leave our nation for economic reasons. We are now throughout all the United States. . . . Mexico is a country that has suffered much, but when Padre Elías returns, we will all be reunited in Mexico City and Padre Elías will bring us together there."

CONCLUSION: DIASPORA RELIGION

While my conversations with temple clergy and laity yielded varying accounts of doctrine and history, they also showed that motivations for con-

versions are remarkably consistent. Most converts had come to *espiritualismo* for a ceremony and received the gift of healing and then decided to
return. Some *espiritualistas* also voiced disenchantment with the Catholic
Church. The Church was believed to be out of touch with the "real" issues affecting the people and interested mostly in collected money. For
those reasons, I was told, people were opting for *espiritualismo*.

 As remarkable as it may seem, *espiritualismo* is a product of modern
urban culture. It also contains key teachings found in parallel nineteenth-
century contexts of rapid industrial growth, urbanization, and socioeconomic marginalization, most notably, a ban on alcohol and an ad-
monishment toward "holiness." But it is also much more than that, and
in fact, because of its poetic theological character, its possibilities—its
conditions for being and becoming—are infinite. However, one of *espiritualismo*'s central discourses involves dispersion and reunification. *Espiritualismo* is intimately tied to the Mexican diaspora in the United
States, to the healing of present-day troubles, and to the hope for a better time. All these beliefs are confirmed through a technology of the body.
The body is the register for knowing the world, for confirming the doctrines of *espiritualismo,* and for a sense experience of the spiritual realm
that locates the believer within an infinite cosmos of wellness and power.
Sylvia Marcos explains as follows:

> According to traditional [Mexican] medicine, the body is porous, perme-
> able and open to the great cosmic currents. It is not a package of blood, vis-
> cera and bones enclosed in a sack of skin which the modern individual
> "has." Also, the body is not the inert terrain of modern anatomical charts.
> Signs of relationship with the universe must be read in the body. Inversely,
> the external world is rich in signals which reveal the small universe which is
> the body. Diagnoses are based on the penetration of entities into the body
> or, inversely, by the movement of various entities out of the body.[41]

Both *espiritualismo* and *curanderismo* create/enact an epistemology
of the body that narrates across boundaries established by modernity—
between the living and the dead, between the impossible and the possible, between the visible and invisible, and between care of the body and
care of the soul. In a time when the Americas were undergoing rapid industrialization and "Republicans," as Takaki says, began "substituting
technology for the body," control over the body—discursive, spiritual,
and otherwise—became a central counter-hegemonic mechanism of resistance.[42] *Espiritualista* practices valorized the body, listened to the
body, trusted it, felt it, stimulated it, recast it as sacred ancestors, colored
it, and healed it. Placing the body at the center of an ontological schema

has resulted in a fresh episteme that relies on premodern conceptual modes. Subsequently, the body charts illness and pain on registers that are sacred—sacred not only because they are inherently so but because they are tied to ancient and distinctively Mexican traditions.

Women, especially, have employed traditional healing techniques by means of which they insert themselves into a social space that has been wrenched open by pain. In *espiritualismo,* the terms and symbols of Mexican gender codes are recast into grammars consistent with the articulation of female power. In *espiritualista* practice, women act as prophets and shamans: they take control over the symbolic constitution of reality—by resignifying time as well as resignifying the space of first the body and then the nation. I. M. Lewis argues that women in traditional cultures achieved social status by channeling male spirits, allowing spirits to speak "through" them, thereby attaining the authority that Catholicism had denied them because of their gender.[43]

Looking to Lewis, Kaja Finkler argues that, in the same way, women in *espiritualismo* are better equipped to negotiate and challenge patriarchy. The spirits serve women well by investing them with authority to manage relationships in their families and in their societies. Authority here is performed; it is mimed and choreographed. *Espiritualistas* mimic Catholic authority and draw from Catholicism, but the movement is also a protest against Catholicism. In protest, religious performance is brought fully to bear, extending what Michael Taussig calls the "mimetic faculty." Mimesis is subversive.[44] In resignifying Catholic rites through mimetic performance, *espiritualistas* have wrenched the symbolic power of Catholicism from ordained men and relocated it in the hands of women, the poor, and the oppressed.

The theme of exile and return permeates the Mexican and Chicano imagination, for ethnic Mexicans live in many diasporas: from the mother country in Mexico and from the economic, political, and cultural mainstream, which, in the U.S. Southwest, their ancestors once occupied. *Espiritualismo*'s doctrines of return symbolically heal the trauma of separation.

I have attempted to understand *espiritualismo* as a poetic borderlands tradition. This analysis runs counter to much of the work on *espiritualismo* heretofore, especially those applying a social "scientific" method. The only book in English on *espiritualismo* was penned by Kaja Finkler, who advances a class analysis. Finkler claims her "book was innovative on several grounds. It combined a *positivist* analysis of how Spiritualist cures heal with the experiential aspects of the healing process. . . . By so

doing [she] attempted to translate Spiritualist understandings into . . .
Western comprehensions of the healing process, using physiological,
psychological, cultural and sociological paradigms."[45] She suggests that
at one psychosomatic level, *espiritualista* rituals work for "peasants" because they cohere with the cultural symbols of Mexicans, whereas
"Western scientific" medicine operates on a different system of symbolization and hence is not effective for Mexicans. She thus bifurcates
Western and Mexican, relegating the latter to a world that cannot be
spatially isolated from the West, so the distinction must be one of temporality—Mexico is in a place temporally prior to the West, where
"West" signifies "scientific" and enfranchised in a world of modern miracles grown out of the European Enlightenment. Based on a single case
study, she arrives at the conclusion that "Spiritualism . . . fails to facili-
tate social mobility for its members by placing emphasis on sustaining
the status quo (as do some pentecostal groups)."[46] This judgment is particularly striking in light of Sister Ester's claim that had the *evangeli-
cos/pentecostes* reached her first, she would have "gone with them."
How do these traditions compare? Let us turn now to a discussion of
borderlands Pentecostals—*evangelicos/alleluias.*

CHAPTER 6

Born Again in East L.A., and Beyond

Although I expect to stay here, you see that I have *serapes* and the Virgin of Guadalupe. The Children are Protestant now.

> "Sra. Ponce," Los Angeles, 1926, quoted in Manuel Gamio,
> *The Mexican Immigrant: His Life Story*

Los Angeles is a veritable Jerusalem. Just the place for a mighty work of God to begin.

> Frank Bartleman, *Azusa Street*

Another speaker had a vision in which he saw the people of Los Angeles flocking in a mighty stream to perdition. He prophesied awful destruction to this city unless its citizens are brought to a belief in the tenets of the new faith.

> *Los Angeles Times,* 18 April 1906

East Los Angeles was our Jerusalem and the birthplace for Victory Outreach. Spiritually speaking, California is our Judea and the United States is our Samaria. The "uttermost parts" is the rest of the world.

> Excerpt from *Victory Outreach Mission Statement*

"Fe" is a petite woman; at twenty-one, she seems without age. She migrated to the United States from Mexico as a teenager. It was on the U.S. side of the border that she became born again; that is, she converted from Catholicism and joined an evangelical/Pentecostal church. But her parents were also evangelicals. Following high-school graduation, she attended East Los Angeles City College and worked in a children's store for a year before marrying. I asked her what she believed to be the most attractive element of her church. "Love!" she responded. What is love? "Well, the love we share here is a very special kind of love. Anyone can love their family, but we show people, strangers, we love them the way they are! No matter if they are drug addicts, prostitutes, whatever—we accept them just like that. Sometimes we take them into our own homes. Now, that is the kind of love that attracted me to this church."[1] The born-again stories of Fe and Esperanza (Esperanza's story was told in chapter 4) are not so unlike each other. Each marks a change, a reversal, and a renewal—as if each had been given a new life.

In Latina/o communities throughout the borderlands, "born-agains" are deemed *los evangélicos* or *los aleluias,* and I too opt for this broad designation, as the people often refer to themselves in this way. In the words of Richard Rodriguez, "*Evangélico:* one who evangelizes; the Christian who preaches the gospel. I use the term loosely to convey a spirit abroad, rather than a church or group of churches. There are evangelical dimensions to all Christian denominations, but those I call evan-

gelical would wish to distinguish themselves from mainline Protestantism, most certainly from Roman Catholicism. . . . Evangelicals are
the most protestant of Protestants." He continues: "Evangelicals are fun-
damentalists. They read scripture literally. Most evangelicals in Latin
America are also Pentecostals . . . trusting most a condition of enrap-
turement by the Holy Spirit. Pentecostalism is rife with prophecy, charis-
mata, healings, and the babble of sacred tongues. Evangelical spirituality hinges upon an unmediated experience of Jesus Christ."[2]

The narrative of dejection and the drama of becoming "born again,"
so central to *los aleluias,* is strikingly akin to the discourses of
Guadalupe devotion and pilgrimage, or, after being healed, to those of
curanderismo or *espiritualismo.* As followers of a borderland religion,
los evangélicos practice spirit possession, religious healing, religious gifting and play, cultural affirmation, as well as trafficking with sacred and
ancestral spirits. My thesis here is that *los evangélicos* continue practical, spiritual, religious, and ecstatic modes of being and becoming that
existed in Mesoamerica prior to Spanish colonization and that have
been articulated so completely with(in) Christianity, Catholicism, and
now evangelicalism that it is difficult to distinguish precise origins. At
the basis of this chapter is the question of why so many Latina/os are
converting to *los evangélicos.* The data are contradictory. One study estimates that sixty thousand *evangélico*-bound Latinos are "defecting"
from the Catholic Church each year, and that over one million converted
to born-again traditions between 1973 and 1988.[3] But more recent studies offer conflicting conclusions. The Hispanic Churches in American
Public Life (HCAPL) project summary of its preliminary findings, based
on telephone surveys conducted with 2,310 adult Latina/os, published
in January of 2003, reported that of the over thirty-seven million Latinos in the U.S., 70 percent remain solidly Catholic, while 23 percent are
Protestant (of which the majority are "evangelical"). Six percent of their
survey identified themselves as "no religious preference" or "other,"
while only 1 percent was of a "world religion" other than Christianity.
Their conclusion is that Latinos are "shifting" toward evangelical,
born-again religions.[4] Another study based on phone interviews with
3,000 adult Latinos, also released in January of 2003, reported different findings:

> In 1990 66% of adult Hispanics identified themselves as Catholics. In 2001
> only 57% of them do so. The proportion of non-Catholic Christians re-
> mains steady at around one quarter of adult Hispanics. It is often assumed
> that the decline in Catholics' share of the Hispanic population has been

mirrored by an equally large increase in the share of Pentecostals. In fact, although the number of Pentecostal Hispanics doubled between 1990 and 2001, their share of the overall Hispanic population increased only modestly from 3% to 4%.[5]

The two reports conflict sharply on (1) the number of Latino Catholics leaving Catholicism, and (2) where those "defectors" are going. Nonetheless, they suggest that Mexicans in America are rejecting in significant numbers the Guadalupe of Mexican Catholicism—or at least her institutional trappings—for new myths and icons. When compared to standard counts of the whole of Protestants in Mexico, 2 percent, it appears that Mexicans are not converting to evangelicalism in significant numbers until they enter the United States.[6] Thus, *evangélico* conversion in East Los Angeles implicates processes of immigration, and this too figures into the narrative that follows.

I explore the impact of the *evangélico* movement on the ethnic Mexican population in East Los Angeles by constructing a genealogy of an evangelical organization, Victory Outreach, and its Spanish churches, Alcance Victoria (hereafter VO/AV), which constitute a group of over five hundred churches.[7] I examine this group through their published writings, newspaper reports, and essays, and through participant observation and interviews. Victory Outreach was founded in East Los Angeles in 1967 as an outreach ministry to Chicano gang members. It now describes itself as an "inner-city" ministry and is known informally as the "junkie church" because of its special mission to drug addicts. Each church supports at least one drug-rehabilitation home for males, and most also support a home for women.

The denomination has its twenty-acre headquarters east of Los Angeles, in La Puente. Given this institutional affiliation, the story of Alcance Victoria is a story within a story, a tale of an elaborate religious organization located strategically within a larger, highly articulated network of religious social organizations. Alcance Victoria provides an exceptional laboratory for understanding *evangélico* dynamics in Latino barrios, for it is comprised equally of recent Mexican immigrants and Mexican-Americans.

As heirs of the Azusa Street Revival, Chicano *evangélicos* live, too, in the fabulous place and time in which the Pentecostal founders believed they lived, but each day brings them closer to the second coming of Christ. It is a time in which material problems such as illness, drug addiction, and poverty are miraculously solved through ritual, particularly shamanic-like spiritual practices and mystical experiences that bring heightened states of knowing and increased spiritual knowledge.[8] This is a world delimited by "signs" signaling the end of history, a mythical (de)construction of time, and enchanted states: God's spirit is pouring out anew on human flesh and spirits. This perspective enables a fresh understanding and expression of body and city: in worship, bodies are surrendered to the collective spirit and to each other—the city.

In Alcance Victoria, Chicanos experience their own bodies, other worshippers' bodies, and indeed the communal body and the city in new and powerful ways, which give them will, determination, and the right to negotiate the precarious social terrain of turn-of-the-century Los Angeles, to survive, and to thrive. As we shall see, the religious machinations of AV reproduce modes of empowerment and mechanisms of domination. Just as in Guadalupe devotion, *curanderismo,* and *espiritualismo,* VO/AV sometimes facilitates tragedy and suffering, enabling people to passively (or prayerfully) accept, or even become agents of, their own oppression and more. It is the discursive engine driving religious agents in their social dialects.

LOS ANGELES OR AMERICAN JERUSALEM?
NEW WORLD BORDER

Between the years 1906 and 1909, in downtown Los Angeles, a multicultural, multiracial, and multilingual group of religious seekers claimed to have experienced a religious healing so profound as to transcend their individual and corporate bodies and extend out to heal the broken city and beyond. In their collective imaginations and bodies, this healing came from a new Pentecost—a fresh outpouring of God's Holy Spirit, which in the Christian scriptures was said to have descended on first-century Christians in Jerusalem and was prophesied to return to initiate the "last days," the period immediately prior to Christ's return: the Holy Ghost was *the* sign that Christ's earthly return was imminent.[9] These events came to be known as the Azusa Street Revival, the longest continuous revival in American religious history. On 18 April 1906, an article reporting the events appeared in the *Los Angeles Times* under the subheading "New Sect of Fanatics Is Breaking Loose." It editorialized that each "night is made hideous in the neighborhood by the howlings of the worshippers, who spend hours swaying forth and back in a nerveracking attitude of prayer and supplication. They claim to have the 'gift of tongues,' and to be able to comprehend the babble."[10]

It is clear from the earliest accounts that issued from the Azusa Street Revival that for the Pentecostals, Los Angeles in 1906 was a designated, enchanted city with a prodigious destiny in a distinguished moment in time. Writing for a revivalist newspaper, *Way of Faith*, Frank Bartleman analogized Los Angeles to Jerusalem. On 1 August 1906 he wrote:

> Pentecost has come to Los Angeles, the American Jerusalem. . . . A cleansing stream is flowing through the city. The Word of God prevails. . . . Every false religion under Heaven is found represented here. Next to old Jerusalem there is nothing like it in the world. (It [Jerusalem] is on the opposite side, near half way around, with natural conditions very similar also.) All nations are represented, as at Jerusalem. Thousands are here from all over the Union, and from many parts of the world, sent of God for "Pentecost." These will scatter the fire to the ends of the earth.[11]

Today's world of wonders for *evangélico angelinos* is not so completely unlike the first generation of Pentecostals who walked the same streets, experienced the same weather, stared off into the same ocean, and lived in the same neighborhoods.

In September 1906, the first edition of *Apostolic Faith*, published by the Azusa Street revivalists, carried an article entitled "Pentecost Has Come: Los Angeles Being Visited by a Revival of Bible Salvation and Pentecost as Recorded in the Book of Acts."[12] In it, the gifts of healing and tongues are proffered as evidence of Christ's second return and of Los Angeles's election as the locus for his millennial manifestation:

> Many are the prophesies spoken in unknown tongues and many the visions that God is giving concerning His soon coming. . . . One prophecy given in an unknown tongue was interpreted, "The time is short, and I am going to send out a large number in the Spirit of God to preach the full gospel in the power of the spirit." About 150 people in Los Angeles, more than on the day of Pentecost, have received the gift of tongues, and many have been saved and sanctified, nobody knows how many.[13]

Los Angeles was for the Pentecostal revivalists a sacred center. It was the meeting place for God's chosen humanity, and it would serve as a base from which they would take the message of "Pentecost" throughout the globe. Moreover, Los Angeles was the place that God had chosen to reveal and manifest his spirit: in the Pentecostal imagination, Azusa Street, like the first temple in Jerusalem, was the locus for the convergence of the sacred and the profane. Indeed, Los Angeles was the gateway to God's millennial kingdom, and as editorials in *Apostolic Faith* hint, Los Angeles, when coupled with Jerusalem, would function as the seat from which God would set up his millennial reign:

> All these 6,000 years we have been fighting against sin and Satan. Soon we shall have a rest of 1,000 years. We are going to rest from our 6,000 years of toil in a reign of 1,000 years. That will be the millennial age. . . . The saints who have part in the first resurrection will return with Jesus and reign over unglorified humanity. (Rev. 20:4). Our place will be higher than the angels. . . . That is when God is going to give some two cities to reign over and some ten.[14]

For the Pentecostals, Los Angeles was a city with a fantastic destiny, for it was from there that God was unleashing his spirit onto the world as a sign that his millennial reign was at hand; it followed, then, that Los Angeles would function as the New Jerusalem during that reign.

For the Chicano imagination, sacred space was shifting, from Mexico City to the city with the second largest concentration of Mexicans in the world, the city of ancestors, of the angels—Los Angeles. But for some, carrying Guadalupe across the border proved too burdensome, and she was left on the other side, at least officially, in favor of the Holy Ghost, heavenly father of the North American Protestant patriarchy. But Guadalupe was central to the L.A. *mexicano* Protestant culture as well, as evangelizers intent on "assimilation" or "cultural integration" concluded that maintaining La Lupe would aid their cause.[15] Many *mexicanos* encountering Los Angeles after having left behind small pueblos also encountered different rhythms and temporal priorities.

Manuel Gamio's famous study of Mexican immigrants to the United States, conducted during 1926–27, spoke directly to attendant religious factors, especially the phenomenon of Protestant, *evangélico* conversion. In Mexico, he claims, there are two religious types: secular humanists and religious enthusiasts. This latter he divides into the following categories: "pre-Columbian religions," "the Catholic mixed religion" (combined with indigenous traditions), "the Catholic religion," and "the Protestant religion." This latter, he claims, is practiced mostly by the middle classes in Mexico, of both "white" and mixed ancestry. According to Gamio, the "religious" Mexican migrating north across the border is subject to one of three fates: "He becomes a normal, non-fanatic Catholic; indifferent or an unbeliever; or a Protestant." Using this formula, Protestant evangelization attracts Mexicans for its material benefits and its criticism of the Catholic Church. But Gamio criticizes the assimilative effects of conversion, which advantage Mexicans in the United

States because of its reorientation of the psyche in conformance with capitalist temporal mandates.[16] In brief, in North America, time is money, and for *evangélicos*, time is short.

The Azusa Street revivalists believed they were the generation chosen to usher in the return of Jesus for his church, that they would be alive to welcome him. One revivalist, writing in *Apostolic Faith,* recounted her prophetic dreams, in which God told her, "If you are faithful, you shall never see death."[17] Likewise, journalist and Azusa Street preacher Frank Bartleman interpreted the events at Azusa Street as signs that theirs was the earthly generation that would be alive to witness Christ's triumphant return. In a 1 August 1906 *Way of Faith* article, Bartleman assured the Azusa followers that "the 'gifts' of the Spirit are being given, the church's panoply restored. Surely we are in the days of restoration, the 'last days,' wonderful days, glorious days. But awful days for the withstanders. They are days of privilege, responsibility, and peril."[18] In September 1906, an outside observer identified by Bartleman as Dr. W. C. Dumble of Toronto explained in the *Way of Faith:* "It is believed that this revival is in its infancy, and the assurance has been given that a great outpouring is imminent, and that we are in the evening of this dispensation. The burden of the 'tongue' is, 'Jesus is coming soon.' "

THE BURDEN OF THE TONGUE

Bartleman was concerned that the people be made aware that their revival would likely end in cataclysmic world destruction. For such, as he pointed out, had happened before. "In all the history of God's world," he reasoned, "there has always been first the offer of divine mercy, then judgment following." He supported this contention with the case of the destruction of Jerusalem in the year 70 of the common era. The impending cataclysmic "carnage" notwithstanding, Bartleman "used often to declare during 1905, that *I* [he] *would rather live six months at that time, than fifty years of ordinary time.*"[19] The notion that the revivalists were living in a time that had been singled out for Christ's return was heightened by the San Francisco earthquake of 18 April 1906—four days after the opening of the Azusa Street mission. For the revivalists, the temblor and fire were God's signs to the unbelievers that his return was fast approaching.

Hence, since the beginning of Pentecostalism, its devotees have read world events as so many "signs" of God's imminent return. In the Revelation of John, which closes the New Testament, Christ's return is to be signaled by the increasing intensity of natural disasters (earthquake, famine, flood), wars (and "rumors of wars"), and the increasing breakdown of society. In this light, time, history, and society all make perfect sense for *evangélicos,* who are ever vigilant, interpreting destruction as portentous in their anxious watch for Christ's millennial return. Even more, especially for the earliest Pentecostals but still applicable today, confirmation of Christ's return is confirmed through the body: speaking in tongues, trance, and divine healing are thought to be evidence of blessings God is to impart in the final days. William J. Seymour, an African-American holiness preacher and leader of the Azusa Street Revival, explains as follows: "The Baptism with the Holy Ghost is a gift of power upon the sanctified life; so when we get it we have the same evidence as the Disciples received on the Day of Pentecost (Acts 2:3, 4), in speaking in new tongues."[20] In addition, Seymour delineates his views that healing is the third blessing parceled out by God in the final earthly days. For Seymour, the first blessing is "forgiveness of sins"; the second is "sanctification through the blood of Jesus," and perhaps most striking in terms of theological appeal to *mexicana/os* is the focus on the body:

> Third. Healing of our bodies. Sickness and disease are destroyed through the precious atonement of Jesus. . . . How we ought to honor that precious body which the father sanctified and sent into the world, not simply set apart, but really sanctified, soul, body, and spirit, free from sickness, disease and everything of the devil. A body that knew no sin and disease was given for these imperfect bodies of ours. Not only is the atonement for the sanctification of our souls, but for the sanctification of our bodies from inherited disease. It matters not what has been in the blood. Every drop of blood we received from our mother is impure. Sickness is born in a child just as original sin was born in the child. He was manifested to destroy the works of the devil. Every sickness is of the devil.[21]

The first editions of *Apostolic Faith* chronicle page after page of religious healings. Again, it is impossible to say how and from where the body and healing were introduced into Pentecostalism. Earliest chronicles describe meetings that were unstructured, with an altar space in the center of the former stable—whereupon whoever felt led could mount and poetically prophesy. Bartleman noted that "Even spiritualists and hypnotists came to investigate [Azusa Street], and to try their influence."[22] It would be unwise to presume the "spiritualists" and "hypnotists" were Euroamerican, though they may have been. Los Angeles had had an Anglo majority for only twenty years at this time, however, which at least casts uncertainty on such a conclusion.

Still, the leadership at Azusa was predominantly black; Seymour, the main preacher, was an illiterate black man with only one eye. The Azusa Street revivalists often wrote of their interaction with people of different races, ethnicities, classes, nationalities, and religions; since its formulation, Pentecostalism has been the product of multiple exchanges with various cultures. Pentecostalism is a product of Los Angeles, a religious phenomenon of the borderlands.[23] As a result, one of Pentecostalism's initial narratives involved healing America's racial dis-ease. An early edition of the Azusa Street newsletter reported: "It is noticeable how free all nationalities feel. If a Mexican or German cannot speak English, he gets up and speaks in his own tongue and feels quite at home for the Spirit interprets through the face and people say amen. No instrument that God can use is rejected on account of color or dress or lack of education. That is why God has so built up the work."[24] Even while the leadership at Azusa Street was mostly African-American, Dañiel Ramírez has documented the formative participation of Mexicans there. The revival's Los Angeles base, and its proximity to Placita Church, ensured that "waves of revival" would crash into that community as well.[25]

Inasmuch as the discourse of Pentecostalism is translated, it mutates and is transformed, shaped to fit cultural idiosyncrasies, it is better to speak not of a single Pentecostal experience but of many *Pentecostalisms,* each with their regional, class, ethnic, gender, and denominational adaptations and expressions. Grant Wacker argues that in spite of the differences among Pentecostals themselves, they all agree that "Conversion must be followed by another life-transforming event known as baptism in the Holy Spirit. Pentecostals believe that a person who has been baptized in the Holy Spirit will normally manifest one or more of the 9 gifts of the Spirit." Certainly other Christian groups are interested in the gifts of the Holy Spirit, but "Pentecostals are distinguished by the emphasis they place upon one of them, the gift of unknown tongues, technically called glossolalia."[26] Gifts of the spirit entail obligation, devotion, and commitment, and they restructure cognitive priorities. The gift of tongues and their interpretation, along with the other gifts, are *conocimientos,* a spiritual intelligence that advantages the devotee in social maneuvers. *Evangélico conocimientos* is not an altogether fresh religious discourse for *mexicana/os* but instead recalls centuries of engagement with the sacred, recasting it into idioms more consistent with the symbolic context of the postmodern world.

Not all people deemed *evangélicos* speak in tongues, but many, perhaps most, in fact do. My research has uncovered tongues speech in

VO/AV churches. In glossolalia, people who lack eloquence, or even the ability to communicate in the dominant language of U.S. society, can forcefully express their deepest desires, dreads, hopes, wishes, and expectations. Glossolalia is most meaningful as public ritual performance. There, among the community of believers, a spell of speaking in tongues loudly declares to the world that the believer is present, in direct communication with God, chosen, special, free, and empowered enough to shout his or her demands to the world. In Pentecostalism, Chicanos have found and shaped a fresh religious idiom through which to speak and be heard.

SAVING BODIES AND SOULS

Battles for the VO/AV devotees are waged through control of the body, and most often, battles occur one at a time—in effect, soul by soul. The life of Art Blajos is exemplary in this regard. His story recounting the battle for his soul has been published in an autobiography entitled *Blood In, Blood Out,* in which Blajos documents the wonders he encountered in VO/AV.[27] Blajos grew up in East Los Angeles, and his narrative reads like a resume of the damned. Abandoned by his parents, raised by a series of reluctant relatives, ultimately he surrendered his body and soul to the familiar path of drugs and gangs. Blajos's life of criminality is *not* dissociable from its place of formation—the gang element of East Los Angeles. He explains, not without hyperbole, that

> cops, gang members, shopkeepers and social workers in East Los Angeles describe their communities as "war zones" these days. I grew up when today's war was just beginning. . . . We big city Chicano kids turned no other cheek. Given our Latin blood and culture, we let no insult—real or imagined—go unchallenged and certainly no disrespect unanswered. We were proud and very poor. We defended our pride with our fists. And our pool cues.[28]

Blajos relates his performance of a particular social script. Overdetermined by the cultural narratives embedded in public representations and social relations, Blajos was convinced that he needed to behave in a particular way—he was socialized into performing a role, and he seems to have been presented few other choices.

In the United States, the conditions of possibility for individuals and groups are circumscribed by many factors, but key among them are the limits of what is culturally imaginable, what is likely or feasible. For Blajos, a Chicano in East Los Angeles without parental support or money, the only *imaginable* possibility was a life of crime. The images of brown men perpetuated in the North American consumer marketplace, perhaps the primary maker of the surrealistic reality characterizing contemporary gnosis, cast the portrait of brown body, the brown self, as the physical container for the souls of criminals and peons. To escape, Blajos, like so many others, needed to reimagine himself. It comes as no surprise, then, that the body—its representation and control—is ground zero for the wars waged by Victory Outreach. Bodies are addicted, given over to drugs and violence, tattooed, and infected with disease. These bodies are in pain, represented as worthless, and suffering from disorientation.

While spending manifold years in prison, Blajos became a "hit man" for the "Mexican Mafia," or "La M" (pronounced in Spanish *em-mé*). In fact, his formidable exposure to evangelicalism came by means of a murder he was expected to commit while in jail. In the course of befriending his intended victim, Eddie, a strategy he often employed, Blajos was at once fascinated and repulsed by Eddie's bizarre and seemingly contradictory behavior. Eddie preached to Blajos about the power of salvation—becoming born again. And yet Eddie himself continued in his drug addiction. Blajos recounts watching him on one memorable occasion. "As he eased the coke into his vein, he jerked with the ecstasy of the rush. Then he said to me, 'You know what, Conejo [Blajos]? Jesus Christ can change your life.'" This angered Blajos, who up to that point had been amused by Eddie's religious discourse. "But now," Blajo explains, "with a needle in his vein, it was sacrilegious."[29] Blajos questioned Eddie about this, and Eddie responded by telling Blajos that he was a "backslider." Blajos did not understand. Eddie explained: "A backslider is a Christian who has stopped going to church, stopped reading his Bible, stopped praying. Eventually, he ends up going back to the filth he came from. That's what happened to me. It's my fault I'm in here, because I turned my back on Jesus. I went back to doing armed robberies and coke."[30]

While Eddie was persuaded by born-again narratives, he was unable to gain control of his body. His mind believed in a particular script, but his body was not behaving accordingly. It was his body he was losing. Simultaneously, Blajos was at war with his own body, suffering from the symptoms of withdrawal from heroin: "I jumped up and began pacing off my cold sweats. I hurt all over. I was trembling." Blajos's experience of *pain* left him receptive to the words of Eddie. "As he talked on and on about God, I paced back and forth in my cell in pain, craving heroin. I

was deeply aware of the futility of my life. Here I was in jail once again.
I had already spent more than half of my life behind bars." Eddie's story
was very different than was Blajos's, for Eddie had experienced some triumph whereas Blajos had not. Blajos was perplexed listening to Eddie's
sad tale, which was at once a lament and an evangelistic appeal:

> Excitedly jabbering away in the cell next to me, this coke fiend went on and
> on talking about how much he loved the dear Jesus Christ. He got more
> and more hyper and animated as the night stretched on.
> "I used to have a nice home, a good wife, a great job and I used to go to
> church," he was telling me in the darkness.
> "So," I yelled, "how come this Jesus didn't stop you from coming to
> jail?"
> "As long as I was obeying him, he protected me. I was off drugs for a
> long time. People warned me about how easy it was to slide back into being
> a junkie, but I didn't listen."[31]

For former drug addicts involved in VO/AV, the body is the border between God's favor and God's indifference or wrath. When Eddie's body
was disciplined into VO mandates, his world opened up for him and he
realized a life of normative capitalist work and consumption, all because
he was under the favor of God. Conversely, when his body relented and
gave way to drugs, the possibilities of his world constricted. The body is
the mechanism through which Victory Outreach members achieve and
gauge the favor of God. Concomitantly, when the body is regulated by
Victory Outreach discipline, the world becomes one of wonders. As
Eddie relates it, the wonders attendant to God's favor require "obedience." According to VO/AV theology, God does not dole out wonders
randomly. God is the head of a complex association of obligation, gift,
and exchange.

This centrality of the body in VO/AV is crystallized in Blajos's conversion. On the verge of the moment of conversion, Blajos was asked to
raise his hands in the air, a bodily posture of complete vulnerability and
surrender. Blajos was reluctant, but his Victory Outreach missionary,
Joseph, insisted: "Pray with your hands up, like you're surrendering to
the Holy Spirit."[32] Finally, Blajos complied, and the result for him was
wonder, which he experienced through his body:

> I felt as if a blast of fresh air had just hit me. I could breathe freely. A
> weight and tension had come into me. In the few seconds it took me to pray
> that simple prayer, the power of God came into my heart and renewed me.
> In that short time Jesus Christ did for me what seventeen years of
> prison, psychiatrists, lawyers, drugs, money, power and sex had been un-

able to do. He had given me a new heart! The realization came upon me that God really had saved me from my sins—just like I had read about in the county jail.

It was a cleansing feeling.

A tremendous load had been taken off my shoulders. I felt a release, a freedom, a peace and a joy I had never known before. . . . Later that first day, I walked outside and there was a beautiful blue sky. . . . Everything seemed different to me now.

It was a time of wonder for me.[33]

Today, after his spiritual—and indeed physical—rebirth in Victory Outreach, "Brother Art" Blajos lives and works as a missionary in London. He travels the world to spread the message of Victory Outreach: you, too, can change. This is the wonder of Chicano *los evangélicos*.

In short, a conversion opens everyday cultural space into sacred space from whence to imagine fresh possibilities for Chicanos. Like *espiritualismo*, the wonder of the new possibility is confirmed through the body—kicking a drug habit, uttering tongues speech in ceremony, or going into spiritual and emotional ecstatic worship and mystical trance.

MORE ORGANIC PROPHECY

The story of VO/AV is best told through the charismatic leadership of Sonny Arguinzoni. Arguinzoni's story, or his "testimony," in *evangélico* vernacular, has become a foundational myth for the VO/AV cosmos; Arguinzoni has been virtually apotheosized in the Victory Outreach sacred pantheon. Arguinzoni's autobiography and an account of the foundation of Victory Outreach can be found in his books *God's Junkie and the Church of the Addicts* and *Internalizing the Vision*, as well as on video and audio tapes.[34] Arguinzoni's narrative poetically inscribes the charter of the Victory Outreach cosmos and instantiates the wonders of VO/AV. The personal narratives or "testimonies" of Sonny and his wife, Julie, are elaborated in a book they coauthored, called *Treasures out of Darkness.*[35] The work is a 287-page paperback, peppered with photographs, in large print, and written in plain and easy language. Its first printing in English was ten thousand copies, and it has been translated into a number of foreign languages. This book is the most complete account of the foundational myth of Victory Outreach. It also reveals Victory Outreach's gender expectations and is required reading at many of the Victory Outreach women's retreats.

The story begins in the Pico-Aliso housing projects in the Boyle

Heights district of East Los Angeles. Victory Outreach has become a vast and highly organized movement that spans the globe in eighteen countries, touching and improving the lives of many. In the Victory Outreach mythological narrative, all thanks for this ministry are due to Sonny Arguinzoni—who emerges in the VO/AV praise literature as God's primary earthbound agent. Indeed, his Web page claims that "one man knows the answer" to the problems of the inner city: Sonny Arguinzoni.

Treasures recounts the early life (perhaps a previous incarnation) of Arguinzoni. A Puerto Rican, or better, Nuyorican, Arguinzoni began using heroin as a youth in Brooklyn. By age fifteen, in 1954, he was addicted to heroin. His parents, however, were both Pentecostals and prayed for their son's salvation. In 1962, after time in jail and increasing addiction and alienation from his parents, Arguinzoni's interest in *evangélico* conversion was aroused by the newly dapper appearance of his former heroin-addicted associate, Ray, who had been born again. Sonny followed him to an evangelical church-related organization, Teen Challenge, founded by David Wilkerson. There, Sonny met evangelist Nicky Cruz, the former president of the infamous Puerto Rican "Mau Mau" gang, who had earned fame in the Bronx for waging war on the police.[36] Cruz physically barred him from leaving the Teen Challenge Center until he was able to renounce drugs. Eventually, Arguinzoni left the streets and attended the Latin American Bible Institute in La Puente, California. There he met Julie Rivera, a Chicana from East Los Angeles and also a student at the college. They got married after graduation in 1964.

Julie Rivera hailed originally from a Catholic home. Her entire family had converted to Pentecostalism, however, after they came to believe that her brother had been revived from the dead after a fatal drug overdose. The family attributed the brother's second chance at life to the prayerful intercession of Julie's aunt, a Pentecostal. The text passages in which Julie reflects on her earliest experiences in "legalistic" Pentecostal churches are filled with disdain. In traditional churches descended from the Holiness movements of the nineteenth century, she was prohibited from cutting her hair or wearing makeup, pants, or jewelry. VO/AV eschews such "household codes."

Sonny and Julie Arguinzoni's first home was a rented unit in the Pico-Aliso public housing projects. There, Sonny began preaching to drug addicts, gang members, and ex-convicts who populated the projects, often taking them into his own tiny unit for rehabilitation. Eventually he rented a church within the inner-city blocks that together comprised the giant housing complex. Even after the church was rented, he and Julie maintained a number of needy Chicanos in their home, helping them to relinquish the drug habit. It was in this way that the idea for a drug rehabilitation and rescue ministry was born.

In *Treasures,* Julie Arguinzoni narrates much of their early life in the ministry. It is a somber and often tragic tale of her husband's neglect of the family for his religious vocation. Indeed, he is unintentionally portrayed as an insensitive and selfish man, totally absorbed in his ministerial projects and, as a result, unable to communicate with or pay much attention to his wife. Julie portrays Sonny as often bringing home recovering addicts to occupy the single bedroom where his five children slept. Julie became so pained by this life that she prayed for her own death, and at one point she attempted suicide, only to be revived. The lesson she learned from this experience was to submit to her husband's will without complaint, in essence, without a will of her own, as all women in the Alcance Victoria ministries are instructed.

Julie Arguinzoni relied on the wonders of God when confronted with the impossible circumstances of poverty and the demands of her husband. One evening the evangelist brought home ten men for dinner without alerting his wife. He instructed her to prepare food for them, but there was no food (and no money) other than a small amount of pancake mix. Julie writes the following story about that event:

> Carefully, I poured the mix into a small bowl and added the correct amount of water. Then I began stirring while I looked up at the ceiling and thanked the Lord for the miracle He was performing. I stirred and prayed and stirred and prayed. When I looked down at the bowl, the mix was ready to run over the edges! Quickly I reached for a larger bowl and piled the mix into it. Then, I continued to stir and pray. This time it wasn't hard to say, "Thank You, Jesus!" The mix grew in the bowl as I stirred, until it reached the rim again. It looked like plenty for the group Sonny had brought home.[37]

Indeed, there was a stack of pancakes left over after all had eaten their fill. In this story, Julie Arguinzoni appealed to God for emotional and psychological support, and for a miracle.

Another example of women's roles is when Julie consoled a friend whose husband, once a pastor, had fallen back into a life of robbery and drugs. In her consolation, Julie revealed what women receive from their active participation in Victory Outreach ministry. "Julie opened the Word of God and told Gina, 'Listen[,] I know right now everything looks hopeless. One day you were a pastor's wife with friends and respect. Now today you feel downcast and alone.' "[38] This suggests that women's active involvement in Victory Outreach is maintained by the opportunity to earn friends and respect, build supportive networks, and become self-authorizing agents. Additionally, women reap material benefits from Victory Outreach ministry, as Julie Arguinzoni's example shows. After years of struggle, she was given her "dream home" outside of Los Angeles. The narrative of Arguinzoni's wife conveys the wonders available to women, the magic and the miracles that follow conversion and dedication to the ministry.

After many years of renting locations for church services—including one discotheque that they would sanitize every Sunday morning, early—Victory Outreach acquired fourteen acres in a former school property in La Puente for 1.7 million dollars. This property now houses the "mother" church of Arguinzoni, the school of ministry, and a bookstore. Several services are held at the mother church sanctuary each Sunday, which seats two thousand people. Currently, congregants are in the process of building a larger temple there.

Today, Victory Outreach is a sophisticated organization spanning the globe. In addition to its La Puente center, it rents office space in West Covina, California, where the ministry offices of Arguinzoni and his staff—their "corporate headquarters," as they call them—are housed. Victory Outreach also has programs designed especially for women under the aegis of United Women in Ministry and the Victory Outreach School of Ministry. The overall VO/AV ministry includes an infrequent television ministry that broadcasts on the Trinity Broadcasting Network (TBN) and various other programs. They have been invited to the White House and have been featured on major newspapers and television networks.

One of their most successful programs, specifically for youth, is called God's Anointed Now Generation (GANG). GANG captures and mimes Los Angeles youth gang culture, creating a parallel Christian aesthetic. Thus, Victory Outreach poetically recreates the popularity of the gang image but refigures that image with *evangélico* signifiers. The denomination has its own rap groups, for example, who sample rhythms and riffs of popular songs but inscribe Christian lyrics over them. Many members of GANG continue to sport the hairstyles, makeup, and baggy clothes of Los Angeles youth culture, but they espouse Christian teachings. In effect, VO/AV presents not an alternative to popular culture but a capitulation, in form if not in essence.

The ministries are elaborate and growing. Ministerial work offers employment, whereby men can improve their lots in life and live comfortably: ministers symbolize the aspirations of the group. Hence, Alcance

Victoria buys a minister a car, or they arrange for his condominium. A man can come to church, marry the woman he has dreamed about, become active in ministry, and move on up through the VO/AV chain of command. Like Sonny Arguinzoni himself, many of the staff drive BMWs, symbols of prosperity. Thus, included in the gospel of rescue and salvation are narratives of prosperity and well-being.

POSEER LA TIERRA/TAKE THE CITY: ANOTHER MESTIZAJE

Central to Pentecostal identity, but often overlooked, is the Azusa Street mythology: the notion that God works through cities and that Los Angeles has been chosen for sacred and evangelical work to be done. As the mission statement indicates, Los Angeles occupies a special discursive place in the VO/AV lexicon: "Los Angeles is our Jerusalem."[39] Richard Rodriguez has noted the emphasis VO locates in the city: "THE CITY IS CORRUPT, THE CITY IS EVIL."[40] One Chicano VO pastor from East Los Angeles summed it up this way: "The city is broken, the city is hurting, Victory Outreach is taking the city for Jesus."[41]

The expressed strategy of VO is to "conquer the world," in a sense, by planting churches and evangelizing city by city—a strategy they refer to as "taking the city for Jesus." In 1996, this theme became the stated objective for the year: *Poseer la tierra* (Possess the land)—their Spanish translation for the English phrase "Take the city." The phrase was ubiquitous on the official material throughout the year, from church programs to fund raising materials to other sorts of literatures. The military signification is intentional; VO/AV imagine themselves engaged in a "spiritual war" that is materialized in bodies and cities.

The first VO church expansion was "launched out" eastward from Boyle Heights to Pico Rivera, California, in the early 1970s. When a male member feels a "burden" to open a church in a particular place, he is "launched out," given one year of support from the organization for that ministry. In that time, the church should become self-supporting, although some exceptions are made and cutoff dates extended. Although women are not officially able to become pastors or heads of churches themselves, they do occasionally. Women can become evangelists and work as leaders among other women. The formal proscription against ordaining women as pastors is unusual for *evangélico* churches.

In fact, across the street from the AV church in Boyle Heights exists another Spanish-based Pentecostal church affiliated with Assemblies of God. The congregation has over three hundred active members, Mexican-Americans and Central Americans, while the pastor is an elder Chicana. The most distinctive aspect of this church is its professional ambiance, elegantly maintained in a building designed during the interwar years specifically as a neighborhood church. Their worship is brilliantly choreographed, elegantly and rhythmically charismatic: men dancing with men, women with women, partnered, every word, every move, every note considered, all members of the church acting as one body, the orchestra—electric organ, guitar, drums—playing enchanting and hypnotic melodies while all sing in unison, locked in a spiritual and erotic dance. This church is certainly different from the church across the street, AV, but they are both *evangélicos,* and one cannot mistake the distinct resemblance—especially in the dance.

The distinct foundational narrative of the Spanish VO churches is that of Eliodoro Esteves, or "Pastor Lolo." Alcance Victoria began in 1983 in an abandoned synagogue on Bridge Street in East Los Angeles. This congregation was taken over by Pastor Lolo in 1989, after the original pastor became too ill to work any longer. Pastor Lolo had been "born again" in Victory Outreach, following his older sisters. Upon his conversion, he immediately felt a "burden" for Mexico. Although he spoke very little Spanish, armed with his Bible, five hundred dollars, and a Chevrolet station wagon and accompanied by his wife, Catalina, and their infant son, he made the pilgrimage to the sacred heart of Mexico, Mexico City, where he planned to win Mexico for Jesus. He can't explain why he chose Mexico City: "I just felt I needed to go to Mexico City, to preach at the Basilica of Guadalupe and at the Zócalo. When I had done that I returned home and began ministry as a changed person."[42] In 1985, the first foreign VO/AV church was established in Mexico City.

Upon returning to the United States several years later, Pastor Lolo assumed the leadership of the Spanish congregation, which, in the meantime, had moved from the synagogue on Bridge Street to a storefront on McDonald Street. Soon the group grew too large, so Pastor Lolo moved them in 1992 into a defunct painters'-union hall on Soto Street in the heart of Boyle Heights, which they rented monthly. In 1994, Pastor Lolo resigned his post once the stress and fatigue of the job had taken its toll on his marriage and family life. The congregation was given over to one of Pastor Lolo's main administrators, "Jesse Garcia," who goes by the nickname "Chuy." At the time Garcia was twenty-two years old, the youngest pastor in the Victory Outreach organization.

In 1994, Alcance Victoria Este de Los Angeles moved from the painters'-union hall in which it held services to the defunct movie theater, also in Boyle Heights, where they currently meet. The theater has an interesting mythology. According to one of the members, during the late fifties and early sixties it was owned by the Mexican singer Pedro Infante. In the late sixties and seventies it was renamed "La Azteca." But as the Chicano movement waned, so did the cinema house, and AV has emerged to take its place. Although they rent the edifice, they have made substantial permanent changes to it and have designs for its eventual purchase; in the words of the pastor, they are "trusting God" for it.

The average Sunday morning and evening attendance is three hundred, of which, according to the pastor's estimates, about one half are recently arrived Mexican immigrants and the other half are Mexican-Americans. Inside, the building is big but spare, with national flags from Latin-American countries hanging from the walls. At the top center of the ceiling hang two flags, one Mexican, the other American. A banner placed behind the pulpit reads "Alcance Victoria E.L.A. Poseer La Tierra." Fresh flowers, a Plexiglas podium, and a red carpet delineate the pulpit. The auditorium has stadium-style seating.

The building's facade is dominated by a marquee, which in times past announced films starring Cantinflas and other Mexican film heroes. It now sports a hand-painted cloth sign announcing Alcance Victoria's presence, the hours of its services, and a welcome to all passersby. On the exterior wall that Alcance Victoria shares with another building, an advertisement reads "You can change your eye color." This message seems an appropriate additional welcome to Alcance Victoria, whose message is one of personal transformation and the omnipotence of God: You, too, can be changed—spiritually, morally, physically. In the wonders of *los evangélicos*, the metanoia is without physical limitations. You can become a different person, a person who can strategically transform at will, an image maker and shape-shifter.[43]

In the center of the church vestibule is a small island where food is prepared and served by the women members. Eating takes place after each service. Excluded officially from official positions of power within the church, women assert authority in their control of food and in other traditionally female arenas. Ushers can be either women or men. Women are routinely positioned on the pulpit during worship services. They tend to be dressed well and to stand behind the song leader. It is impossible to overlook the allure of this women's chorus to the typically single male audience members. This is, indeed, a strategy for attracting men who want to find a "virgin" to marry and impregnate. Even the posture of the women resembles Guadalupe: head slightly bowed, hands folded,

compassionate, nurturing, motherly. In spite of the *evangélico* iconoclastic rejection of the Virgin of Guadalupe, the realm of women's possibilities that she symbolizes and circumscribes still dominates the Chicano imagination.

Worship is lively; the band plays many styles, but most popular is a
distinctive *conjunto* sound, a northern Mexico fusion of Spanish trum-
peters with polka, rock and roll, and soulful rhythms.[44] Men and women
spill out of the aisles and dance to the beats. People are dressed formally,
with men in ties and women in modest professional dresses and skirts.
Sunday morning services begin at ten-thirty and last until noon. The ceremony opens with prayer, scriptural reading, and congregational
singing—a typical sequence for *evangélico* services. The pastor makes a
dramatic entrance, walking briskly from the rear of the church with two
or more of his officers in suits and ties, all young men in their twenties,
well groomed and in good physical shape, who assume the places reserved for them in the first row and do not stop to greet anyone. The pastor assumes the pulpit about one hour to ninety minutes after the service
begins. He makes announcements, leads songs, reads from the Bible, and
begins to preach.

Pastor Chuy's sermons are animated and compelling. He illustrates
(most often indirectly) how his chosen biblical passage is relevant to the
congregational life, using some example close to the present reality. His
preaching contains a poetic interpretation of the Bible, making the
themes of personal responsibility and the transformative power of God
fit the needs of the East L.A. community. He typically exhorts the congregation to maintain their faith, work hard for Jesus, continue coming
to church, and love and help one another—for the time of Jesus' return
is at hand. Pastor Chuy preaches God's wondrous power to work miracles for those who obey. His sermons average between forty-five minutes and one hour. On Father's Day, 1995, his message focused on responsible fatherhood. He related a sad story about his own father, who
abandoned his family when Pastor Chuy was very young. When he contacted his estranged father to invite him to his high-school graduation,
Pastor Chuy's father declined. All he wanted, he explained, was his father's friendship. The point of the message was forgiveness: Pastor Chuy
was admonishing his congregants to behave in kind and to forgive their
fathers.

Women do not typically preach in the congregation, but occasionally
they do—the decision is made by each pastor. In fact, it is common, especially in the English-language churches, for the pastor's wife to take the

microphone in front of the congregation and begin to prophetically sermonize on a recent event or theological issue. Pastor's wives do indeed have ministry *de facto* if not *de jure*. Two women preached at AV in East Los Angeles on Mother's Day, 1996. The first woman, in her fifties, was a native Angeleno. She offered a *consejo*—sage advice, proverbial wisdom—about the power of a mother's love and the witness of a Christian mother to her children. She poetically analogized a mother's unconditional love to that of God. The next speaker, in her early twenties and recently arrived from Mexico, began by asking the women present, "What kind of influence are you on your husband?" She stated that Jezebel was a negative influence on her husband because Jezebel was always speaking her mind and giving her kingly husband advice, habits that proved his ruin. After the woman had spoken for about thirty minutes, there was dead silence in the congregation as she left the pulpit. The first speaker, by contrast, was remarkably well received.

Preaching culminates in a climactic moment of collective effervescence with the altar call. Most parishioners make their way up to the altar, a movement resulting in heated crowding and sensual body contact. The music, the massage of the crowd and prayer leaders, the emotion, the sounds, and the passion all intensify the sensuality of the moment. Generally, men make much physical, emotional, and spiritual contact with other men during these periods of intense prayer. They embrace one another, hold hands, place their arms around one another, kneel down together, and hold each other tightly, making full body contact while weeping, praying, and shaking. Women behave likewise among themselves. Congregants speak in tongues and experience ecstatic trances as their bodies are repossessed anew by the Holy Ghost. The charismatic worship lasts up to thirty minutes and is followed by a period of brief singing before the close of the service. In charismatic worship, women and men give their bodies to God and to each other: central to the wonder of Victory Outreach is the construction of a new, physical, sensual, and spiritual membership, a new collective body.

Binding these congregates to each other is the ritual of laying on of hands. Members are joined together, somewhat ironically, in what seems a fresh spiritual union in a new *nepantla* place, by relying on the ancient Mexican ritual of touch. The pastor, the pastor's wife, or another congregational leader at some point retrieves the microphone, positions himself or herself in a conspicuous place, and calls the "elders" of the congregation to pray for the sick, the troubled, the lost, the hurting. A circle forms, people join hands, oil is removed from a bottle previously blessed.

A member known to be "hurting" is asked to come and kneel in the center of the circle to be anointed with oil and healed. All together, the group lays on hands. Another ritual involves women and men lining up on the pulpit and congregants forming a line to receive prayer and the laying on of hands. Those receiving prayer weep, speak in tongues, faint, clap, tremble, prophesy, and heal.

MARIACHI GENESIS: *CONJUNTO* SPIRITUALITY

The ensemble rhythms of *conjunto* music characterize not only a Chicano VO/AV sound but also an attitude inclined to experimentation with fresh existential forms—this is what I call religious poetics. The cultural organization found at VO/AV is an organic practice, a *nepantla*/borderlands "cultural coalescence," central to the *mexicano* experience.

Take, for example, the family of born-again trumpet players called Mariachi Genesis. When they play in the church, their music is combined with the drums, accordion, tambourines, guitars, and the sounds of the people singing, laughing, crying, dancing, and manifesting love—a *conjunto* chorus. Often band members wear the tight-fitting red-and-black slacks and coats with gold trim and big sombreros that define mariachi style. They have a good number of songs in their repertoire, all of which, in classic mariachi fashion, are based on lead trumpets, but with lyrics expressing evangelical theology. Occasionally they will perform traditional Mexican songs that have no explicit religious message but convey instead a strong spiritual yearning for Mexico—a melancholic mood or feeling acquired during the long and difficult years spent in exile. One of Mariachi Genesis's most popular songs is entitled "Mexico para Cristo" (Mexico for Christ). The chorus declares: "I love my Mexico; I love the Lord; I love my race with all of my heart; I'm not ashamed of the gospel, because it is power and salvation." At AV, this song draws passionate applause and vocal responses.

This willingness to address the needs of the people by appealing to cultural narratives provides a key piece to the complex puzzle of VO/AV success.[45] Mariachi Genesis is but one product of this cultural strategy that throws mysticism in the mix with pragmatism and arranges it around Mexican symbolism to produce a new cultural matrix that can sustain what at one time might have been a cultural oxymoron: *evangélico* mariachis, a borderland religion. Pastor Chuy explains that the church needs to become "culturally relevant" for a ministry aimed, at least initially, at the gang culture of East Los Angeles. To achieve cultural relevance involves rehabilitation—one of Pentecostalisms main narratives. AV in East Los Angeles sponsors four drug-rehabilitation homes, one located directly across the street from the church and the others nearby. Three of the four shelters house men, and one is exclusively for women. On average, the "rehabs" enroll fifteen people each, although turnover rates are high and most of the members do not withstand the nine-month duration of the program. In fact, the church's rehabilitation center directly across the street from the church was until recently a "transitional" space, where rules were lax and most men had individual jobs outside the home. It soon reverted to a home for men in the initial stages of drug rehabilitation.

The men in the homes, or *casas,* are not allowed to leave without supervision. They sleep on bunk beds in crowded rooms. Throughout the day they busy themselves with chores, prayers, worship, evangelization, common meals, and fellowship. Since the homes are self-supporting, the men and women are hired out by the home's director as laborers to do menial odd jobs. Very early on, VO accepted a government grant, which, however, they eventually refused because, in the words of one home director, the home became more of a "business" than a ministry. They live on faith, says "Brother Saul," the current director. Saul does what he can to make money to run the home, including hiring "the guys" out for various jobs. "I'm not like the other home directors worrying about where the next rent will come from. Like this month rent is due in two weeks and I'm 160 short but I'm just trusting the Lord." He had to cut our conversation off to deal with defective plumbing in the first-floor bathroom.[46]

Another home director, "Kiko," who appeared to be much older than his eighteen years, recounted to me his daily tasks dealing with gang members. "I get in their face and tell them who we are and what we are about; they respect us." Recently, he nearly evicted someone for speaking badly about him; this tough young warrior was reduced to tears by vicious gossip.[47]

Alcance Victoria has experienced marked growth in the two years that Pastor Chuy has been at the helm. Chuy himself attended Alcance Victoria as a member before Pastor Lolo brought him into the ministry full-time. Pastor Lolo made Chuy—at the time still "Jesse Garcia"—a much-coveted offer to work as an assistant for six dollars an hour. At the time, however, Garcia was working for a Los Angeles high school earning twelve dollars an hour, and the school was paying for him to pursue a bachelor's degree in business administration. Hence, Garcia told Pastor

Lolo that he would "pray about it." He recalls his conversion and the critical moment when he made the decision for full-time ministry. He calls it his "road to Damascus" experience.

> When my brother first started coming here to this church, I thought it was good for him because it changed him. Then he started preaching to me. But, I wasn't in any trouble, everything was going fine for me, I didn't need church. But deep inside of me something was missing. I was getting good grades but in my heart I was wondering what was the purpose of this life. Why are we here? I use to lie awake at night meditating about this. It was the Lord speaking to me. So I accepted Jesus into my life. . . . I began to feel a burden for the full-time ministry. I didn't want to, I thought God had blessed me with my job and school, and I knew that God was not an Indian giver [sic]. But shortly after that, I was witnessing to a sister and her husband at her home, and when I left the sister gave me the *pentecostal* [hand] *shake*. She slipped a bill into my hand while shaking it. Usually this is about ten or twenty dollars. But, later, driving in my car, I took out the bill, thinking it might be enough to get some tacos or a hamburger, and it was actually four twenty-dollar bills all folded up! I began to cry in my car. I cried and knew at that point that God would take care of me in ministry. It was the Holy Spirit who spoke to me.[48]

When Garcia was tapped for the Alcance Victoria pastorship in 1995, he was newly married and was planning on "launching" a Victory Outreach church in Brazil. He claims, however, that God had other plans for him.

Pastor Chuy's "road to Damascus" experience has proved a harbinger of the "blessings" he was destined to receive in ministry. In 1995 a member of the church arranged for him to buy a new condominium in Monterey Park Hills. At the Father's Day morning service in 1995, much to Pastor Chuy's surprise, the congregation ceremoniously handed him a check that he was instructed to use as a down payment on a new car. Later that day at the drug rehabilitation home property in El Sereno, an energetic Pastor Chuy was busily walking around giving orders, supervising the making of the *carne asada* (roasted meat), greeting people, choosing the tapes that were being played on the huge boom box, and counseling members. There were to be Christian baptisms in the aboveground pool that sits on the property. He sat briefly to chat with me. "We baptize before we eat," Figueroa explained, "or else everyone will leave before the baptisms." He is a *güerito,* or a light-skinned Latino. He stands about five feet, ten inches tall and wears a thick mustache. For this occasion he was wearing long athletic shorts, basketball shoes, and an oversized T-shirt with a picture of the Tasmanian Devil that read "Houston Rockets." He had recently returned from supervising the opening of a church in Houston.

"I'm the youngest pastor here in Victory Outreach," he told me. His biggest challenge, he explained, was getting the older men to respect him, and so he tries to look older. The sacred value of respect, or *la dignidad*, has not faded away with Catholicism; nor have the other defining *mexicano* traits. What happens instead is that the local *evangélico* congregation opens a social space where people negotiate and rework their identities, not by retreating from reality but by directly confronting and engaging realistic conditions. This they do by spinning understandings of time and place, together with self and society, into webs of religious meaning systems. What follows attempts to unravel the Alcance Victoria web to tell the stories of the individual lives that together constitute what I call the "congregational narrative."

LAZARUS ARISEN: VOICES FROM BEYOND THE GRAVE

One Victory Outreach preacher has called the movement's membership the "Lazarus Generation," a designation meant as an allegory for those who have been raised, metaphorically, from the dead—like Lazarus in the Christian scriptures. According to *evangélico* theology, all are born into sin and sinful nature and all must experience rebirth; the time prior to rebirth is their "death" period. "Spiritual death" refers especially to gang members, drug addicts, prostitutes, and the like—who were "dead in sin," in VO/AV language. Inasmuch as *evangélicos* preach a necessary period of "death" or darkness—*tinieblas*—a natural state of the living that precedes new life, they echo a tradition that has circulated in borderlands discourse for centuries, at least. There are several socioeconomic classes represented in the VO/AV East L.A. congregation: everything from former gang-bangers to immigrant and Chicano managerial, artisan, and professional classes. Emergent, too, is the generation of Chicanas and Chicanos raised in *evangélico* churches.[49]

But even those raised in *evangélico* churches can mark their date of first spiritual conversion, becoming "born again." The stories of *evangélicos* include more than one single conversion. Rather, each narrative involves periods of lapse, or "backsliding," and periods of return—with a stronger, renewed, spiritual resolve. Some don't return at all, and some don't "backslide" completely, but everyone in the congregation can narrate their spiritual state by periods of temporary "lapse,"

when the issue of one's salvation was in question—a period, even mo-
mentary, of "spiritual death." This narrative trope of journey and return,
so familiar to the borderlands, provides the emotional binds for the various constituencies of the church.

AV welcomes newly arrived Mexican immigrants and their young
families, in addition to widows and widowers, divorcees, and young single men and women, some of whom are college and high-school students. Many of the young congregates have never been on drugs and
have other motivations for joining this rescue ministry. The wondrous
world of VO/AV is fashioned to address many different needs. Through
this research, I have identified several different life situations of individuals who attend the VO/AV. The AV congregation is a bridge between
various class, generation, and linguistic groups among Mexicans and
Mexican-Americans themselves in Los Angeles.

The former drug addicts, gang members, and prostitutes are in many
respects the cornerstone of the congregation, for they are the foot soldiers that march and fight most loyally in the Victory Outreach army.
Collectively, this "Lazarus Generation" has done more to shape the congregational narrative than any other VO/AV group; they act as ushers,
deacons, musicians, rehabilitation-home leaders, and church administrators. More than any other, this group has stressed the wonder of "the
change." Twenty-seven-year-old "Manny Martinez," a former gang
member who works as an usher in the church, spoke for them:

> The change, the change is the most important thing. I was a drug addict be-
> fore [I came here]. I went to jail and everything, but now God has changed
> my life. Twenty-five years ago Pastor Sonny [Arguinzoni] got the burden,
> and that's why he opened the first church. So when people come here they
> can see with their own eyes, people can see the results. People are always
> happy here! It's knowing God. It's knowing who he really is. I know God is
> love, peace, happiness; God is like air—you don't see it, but you feel it.[50]

"The change" enables former gang members to take control of their lives
and to imagine and live in a coherent world.

As Martinez notes, there is a sensual, corporeal quality to Alcance
Victoria worship. It is experienced as electric charges and ecstatic trancelike states that assure the believer that God is real and that he or she has
directly tapped the infinite power of God. Martinez also notes the centrality of Arguinzoni to the Victory Outreach cosmogony. Arguinzoni is
the living embodiment of the power of God, of the capacity for the quick
change, of divine election and material success. Arguinzoni lives in a

large house in a fashionable Los Angeles suburb, drives a new 5-Series BMW, and travels extensively. In his rise from gang membership and drug addiction on the streets of Brooklyn to successful religious entrepreneurship, Sonny Arguinzoni is a walking and preaching symbol of the American success story—from rags to riches.

The Victory Outreach empire was built by preaching that other men can do the same: become "born again," marry a "nice girl," pastor a church, and make your way up the "corporation." The wonder for the Lazarus Generation is delimited by the renewal and progress: symbolic, spiritual, and material. All involved in the leadership of Victory Outreach will vehemently insist that the motivation to pastor a church is entirely spiritual. Nonetheless, they will in the same breath concede the draw of financial independence and (lower-)middle-class respectability. "I'd like to have a nice home in the suburbs, a nice wife, a family"; this is their (Mexican-)American dream. Single men arrive at the church looking for "nice girls" who seem to come as part of the conversion package. VO/AV encourages men to realize their individual calling as pastors and to open their own churches. This is the path taken by hundreds of men in the organization. Certainly Manny is following this path. Less than a year before our interview he married a young woman he had met in the church; he had been active in the church leadership and was planning eventually to pastor his own church. Meanwhile, like the majority of the Chicanos in the congregation, he worked seasonally in construction.

Kiko, the former director of the men's transition home, was actively working in the Alcance Victoria offices, running errands for Pastor Chuy. He explained that he did not receive a regular salary for this work but that the pastor "blesses" him often. This means that the pastor will spontaneously hand Kiko some cash. The pastor of each church controls the financial resources. While becoming a pastor is the most common goal, it is not the sole upward path open to VO/AV men. Kiko plays keyboards in the church and would like eventually to earn a living as an evangelist and marry a woman from Alcance Victoria.

Women, too, have entrepreneurial opportunities. Certainly, when a woman and man open a church together, each one is responsible for the leadership of the church, even if the male is the primary figurehead. Many of the women in the congregation have also gone through the rehabilitation programs, and their stories typically involve children. One such woman, "Magdalena," had been in the United States for four years at the time of our interview; an active member of VO/AV for three of those years, she is now forty-two years old and a director of an AV women's home. Her change, as in the case of others who eventually darken the doorstep of VO/AV, took place at a dramatic low point in her life, when she was put into a mental hospital. "I was going crazy," she recounts. "I was looking for answers, but only Jesus is the answer."[51] The answer to Magdalena's existential crisis came first in the form of witchcraft *(hechicería)* and lesbianism, which she now attributes to her witchcraft practices—all while she was a confirmed Catholic living in Mexico City. Her physical change occurred while she was confined to a bed in a mental hospital. It was Magdalena's sister who preached the evangelical gospel to her, as refracted through the AV prism. She freely employs military metaphors in explaining that only God can help to "fight that battle" with temptation, the enemy. She leads six other women who live in the home. One is a former gang member, a twenty-two-year-old Chicana who has a baby. Four others are Mexican immigrants who have nowhere else to go. A pregnant woman from Guatemala also lives there with her first child, a toddler; she came to the United States to earn money to support her husband back home.

Magdalena claimed that the mission of the home is to restore women's "dignity" and to teach them to be "blessings in their homes and with their children." Some women have had their children taken away from them by the county, she lamented. Therefore, the home helps to rehabilitate these women and to have their children returned to them. In these efforts, the women are hired out to help support the basic needs of the home.

That women are to help their husbands is the teaching expressed by the cofounder of VO, Julie Arguinzoni. In "Preparing Women for the Vision 2000," a sermon recorded on 25 June 1996 at a Victory Outreach women's retreat, Julie Arguinzoni defined women's roles in ministry, explaining that women regularly approached her to declare their desire for ministry. In response, she tells them that they don't really know what they want, because to be a woman in ministry "you must suffer." She explains that, yes, being in ministry will mean dressing "real pretty" and "sitting in the front of the church." Additionally, however, women must be prepared to do "whatever it takes" to help the ministry grow. But, overall, they must "love the Lord." When Julie Arguinzoni referred to women in ministry, she meant women who were married to a pastor.

I asked young VO women and men what they imagine themselves doing in five or ten years. Magdalena expressed a desire to return to Mexico City to work with the children of the streets there. "This country [the United States] is blessed; this God will bless us [Mexicans too], not with money but with faith in God." Magdalena said she knew of Mexican mothers who, in a twist on the myth of La Llorona, had killed their children because they could not afford to feed them. She believed that her work in the Alcance Victoria rehabilitation center was "preparation" for the work she felt called to do in Mexico City.

When this same question about life ten years hence was posed to the former gang members, most men seemed puzzled and had to meditate solemnly before responding. One twenty-nine-year-old Chicano spoke to me in Spanish; he had been in the home for eight weeks and just wanted to make it in the home for three months without "messing up" by injecting heroin into his body. If he could make it for that long, he was almost certain that he could go the full nine months. Ultimately, he said, he would like to be married with a family and "have a regular life." I asked him if he would like to work in the ministry, and like all the others in the Lazarus category, he said he definitely would. At the moment, however, his energies were focused on overcoming a five-balloon-daily heroin habit. He could not think much farther than tomorrow or the next week.

I also interviewed the pastor of an English-language VO church in Boyle Heights, "Pastor Felix," and his wife, "Lola Felix." Their church is comprised almost entirely of former gang members, and Pastor Felix was himself once a violent gang member. He stressed the "inner-city" nature of Victory Outreach, explaining their mission to reach the "hurting" people of the inner city. "We take church to the different neighborhoods," identifying them by gang affiliation. "There is a lot of hurt in the city, and we are able to come and to be effective because we come from that lifestyle ourselves." I asked Lola and Pastor Felix how effective socioeconomic help could be to improving conditions around the neighborhood. Lola nodded her head in response, saying, "That is what this community needs." Pastor Felix disagreed, lamenting: "That would help for a little while, but eventually the gang members are going to keep coming back; back to their roots, back to the neighborhoods, back to the drugs, back to violence."[52]

BORN AGAIN, AND AGAIN

The "First Second Generation" (FSG) is the first cohort of Chicanos to be born second-generation VO/AV: they have Pentecostal parents, but they did not convert from Catholicism as did the rest of the church. These people's lives have followed two distinct patterns. Some in the FSG were involved in drugs and gang warfare; others were not. Of those who were not, many are pursuing an education and have ambitious career goals, but they too narrate their lives in tropes of rebirth.

"Lulu," a thirty-year-old homemaker, volunteered several hours each week in the business office of Alcance Victoria. Born in Mexico, she came to the United States as a young girl and dropped out of school when she was fourteen to help at home with her family. Although her parents are Pentecostal, she marks her own "conversion" at age fifteen. While Sister Lulu was not involved in gangs, she explained that she had been "looking for love" and found it in Jesus and the "love of God" located in the Alcance Victoria congregation:

> All my friends were either killed or overdosed on drugs. If it wasn't for Jesus, I wouldn't be here right now! Fourteen of my friends from school have died! But my family was different: we were the only Pentecostals on our block, and we are the only ones left. The most important thing he [God] has done for me is the change, that love he gave to me. If I didn't have love I couldn't be going out to another person, a stranger, and telling them about God.[53]

Another FSG man, "Noé," had similar responses. At the time of our interview, Noé was twenty-one years old. He was born in Guadalajara, Mexico, and has been in the United States since age five. He plays the trumpet in the church with his brothers and is part of Mariachi Genesis. Never involved in gangs or drugs, he graduated from high school and attended East Los Angeles City College for one semester; Then he worked delivering phone books around East Los Angeles until he was injured on the job in a car accident. At the time of our interview, he was settling this claim and looking for a job while living with his parents. His narrative typifies many of the FSG in faith crisis resolved in an epiphany, resulting in a renewed and deeper commitment to the church. He explains, "I never really experienced the streets. But at one point a few years ago I just got real cold in the Lord. I was addicted to sports. That's all I wanted to do—watch sports on TV, play basketball, and read about sports. If you would ask me anything about sports I would know. I put that first before God. Sports is [sic] not a sin, but it shouldn't be your number one priority. For a Christian the number one priority is God. I realize that now."[54]

I interviewed a group of eight second-generation Americans, four women and four men, ranging in ages from fifteen to twenty.[55] Seven of the eight had "rebelled" briefly, experimenting with the "things of this world," before returning to the church with a deeper commitment. All participants in the interview were committed to their education, whether in high school heading to college, or in a local state or community college. All in this group were single and childless. One sixteen-year-old woman in the group had a straight-A record in her college preparatory courses, and because of this she had assumed the identity, bestowed by her peers, as someone heading for Harvard. "I'm going to apply there," she told me when I asked if she was indeed Harvard-bound. "We'll see what happens." Most in the group were introduced to the church through their parents, or they were invited by a family member or friends close to their own age. Interestingly, many of their parents had ceased regular church attendance themselves.

The men dominated the conversation, but the women expressed non-verbally their dissatisfaction with the men's manipulation of the interview. Three of the men took the opportunity to relate long, detailed narratives about their lives, while the women were very aware of the project as a group effort and kept their responses short. One twenty-year-old man, Cyrus, lead the group. Cyrus is currently president of the student body at his California State University campus. He is torn between pursuing a career in public service or in church ministry. At the time of our interview he was working in the offices of his local state assemblyman, who is also Mexican-American.

Two of the women explained that they had been attending another Protestant church, but that the other church did not have the active youth programs they found in Alcance Victoria. The meaningful participation of the youth in the life of the congregation was the attraction for these women. Another woman had been attending an all-white Protestant church in Burbank, where she did not feel entirely at home. At Alcance Victoria, the music combined with the general enthusiasm put her at ease, reminding her of the church she had attended with her parents as a child, whereas in the Anglo church she felt isolated by the cold formality. Most members in this group were connected to each other through bonds of kinship, or in the case of the men, by "homeboy" bonds. They invited one another. One of the men, Ramón, spoke of the inspiration he found in church:

> The thing that keeps me motivated in coming to church is that whenever I'm feeling down, or whenever I need help with whatever part of my life, with anything at school or here at church, my social life or my family . . . I can bend my knees and just look up to heaven and ask God for that extra help and that extra push that I need in my life, and that just keeps me motivated and keeps me going on. So I thank God for that.

Another twenty-year-old man, Eddie, echoed Ramón's testimony, claiming that the key to understanding God and having a rewarding life is obedience to church doctrine. He contended that God must be the priority in one's life and all other goals will follow. His aphorism was greeted with cheerful agreement: "If you just listen to his word and everything, make God first, everything will go all right."

The youngest woman, Flora, fifteen years old, said that she liked Alcance Victoria because all her cousins attended and there were many teenagers in the congregation. Another young woman, Gabby, claimed that she had come to Alcance Victoria because her cousins were there, and she found what she "needed" in Alcance Victoria. Like the others, she broke into a rehearsed testimony: "That emptiness. I don't have it anymore. I don't need anything because here I found what I needed. I know that God will supply the things that I need. Because he is there for us, to do for us."

I asked them to compare themselves to their parents. The women said that they differed from their mothers because their mothers are "traditional" homemakers. The men said that they differed from their fathers because their fathers worked in factories. All agreed that the critical difference was that they now had the opportunity for education that was denied their parents. The opportunity "to have a better life," Cyrus and others explained. They recognized that their parents' lives were much harder than their own. When asked what they imagined themselves doing in ten years, none identified the ministry as an option except for Cyrus, who was still considering it. All said they wanted to finish their education. One wanted to become a sociologist, another wanted to become a doctor, another a teacher, another a child psychologist, and another a police officer. All claimed that they wanted, "of course," to be doing "big things for God" and to have families.

All members of this group identified themselves as Chicano or Chicana. However, they were ambivalent about political issues. All hesitated to express favor for either the Democratic or Republican parties but claimed instead to vote on particular issues and identified themselves as nonpartisan. Many of the members of the church did not maintain strong ties to any political party or to Catholicism before conversion; they simply started attending AV because they were energetically pursued. The people in this category were not battling drug problems, involved with gangs, old and alone, or recent immigrants without established ties in the community. "I came to Alcance Victoria because they invited me."[56]

Most of the "lapsed Catholics" came to Alcance Victoria because they enjoyed the company of others, the feeling of belonging, the music, the message of security and control over life. In the congregation they found emotional fulfillment, friendship, and intimacy. For immigrants and Mexican-Americans who found themselves on the margins of society, the congregation functions as a mechanism of cultural brokerage. Symbolically and physically excluded from so many other centers in Los Angeles, in Alcance Victoria they encountered a vibrant fellowship where they remake self, community, and the nation.

In an utterly pragmatic and pithy explanation, perhaps Pastor Chuy said it best: "Alcance Victoria is successful because we are meeting the needs of the people!"

(MEXICAN-)AMERICAN DREAMING: *EVANGÉLICO* RELIGIOUS PERFORMANCE

The seeming rigidity of fundamentalist *evangélico* ethics allures (post)moderns of all classes who find themselves lost in a world of moral relativism and confusion: *los evangélicos* give simple and plausible answers to profound existential questions. This rigidity appeals also to immigrants who are suffering the anomie and trauma of displacement, and perhaps suffering from the ravages of war in their home countries, and to the young women and men who suffer the ravages of poverty and gang warfare in inner cities across America. *Evangélicos* appear to offer entry into the lower North American middle class: Protestant cultural drama is mimed, that is, performed mimetically, without essence.

Mexican-American *evangélicos* wear suits and ties on Sundays, carry Bibles, and speak the dominant religious language of the country, performing its hegemonic religious codes. In mimesis, however, there is always appropriation and subversion: Chicano *evangélicos* appropriate Protestantism, inflect it and mirror it back, changing the Protestant symbolic language of North America, figuring it with distinctively Mexican-American grammars. The emergence of a Chicana/o and Latina/o middle class, of whatever religion, affects the dominant culture by creating an identifiable consumer market that demands public representation.

VO/AV is known throughout California for its elaborate stage plays that dramatize the Chicano gang lifestyle and end with the protagonist's conversion to born-again Christianity through the efforts of Victory Outreach evangelism. These plays are in English, and they portray a distinctively Chicano, that is, Mexican-American, experience, rather than an immigrant one. They are performed at churches, schools, and other meeting halls. The Spanish churches have produced their own play, *Sueño americano* (American dream). This play represents the experience of one Mexican immigrant family in Los Angeles, whose "American dream" is for the children to have a better life in the United States. Written and produced by an Alcance Victoria congregation, the play is a native, organic dramatization of the Alcance Victoria congregational narrative. The theme song is called "Just a Dream," the chorus of which expresses in lyrical melody the message of the play: "Just a dream, just a dream, all our hopes and all our schemes." That is, the social aspirations of immigrants into the United States are without essence, "just a dream," nothing else.

The story of the play goes as follows: A Mexican family preparing to embark upon a journey to the United States is visited at home by a *compadre* recently returned from there. The *compadre* urges the family to stay in Mexico, where, he says, education is available and kids can have a good career. Things up north are very hard, he cautions. There is no work and people fall into despair. He had been so desperate that he began drinking and became an alcoholic. He even began using drugs, until someone from AV preached to him; then he converted and found "true happiness." The father of the family responds that, despite how ill-disposed he is toward Los Angeles, there is literally nothing for him in his own country and the only hope he has is to emigrate to the United States; he has faith in the saints and especially in La Virgen de Guadalupe: his children will be well and everything will work out fine. He says that his great "American dream" is for his daughter to become a doctor, for his son to become a lawyer, and for his younger son to become a police officer. The *compadre* then tells the father that only the Bible has the answers, and as he begins preaching in this way he gets ejected from the family's home, the father pointedly calling him crazy.

Before the evangelist leaves, he exhorts the father to remember, in times of trouble, that Christ loves him and (pounding again on his huge Bible for emphasis) that Christ is the answer to all his problems. The rest of the story is predictable. Life in the United States results in the father's becoming an alcoholic and the children's ending up in gangs. The family converts to *los evangélicos,* and the final scene becomes an altar call as the actors break character to invite the audience to the stage to receive prayer. Evangelical salvation is presented as a panacea, an antidote to social ills. Through conversion, one can become changed and rechannel one's frustrated energies into constructive pursuits with modern, Protestant measures. In his essay on VO, Richard Rodriguez characterizes this change: "To immigrants who came to the American city expecting new beginnings, and who found instead the city corrupt, the evangelical missionary offers the possibility of refreshment, of cleansing. To the children of immigrants, trapped by inherited failures, the evangelical offers the assurance of power over life. The promise of the quick change."[57] The metanoia is key to the experience of *los evangélicos;* it is the initiatory event that signifies membership in the wondrous world of Alcance Victoria. As Ramón indicated, "If you just listen to his word and everything, make God first, everything will go all right." Some members look to God not as an antidote for failed social dreams and to the congregation not as a way to redirect failed ambitions; rather, they see them as vehicles for fulfilling their dreams—dreams that remain unimaginable, undreamable, to many of their Chicana and Chicano peers.

CONCLUSION: CONVERSION AS SOCIAL PROCESS: PENTECOSTAL ETERNAL RETURNS

In November 1994, nearly ninety years after the *Los Angeles Times* first ran the series on the Azusa Street Revival, the paper printed a long feature on Victory Outreach's work in Los Angeles. The article, entitled "Body and Soul," describes the wondrous world of Victory Outreach, including several stories of the members, focusing on the triumphs and tragedies of these often hapless individuals who oscillate between the pull of drugs and the refuge for their bodies and souls they find in Victory Outreach.[58] Color photographs accompanying the story depict passionate men locked in each other's arms or staring at each other while holding one another, their faces only inches apart. The image in which one man is holding a Bible is meant to represent an evangelistic moment on the street in the barrio. The next photograph reveals the two men locked in an affectionate embrace, while one holds a large Bible. Alcance Victoria performance reifies and essentializes masculinity at the same time that it subverts and challenges those strictly defined male roles of stoicism and aloofness. This is the macho paradox: passion and stoicism.

The emphasis on the social body, captured in the phrase "Take the city for Jesus," mandates that men in Alcance Victoria unite the individual body and the collective body in their concern for the city; that is, the city as built and bounded social unit, and the city as the collectivity. Even for those who were not involved in gangs or drugs, the mythological and ritual modes of the system require that they become instated in the economies of men's individual and social bodies: in Victory Outreach, their bodies belong to one another, creating an ecology of religion, commitment, and devotion, where the boundaries between erotic and philanthropic emotions are fluid and shifting. Alcance Victoria men warmly embrace one another when greeting or parting, and they sustain warm embraces when praying for one another. Many take every opportunity to lay hands on each other.

During worship they speak in tongues, dancing, crying, and shouting in rapture. They express emotion and experience their own and each other's bodies in emotional and tactile ways. Manny Martinez identified this body contact and consequent troubling of traditional male gender norms as one of the key attractions of the congregation. He said, "A guy can hug another guy here and, you know, it's different, it's not like people will make fun of you. Like this morning you saw the preacher, he just started crying up on the pulpit because he felt a burden. It is okay to do that here." *Evangélicos* too recast and replay the male devotional formation that I call El Lloron.[59]

In traditional modes of masculinity the body is a marker of power and strength, but otherwise men are alienated from its sensual, emotional aspects. In Alcance Victoria, the experience of the body is central to worship and to the construction of a social body that coheres with other male bodies; men's bodies are ritually, emotionally, spiritually, and physically connected to one another—especially in the performance of tongues speech and the atmosphere that that act engenders, an atmosphere that can be seen as a kind of "antistructure." Thus, women and men of VO/AV establish a corporate body from which base they experience the city in a new and empowering light, reassured that they are not alone but are part of a collective body that is part of God. "For all of their obvious differences from Catholicism," writes Rodriguez, "I sense among [Chicano] evangelicals a longing for some lost Catholic village, some relief from loneliness. Perhaps this is inherent in Protestantism; the reason why Protestants enjoy such intensely communal worship. . . . In the small evangelical church, people who are demoralized by the city turn to the assurance of community. . . . Hymns resound over the city, wild with grace, and the world becomes certain and small."[60]

Pentecostal conversion is, in a sense, a social process—a transitional passage, from one life state to the next, that is marked by crisis, separation, and modified reintegration. Separation is the liminal phase, or the *communitas,* in which the social structure of life is rejected and a time of freedom reigns. It is in the *communitas* that men have the freedom to experience their own and each other's bodies with freedom, in poetic religious performance. In the practice of ecstatic worship, men participate in the *communitas* anew. Victory Outreach men agree: they are rejuvenated in charismatic ceremony by a fresh experience of God and one another. The charisma in worship allows men to become separated from self and to become freshly yoked to one another. During the expansive social space of *communitas,* of charismatic worship, the men give themselves to the passion of the moment, to God, and to one another in an unstructured ceremony of union and renewal. As literal interpreters of the Bible, Pentecostals take as a model for gender relations the Pauline teachings regarding women, men, and sexuality, but even here too power and subjection are dialectical and spiritual priorities that often trump too literal a reading of the scriptures.[61]

However, as the leadership of Victory Outreach and others attest, there is an elite class emerging in *los evangélicos* that is removed from the problems and quotidian politics of everyday workers. Sonny Arguinzoni has written that the VO ministry must always come before spending energies on social-justice "causes." "It is not our job to propose legislation resolving immigration conflicts," writes Arguinzoni. "The enemy has a way of diverting us, getting us involved in so many things that we are unable to accomplish anything. James Chapter 1:8 tells us that the life of a man with divided loyalty will reveal instability in every turn. You simply ask, 'What will this program do to help fulfill our vision?'"[62] *Evangélicos* are not offering the community new ways to address old issues but new ways to address what I call "new wars": the terror of the postmodern age.

Many in the congregation are undocumented workers—in effect, living a lie. Pastor Chuy overlooks this fact, as do the others, and will agree to requests that he pray for the successful illegal border crossings of his congregants and their families. He explains that this issue is a matter of personal conscience. In this regard, as in many others, Alcance Victorians exhibit a tolerance for ambiguity and contradictions. If VO/AV is motivated by "growth" and "corporate" concerns and uses popular culture, perhaps even rendering it "sacred," then basic "theological" tenets too are subject to the "popular" will that drives cultural fashion, and I suspect that teachings on subjects such as (homo)sexualities and other controversial issues will likewise begin reflecting mainstream tolerant attitudes. Borderlands movements are in continuous formation.

By way of conclusion, I want to stress borderlands movements, and other ideologies constituting VO, as captured and summarized in the

Victory Outreach Mission Statement: "Since we pattern ourselves after *Acts 1:8* we move geographically and ethnically through these steps. Our aim is to cross all cultural, language, and geographical barriers to reach hurting people from all cities. . . . Drug addiction affects every race, color, and creed with a vengeance. Those who are heavily involved with it live within their own distinct culture."[63] Victory Outreach defines itself in movements—border crossings. In addition, recidivism and the social process of conversion and ecstatic worship bind members together in ritual and mythical ties of body, space, and time. *Evangélico* conversion too involves a ritual of eternal returns.

VO/AV does not ask believers to eschew their ethnic heritage—it is a borderlands phenomenon, one that combines Mexican, American, and Christian archetypes, mythologies, religious practices, and complex spirituality into a fresh identity, one that can produce and support *evangélico* mariachis. VO/AV respects and affirms *mexicano* roots, but it especially celebrates *el Chicano,* not as an aberration but as another *mestizaje.* That is, rather than understanding *evangélico* conversion as a *malinche* narrative of treason and cultural abandon, *los evangélicos* understand themselves as continuing the essence of *lo mexicano* (food, language, calendar, song, place), and also availing themselves of Protestant cultural symbols of faith and material success. *Mestizaje* is not only a condition, a state of being, but an ongoing dialectical process of opposites that move and synthesize with each other. This movement of religious innovation has come to characterize spirituality and cultural expression in the borderlands—perhaps a *rasquache* spirituality.

These religious elements, which we have isolated and examined as parts of a whole, in aggregate characterize borderland religions. It is to this conclusion that we now turn.

Fin de Siglo
in the Borderlands

So Far from God, So Close to the United States

Nothing is so close to man as his biological being. So near, and at the same time, so universal.

Alfredo Austin López, *The Human Body and Ideology: Concepts of the Ancient Nahuas,* trans. Thelma Ortiz de Montellano and Bernard Ortiz de Montellano

People are free to feel as they choose, but rarely do they respond to the call of that freedom.

Tomás Eloy Martínez, *Santa Evita*

What are the limits of the sacred in contexts of extreme deprivation? In Mexico and in Latin America, the universe of myths, rituals, centres of worship, of socially uncontrolled emotions and annual pilgrimages to the most inconceivable of sacred places, of marvelous tales, charismatic heroes and stories of saints whose names are not even included in the calendar of days, are all reproduced as dense cultural formations.

Carlos Monsiváis, *Mexican Postcards,* trans. John Kraniauskas

The reality of human suffering—of extreme deprivation—begs the limits of the sacred. But so too do the limits of pleasure or ecstasy. As Monsiváis notes, at its limits or boundaries the sacred is extended into, crosses into, Latina/o culture. At the border, the limit, separating the sacred realms of pleasure, joy, and ecstasy and the profane realm of suffering and pain, the sacred is recoded, idiomatically, idiosyncratically, and poetically, and densely (re)emerges in cultural practice so that misery and agony too become sacred. But what modern idioms classify "the sacred" as a category for study and knowledge? How do we understand the sacred as believers themselves do, as a *reality?* How does one translate religious experience? Is linguistic reduction the modern answer to ineffability? How can religion in the borderlands be captured, contained, and reiterated in the idioms acceptable to a post-Enlightenment academy?

In Monsiváis's "dense cultural formations," religion and culture are dissociable from one another. Therefore, in contrast to Geertz, rather than religion acting singularly as a cultural system, culture too is deployed as a religious system. But religion and culture are woven together into complex patterns of power, submission, change, and return in constant movements. To isolate a particular area—culture, for example, as distinct from religion and politics—treats human ideas and relationships as unidimensional, rather than as complex and uneven and tied to multiple realities that are fluid and evolve. But neither does continuing progress fully describe the charter of the human world, as historians would have it, for advance is tempered by the inevitable retreat.

The borderlands—that interstitial place straddling U.S. and Mexican ideals, existing at the crossroads of what Homi Bhabha calls the "normative" and the "performative"[1]—constitutes a distinct area of spiritual and political formation that has occasioned a religious narrative marked by ancient Mexican philosophy and all that has come since. For many of the Nahuas, truth was illusive, fleeting, and found in beauty, song, poetry—religious poetics, a Latino ethics of beauty.[2] This book has attempted to show the poetic impulse in religious practice, an enduring spirit or consciousness, Foucault's soul and more, formed through space, time, and the body. Concluding here is akin to unlayering, unpeeling, and erasing the layers of inscriptions coding the "Aztec palimpsest," while simultaneously adding a new interpretive layer.

THE CROSS: MAKING A NEW *MESTIZAJE*

Mexican President Porfirio Díaz once lamented the geopolitical position of Mexico, opining, "How unfortunate is Mexico, so far from God, so close to the United States." Díaz's remark observed the spatial fact that binds the two countries' histories and destinies: Mexico is inextricably tied to the United States, and vice versa. Mexicans and Chicanos in Los Angeles exist within the possibility of a relatively short drive to Mexico. And while ethnicity theorists have unwittingly forced Mexicans under the rubric of European immigration models, no other immigrant group in the United States, except perhaps for Canadians, is as spatially connected with their homeland as are Mexican-Americans to Mexico. This spatial relation is instructive in guiding analysis of religion in the borderlands. Religion in Chicano communities is a continuation and radical modification of religion in Mexico, and religion in Mexico is inevitably affected by religious developments north of the border: the transnational movements of people back and forth across the border necessarily result in the two mutually influencing one another.

The symbol of the cross is at the base of Mexican-American and religious experience. In Christian mythology, the cross symbolizes the intersection of the human, profane realm with the sacred realm, the meeting of life and death, the reconciliation of sin with grace, humanity with God. In African diasporic religions, Vodou and Santería, the crossroads is the meeting place of the living and the dead. The cross symbolizes action, movement, transformation: the "cross" is a verb. Pilgrims carry and enact the cross from South to North America, from the Third World to the First, from certain poverty to uncertain poverty, from the old to the new, refiguring multiple covenants of grace and hope. The cross bears seemingly infinite meanings but becomes most significant in religious poetics as both symbol and verb. Migrants intersecting the northern border reenact a drama of religious transformation that is centuries old, at least: a life translation. Conversion, new life, transformation, a renewal of spirit are realized in the intersections created by the cross. The initiation of the cross is central to the most recent work of Chicano artist El Vez: the opening to his record *Boxing with God* and to the attendant stage performance, "The Gospel Show," is a song entitled "Oralé," a Chicano idiom for "right on!" The song is recorded to the tune of "Oh Happy Day." The first sounds on the record are of splashes—the sound of immigrants crossing the river and, simultaneously, receiving a religious baptism:

> Oh Oralé oh Oralé / when Jesus walked Oh when he walked Oh when he walked into the USA / into the USA oh Oralé oh Oralé / oh Oralé oh Oralé / When Jesus crossed Oh when he crossed Oh when he crossed into the USA / oh Oralé oh Oralé / He crossed the land to stand be part of the USA / To earn a wage a way to be part of the USA / . . . a new begin family and friends / To share a better working way / Sail on silver girl oh happy day / Sail on by oh happy day / Your time has come to fly / You have no borders / See how they run across freeways / And peace just can't be found. / Like a bridge over troubled borders I will lay me down.[3]

Recalling the multiple transformations the Mexican indigenous continue to give to the cross—such as "our sacred cross, our sacred virgin of whom we eat, our lady of the earth that we sow"[4]—Anzaldúa employs Santería tropes to describe what she calls "*La encrucijada* [The crucified woman]/The Crossroads"—the somatic sacrifice that prefigures change:

> A chicken is being sacrificed
> at a crossroads, a simple mound of earth
> a mud shrine for *Eshu,*
> Yoruba god of indeterminacy,
> who blesses her choice of path.
> She begins her journey.[5]

THE BODY

Control of the body was achieved by the Aztecs, who didn't appear willing to relinquish it to the Spanish. In Aztec ritual, "the decoration, move-

ment and changes of the human body and its most potent parts, including the head, the heart, hair, and blood, constituted a significant portion
of the nexus of ceremonial life."[6] Indeed, Aztec cosmology was constructed to replicate the human body, and ancient Mexican knowledge
of the human body was empirical, extensive, and tied intimately to religious thought. When the Spaniards arrived, Mexican discourse on the
body had to contend with Christian conceptions of the body, rejection
and assimilation of European ideas. This negotiation continues today. In
a sense, these practices contribute to unfocusing the "scientific" gaze on
legitimacy and contributes to Dussel's demythologization of modernity:
"Transmodernity is a new liberation project with multiple dimensions:
political, economic, ecological, erotic, pedagogic, religious."[7] At times, of
course, reliance on ancient healing facilitates tragedy—perhaps narrating suffering in ways that makes it meaningful, sacred, and thus bear-
able. In any case, spiritual command of the body undercuts the medical
industry, elaborating ancient technologies of the body not vouchsafed by
modern institutions and specialists.

Spiritual healing—long a practice in ancient Mesoamerica—was instantiated by Guadalupe, who came to heal the wounds of colonialism
and the bodies of the Indians. Her body was *un poco morenito*, a little
bit dark. Guadalupe was then, as now, a *curandera*. *Curanderismo* has
thrived and become institutionalized in *espiritualismo*. Spiritual healing
and the vocation of charismatic religious healer persist in *evangélico*
practices, as there are evangelists, women and men, whose ministries are
focused on healing; they too are *curanderas* and *curanderos*, healing by
the laying on of hands.

When speaking of the body and epistemology in the history of religions, Lawrence Sullivan argues as follows: "The well constructed
human body, when acting properly, is an effective sign of that [periodic]
cosmos, which is sustained through the periodic rhythms of production,
reproduction, consumption, and exchange. In so many cultures around
the world, knowledge of the body is a religious affair."[8] The body is at
the "center of a political playing field," as Foucault argues,[9] yet access
to it is utterly democratic. Ideology, the limits of personal experience,
and forgetting block access to the body. Religious poetics enables the re-
trieval of the body in a primal, powerful form. In order to practice religious healing, spiritual ecstasy, and physical mortification, for example, practitioners must defy the restrictions of medical science—their
acceptability, even legality, is beyond what is delimited in modern cultural scripts. Everyday religious practices can be understood not as an

escape from modern realities but as old methods of engaging in new struggles.

Chicana altar-installation artist Amalia Mesa-Bains describes her work as continuing Chicana religious practices, invoking physical sites of "spiritual mediation," while "reclaiming with a politicized spirituality." The mostly ethereal and itinerant character of her altars captures the contextual action of religious poetics. Echoing the situational tactics of Michel de Certeau, Mesa-Bains claims that "spiritual acts create protective space." For her, building the home altar is not a completed project—it is one in continuing states of completion. The altar is a "document of family history, connecting mind, spirit, and body with the community and the individual."[10]

Yolanda López, a pioneer of Chicana art, explains her process of creating an enduring and powerful image of Guadalupe, whose body is inhabited by the ancient Nahuatl goddess Coatlicue, entitled *Nuestra Madre,* or Our Mother:

> I came to realize that Guadalupe represents what is sacred about women and, as importantly, I concluded that the Virgin of Guadalupe is an ancient Goddess coated with a thin veneer of Christianity. . . . The final work . . . is my way of connecting our past with our present. It is also an offering to Chicanas and Chicanos to rethink our roles as men and women, and the values we have created for ourselves. And as an artist, I ask you to examine how those values are expressed in the images we make. . . . We are in the process of reinventing ourselves and our history. That is what the Chicano movement is about. Chicano culture is fluid and negotiable. Chicano culture will be brought with us on our way to social, political and economic justice; it is one of the gifts we bear as we travel this very focused path. And it is our job to shape it as we go.[11]

In contrast, volumes of "medical anthropology" have classified sacred poetics as a social malady. In other words, the episteme of "medical anthropology" has placed Mexican religious healing under the categorical gaze of nosology, or medical sciences of classification and terminology, especially psychology. Religious healing practices, *curanderismo* particularly, articulated for centuries using idiosyncratic grammar codes, when translated into the vernacular of Western medicine become a Mexican pathology: an "obsessive behavior," a "placebo" among the "uneducated," "paranoid"; the product of "primitive" masses who struggled to make sense of a modern industrial world. At best, *curanderismo* has been dismissed as a form of half-baked "folk" psychiatry, functioning as a free and accessible panacea to assuage a poor and superstitious population.[12]

These attitudes, scientific mandates, traceable to the emergence of the modern clinic, enabled a new "positivistic" relation to the body. New ways of seeing the body, and new places to see in the body, engendered paradigm shifts in perception and a scientific discourse that regulated speaking about corporeality, illness, and health in idioms circumscribing the limits of acceptable experience and understanding—between sanity and madness. Through an intimate and scientific relation to the body, paradoxically, patients were at once objectified and individualized. That is, the clinic provided the space for the body to be spatialized, mapped, and coded—concomitant to the rise of nosology. Diagnosing individual diseases became possible only in relation to a discursive technology of the body and classification of illness. In the space of the clinic, the relation between the physician (representing science and reason) and the objectified space of the body became intricately woven into an Enlightenment technology of social control and invested with a matrix of larger, indeed universal, meanings. A key part of this process was the classification of the "invisible," or the uncontrollable, as the realm of the unknowable, the nonpositivistic irrational, prohibited knowledge.

With the practice of autopsy, the burden of the Enlightenment was brought to bear on the cadaver via what Foucault calls the "medical gaze." Through the medical gaze, the formerly invisible—those parts of the body hidden from medical perception—become open, accessible spaces where the positive knowledge of science is manifested. This is what Foucault calls "invisible visibility." In this way, the nonmaterial becomes the truly invisible—unknowable and forbidden. "That which is not on the scale of the gaze," writes Foucault, "falls outside the domain of possible knowledge. Hence the rejection of a number of scientific techniques that were nonetheless used by doctors in earlier years."[13] In this technology of the body, religious healing is deemed useless and is summarily rejected, and the measure of individual achievement becomes the degree to which one is able to apply standard, yet changing, scientific codes.

It is out of the space constituted by the gaze, between science and the knowable world, that universal normativity and order are made, deviance defined, and aberration classified and managed. This is the space disrupted by the persistence of religious poetics. Religious poetics provides an alternative mode of knowing based on knowledges of the body, which, if not posing a direct threat to modern forms of knowing, competes with them for authority. Spiritual healing, in particular, challenges modern reliance on empiricism and colonial forms of knowledge.

Isabel Attais notes that an entire gamut of traditional healers thrive in *mexicano* communities: "*espiritistas,* Pentecostals, Catholic charismatics and Marian Trinitarian Spiritualists." These last she describes as "shamans." Pentecostals, she claims, are not shamans because they belong to a "cult of spirit possession," wherein they lose control of the trance state.[14] However, my research demonstrates that (1) Pentecostal theologians do not regard Holy Ghost spirit possession as complete surrender and cite biblical precedence toward this end, and (2) *espiritualistas* claim they work with their cognitive and motor functions under the control of their protector spirit: they retain no memory of the trance state. To do otherwise is known as "working dirty."[15] The similarities are remarkable: in religious healing, a sacred poetics reclaims the space of the body and troubles the configuration of the nation by claiming healing spaces as sites of spiritual power, as sacred places.

SPACE

"Am I not here?" In her apparition, the Virgin of Guadalupe sanctified the profane place of colonization in Mexico; from Tepeyac she symbolically healed the violated womb that birthed *mestizaje.* She furnishes Mexican and Chicano Catholics with a claim to sanctity, election, and place. While in exile in Los Angeles and points beyond, she remakes seemingly foreign, often hostile, space into familiar place. From her throne in Mexico City, she imbues the city with an extra layer of sacrality and memory. The city itself functions as a sacred center of memory, where the past is structured into the built environment of the place. Since its first settlement, Mexico City has served as a veritable canvas on which artists painted their vision of place, nation, and Mexican identity. Throughout all of Mexico City, statuary and ritual centers act as mnemonic devices for triggering mythical memory. These ritual centers include auxiliary shrines to Mexican Virgins and saints who round out the pantheon of Mexican Catholicism.

For Jonathan Smith, articulating "the question of the character of the place on which one stands is *the* fundamental symbolic and social question. Once an individual or culture has expressed its vision of place, a whole language of symbols and social structures will follow." Hence, deconstructing the symbolic constitution of the world enables social change. "To change stance is to totally alter one's symbols," argues Smith, "and to inhabit a different world."[16] This takes the form of a "utopian" map of place—the expansive, versus the "locative," vision of place, which for Smith signifies retreat into a finite world. Davíd Carrasco, in light of Smith's formulation, proposes a third vision, which he argues is exemplified especially in the "festival of Toxcatl, dedicated to the protean God Tezcatlipoca, we are presented with an arresting example of this 'metamorphic vision of place.' It is a vision of place in which change and transformation are the sustained pattern." My research adduces this "metamorphic vision of place."[17]

Metamorphism defines sacred space in the contemporary borderlands. Since colonialism, place shifted temporarily to foreign space, and then back again with "idols behind altars."[18] In the new *mestizaje*, a transnational profane/sacred pilgrimage and ceremony of crossings, memories and nostalgias, persistences and innovations, place continues to shift and convert—where "change and transformation" are the norm, recalling the spirit of the festival of Tezcatlipoca. Guadalupe moved north and shifted sacred space with her. She continues to move throughout the borderlands. Saints move, and bodies follow. Now, another seismic shift occurs, as *evangélicos* formulate fresh tactics to shift sacred space—the church, the congregation—and in some ways are unable to escape the inevitable return to the city and the body, familiar tropes that also continue shifting ritual patterns.

To VO/AV and other *evangélico* groups who accept literally the biblical mandate to evangelize the world, East Los Angeles is the battleground in an intense war for the soul of the community. VO/AV members understand with grave seriousness their dictate: "Take the city!" That the city becomes isomorphic with the body in Victory Outreach discourse and practice is captured in their language of "broken streets," "broken hearts," "broken bodies/broken city." VO/AV seeks to repair and restore the Chicano body and the city, which, especially for men, become intimately, if not erotically, conjoined in ecstatic worship. In movements across geopolitical borders, ethnic Mexicans shift and rearticulate their vision of place, body, and temporality—which leads to the redrawing of world boundaries and results in various forms of social change. Symbolic reordering enables shifts in perceptions of time and place. Los Angeles is invested with a sacred history: it is the chosen place for the emergence of the Holy Ghost during the last days, the period of Pentecost. Chicanos have discovered a fresh sacred significance to impute to East Los Angeles. According to the *Victory Outreach Mission Statement,* East Los Angeles is the "Jerusalem" of believers and California their Samaria—the "outermost parts" are the rest of the world.

Peter van der Veer offers a compelling definition for the postmodern world:

> Sacred centers are the foci of religious identity. They are the places on the surface of the earth that express most clearly a relation between cosmology and private experience. A journey to one of these centers is a discovery of one's identity in relation to the other world and to the community of believers—a ritual construction of self that not only integrates the believers but also places a symbolic boundary between them and "outsiders." This is not an unambiguous boundary, however, but a contested and negotiated one. It allows for negotiation, revision, and reinterpretation.[19]

In movement, borders between "us" and "them" are reconstructed, while sacred centers arise to represent these unions and tensions.

AND TIME

Mexican ethnographers have documented the persistence of ancient temporal worldviews among contemporary Mayas: "The task of bearing the sun in its daily cycle is closely tied to the Maya notion of time as a 'burden' that the gods bear with man's help."[20] The time of the borderlands is a contested field of religious meanings, both new and old. Even the Mexican Catholic calendar and liturgy are celebrated differently than those of American and other national Catholicisms: the Mexican annual liturgy is organized around the central 12 December ritual—the feast of Guadalupe. The Mexican Catholic calendar is rounded out by various saint's days. In Mexico, the most significant date of one's life is not the day one enters the world but the saint's day—the feast to which one's birthday is closest. The meanings of time are set not in astronomy but rather in memory and the imaginary. Thus, in the 12 December pilgrimage to Tepeyac, the time of colonialism is recast into a time when the indigenous reign supreme—it is a semiotic victory.

Espiritualistas, too, have created their own calendar of days, wherein venerated saints and holidays are clearly marked as distinct from profane time. In this way, time is assigned a meaning that belongs exclusively to the espiritualistas. But perhaps even more significantly, in espiritualista mythology, the space of Mexico City and the time of (post)colonialism are imbued with religious significance and rendered sacred in the myth of the return of Roque Rojas. In 3861, believers are assured, Rojas will return for his followers. Together, they will lead the nations in judgment in the newly restored sacred center, Mexico City. The Mexican nation, according to the myth of Padre Elías, will rule the globe as espiritualistas celebrate their collective.

Similarly, VO/AV, like all evangélica/os, are invested in a millennial

myth of their own choosing and reworking: Christ's return—the pre-mil-
lennialist myth of Christ's imminent return for his church prior to a thou-
sand-year earthly tribulation.[21] Having grafted this myth onto the increasingly violent conditions in the barrio, the lives of those who inhabit
this exploited space make sense: the increase of violence, hunger, death,
starvation, disease, and fear are read as signs that Christ's return is fast
approaching. All these events assume cosmic significance when placed
within the mythical temporality of Christ's return. Indeed, all occasions
of crisis are interpreted as signs, God's cryptic and destructive warnings
to the world that his apocalyptic return is near. The lapse of time, in this
instance, has redemptive meanings.

In book 10 of his *Confessions,* Saint Augustine argued that even
though he was readily aware of time's definition, when asked to explain
it, he was at a loss. Time, duration through space, is measured in context. In modern times, temporality is thought of largely in terms of
work—hours worked, time paid, "time off." But the products of one's
labor are foreign to the worker himself, or herself—a condition referred
to by Marx as "alienation." In his theory of "relative value" Marx argued that the amount of human labor required to produce a commodity
is the measure of its worth. "Human labour-power in motion, or human
labour, creates value, but it is not itself value. It becomes value only in
its congealed state, when embodied in the form of some object."[22] In capitalism, time underpins systems of production and exchange. Space, then,
becomes utterly meaningless as cycles of production, dissemination, and
obsolescence render the place of exchange merely a temporal hurdle to
be overcome. "Virtual" or "cyber" space, wherein space is merely an
electronic place of exchange, is a triumph of Marx's theory.

The idea of "relative value" is given fuller meaning in light of Marcel
Maus, who argued that capitalist social and thus temporal patterns are
delimited by three particular modes of exchange: the obligation to receive, the obligation to reciprocate, and the obligation to gift. More recently, Jacques Derrida questions whether or not the true "gift" is not itself *the* impossible, for only a gift given without expectation is a true gift;
for all acts of gifting imply obligation, and obligation and gifting require
time—the modern priority.[23] Thus, conceptions of time—the use and
misuse of time, the prioritization of time, the commodification of time—
become impressed upon the modern consciousness and work to create a
uniformity of thought and action. In North America, time is money.

Thus, in the United States, capitalist consumer time is sacralized and
transmuted into a national calendar punctuated by rituals of produc-

tion/work and consumption/play—culminating in the grand orgiastic consumer ritual of Christmas.[24] Holidays, vacations, leisure, and worship are thought of as ends in themselves, that is, as a goal, work to be achieved, as reward. Even simple "relaxation" is thought of as a consumer "luxury" that must be earned, and then spent, to achieve a state of "rest" that ultimately enables one to return to work and repeat the pattern. In the language of an earlier generation of analysts, to "culturally assimilate," on one level, is to conform to capitalist rhythms and to adopt a set of temporal priorities—a new devotion.

Richard Flores calls attention to the subtle yet nonetheless subversive ways capitalist priorities are challenged by the religious performance of *Los Pastores:*

> I refer to these [ritual] tasks as the "gifting of performance." In brief, cultural performances, especially those structured by ritual elements, are dynamic events that call forth a special commitment on the part of the performers and spectators marked by a process of gifting and reciprocity. . . . But gifts, especially those dealing with ritual, must be reciprocated if they are to be efficacious.[25]

Religious performers organize into communities of time, who "work to form a collective, however indeterminate and fleeting it may be, and it is this emergent, ritually constituted, collectivity that is responsive to the forces of the dominant by 'struggling in history.' "[26]

Religious poetics rearrange temporal devotions. Time, value, and gift are intricately woven into economies of resignified desire and exchange. Similarly, at VO/AV performances, even though performers do not openly consume beer, the play has its own kind of intoxication. The festival of the Virgin of Guadalupe invokes a similar radical play and challenge to capitalist mandates of purposeful and nervous work. In fact, in Mexico City and throughout the borderlands, festivals assume elements of the carnivalesque, which, as was discussed in chapter 2, reverses dominant class values, resulting in semiotic victories.

PROPHECY AND PERFORMANCE

"Prophet" is not a vocation exclusively for Biblical Hebrew men. *Espiritualista* women prophesize in church while they are presumably under the influence of the spirits. Similarly, *curanderas* and *evangélicas* and women and men utter prophecy when under the influence of the Holy Spirit or when they are preaching and evangelizing. The guidance of the

Holy Spirit trumps even biblical teaching in *evangélico* practice.[27] In ways that follow similar tropes, patterns, and ends, if not forms, women and men become prophets by theologizing around a home altar or shrine to Guadalupe, Juan Soldado, or another community saint.

For Nietzsche, religions arise discursively by emphasizing things about an extant religion that have not been sufficiently noticed, while simultaneously criticizing and re-creating that religion anew. Key to this formation is what Max Weber called "the prophet"—a nonordained, *lay* religious leader who proclaims a divine plan of redemption and salvation as if it were a new message from God. The prophet speaks on behalf of the poor and the oppressed.[28] Prophecy issues from the virtue of "charisma," which is conferred by an office such as "priest," or inheres naturally by "endowment." The latter is the more powerful, and by means of it the prophet "seizes" rather than "submits" to power. Prophecy, as I see it, particularly in the borderlands, is strategically connected to religious performances—especially subversive acts of mimesis.

Prophecy, or what I call poetic religious narrative, gives public expression to personal pain and concomitantly identifies, names, and condemns suffering and injustice. In a storefront or in front of a saint, prophecy and performance are, in turn, types of rituals, which, in the words of Catherine Bell, "*create* culture, authority, transcendence, and whatever forms of holistic ordering are required for people to act in meaningful and effective ways." In symbolic performance we can understand "both religious and secular rituals as orchestrated events that construct people's perceptions and interpretations." The power of performance for the believer "lies in how she creates and modifies such realities while never quite seeing the creation or the system as such."[29] Effective "misrecognition" enables religious empowerment, but the term is limiting inasmuch as it blinds the believer to those things worth seeing, deemed worthy by modernity.[30] Perhaps it is the invisible realm that comes into focus during religious performance and is clearly recognized.

In *espiritualismo* and *curanderismo,* healers mimic priests and doctors, altar-makers mime theologians from their devotional sites, and *evangélicos* mime and perform grand prophetic narratives and acts of healing. Moreover, *evangélicos* mimic a middle-class Protestant ethos, dressing in suits and ties on Sundays, driving BMWs, espousing conservative Republican tropes (even to the detriment of the communities they claim to serve). This sanitized Protestant aesthetic is all the more difficult for VO/AV, whose bodies are tattooed with gang insignias and who once represented the direct object of scorn for the classes many of them now wish to imitate. In a sense, then, the performance of *los evangéli-cos*—many *cholos,* or gang-bangers, in bourgeois drag—troubles no-tions of a normal or natural Euroamerican professional subject. This identity, too, is manufactured by American capitalism and doled out by industry as if normal.

But "performance" is not without its limits, for individuals are equipped with the finitude of the individual body, and are as a result cir-cumscribed in the extent of roles to be played and the ability to play them. Judith Butler proposes "performativity" instead, based on her study of drag, describing the multiple levels of consciousness and agency operative during performance.[31] Thus, performance of another gender is subversive insofar as it demonstrates that gender *can* be performed and mimed—the mimetic impulse here is the norm—disclosing the artificial nature of gender. In mimesis there is criticism and subversion. Similarly, when ethnic Mexicans mime the roles of religious specialists, doctors, priests, and saints, they demonstrate to the world the often arbitrary na-ture of existing religious authority, thus relocating influence, weight, ex-pertise, and right. Such miming also shifts modes of attaining permis-sions and authorizations to benefit those on the margins of recorded history.

In Ruth Behar's *Translated Woman,* a *mexicana* elder, Esperanza, re-lies on and is possessed by the spirit of Mexican revolutionary Pancho Villa. Behar argues that in channeling Villa, Esperanza inscribes "herself back into national epic history by reenacting that history and appropri-ating that history as performance and as healing. Refused to be seduced into femininity, she is cutting out a new window from which to view, and enter, a male narrative that seems to be sealed off to her gaze. But the win-dow, once cut out, turns out to be a looking glass." Behar also pays close attention to the how gender's artificiality is unveiled in spiritual practice:

> In the course of the spiritist performance, a key transformation takes place: gender is released from its fixity. Femininity and masculinity become masks, not essential identities. It may well be that the stereo-typed gender casting of "real life" left Chencha with little choice but to play a male lead in the theater of spiritism; yet her performances, both in real life and in spiritism, seem to turn both womanliness and manliness into masquerades, in which there truly is no difference between the genuinely gendered identity and the mask.[32]

Religious performance often functions to produce and subvert percep-tions of cultural norms through what Taussig calls the "mimetic faculty," which parallels Anzaldúa's *la facultad.* Taussig has demonstrated how mimesis operates as a mechanism by means of which the oppressed capture and reflect back techniques aimed at their social domination. Mimetic performance by the dominated classes has a corrosive effect on the authority of the status quo.[33] In Victory Outreach performance, for example, Euroamerican bourgeois life is not replicated wholesale. Rather, it is inflected with Mexican-American cultural codes and religious sensibilities that, when added to the American scene in public performance, refigure and change the character of what it means to be an American—and especially what it means to be an evangelical Christian. Religious performance blurs lines of authority and refigures cultural values, even while affirming oppressive structures. It not only generates new religious specialists who authorize techniques, new and old; it also legitimizes new specializations and new modes of authority.

In Cadena's "*abuelita* theology," or "grandmother theology," the narrative of world order is determined and transmitted by women as so many prophetic *cuentos, dichos, consejos*—what Alberto Pulido calls "stories" and what I call myths and prophecies.[34] Following the classic thesis of I. M. Lewis, it can be said that in the poetic spirituality of *evangélicas* and *espiritualistas*, women, especially, are empowered by spirit possession—inasmuch as spirits prophetically declare through women what is otherwise prohibited in profane speech.[35] Indeed, women gain status in *espiritualismo* and in *curanderismo* that they find difficult to relinquish when not in their symbolic places of authority: they carry authority in their bodies, which enables other public performances. In religious healing, women become the producers of knowledge and power—not unlike women exercising authority in the Guadalupe home-altar tradition, or women claiming the authority of the Holy Spirit in *evangélico* practices: prophetic spiritual performance enables the transgression of many borders.

SPIRITUAL (TRANS)NATIONALISM

For *espiritualistas*, there can be no stronger affirmation of their homeland and heritage than the myth of the return of Padre Elías. In this grand narrative, Mexican identity becomes pivotal to a cosmic drama that begins and ends with the special election of the Mexican people, (re)positioning them above all others. Similarly, in the myth of Guadalupe, God chose the Mexican nation for the manifestation of the "Queen of the Americas," and chose also the *mestizo*—Aztec and Spanish—body as the divine corporeal form that brought Christianity to the new world. *Evangélicos* feel a special burden—received at Azusa in the primordium—to evangelize the Latino world, their Israel.

What I call "spiritual (trans)nationalism" denotes the ways in which believers deploy religion to affirm national identity, particularly in exile—"cultural nationalism"—but also create spiritual and symbolic ties to their heritage. Manny Vasquez argues that "flexibility" in Latino Pentecostalism "allows local deployments." This adaptability enables a transnational strategy whereby immigrants assert "their national origin and cultural roots in the face of perceived exclusion from the dominant Anglo world."[36] Mexican immigrants have deftly reproduced religious systems that enable them to straddle a world divided by various material and symbolic borders. Spiritual transnationalism enables a fresh redrawing of center and periphery by imagining alternative modes of exchange.

The material benefits of *los evangélicos,* for example, only accrue through bonds of gifting, obligation, and exchange with the congregation and God. In Guadalupe devotion and saint traditions, *curanderismo,* and *espiritualismo* saints are propitiated, requests proffered, and favors granted. The biggest gift in borderland religions is "rebirth," or "renewal," a "death" that anticipates a rebirth as shamanic-like healer, or the "born again" practices of the *evangélicos.* Once believers receives the gift of "new life," they are locked into a mode of exchange with the sacred. Even while believers claim that they could never "repay" the gift, gifts nonetheless obligate the believer to perform certain duties, to behave in particular ways, to attend church regularly and submit to devotional acts.

In religious poetics, each believer is gifted by God and the spirits to heal—*el don*—the gift(s) of the S/spirit(s). In return, the followers must gift others, returning the same gift they have been given. The spirits in *curanderismo* and *espiritualismo* gift the devotees with healing and life—indeed, *time*—thus obligating followers to gift the spirits in bonds of reciprocity. The same pattern is also true for *los evangélicos:* the gift from God is believed to be administered by the Holy Spirit. Gifts are mediated in *curanderismo* and *espiritualismo* by spirit "protectors" or guides. In *espiritualismo,* spirits are mitigated in devotional practices. *Evangélicos* owe "obedience" and "submission" to the Holy Ghost and must observe the great mandate to "evangelize," or spread the gift to others.

Public ceremonies are also a way in which Guadalupe and the saints are mitigated in bonds of exchange, gifting, and obligation. From the very first narratives of Guadalupe ritual, Guadalupe obligated Juan Diego with a favor, a *promesa* or *manda.* She sent him to implore the bishop to build a temple to her at Tepeyac. She told Juan Diego that she would repay or reward him richly for his service. In ethnic Mexican tradition, Guadalupe, like the saints generally, gifts devotees with power over life. Guadalupe and the saints gift healing and power, while they are repaid in turn with devotion. The more intensive a public display of devotion, the more the gift is thought to be worth. That is, the more the cost to the devotee, cast usually in terms of ritual bodily mortification, the greater will be the reward gifted back to the acolyte. Thus, a women wrenching in pain as she makes a pilgrimage to Guadalupe on her knees does so for the expectation that her suffering, her sacrifice, her bodily mortification are accepted by Guadalupe in exchange for Guadalupe's gifts.

Religious poetics operates on a symbolic economy of gifting and exchange; it ties believers to each other in spiritual and cultural bonds with its own distinct logics—"spiritual nationalisms"—but also reinforces spiritual and national ties of immigrants to the mother country, Mexico, and Mexicans—spiritual transnationalism. Without doubt, this symbolic economy is intimately tied to economic entrepreneurial ambitions. Certainly many healers, VO/AV ministers, and curators of Catholic devotional sites profit economically from the symbolic economy of exchange. Like all human economies, motivations for action are never singular; relationships are complex and desires are riddled with contradictions. Various interests are served and left (un)satisfied in systems of religious exchange. And yet, despite the sometimes disappointing outcome, spiritual transmigration continues and grows.

MOVEMENT: CONVERSION AND ETERNAL RETURNS

Mexican migrants typically follow the seasonal patterns of crops and other labor rhythms (the demand for construction workers being greater during the non-rainy months, for example). And inasmuch as migrants touch and inform the lives of permanent residents in the spaces they inhabit, entire communities are affected by cycles of return: various communities and social collectives experience ebb and swell as a function of migration. For a community delimited by border crossing, fluidity, and movement, religion is experienced as flux and flow; the greatest religious movements occur at times of crisis.

When people come to the United States, they bring their religious traditions with them; when they come as temporary workers, they return to Mexico with the commodities and cultural influences they accumulated while in exile—both are disseminated in their homelands. Thus, the cultural rhythms of the United States pulsate into Mexican religious systems, and vice versa, in various means of transnational exchanges. Both nations are influenced by the transnational movement of peoples—bodies and souls. As a result, borderland religions are dynamic, like the New Fire Ceremony dedicated to Tezcatlipoca—never static but always in flux—whereby Mexican religious structures are disembedded from their places of origin in Mexico and reembedded into United States contexts, a cycle that takes place again and again.[37]

Borderlands Catholicism is delimited by movements circulating around the fulcrum of the Virgin of Guadalupe. In what was perhaps her most significant movement, Guadalupe shifted from the sacred center in Mexico City, Tepeyac, to East Los Angeles. Concomitantly, she moved to several nodal points throughout the United States that delineate Chicano sacred geography. In East Los Angeles, Catholicism is circumscribed by movements between the Catholic Church and the home altar, between the saints; all the while, the saints are moving as well. Catholicism emerges in East Los Angeles also in political movements for reform and social justice. In each movement, religious agents contest the authority of the male-dominated Catholic institution.

Similarly, in *curanderismo* and *espiritualismo,* devotees practice a symbolic and cognitive flux between the mandates of the Enlightenment, science, and medical technology, and the premodern forms of ritual healing. In healing, especially, the movement between the living and the dead is brought centrally to bear and rendered a definitive ritual of religious practice. The vast majority of Chicano *evangélicos* were not born as Protestants but converted from Catholicism. Thus, the definitive movement for Chicano *evangélicos* is *conversion.* Conversion in Chicano evangelism exhibits the classic characteristics of a social drama: crisis, separation, and reintegration. *Evangélicos* migrate too between various preachers.

The predicament of "liminality," of the place in between, *nepantla,* characterizes not only religious movement in the borderlands, but cultural, social, and political movements more generally. In the borderlands, Mexicans move temporarily from Mexico to the United States and back again, between the home altar and the Catholic Church, from Catholicism to Pentecostalism and back again, from Catholicism and Pentecostalism to *curanderismo* and *espiritualismo* and oscillations in all places in between, in an endless cycle of returns—transgressing and recreating geopolitical, cultural, and symbolic borders. Religion, work, community, family, and place are all poetically rearticulated through the

matrix created by eternal returns: religion in the U.S.-Mexico borderlands is delimited by several intersecting rituals of returns. Insofar as
Mexicans transform space through their back-and-forth movement, they
reconstruct symbolic systems. In this way, ethnic *mexicana/os* flee from,
perhaps escape, the terror of a postcolonial history, living in a sense outside of profane time and within a mythical cycle of seasonal, almost
mythical, returns. Each destination promises greater hope, yet it is in the
cycle of returns itself that time and place become meaningful.

Movement implies and involves conversion—fresh places, symbolic
referents, spiritual energies. Movement and conversion are strategic, responding to and negotiating power in what Chela Sandoval calls "differential movement,"[38] which, as I see it, is a triumph of a will to power
and the eternal returns—inasmuch as a return is a victory of memory
against forgetting. Eliade critiqued the Hegelian linear vision of (movement in) history, promoting (perhaps romanticizing) the myth of the
eternal return. Nietzsche theorized the relentless and ironic return of all
things in endless cycles of change and stability—including religion, de-
bunking too the Western Christian myth of forward progress and advance. Victor and Edith Turner understood "movement itself, [as] a symbol of communitas, which changes with time, as against stasis, which
represents structure; individuality posed against the institutionalized mi-
lieu; and so forth."[39] Movement, conversion, change—the social
drama—provided an antidote to the confines of social structure, the
predicament of oppression. Walter Benjamin argued that "the condition
of the oppressed teaches us that the 'state of emergency' in which we live
is not the exception but the rule. We must attain to an understanding of
history that is in keeping with this insight."[40] In keeping with this insight,
by way of conclusion, I want to suggest that religion in the borderlands
is characterized by a matrix of intersecting movements—all of which are
framed within the larger pattern of transnational movements between
Mexico and the United States, eternal returns in the borderlands.

There is both tragedy and comedy (or triumph) in the religious expressions of Mexican-Americans. In the ritual of return, ethnic Mexicans
attempt to escape the terror of postcolonial history—seeking improved
economic conditions for themselves and their children. Ethnic Mexicans,
located at the borders of power, commonly engage in continual processes
of circumscribing and reimagining their worlds—insofar as social-spatial
conditions allow—creating the conceptual, social, cultural, and geo-
graphic space that frames religious production: the borderlands. Momentum for religious movement comes in crisis situations. It is through

religious movement that Mexicans usurp authority and power from the hands of institutions and become their own religious specialists: decentering reference and institutions, blurring lines, and reinscribing grammars of justice and injustice in order to survive.

This poetic ethic of justice, beauty, and return, or survival, constituted in dissonance, returns to the ancient idea of *difrasismo*. Recently, the *difrasismo* of Aztec *flor y canto*—conditions of truth—was reinscribed into the *Codex Espangliensis: From Columbus to the Border Patrol*.[41] Produced in the ancient style, the book opens from right to left, unfolding as a cylinder with accordion folds. Rather than each section superseding what has come before it, they overlap and complement each other and, yes, advance a narrative across a terrain that is at once old and new. Images for the *Codex Espangliensis* were produced by San Francisco–based artist Enrique Chagoya and the narrative by Mexico City–San Diego–based Guillermo Gómez-Peña. The pages are not numbered, and images can be read from either direction.

A story of colonial encounters is told if the pages are read from left to right (while unfolding right to left). Images are wildly incongruent, including a comic-book image of the Spiderman hero, with the head of George Washington, poised over a scene of ritual Indian massacre at the hands of the Spanish. The page is stained by red fingerprints. In the center, joining two pages, is a passionate, penitent Christ, also bloodied; behind him, in red text, an inquisition of NAFTA, signed, "From a Speech by Cross-Cultural Salesman El Aztec High-Tech." On the right-hand corner, directly above a text of the Inquisition, where the witness points to a giant Spaceship, Gómez-Peña has penned the following poem:

> I Travel across a different America. My
> America is a continent (not a country) which
> is not described by the outlines of any of the
> standard maps. In my America, "West"
> and "North" are mere nostalgic abstract-
> ions—the South and the East have
> slipped into their mythical space. Quebec
> seems closer to Latin America than its
> Anglophone twin. My America in-
> cludes different peoples, cities, borders, &
> nations. The Indian nations of Canada
> and the U.S. and also the multiracial
> neighborhoods in the larger cities all seem
> more like Third World micro-republics than

like communities which are part of some
"western democracy."[42]

The movement of the narrative is circular but always in movement. Rather than a linear colonial triumph, that is, one regime's victory over another, what emerges instead is a series of random encounters, borrowings, crossings, exchanges, and repulsions—a palimpsest of religion, society, history, and myth—an uncanny cultural text that is understood only from a hermeneutics of *difrasismo: difrasismo* is the hermeneutic of the borderlands.

REQUIEM FOR THE LIVING: THE ETERNAL RETURN OF LA LLORONA'S CHILDREN

Today Latinos are no longer a minority in California. The millennial census demonstrated that nearly one-third of all Californians, and 45 percent of Angelenos, are Latino. Of these, more than half are native-born Americans. Yet their demographic, their materiality, alone does not equal democratic representation. That the exact number of undocumented Mexican workers in the United States cannot be determined is a fact that should give us occasion for pause. Mexicans entering the United States to work must disappear from view even before they arrive. They must live without visibility, as ghosts in a political economy that requires their labor for its maintenance. Thus, they exist as specters raised against a backdrop of a volatile economy. Other Chicanas and Chicanos, gang members, unlucky residents of the barrios, live as phantoms, hiding from the police who relentlessly hunt them. Still other, law-abiding Mexican-American citizens live invisibly in a society that fetishizes idealized European body images. Borderland dwellers must shed their bodies. Their bodies must be dissipated, they must exist in opacity, their materiality denied them in order to conform to Western capitalism, which, as Judith Butler argues, is "a materialization of reason which operates through the dematerialization of other bodies."[43] Chicanos are invisible also in a racialized political and academic project that cuts racial categories exclusively down the black/white divide. Together, these are the children of La Llorona, who have been, in effect, killed by U.S. society; and yet, they are the ones who multiply. In this sense, spirituality, particularly ancestor veneration and trafficking with spirits, becomes a powerful force at the core of borderland religions.

Ethnographic death narratives collected from Mexicans in Los Angeles in the late 1960s indicate a strong belief in the presence of the dead among the living: Chicanas and Chicanos traffic with the dead.[44] Informants referred to these ghosts as the *ánima,* or soul. Hence, while bodies are shed and decompose, the souls of the dead continue to inform everyday life. Most of the informants, women of various religions whose stories were recorded and published verbatim, told of dead relatives who materialized among the living to request that the surviving family member complete a vow the deceased had left unfulfilled. Other spirits return to make retribution for some wicked deed before receiving admittance to the heavenly paradise, and still others bring good fortune and money to their kinsmen.

Narrations of the dead, however, typically occur for didactic purposes: these stories are meant to be instructive to those living on earth, the weaker beings, those with incomplete knowledge of the next spiritual realm. In the pedagogy of the dead, the living poetically redraw the boundaries of reality so that they connect with allies on the other side of the existential divide. Stories of ghosts inhabiting the borderlands is a discursive resource deployed particularly by women.

Take, for example, the following tale recounted by a woman who learned it from another women, an elder, of the Mexican Yucatán region:

> A women was accustomed to come out from the trees in the land of the Yucateca[,] she had long hair and a white tunic with big black eyes, very pretty, who would call to the men that . . . let's say . . . go out in the small hours of the night. This woman, clearly very attractive, invites these men to make love. These men, attracted of course by her beauty, approach her, make love to her, and quickly this woman turns into a venomous serpent.[45]

The message conveyed by this woman is cautionary, intended to discourage would-be promiscuous men. The incarnation of evil spirits to engage in sex with humans, though perhaps lacking suasion in its literal form, nonetheless functions as a reminder that people are not always what they appear to be—especially if that person is a seductress of married men. And more, the lesson teaches the high costs of infidelity: scarred memories, ghosts, and hauntings.

Sandra Cisneros has told a powerful and poetic story of spiritual transformation, entitled *Woman Hollering Creek*—the title refers to "La Gritona," or the screaming woman, as the local Chicanas in the story call the creek. Cleofilas, a Mexican woman, is taken to live near the creek; her neighbors are Soledad, "solitude" and Dolores, "pains." The creek itself has life, movement, change.

The stream sometimes only a muddy puddle in the summer, though now in the springtime, because of the rains, a good-size alive thing, a thing with a voice all its own, all day and all night calling in its high, silver voice. Is it La Llorona, the weeping woman? La Llorona, who drowned her own children. Perhaps La Llorona is the one they named the creek after, she thinks, remembering all the stories she learned as a child. . . . La Llorona calling to her. She is sure of it. . . . The day sky turning to night . . . La Llorona. Wonders if something as quiet as this drives a woman to the darkness under the trees.[46]

The haunting aesthetic of La Gritona/Woman Hollering Creek captures and reflects the tragic stories of local women found dead in the creek. Cleofilas's new home, Woman Hollering, is a place haunted by the ghosts of suffering and dead women who attain voice in the cries of La Llorona. Cleofilas's own expectations of a life "happily ever after" soon turn to dread of her abusive husband. She is rescued by an unlikely friend, Felice, "joy," who takes Cleofilas across the creek to freedom. In Felice, Cisneros reverses the image of the black-cloaked sorrowful woman—when driving across Woman Hollering Creek, Felice "opened her mouth and let out a yell as loud as any mariachi." She explains to Cleofilas that that is what she does every time she crosses Woman Hollering Creek.[47] She releases her own joyful spirit over the canyon alive with ghosts, as comfort, as triumph, as a siren to new life and pleasure. This is the return of La Llorona's children.

CONCLUSION: *FIN DE SIGLO* IN THE BORDERLANDS: NEW WARS

Ghosts cannot be reduced to the realm of memory, myth, and history. "The ghost is not simply a dead or missing person," argues Avery Gordon, "but a social figure."[48] The undocumented Chicano population, the outcasts, are the ghostly presences of Los Angeles and throughout the borderlands. La Llorona's children, they are the walking invisible dead known as the "illegal" population; they haunt society with their invisibility. As Los Angeles rushes into the millennium, its inner city has become the social, economic, and political periphery: the inner city is increasingly occupied by Mexicans and other easily exploitable minority wage laborers—a process Edward Soja calls the "peripheralization of the core." This burgeoning labor market has created "an overflowing pool of cheap, relatively docile labour that is not only locally competitive but also able to compete with the new industrial concentrations of the Third World." In *fin de siglo* Los Angeles, there are more Mexicans than in any

other city except for Mexico City. Soja has called attention to the invisibility of this population, explaining that Mexican urban life is characterized by "the underground economy [that] thrives in the interstices of
urban life, succoring ethnicities and providing the necessary niches for
personal survival. Only when it breaks out from its niches into wider networks of criminal gang—and drug-related activities does it threaten the
restructured order."[49] Ghosts move with freedom to haunt and transform
a place. In fact, perhaps the most powerful movement in religious poetics is between the living and the dead, and the movements of the walking dead.

The dead are the protagonists in Ana Castillo's vision of place. In her
So Far from God, the magical lands of New Mexico are haunted by
ghosts—sisters, who, even after death, continue to work together for the
family's survival.[50] The salvation of the entire family, a mother (Sofie)
and four sisters (Faith, Hope, Charity, and La Loca), occurs through the
agency of the youngest sister, La Loca, or "the crazy one." The novel
opens to the funeral of La Loca, dead at age three, who miraculously returns to life, flying out of the casket. Thereafter, La Loca is averse to
human contact; only her mother is allowed to touch her. She is the mystic of the family who brings salvation through sacrifice. She becomes a
patron saint, especially for those suffering the ravages of AIDS. Her message is clear: "Have faith in La Loca."

La Loca is represented as a trickster figure and more—she is akin to
Carrasco's description of the "gifted shamaness." Carrasco describes
Gloria Anzaldúa in the condition of "*loco-centric*, or *loca-centric*, with
a wild tongue, an oscillating mind, and a whirling spirit focused in [*Bor-
derlands/La Frontera*] to describe a profound crisis of political, cultural
and personal identity and to stimulate forces to heal it. This healing, to
the extent that it takes place feeds off of a mythic awareness that is loco
centric. *Loco*-centric is a *puro* borderlands category."[51] Carrasco's interpretation is confirmed later, when Anzaldúa says, "The grounding of my
spiritual reality is based on indigenous Mexican spirituality, which is
Nahualismo, which loosely translates as 'shamanism.' But the Nahuatl
was a shapeshifter, a shaman that could shift shapes, that could become
a person or an animal." In these magical endeavors, she returns to the
wisdom of the ancients:

> The philosophy I am now trying to unravel also goes back to Mexican in-
> digenous times where I use the words like Nepantla, like conocimiento, so
> things that come from the indigenous, the Mexican or the Chicano. . . .
> With the spiritual *mestizaje* there is a component of folk Catholicism in

it. . . . The Catholicism that Mexicans in South Texas participate in is more of a folk Catholicism, as it has a lot of indigenous elements in there. But on top of the indigenous elements are put the Catholic scenes.[52]

From Anzaldúa's perspective, the mystic, ecstatic, and *loca*-centric/shamanic aspects of "spiritual *mestizaje*" lead to transformation and power: a pattern of death and rebirth she calls the Coatlique State: the death period she must undergo, a descent into the underworld, to reemerge into the upper world as a transformed being. Though fraught with sacrifice, *la encrucijada,* the new *mestiza,* the shape-shifter is ultimately triumphant. This argument comes in contrast to the writings of Monsiváis on the plight of Indians and *mestizos* in Mexico.

Take, for example, the brilliant ambivalence with which Monsiváis regards El Niño Fidencio, who, for him, is "the supreme symbol of a kind of popular religiosity that is self-sacrificing, violent in its self-flagellation, incapable of despair and discouragement, and born again in every cult or ritual."[53] Monsiváis calls these practices "marginal mysticism," which, as he sees it, "combines Catholicism as a mass social practice, with pilgrimage as an end in itself (the road to the sacred place is always the most rewarding), faith healing, Marianist spiritualism, and those charismatic personalities who, whether they attempt to found a religion or not, use themselves as a filter for religious experience." Central characteristics of "marginal mysticism" include

> faith in the unbreakable bond between everyday life and the liturgical representation of the beyond. Everything (Heaven, Hell, Limbo, virgins, apparitions, miracles, satanic and seraphic possession) is natural, because the secular world does not exist and history happens only at a distance. . . . Life is lived to accomplish essential goals, those in which the will to sacrifice is a form of transfiguration. In this case, mysticism is the abandonment of self, the renunciation of possessions, the battle for primordial ideals . . . the pronouncement of prophecies, the embodiment of nature . . . and the presumption of living as God commanded.[54]

Monsiváis uses a *difrasismo* hermeneutic himself, one fully aware of the irony, parody, and play, intimately bound up with Marxist mystification, "marginal mysticism" functioning as a double entendre, for those on the edge of "legitimate" society, occupying a place of mystification. There is tragedy and ambivalence in Monsiváis, as in life itself—all of these paths are reiterated in religious poetics: comedy and tragedy. Monsiváis's vantage point, like that of Mexican Nobel laureate Octavio Paz, is that of a "bourgeois intellectual from the South."[55] Southern Mexican intellectuals have long held idealized, nostalgic, yet ultimately ambivalent discursive positions in relation to the indigenous past and present that are at once alike and unlike those of Chicana/o scholars. The latter tend more toward romantic and powerfully strategic relations with present memories of ancestors.

Gómez-Peña highlights this difference with specific reference to La Virgen de Guadalupe, documenting cases in Mexico in which "militant" *guadalupanos* terrorized exhibits of Guadalupe they deemed offensive. For Gómez-Peña, as for other Mexican intelligentsia, Guadalupe is innocent to the fact that "in her name many people in Mexico have been forced into social submission, political passivity, and fear: fear of religious and cultural difference, fear of sex and 'sin,' fear of eternal punishment, fear of contradicting the majority, fear of being an inadequate Mexican. And ultimately, fear of metaphysical orphanhood, of not belonging to the great and harmonious Mexican family."[56] But in the North Mexican Americas, what I call the family romance of Guadalupe and Christ is also lived, as pious *católicos* enact Oedipal dramas wherein Christ becomes associated with the colonizer, patriarch, father—becomes self—and killed: *el crucificado;* Guadalupe is elevated as *mestiza* mother and incorporated into self: thus, the conflict of *mexicano* identity is resolved in the crucifixion of Christ: that part of self that betrays, rapes, violates, is ritually killed. Perhaps this is El Lloron, the male counterpart to La Llorona? Gómez-Peña confesses: "Like every other Mexican, whether I like it or not, I may suffer from an acute oedipal complex. Like most agnostic Mexicans, I might in fact be a very religious individual."[57]

Back on the U.S. side of the border, Gómez-Peña encounters another Guadalupe and yet an additional layer of being a religious individual and a political being, adding a distinctly North American romanticism (perhaps transcendentalism): "I also discovered that my Chicano colleagues had a very different connection to the Guadalupan imagery. They had expropriated it, reactivated it, recontextualized it, and turned it into a symbol of resistance, something that Mexicans have never been able to understand."[58]

Guadalupe, transformed by the Chicana/o romantic impulse, religious poetics, participates in "civil disobedience." Nowhere is this romanticizing clearer than in the myth of Aztlán, which at once constitutes a beginning and an end—the exile of the Aztecs and the return of the Chicana/os. Alurista, the "poet laureate of Aztlán," explains his view of Aztlán as "the mythological time space that unifies the personal and historical times spaces. All of us are using one level and, more often than not, at least two: historical and personal are the most common. But we're coming of age where we will use mythological time-space."[59] Mythological uses of time arise from religious poetics; "when beliefs become institutionalized (like certain aspects of La Virgen de Guadalupe), that becomes an opiate for the people. But if you maintain a connection that doesn't have all these institutional trappings, it's political."[60] The political and the religious are inseparable, as far as I see it, and their connection enacts a mythological time-space directly affecting the body.

The method and theory of religious poetics have emerged in the previous pages as various social strategies and tactics, through fragmented genealogies of borderlands religious products, focusing on the body, space, and time. Though the scope has been broad, it is nonetheless incomplete without a genealogy of the modern borderlands soul, its psyche and imagination, the politics and erotics.

Notes

1. Throughout this book I use the term "Mexican Americas" to designate the places occupied by Mexican-origin people on both sides of the U.S.-Mexican border; the term *mexicana/o* signifies people of Mexican origin in what José Limón calls "greater Mexico." I use the term "Latino" to refer to people of Latin American origin—the term is inclusive of Mexican-Americans, Mexicans, and those living in the Latin Americas. "Chicano" refers to people of Mexican heritage who live most of their lives in the United States. There is no "pure," unproblematic, or universally accepted way to name Latinos, and I keep this term in continual formation. However, the act of naming is itself political. Pierre Bourdieu argues:

> Struggles over ethnic or regional identity . . . are a particular case of the different struggles over classifications, struggles over the monopoly of power to make people see and believe, to get them to know and recognize, to impose the legitimate definition of the divisions of the social world and, thereby, to *make and unmake groups.* What is at stake here is the power of imposing a vision of the social world through principles of di-vision which, when they are imposed on a whole group, establish meaning and a consensus about meaning, and in particular about the identity and unity of the group, which creates the reality of the unity and the identity of the group. (Pierre Bourdieu, *Language and Symbolic Power,* trans. Gino Raymond and Matthew Adamson [Cambridge, Mass.: Harvard University Press, 1991], 221; emphasis original)

On the racialization process of Mexicans in the United States, I follow here David Montejano, who argues that framing this problem as a sociological and political question "helps to clear the ambiguity concerning the sociological classification of Mexicans. The bonds of culture, language, and common historical experience make Mexican people of the Southwest a distinct ethnic population. But Mexicans, following the above definition, were also a 'race' when subjected to policies of discrimination and control." Montejano, *Anglos and Mexicans in the Making of Texas, 1836–1986* (Austin: University of Texas Press, 1987), 96.

2. See James S. Griffith, "El Tiradito and Juan Soldado: Two Victim Intercessors in the Western Borderlands," in Griffith, *A Shared Space: Folklife in the Arizona-Sonora Borderlands* (Logan: Utah State University Press, 1995), 67–86; and Patrick McDonnell, "I Believe in Juan Soldado: Soldier Executed in 1938 Revered as Tijuana Miracle Worker," *Los Angeles Times*, 5 November 1998.

3. Here and throughout, I opt for the broadest definition of "myth," as sacred and symbolic narrative. I follow Ninian Smart, who argues, "I do not think any one theory of myth will work" in all cases. "Certainly some notions appear simply false, for instance the idea that all myths deal with a special sort of time. Some do and some do not." Smart, *Dimensions of the Sacred: An Anatomy of the World's Beliefs* (Berkeley: University of California Press, 1996), 131. See also Bruce Lincoln, who argues that myth, as opposed to history, relies on an internal authority, a symbolic authority, not only an implied truth but a truth that serves as a template for world narration. According to Lincoln, myth is a narrative "for which successful claims are made not only to the status of truth, but what is more to the status of paradigmatic truth, through the recitation of myth one may effectively mobilize a social grouping." He continues: "Like myth, ritual is best understood as an authoritative mode of symbolic discourse and a powerful instrument for the evocation of those sentiments (affinity and estrangement) out of which society is constructed." Lincoln, *Discourse and the Construction of Society: Comparative Studies of Myth, Ritual, and Classification* (New York: Oxford University Press, 1989), 53. "Sign" and "symbol" are distinguished throughout: "sign" is a direct reference, whereas the signification of the "symbol" is purposefully unclear; there is a poetic and contemplative—spiritual—quality to the symbol that is much more personal than that of the sign.

4. The style in which a community, especially a religious community, is imagined and reimagined is a product of the ways that symbols are combined and fashioned into a system that is at once volatile (i.e., subject to constant revisions) and absolute. Benedict Anderson has argued against genuine communities, proposing that "communities are to be distinguished, not by their falsity/genuineness, but by the style in which they are imagined." Anderson, *Imagined Communities: Reflections on the Origins and Spread of Nationalism* (London: Verso, 1983), 6. Lincoln argues that only symbolic memory "could legitimate the actions and mobilize the social groupings that would enable them to deal with the initially problematic situation. Beginning in the present, they sought and appropriated that piece of the past—real or imagined, familiar or novel—that could best serve them as an instrument with which to confront and reshape their present moment." Lincoln, *Discourse and the Construction of Society*, 28.

5. Salvador Cisneros, quoted in Anne-Marie O'Connor, "A Host of Populist Saints Venerated by the People If Not Approved by the Catholic Church Attract Devoted Followings Despite Checkered Pasts," *Los Angeles Times*, July 18, 1997.

6. Bruce Lincoln has argued that the power of myth is fluid and shifting—and is contained in the various embodiments able to confer religious authority. See

Lincoln, *Authority: Construction and Corrosion* (Chicago: University of Chicago Press, 1994).

7. I resist attempts to describe such practices against an institutional referent; thus the designation "popular religion." In fact, the figuration "popular religion" can be understood on one level through the prism of Foucault's "discursive practices," which reassign democratic privilege. Scott describes this in terms of "stigmatization." He notes that "the power to call a cabbage a rose and make it stick in the public sphere implies the power to do the opposite, to stigmatize activities or persons that seem to call into question official realities. . . . Rebels or revolutionaries are labeled bandits, criminals, hooligans in a way that attempts to divert attention from their political claims. Religious practices that meet with disapproval might similarly be termed heresy, Satanism, or witchcraft," or they might also be termed "popular religion." James Scott, *Domination and the Arts of Resistance: Hidden Transcripts* (New Haven, Conn.: Yale University Press, 1990), 55. My disagreement with Scott stems from his simple bifurcation of social groups and the seemingly monolithic transcripts they enact.

8. David Kertzer, *Ritual, Politics, and Power* (New Haven, Conn.: Yale University Press, 1988), 11.

9. Scott, *Domination and the Arts of Resistance,* 184.

10. See Renato Rosaldo, "Imperialist Nostagia," in Rosaldo, *Culture and Truth: The Remaking of Social Analysis* (Boston: Beacon Press, 1989), 68–87.

11. Davíd Carrasco, "A Perspective for a Study of Religious Dimensions in Chicano Experience: *Bless Me, Ultima* as a Religious Text," *Aztlán: International Journal of Chicano Studies Research* 3 (1982): 195–222, quote from 198.

12. Note especially the ethnicity/assimilation model employed for historical research on "ethnic religion"; see, for example, Jay Dolan's edited volume *Hispanic Catholic Culture in the United States* (Notre Dame, Ind.: University of Notre Dame Press, 1994). For its originator, see especially Will Herberg's classic study *Protestant, Catholic, Jew: An Essay in American Religious Sociology* (Chicago: University of Chicago Press, 1955). Perhaps the definitive statement of the "ethnicity assimilationist paradigm" comes from Milton Gordon's "Assimilation in America: Theory and Reality," *Daedalus: Journal of the American Academy of Arts and Sciences* 2 (Spring 1961): 263–85. See also Raymond Brady Williams, *Religions of Immigrants from India and Pakistan: New Threads in the American Tapestry* (Cambridge, Eng.: Cambridge University Press, 1988).

13. Rudy Busto, "The Ring of Fire: Religious Eruptions and Flows along the Pacific Rim" (paper presented at the American Academy of Religion and Lilly Endowment/Henry Luce Foundation Teaching Workshop, Cuernavaca, Mexico, June 2001).

14. For example, see George M. Marsden, *Religion and American Culture* (New York: Harcourt Brace Jovanovich, 1990), which, while professing a focus on the role of religion in American culture since the Civil War, fails to mention Latinos save in one sentence where "Asians" and "Hispanics" are identified as "new outsiders." Perhaps the quintessential example of this impulse in the writing of American religious history is Winthrop S. Hudson's *Religion in America,* 5th ed. (New York: Macmillan, 1992). Indeed, it is not until the fifth edition and

the addition of John Corrigan as coauthor that Latinos are even mentioned in the text, and this in the form of a one-page section under the heading "The Emergence of Hispanic Catholicism" (383–84). Sydney E. Alhstrom's 1,158-page tome, *A Religious History of the American People* (New Haven, Conn.: Yale University Press, 1972), received *The Christian Century*'s Religious Book of the Decade Award. It contains three paragraphs on the Catholicism of the "Spanish-speaking" (1000–1001). Edwin Scott Gaustad's *A Religious History of America* (San Francisco: Harper and Row, 1990) devotes nearly one and a half pages to a discussion of "Hispanic Catholicism" (334–35). Martin Marty's classic narrative move is to group those who do not fall under his determination of normative into categories of "ethnic religion"; this discussion included a cursory discussion of "Hispanic Catholicism." See Marty, *A Nation of Behavers* (Chicago: University of Chicago Press, 1976), and *Modern American Religion: The Irony of It All: 1893–1819*, vol. 1 (Chicago: University of Chicago Press, 1986). For an example of borderland religions as addendum to North American Protestant church history, see Edwin E. Sylvest, Jr., "Religion in Hispanic America since the Era of Independence," in Charles H. Lippy and Peter W. Williams, eds., *The Encyclopedia of the American Religious Experience: Studies of Traditions and Movements*, 3 vols. (New York: Scribners, 1988), 201–22. Chicano studies, too, has dismissed the importance of religious categories in studies of community because of its early adherence to Marxist and cultural nationalist paradigms. For an elaboration of these positions within Chicano studies, see Carlos Muñoz, *Youth, Identity, Power: The Chicano Generation* (London: Verso, 1989).

15. Laura Pérez, "Spirit Glyphs: Reimagining Art and Artist in the Work of Chicana Tlamantine," *Modern Fiction Studies* 44 (Spring 1998): 36–76, 39–40.

16. On the question of human agency in social formation, I follow Pierre Bourdieu's theories of human practice, led by what he calls the *habitus:* "action guided by a 'feel for the game' [which] has all the appearances of the rational action that an impartial observer, endowed with all the necessary information and capable of mastering it rationally, would deduce. And yet it is not based on reason." Pierre Bourdieu, *In Other Words: Essays Towards a Reflexive Sociology,* trans. Matthew Adamson (Stanford, Calif.: Stanford University Press, 1990), 11. Religious poetics are a triumph, on one level, of those cultural micropractices, what Michel de Certeau calls "tactics," the mobile and opportunistic maneuverings of those without recourse to conventional power. Through tactical maneuvers, religion is utilized in the quotidian struggle of "making do." A "tactic" is a victory of time over space, "a calculus which cannot count on a 'proper' [institutional place] (a spatial or institutional localization), nor thus on a borderline distinguishing the other as a visible totality. . . . It must constantly manipulate events in order to turn them into 'opportunities.'" Michel de Certeau, *The Practice of Everyday Life,* trans. Steven F. Rendall (Berkeley: University of California Press, 1984), xx.

17. I make no distinction between "ritual," as such, and "performance" when it refers to actions done with religious consciousness by the actors before a real or imagined audience. For an elaborate distinction, see Ronald Grimes, "Ritual and Performance," in Gary Laderman and Luis D. León, eds. *Religion*

and American Cultures: Multicultural Traditions and Popular Expressions, 3 vols. (Santa Barbara: ABC-CLIO Press, 2003). Catherine Bell has attributed the power of ritual to what she calls "redemptive hegemony," wherein ritual actors believe themselves to be redeemed, or redeemable, even if such apprehensions are predicated upon a false consciousness. Bell argues that ritual "schemes become socially instinctive automatisms of the body and implicit strategies for shifting the power relationships among symbols." In this way, space and time are redefined. As she sees it, "ritualization is the way to construct power relations when the power is claimed to be from God, not from military might or economic superiority; it is also the way for people to experience a vision of a community order that is empowering." This sense of empowerment is in part a product of what Bell calls "strategic misrecognition," or the sense of well-being derived from the mystification of real power relations. Catherine Bell, *Ritual Theory, Ritual Practice* (New York: Oxford University Press, 1992), 99, 115, 116. Unfortunately, Bell only looks to modernist-sanctioned language for what can be "real consciousness."

18. See Margaret Miles, *Seeing and Believing: Religion and Values in the Movies* (Boston: Beacon Press, 1996), 9. On the use of literature in the study of religion, see Giles Gunn, *The Interpretation of Otherness: Literature, Religion, and the American Imagination* (New York: Oxford University Press, 1979). Also see Luis D. León, "The Poetic Uses of Religion in the Miraculous Day of Amalia Gomez," *Journal of Religion and American Culture* 1 (1999): 205–32.

19. Here, I follow Geertz's notions of thick description: "to uncover the conceptual structures that inform our subjects' acts, the 'said' of social discourse, and to construct a system of analysis in whose terms what is generic to those structures, what belongs to them because they are what they are, will stand out against the other determinants of human behavior." Clifford Geertz, "Thick Description: Toward an Interpretive Theory of Culture," in Geertz, *The Interpretation of Cultures* (New York: Basic Books, 1973), 27. On questions of verifiability and truth, I look to James Clifford, who proposes instead "partial truths." See James Clifford, "Partial Truths," introduction to Clifford, *Writing Culture: The Poetics and Politics of Ethnography* (Berkeley: University of California Press, 1986), 1–26. See *The Fate of Culture: Geertz and Beyond,* a special issue of *Representations* 59 (Summer 1997), ed. Sherry B. Ortner.

20. I approached fieldwork as the creation of my own text, the speech act as event captured, which I would then interpret and verify, following Paul Ricoeur in "The Model of the Text: Meaningful Action Considered as a Text," *Social Research* 38:3 (Autumn 1971): 73–101.

Many of the Spanish-to-English translations of texts and interviews cited in this book are my own. All persons interviewed have been given pseudonyms, and unless otherwise indicated, no recording devices were used. Many of my interviews were conducted in Spanish, and I have translated some passages into English. My translations of both oral and written texts are rendered more literally than colloquially in an attempt to preserve the integrity of the original Spanish. Those unfamiliar with Spanish can grasp the meaning, and those who know Spanish will recognize the Spanish syntax.

INTRODUCTION. IN SEARCH OF LA LLORONA'S CHILDREN

1. For a discussion of Chicano battles for La Placita and the adjacent Olvera Street, see Rodolfo F. Acuña, introduction to Acuña, *Anything but Mexican: Chicanos in Contemporary Los Angeles* (New York: Verso, 1996).

2. See www.lavirgenperegrina.org, web page, Los Angeles Archdiocese.

3. Emma Perez, quoted in Margaret Ramirez, "Huge Throng Hails Virgin of Guadalupe," *Los Angeles Times,* 12 December 1999, B-1.

4. The term "presencing" is from Douglas Monroy, *Rebirth: Mexican Los Angeles from the Great Migration to the Great Depression* (Berkeley: University of California Press, 1999).

5. See Gregory Rodriguez, "A Church, Changing," *Wall Street Journal,* 8 March 2002, and Anne-Marie O'Connor, "Church's New Wave of Change," *Los Angeles Times,* 25 March 1998.

6. This reordering of symbolic value resonates with Nietzsche's "transvaluation" of ethics in his genealogy of morals. See Friedrich Nietzsche, *On the Genealogy of Morals,* trans. Walter Kaufmann and R. J. Hollingdale (New York: Vintage Books, 1969 [1887]). For an application, see Jerome Levi, "Pillars of the Sky: The Genealogy of Ethnic Identity among the Raramuri-Simaroni (Tarahumara-Gentiles) of Northwest Mexico" (Ph.D. diss., Harvard University, 1993). I am aware of the recent critique leveled by Bruce Lincoln against the usage of Nietzsche in the study of religion: "Blond Beast," in *Theorizing Myth: Narrative, Ideology, and Scholarship* (Chicago: University of Chicago Press, 1999), 101–20. However, here I follow Levi, who, as others do, stresses Nietzsche's employment of irony, parody, and dissimulation, and how Nietzsche is often read too literally instead.

7. See Pierre Bourdieu, "Genesis and Structure of the Religious Field," *Comparative Social Research* 13 (1991): 1–43.

8. Clive Kessler, *Islam and Politics in a Malay State* (Ithaca, N.Y.: Cornell University Press), 244–45.

9. In *Discourse and the Construction of Society: Comparative Studies of Myth, Ritual, and Classification* (New York: Oxford University Press, 1989), Lincoln illuminates the social force of symbols, not only in the construction of society, but also in its effective deconstruction and reconstitution. See also David Kertzer, *Ritual, Politics, and Power* (New Haven, Conn.: Yale University Press, 1988).

10. David Carrasco, "A Perspective for a Study of Religious Dimensions in Chicano Experience: *Bless Me, Ultima* as a Religious Text," in *Aztlán: International Journal of Chicano Studies Research* 3 (1982): 195–222; José Saldívar, *Border Matters: Remapping American Cultural Studies* (Berkeley: University of California Press, 1997), 188.

11. See Chela Sandoval, *Methodology of the Oppressed* (Minneapolis: University of Minnesota Press, 2000); and Laura Pérez, "El Desorden, Nationalism and Chicana/o Aesthetics," in Caren Kaplan, Norma Alarcón, and Minoo Moallem, eds., *Between Woman and Nation: Nationalisms, Transnational Feminisms, and the State* (Durham, N.C.: Duke University Press, 1999), 19–46.

12. Vicki L. Ruíz, *Out of the Shadows: Mexican Women in Twentieth-Century America* (New York: Oxford University Press, 1998).

13. José E. Limón, *Dancing with the Devil: Society and Cultural Poetics in Mexican American South Texas* (Madison: University of Wisconsin Press, 1994), and Limón, *American Encounters: Greater Mexico, the United States, and the Erotics of Cultures* (Boston: Beacon Press, 1998).

14. Gloria Anzaldúa, quoted in Anzaldúa, *Interviews/Intrevistas*, ed. Ana-Louise Keating (New York: Routledge, 2000), 96.

15. Ibid.

16. Bernardino de Sahagún, *Florentine Codex: General History of the Things of New Spain*, vol. 2, trans. Arthur J. O. Anderson and Charles Dibble (Santa Fe: School of American Research, 1970), 11.

17. From the *Florentine Codex*, reprinted in Miguel Léon-Portilla, ed., *The Broken Spears: The Aztec Account of the Conquest of Mexico* (Boston: Beacon Press, 1992), 6.

18. Don Luis González Obregón, *The Streets of Mexico*, trans. Blach Collet Wagner (San Francisco: George Fields, 1937), 15.

19. Betty Leddy, "La Llorona in Southern Arizona," *Western Folklore* 3 (July 1948): 272–77, 272. See also Bess Lomax Hawes, "La Llorona in Juvenile Hall," *Western Folklore* 3 (July 1968): 153–70; and Bacil F. Kirtley, " 'La Lorona' and Related Themes," *Western Folklore* 19 (1960): 155–68.

20. Octavio Paz, "Sons of La Malinche," in *The Labyrinth of Solitude*, trans. Lysander Kemp (New York: Grove Press, 1985), 75.

21. This narrative appears in a collection edited by Edward Garcia Kraul and Judith Beatty, *The Weeping Woman: Encounters with La Llorona* (Santa Fe: Word Process, 1988), 1.

22. *La Opinión*, Los Angeles, 15 and 16 December 1944; recounted in Monroy, *Rebirth*, 267.

23. Manuel Terán Lira, *El Niño Fidenco* (Mexico: Editorial Maconda, 1980). I elaborate the discussion of El Niño in chapter 4.

24. See Virgil Elizondo, *Galilean Journey: The Mexican American Promise* (Maryknoll, N.Y.: Orbis Books, 1983); and Jacques Lafaye, *Quetzalcóatl and Guadalupe: The Formation of Mexican National Consciousness, 1531–1813*, trans. Benjamin Keen (Chicago: University of Chicago Press, 1976).

25. See Sandra Messinger Cypress, *La Malinche in Mexican Literature: From History to Myth* (Austin: University of Texas Press, 1991).

26. Paz, "Sons of La Malinche," 85.

27. See www.lallorona.com, which offers a brilliant postmodern interpretation of the myth.

28. José E. Limón, "La Llorona, The Third Legend of Greater Mexico: Cultural Symbols, Women, and the Political Unconscious," in Adelaida R. Del Castillo, ed., *Between Borders: Essays on Mexicana and Chicana History* (Encino, Calif.: Floricanto Press, 1990), 417; emphasis mine.

29. Bourdieu, "Genesis and Structure of the Religious Field."

30. Cordelia Candelaria, "La Malinche, Feminist Prototype," *Frontiers* 2 (1980): 1–6.

31. See Norma Alarcón, "Traddutora, Traditora: A Paradigmatic Figure of Chicana Feminism," *Cultural Critique* 13 (Fall 1989): 57–87; Candelaria, "La Malinche"; and Adelaida R. Del Castillo, "*Malintzín Tenepal*: A Preliminary

Look into a New Perspective," in Alma M. García, ed., *Chicana Feminist Thought: The Basic Historical Writings* (Routledge, 1997), 122–26.

32. Paz, "Sons of La Malinche," 85.

33. Saldívar, *Borders Matters*, 148.

34. See also Deena Gonzalez's feminist historical revision of La Malinche, "Encountering Columbus," in Teresa Cordova, ed., *Chicano Studies: Critical Connection between Research and Community* (Albuquerque: The National Association for Chicano Studies, 1992), 13–19.

35. Ana Castillo, ed., *Goddess of the Americas, La Diosa de las Americas: Writings on the Virgin of Guadalupe* (New York: Riverhead Books, 1996), xxi.

36. Sandra Cisneros, "Guadalupe the Sex Goddess," in Castillo, ed., *Goddess of the Americas*, 47, 48.

37. Ibid., 51; ellipses original.

38. Carla Trujillo, "La Virgen de Guadalupe and Her Reconstruction in Chicana Lesbian Desire," in Carla Trujillo, ed., *Living Chicana Theory* (Berkeley: Third Woman Press, 1998), 212–31.

39. Lupe Reyes, quoted in E. J. Gong, Jr., "A Show of Faith in a Saint," *Los Angeles Times*, 13 December 1993.

40. See especially Rudolfo Anaya, *The Legend of La Llorona* (Berkeley, Calif.: Quinto Sol, 1984).

41. Limón, *Dancing with the Devil*, x.

42. Ruth Behar, *Translated Woman: Crossing the Border with Esperanza's Story* (Boston: Beacon Press, 1993), 235; James Clifford, "Partial Truths," introduction to Clifford, ed., *Writing Culture: The Poetics and Politics of Ethnography* (Berkeley: University of California Press, 1986), 1–26; see also Michael Taussig, *The Nervous System* (New York: Routledge, 1992).

43. Laura Pérez, "Spirit Glyphs: Reimagining Art and Artist in the Work of Chicana *Tlamatinime*," *Modern Fiction Studies* 44 (Spring 1998): 36.

44. Richard D. Hecht has termed this type of analysis a "cultural history of religions" for its focus on the religious strategies used to control the meanings of sacred space and time. "From History to Politics: Theorizing a Cultural History of Religions" (paper presented to the Department of Religious Studies, University of California, Santa Barbara, 28 October 1992), 22.

45. Pragmatism, or the "prophetic pragmatism" of Cornel West, informs my articulation of religious poetics for the ideals of scholarly "material force," or the real-world consequences of scholarly production. See Cornel West, *The American Evasion of Philosophy: A Genealogy of Pragmatism* (Madison: University of Wisconsin Press, 1989), esp. "Prophetic Pragmatism: Cultural Criticism and Political Engagement," 211–39. I disagree with West's conclusions on Foucault and will elaborate my points in future writings. On questions of truth and verification, I follow William James, who argues that truth is a process, that ideas *become* truth. See "Pragmatism's Conception of Truth," in William James, *Pragmatism* (New York: Dover, 1995), 76–91. This broad definition helps also to resolve a discussion among Latina/o theologians between *poesis* and *praxis*—the former more concerned with beauty and the latter more directly coincident with transformation and change. On this question, I follow Roberto Goizueta, who insists, "Precisely as embodied, human praxis is also beautiful." Roberto S.

Goizueta, "Beauty and Justice," in Goizueta, *Caminemos Con Jesús: Toward a Hispanic/Latino Theology of Accompaniment* (New York: Orbis Press, 1995), 106.

46. Behar, *Translated Woman*, 270.

47. See Renato Rosaldo, *Culture and Truth: The Remaking of Social Analysis* (Boston: Beacon Press, 1989).

48. See also Talal Asad, *Genealogies of Religion: Discipline and Reasons of Power in Christianity and Islam* (Baltimore: Johns Hopkins University Press, 1993), a collection of previously published essays that are equivocally described as "genealogies." Genealogy figures questions of origins, recovery, and recuperations, and current manifestations, unlike a "long history" that poses spatial and temporal limitations. See Fernand Braudel, "History and Social Sciences: The *Longue Dureé*," in Braudel, *On History*, trans. Sarah Matthews (Chicago: University of Chicago Press, 1980), 25–55.

49. Emile Durkheim, "Concerning the Definition of Religious Phenomena," in Durkheim, *Durkheim on Religion*, ed. and trans. W. S. F. Pickering (Atlanta: Scholars Press, 1994), 74–99, 74.

50. I. M. Lewis, foreword to John Eade and Michael J. Sallnow, eds., *Contesting the Sacred: The Anthropology of Christian Pilgrimage* (New York: Routledge, 1991), x.

51. See Victor Turner and Edith Turner, *Image and Pilgrimage in Christian Culture: Anthropological Perspectives* (New York: Columbia University Press, 1978).

52. Max Weber, "The Prophet," in Weber, *The Sociology of Religion*, trans. Ephraim Fischoff (Boston: Beacon Press, 1963), 46; see Nietzsche, *Thus Spoke Zarathustra*, trans. Walter Kaufmann, in *The Portable Nietzsche* (New York: Vintage Books, 1954).

53. Lewis, foreword to Eade and Sallnow, xi.

54. Weber, "The Prophet," 46.

55. Aristotle, *Poetics*, trans. Ingram Bywater (New York: Modern Library, 1954).

56. Durkheim, "Concerning the Definition," 91. Even while Durkheim went far for his time to avoid hierarchical distinctions between "primitive" and "civilized" in his definition of "religious phenomena," I disagree strongly with the evolutionary model that ultimately informs his thinking.

57. See Milan Kundera, *The Book of Laughter and Forgetting*, trans. Aaron Fisher (New York: Harper Perennial, 1999).

58. Daniel Cooper Alarcon, *The Aztec Palimpsest: Mexico in the Modern Imagination* (Tucson: University of Arizona Press, 1997).

59. See Henri Bergson, *Matter and Memory*, trans. Nancy Margaret Paul and W. Scott Palmer (New York: Zone Books, 1988).

60. Walter Benjamin, "A Berlin Chronicle," *Reflections: Essays, Aphorisms, Autobiographical Writings*, ed. Peter Demetz, trans. Edmund Jephcott (New York: Schocken Books, 1978), 25; Lawrence Sullivan, "Bodyworks: Knowledge of the Body in the Study of Religion," *History of Religions* 30:1 (August 1990): 86–99, 87; Bryan Turner, *Religion and Social Theory: A Materialist Perspective* (London: Heinemann Educational Books, 1983), 2.

61. Alfredo Austin López, *The Human Body and Ideology: Concepts of the Ancient Nahuas,* trans. Thelma Ortíz de Montellano and Bernardo Ortíz de Montellano (Salt Lake City: University of Utah Press, 1988), 417.

62. See Bernardo Ortíz de Montellano, *Aztec Health, Medicine, and Nutrition* (New Brunswick, N.J.: Rutgers University Press, 1990).

63. Michel Foucault, *Discipline and Punish: The Birth of the Prison,* trans. Alan Sheridan (New York: Vintage Books, 1979), 25.

64. Charles H. Long, *Significations: Signs and Symbols in the Interpretation of Religion* (Philadelphia: Temple University Press, 1986), 197. Long has pointed elsewhere to the ways in which this colonial discourse, premised upon a distinction between primitive/civilized, has folded into discourses on "popular religion," which are inevitably racialized discursive practices posing a binary structural relationship between subject/object, that is, "official religion" and abject, popular, racialized religion. See Charles Long, "Popular Religion," in Mircea Eliade, ed., *Encyclopedia of Religion* (Chicago: University of Chicago Press, 1986), 442–52.

65. Thomas Jefferson, "Laws," in Jefferson, *Notes on the State of Virginia* (New York: W. W. Norton, 1982 [1789]), 138, 139.

66. See Howard Omi and Michael Winnant, *Racial Formation in the U.S.: From the 1960s to 1990,* 2nd ed. (New York: Routledge, 1990).

67. Ronald Takaki, *Iron Cages: Race and Class in 19th Century America,* 2nd ed. (New York: Oxford University Press, 1990), 225.

68. Partha Chatterjee, "Whose Imagined Community?" in Chatterjee, *The Nation and Its Fragments: Colonial and Postcolonial Histories* (Princeton, N.J.: Princeton University Press, 1993), 6. Chatterjee argues in part that the impact of colonialism in India was to form a civil society vis-à-vis the state; the former worked to galvanize popular sentiment around spirituality that subverted British attempts at social control à la Indian nationalism.

69. Durkheim, "Concerning the Definition," 94.

70. On "cultural" and "psychic" death, see Judith Butler, *The Psychic Life of Power: Theories in Subjection* (Stanford, Calif.: Stanford University Press, 1997).

71. Benjamin, "A Berlin Chronicle," 25.

72. Ibid., 28.

73. See Jacques Derrida and Gianni Vattimo, eds., *Religion* (Stanford: Stanford University Press, 1996); Jacques Derrida, *Given Time: 1. Counterfeit Money,* trans. Peggy Kamuf (Chicago: University of Chicago Press, 1992).

74. On the specters of terror as social hauntings, see Avery Gordon, *Ghostly Matters: Haunting and the Sociological Imagination* (Minneapolis: University of Minnesota Press, 1997).

CHAPTER 1. THE TERROR OF POSTCOLONIAL HISTORY

1. Ramón Gutiérrez, *When Jesus Came, the Corn Mothers Went Away: Marriage, Sexuality, and Power in New Mexico, 1500–1846* (Stanford, Calif.: Stanford University Press, 1991), xvii.

2. J. Jorge Klor de Alva, "Spiritual Conflict and Accommodation in New Spain: Toward a Typology of Aztec Responses to Christianity," in George A. Col-

lier et al., eds., *The Inca and Aztec States, 1400–1800: Anthropology and History* (New York: Academic Press, 1982): 345–66, 346.

3. Gloria Anzaldúa, interview in Louise Keating, ed., *Interviews/Entrevistas* (New York: Routledge, 2000), 96.

4. Diego Dúran, *Book of the Gods and Rites and the Ancient Calendar*, eds. and trans. Fernando Horcasistas and Doris Heyden (Norman: University of Oklahoma Press, 1983), 410–11.

5. See Klor de Alva, "Spiritual Conflict," 353.

6. Gloria Anzaldúa, *Borderlands/La Frontera: The New Mestiza,* 2nd ed. (San Francisco: Aunt Lute Books, 1999).

7. Rudy Busto, "The Predicament of Nepantla: Chicana/o Religions into the 21st Century," in *Perspectivas/Occasional Papers* (Fall 1998): 7–21, 8.

8. Klor de Alva, "Spiritual Conflict," 354.

9. June Nash, "Gendered Deities and the Survival of Culture," in Sylvia Marcos, ed., *Genders/Bodies/Religions* (Cuernavaca, Mex.: ALER, 2000), 297, 300.

10. Miguel León-Portilla, *Aztec Thought and Culture: A Study of the Ancient Nahuatl Mind,* trans. Jack Emory Davis (Norman: University of Oklahoma Press, 1963), 3.

11. Ibid., 45, 46.

12. See Davíd Carrasco, "Myth, Cosmic Terror, and the Templo Mayor," in Johanna Broda, Davíd Carrasco, and Eduardo Matos Moctezuma, eds., *The Great Temple of Tenochtitlan* (Berkeley: University of California Press, 1992), 124–62.

13. Tzvetan Todorov, *The Conquest of America: The Question of the Other,* trans. Richard Howard (New York: Harper, 1984), 84.

14. "Sorrowful Certainty of Death" (ancient Nahuatl poem), in Miguel León-Portilla et al., eds. and trans., *Native Mesoamerican Spirituality* (Mahwah, N.J.: Paulist Press, 1980), 181.

15. León-Portilla, *Aztec Thought and Culture,* 99.

16. Davíd Carrasco, "Jaguar Christians in the Contact Zone," in Anthony M. Stevens Arroyo and Andres I. Pérez y Mena, eds., *Enigmatic Powers: Syncretism with African and Indigenous People's Religions among Latinos* (New York: Bildner Center, 1995), 60.

17. Stephen Greenblatt, *Marvelous Possessions: The Wonder of the New World* (Chicago: University of Chicago Press, 1991), 132.

18. See Beatriz Pastor, *The Armature of Conquest: Spanish Accounts of the Discovery of America, 1492–1589,* trans. Lydia Hunt (Stanford, Calif.: Stanford University Press, 1992).

19. For a definitive collection on Nahua myths of Quetzalcoatl, see "The Story of Quetzalcoatl," in Miguel León-Portilla, *Native Mesoamerican Spirituality* (Mahwah, N.J.: Paulist Press, 1980), 151–277.

20. See Davíd Carrasco, *Quetzalcoatl and the Irony of Empire: Myths and Prophecies in the Aztec Tradition,* 2nd ed. (Boulder: University Press of Colorado, 2000).

21. See Jacques Lafaye, *Quetzalcóatl and Guadalupe: The Formation of Mexican National Consciousness, 1531–1813,* trans. Benjamin Keen (Chicago: University of Chicago Press, 1974).

22. On the images of Christ in medieval art, see Carolyn Walker Bynum, "The Body of Christ in the Later Middle Ages: A Reply to Leo Steinberg," in *Fragmentation and Redemption: Essays on Gender and the Human Body in Medieval Religion* (New York: Zone Books, 1991), 79–118.

23. Nash, "Gendered Deities," 308.

24. See especially Bartolomé de las Casas, *Historia de las Indias* (Mexico: Mexico, Fondo de Cultura Económica, 1951).

25. Bartolomé de las Casas, *The Devastation of the Indies: A Brief Account,* trans. Herma Briffault (New York: Seabury Press, 1974), 40–42.

26. Todorov, *Conquest of America,* 146.

27. Enrique Dussel, "Europe, Modernity, and Eurocentrism," *Nepantla: Views from South* 1:3 (2000): 465–78, 474.

28. For an extensive discussion of the *encomienda* and *repartimiento* systems, see James Lockhart and Stuart B. Schwartz, *Early Latin America: A History of Colonial Spanish America and Brazil* (Cambridge, Eng.: Cambridge University Press, 1983).

29. Bartolomé de las Casas, *A Short Account of the Destruction of the Indies,* ed. and trans. Anthony Padgen (London: Penguin Books, 1992), 145.

30. See Ronald Grimes, *Symbol and Conquest: Public Ritual and Drama in Santa Fe* (Albuquerque: University of New Mexico Press, 1992).

31. On this incident, see especially Gutiérrez, *When Jesus Came,* 143–75.

32. Pedro Naranjo, quoted in Timothy Matovina and Gerald E. Poyo, eds., *¡Presente!: U.S. Latino Catholics from Colonial Origins to the Present* (Maryknoll, N.Y.: Orbis Press, 2000), 15.

33. William Taylor, *Magistrates of the Sacred: Priests and Parishioners in Eighteenth-Century Mexico* (Stanford, Calif.: Stanford University Press, 1996), 294.

34. Howard Lamar, "From Bondage to Contract: Ethnic Labor in the American West, 1600–1890," in Steven Hahn et al., eds., *The Countryside in the Age of Capitalist Transformation: Essays in the Social History of Rural America* (Chapel Hill: University of North Carolina Press, 1986), 314.

35. See Sherburne Cook, *The Conflict between the California Indian and White Civilization* (Berkeley: University of California Press, 1976).

36. See Carey McWilliams, *North from Mexico: The Spanish-Speaking People of the United States* (New York: Greenwood Press, 1968).

37. Roberto Lint-Sagarena, "Image and History: Mission Revival Architecture and Cultural Rhetoric in California" (paper presented to the American Academy of Religion annual meeting, 24 November 1997, San Francisco).

38. Douglas Monroy, *Thrown among Strangers: The Making of Mexican Culture in Frontier California* (Berkeley: University of California Press, 1990).

39. See Ramón Gutiérrez, "The Pueblo Indian World in the 16th Century," in *When Jesus Came,* 3–38.

40. Monroy, *Thrown among Strangers,* 25, 27.

41. Harrison G. Rogers, cited in Harrison C. Dale, ed., *The Ashley-Smith Explorations* (Glendale: Arthur H. Clark, 1941), 196.

42. Ibid., 204.

43. Carey McWilliams, cited in Monroy, *Thrown among Strangers,* 102.

44. Monroy, *Thrown among Strangers,* 127.

45. For a discussion of the well-known doctrine of Manifest Destiny, see Robert Bellah, *The Broken Convenant: American Civil Religion in Time of Trial*, 2nd ed. (Chicago: University of Chicago Press, 1975). For a treatment of westward movement, see Richard Slotkin, *Regeneration through Violence* (Middletown, Conn: Wesleyan University Press, 1973); and Patricia Nelson Limerick, *The Legacy of Conquest: The Unbroken Past of the American West* (New York: W. W. Norton, 1987).

46. Richard Henry Dana, *Two Years before the Mast* (Los Angeles: Ward Ritchie Press, 1964), 92, 98.

47. Hubert Howe Bancroft, *California Pastoral, 1769–1848* (San Francisco: History Company, 1897), 180.

48. Ibid., 559.

49. Ibid., 561.

50. Quoted in Taylor, *Magistrates of the Sacred*, 174.

51. "They Wait for Us," quoted in Antonia Castañeda, "Gender, Race, and Culture: Spanish-Mexican Women in the Historiography of Frontier California," *Frontiers* 1 (1990): 8–20, 10.

52. Cited in Richard Griswold del Castillo, *The Los Angeles Barrio* (Berkeley: University of California Press, 1979), 23.

53. James Alexander Forbes, cited in Francis J. Weber, ed., *Documents of California Catholic History* (Los Angeles: Dawson's Bookshop, 1965), 50.

54. Jonathan D. Stevenson, quoted in Weber, *Documents of California Catholic History*, 53.

55. See Orlando O. Espín, "Trinitarian Monotheism and the Birth of Popular Catholicism: The Case of Sixteenth-Century Mexico," in *The Faith of the People: Theological Reflections on Popular Catholicism* (Maryknoll, N.Y.: Orbis, 1997), 32–62.

56. For a review of the literature on the relationship between Indian religion and Spanish colonial Catholicism, see Jeffery S. Thies, *Mexican Catholicism in Southern California* (New York: Peter Lang, 1993).

57. Griswold del Castillo, *The Los Angeles Barrio*, 13.

58. Gregory Singleton, *Religion in the City of Angels: American Protestant Culture and Urbanization in Los Angeles, 1850–1930* (Ann Arbor, Mich.: UMI Research Press, 1977), 33.

59. For the complete numerical table, see "Dynamics of the Catholic Church: From Pastoral to Social Concern," in Leo Grebler et al., eds., *The Mexican-American People: The Nation's Second Largest Minority* (New York: Free Press, 1970), esp. app. J, 668–70.

60. See Jay P. Dolan, *The American Catholic Experience* (Garden City, N.Y.: Doubleday, 1985).

61. Catherine L. Albanese, *America: Religions and Religion*, 2nd ed. (Belmont, Calif.: Wadsworth, 1992), 87.

62. See especially Gilbert Cadena, "Chicanos and the Catholic Church: Liberation Theology as a Form of Empowerment" (Ph.D. diss., University of California, Riverside, 1987); and Antonio R. Soto, "The Chicano and the Church in Northern California, 1848–1979: A Study of an Ethnic Minority within the Roman Catholic Church" (Ph.D. diss., University of California, Berkeley, 1978).

63. See Robert O. Orsi, *The Madonna of 115th Street: Faith and Community in Italian Harlem, 1880–1950* (New Haven, Conn.: Yale University Press, 1985).

64. Dolan, *The American Catholic Experience,* 372.

65. Michael E. Engh, "From Frontera Faith to Roman Rubrics: Altering Hispanic Religious Customs in Los Angeles, 1855–1880," *U.S. Catholic Historian* 4 (Fall 1994): 85–106.

66. Bishop Thaddeus Amat, C.M., pastoral letter to Diocese of Southern California, 28 December 1855, Los Angeles, Santa Barbara Mission Archives, 5.

67. Engh, "Frontera Faith to Roman Rubrics," 89, 91.

68. Father Dominic Manucy, cited in Moises Sandoval, *On the Move: A History of the Hispanic Church in the United States* (Maryknoll, N.Y.: Orbis Press, 1991), 32; see Timothy Matovina, *Tejano Religion and Ethnicity: San Antonio, 1821–1860* (Austin: University of Texas Press, 1995).

69. See Alberto Pulido, *The Sacred World of the Penitentes* (Washington, D.C.: Smithsonian Institution Press, 2000).

70. See James Griffith, *Beliefs and Holy Places: A Spiritual Geography of the Pimeria Alta* (Tucson: University of Arizona Press, 1992).

71. Edward Hanna, letter, *San Francisco Chronicle,* 10 March 1926. For an overview of various regional confrontations between Euroamerican and Mexican Catholics throughout the Southwest following the American takeover, see Sandoval, *On the Move;* Jay P. Dolan and Gilberto Hinojosa, eds., *Mexican Americans and the Catholic Church, 1900–1965* (Notre Dame, Ind.: University of Notre Dame Press, 1994), also contains useful information.

72. See Singleton, *Religion in the City of Angels.*

73. Ibid., 2.

74. Alden Buell Case, *Thirty Years with the Mexicans: In Peace and Revolution* (New York: Fleming H. Revell, 1917), 243, 242.

75. Patrick H. McNamara, "Catholicism, Assimilation, and the Chicano Movement," in *Chicanos and Native Americans: The Territorial Minorities,* Rudolph O. de la Garza et al., eds. (Englewood Cliffs, N.J.: Prentice-Hall, 1973).

76. George J. Sánchez, *Becoming Mexican American: Ethnicity, Culture, and Identity in Chicano Los Angeles, 1900–1945* (New York: Oxford University Press, 1993), 164.

77. See Mario T. Garcia, *Mexican Americans: Leadership, Ideology, and Identity, 1930–1960* (New Haven, Conn.: Yale University Press, 1989).

78. Sánchez, *Becoming Mexican American,* 164.

79. On the ratio of U.S.-born Chicanos to Mexicans, see Grebler et al., eds., *The Mexican-American People,* 84; Griswold del Castillo, *The Los Angeles Barrio.*

80. Sánchez, *Becoming Mexican American.*

81. Robert Blauner, *Racial Oppression in America* (New York: Harper and Row, 1972), 56.

82. For an extensive discussion of the Treaty of Guadalupe Hidalgo, see Richard Griswold del Castillo, *The Treaty of Guadalupe Hidalgo: A Legacy of Conflict* (Norman: University of Oklahoma Press, 1996).

83. For histories of these events, see Albert Camarillo, *Chicanos in a Chang-*

ing Society: From Mexican Pueblos to American Barrios in Santa Barbara and Southern California, 1848–1930 (Cambridge, Mass.: Harvard University Press, 1979); and Griswold del Castillo, *The Los Angeles Barrio.* See also Tomás Almaguer, *Racial Fault Lines: The Historical Origins of White Supremacy in California* (Berkeley: University of California Press, 1994).

84. Tomás Almaguer, "Interpreting Chicano History: The World-System Approach to Nineteenth-Century California," *Review* 4 (Winter 1981): 459–508.

85. "East Los Angeles" is commonly used euphemistically to denote the communities east of downtown Los Angeles and across the Los Angeles River. Mary Pardo explains as follows:

> The designations "Eastside" Los Angeles and East Los Angeles are used to refer to the area east of the downtown civic center. Often used interchangeably and similarly in demographic profiles, the geographical area East Los Angeles proper, is unincorporated; Eastside Los Angeles immediately east of the Los Angeles river is part of the city of Los Angeles and represented by the same political structure. The neighborhoods immediately east of the river include Boyle Heights, Lincoln Heights, and El Sereno. . . . all have historically shared public services and territory. (Pardo, *Mexican American Women Activists: Identity and Resistance in Two Los Angeles Communities* [Philadelphia: Temple University Press, 1998])

My fieldwork in Los Angeles focused on Boyle Heights, which has historically been the center of the region. Boyle Heights occupies a spatial area of 3.27 square miles. Its population of 55,157 consists of 2 percent African-Americans, 4 percent Asian-Pacific Islanders, 93 percent Latina/os, and 1 percent others. Thirty-nine percent of these households earn below $15,000 dollars per year, and another 39 percent of households earn between $15,000 and $35,000 dollars per year (Pardo, *Mexican American Women Activists*).

Eighty-nine thousand residents were counted in this area during the 1990 census (which most agree is an undercount). The median family income for the 96 percent of the "Spanish-origin" residents was $12,767, and 25 percent of residents fell below the poverty line. The 2000 census counted 124,283 residents of East Los Angeles.

86. Sánchez, *Becoming Mexican American,* 13.

87. José Vasconcelos, *The Cosmic Race: The Mission of the Iberian Americans,* 1st English ed. (Los Angeles: Centro de Publicaciones, California State University, 1979); Garcia, *Mexican Americans;* Andrés G. Guerrero, *A Chicano Theology* (Maryknoll, N.Y.: Orbis Press, 1987); Roberto Goizueta, *Caminemos Con Jesus: Toward a Hispanic/Latino Theology of Accompaniment* (Maryknoll, N.Y.: New York: Orbis Press, 1995).

88. José Vasconcelos, *A Mexican Ulysses: An Autobiography,* trans. W. Rex Crawford (Bloomington: Indiana University Press, 1963).

89. Vasconcelos, *The Cosmic Race,* 1.

90. Ibid., 30.

91. Ibid., 32.

92. Ibid., 30.

93. Ibid., 3.

94. See Vicki L. Ruíz, *Cannery Women, Cannery Lives: Mexican Women,*

Unionization, and the California Food Processing Industry, 1930–1950 (Albuquerque: University of New Mexico Press, 1987). See also Max Vorspan and Lloyd P. Gartner, *History of the Jews of Los Angeles* (Philadelphia: Jewish Publication Society of America, 1970); and Deborah Moore Dash, *To the Golden Cities: Pursuing the American Jewish Dream in Miama and L.A.* (Cambridge, Mass.: Harvard University Press, 1994).

95. See Mike Davis, *City of Quartz: Excavating the Future in Los Angeles* (New York: Vintage Books, 1990).

96. Alurista, "Cultural Nationalism and Xicano Literature during the Decade of 1965–1975," *Melus* 8:2 (Summer 1981): 22–34.

97. For an account of the life of Joaquín Murieta, see John Rollin Ridge, *The Life and Adventures of Joaquin Murieta* (Norman: University of Oklahoma Press, 1986 [1955]).

98. Pedro Castillo and Albert Camarillo, *Furia y Muerte: Los Bandidos Chicanos* (Los Angeles: Aztlán Publications, UCLA Chicano Studies Center, 1973), 35.

99. Rodolfo "Corky" Gonzales, *I Am Joaquín* (Denver: *El Gallo* Newspaper, 1967).

100. Antonia Castañeda, personal communication, 1 March 1993.

101. John R. Chávez, *The Lost Land: The Chicano Image of the Southwest* (Albuquerque: University of New Mexico Press, 1985), 5.

102. Alurista, from "Mesa Redonda," in Cesár A González-T, ed., *Rudolfo A. Anaya: Focus on Criticism* (La Jolla, Calif.: Lalo Press, 1990), 449.

103. Carlos Muñoz, *Youth, Identity, Power: The Chicano Generation* (London: Verso, 1989), 78.

104. Luis Leal, "In Search of Aztlán," in Rudolfo A. Anaya and Francisco Lomeli, eds., *Aztlán: Essays on the Chicano Homeland* (Albuquerque: University of New Mexico Press, 1989), 11.

105. Rodolfo "Corky" Gonzalez, cited in Stan Steiner, *The Mexican Americans* (New York: Harper and Row, 1969), 385. See especially Jack D. Forbes, "The New Aztlanes: Fact or Fantasy?" in Forbes, *Aztecas del Norte: The Chicanos of Aztlán* (Greenwich, Conn.: Fawcett Publications, 1973).

106. Michael Pina, "The Archaic, Historical, and Mythicized Dimensions of Aztlán," in Anaya and Lomeli, *Aztlán*, 35.

107. Muñoz, *Youth, Identity, and Power*, 76–77; emphasis added.

108. Anaya and Lomeli, *Aztlán*.

109. Ruben Salazar, "Chicano Conferees Plan 5-State School Walkout," *Los Angeles Times*, 1 April 1969, 206.

110. Forbes, *Aztecas del Norte*, 297.

111. "El Plan de Aztlán," reprinted in Anaya and Lomeli, *Aztlán*, 4.

112. Diego Dúran, *The History of the Indies of New Spain*, trans. Doris Heyden and Fernando Horcasitas (New York: Orion Press, 1964), 9–14.

113. Davíd Carrasco, *Quetzalcoatl and the Irony of Empire: Myths and Prophecies in the Aztec Tradition* (Chicago: University of Chicago Press, 1982), 168.

114. Cherríe Moraga, *The Last Generation* (Boston: South End Press, 1993), 150.

115. Rafael Pérez-Torres, "From the Homelands to the Borderlands: The Reformation of Aztlán," in Pérez-Torres, *Movements in Chicano Poetry: Against Myths, Against Margins* (New York: Cambridge University Press, 1995), 56–96.

116. See Victor Turner, *Drama, Fields, and Metaphors: Symbolic Action in Human Societies* (Ithaca, N.Y.: Cornell University Press, 1974).

117. See Carl Gutiérrez-Jones, *Rethinking the Borderlands: Between Chicano Cultural Discourse and Legal Discourse* (Berkeley: University of California, 1995).

118. Virgilio Elizondo, "Mestizaje," in Elizondo, *Galilean Journey: The Mexican American Promise* (Maryknoll, N.Y.: Orbis Press, 1983), 5, 14.

119. Sánchez, *Becoming Mexican American,* 9.

120. Gloria Anzaldúa, "La Prieta," in Cherríe Moraga and Gloria Anzaldúa, eds., *This Bridge Called My Back: Writings by Radical Women of Color* (New York: Kitchen Table Press, 1983), 205.

121. The word *mestizo* is Spanish for "miscegenation." It has come to denote the race of people who emerged from the mix of Spanish and Indians in the colonization of Mexico.

122. Chela Sandoval, "Mestizaje as Method," in Carla Trujillo, ed., *Living Chicana Theory* (Berkeley, Calif.: Third Woman Press, 1998), 359.

123. Davíd Carrasco, "The Myth of the Chicano Borderlands: Shamanism and the Loco-Centric Imagination in the Work of Gloria Anzaldúa and Dr. Loco" (paper presented at the New Directions in Chicano Religions Conference, 17 February 1997, Santa Barbara, Calif.).

CHAPTER 2. VIRTUAL VIRGIN NATION

1. Sandra Cisneros, "Guadalupe the Sex Goddess," in Ana Castillo, ed., *Goddess of the Americas: La Diosa de las Americas: Writings on the Virgin of Guadalupe* (New York: Riverhead Books, 1996), 46–51, 51.

2. See Victor Turner, "Social Drama," in Victor Turner, *Dramas, Fields, and Metaphors: Symbolic Action in Human Society* (Ithaca, N.Y.: Cornell University Press, 1974); and Eric Wolf, "The Virgin of Guadalupe as a Mexican National Symbol," *Journal of American Folklore* 71 (1958): 34–49.

3. For a discussion of the carnivalesque, see Peter Stallybrass and Allon White, *The Politics and Poetics of Transgression* (Ithaca, N.Y.: Cornell University Press, 1986). Stallybrass and White elaborate Mikhail Bakhtin's understanding of the carnival as a form of "populist inversion" and subversion of social mandates.

4. *Nican Mophua,* reprinted in Ernesto de la Torre Villar and Ramiro Navarro de Anda, eds., *Testimonios Históricos Guadalupanos* (Mexico City: Fondo de Cultura Económica, 1982).

5. Ibid., 28. While the original text is said to have been written in Nahuatl, the Spanish edition was and is the standard reference text.

6. *A Brief History of the Guadalupe Apparitions,* distributed by Guadalupe Basilica (Mexico City: n.p., n.d.).

7. Ibid, 28.

8. Ibid.

9. Ibid., 28, 29.

10. Ibid.

11. For a discussion of the *retablo* tradition, see Jorge Druand and Douglas S. Massey, *Miracles on the Border: Retablos of Mexican Migrants to the United States* (Tucson: University of Arizona Press, 1995).

12. *A Brief History of the Guadalupe Apparitions,* 24.

13. Ibid., 31, 32.

14. Jacques Lafaye, *Quetzalcóatl and Guadalupe: The Formation of Mexican National Consciousness, 1531–1813,* trans. Benjamin Keen (Chicago: University of Chicago Press, 1974), 297–98.

15. Jonathan Kendall, *La Capital: The Biography of Mexico City* (New York: Henry Holt, 1988), 164.

16. Fray Toribio de Benavente Motolinía, *Memoriales* (Mexico: Universidad Nacional Autónoma de México, Instituto de Investigaciones Históricas, 1971), 34, 35.

17. Kendall, *La Capital,* 165.

18. See especially Virgilio Elizondo, *Galilean Journey: The Mexican American Promise* (Maryknoll, N.Y.: Orbis Press, 1983). See also Andrés G. Guerrero, *A Chicano Theology* (Maryknoll, N.Y.: Orbis Press, 1987); and Jeanette Rodriguez, *Our Lady of Guadalupe: Faith and Empowerment among Mexican American Women* (Austin: University of Texas Press, 1994).

19. Rodriguez, *Our Lady of Guadalupe,* 127.

20. Stafford Poole, *Our Lady of Guadalupe: The Origins and Sources of a Mexican National Symbol, 1531–1797* (Tucson: University of Arizona Press, 1995).

21. Davíd Carrizales, quoted in James F. Smith and Margaret Ramirez, "Challenge to Sainthood Evokes Charges of Racism," *Los Angeles Times,* 11 December 2000; Robert E. Quirk, *The Mexican Revolution and the Catholic Church, 1910–1929* (Bloomington: Indiana University Press, 1973), 4.

22. See especially "Myth, Cosmic Terror, and the Templo Mayor," in Johanna Broda, Davíd Carrasco, and Eduardo Matos Moctezuma, eds., *The Great Temple of Tenochtitlan* (Berkeley: University of California Press, 1992), 124–62.

23. Ibid., 130.

24. Aztec poem, translated from Nahuatl into Spanish by Angel Maria Garibay K., in Miguel León-Portilla, ed., *Broken Spears: The Aztec Account of the Conquest of Mexico,* trans. into English by Lysander Kemp (Boston: Beacon Press, [1962] 1990), 149.

25. Davíd Carrasco, *Quetzalcoatl and the Irony of Empire: Myths and Prophecies in the Aztec Tradition* (Chicago: University of Chicago Press, 1982), 130.

26. Alfredo López Austin, *The Human Body and Ideology: Concepts of the Ancient Nahuas,* trans. by Thelma Ortiz de Montellaño (Salt Lake City: University of Utah Press, 1988), 417.

27. Davíd Carrasco, "The Sacrifice of Tezcatlipoca: To Change Place," in Carrasco, ed., *To Change Place: Aztec Ceremonial Landscapes* (Boulder: University of Colorado Press, 1988), 33.

28. Brian Wilson, "The New World's Jerusalems: Franciscans, Puritans, and Sacred Space in the Colonial Americas, 1519–1820" (Ph.D. diss., University of California, Santa Barbara, 1996), 1.

29. Lauro López Beltrán, "Guadalupe Eucharist Congress, 1949," published as *El Santuario del Tepeyac* (Mexico City: Editorial "Juan Diego," 1951), 15.

30. Jeffrey F. Meyer, *The Dragons of Tiananmen: Beijing as Sacred City* (Columbia: University of South Carolina Press, 1991), 149, 153, 157.

31. Bernardino de Sahagún, *Florentine Codex: General History of the Things of New Spain*, vol. 2, trans. Arthur J. O. Anderson and Charles Dibble (Santa Fe: School of American Research, 1970), 352.

32. See Ramón Ruíz, *Triumphs and Tragedy: A History of the Mexican People* (New York: W. W. Norton, 1992).

33. See Kendall, "Independence," in *La Capital,* 266–91.

34. Cited in Quirk, *Mexican Revolution,* 42, 43.

35. On the Cristero revolt, see David C. Bailey, *Viva Cristo Rey!: The Cristero Rebellion and the Church-State Conflict in Mexico* (Austin: University of Texas Press, 1974).

36. Guadalupe Ortega, "Catholic Women Plead with Senora [*sic*] Calles to Get President to Revoke Religious Laws," *New York Times,* 29 July 1926, 1.

37. Ibid., 1.

38. Ibid., 2.

39. Ibid.

40. Quirk, *Mexican Revolution,* 243–45.

41. In 1994, 1995, and 1996 I attended the 12 December pilgrimage to Guadalupe.

42. See Diana Eck, *Banaras: City of Light* (New York: Alfred A. Knopf, 1982).

43. "Rosa Hernández," 10 December 1994, Mexico City, interview by author in Spanish.

44. Rubén Martinez, "Mexico's Lady of Hope," *San Francisco Weekly,* 4 January 1995.

45. Paolo Giuriati and Elio Masferrer Kan, eds., *No temas . . . yo soy tu madre: Estudios socioantropológicos de los peregrinos a la basílica* (Mexico City: Plaza y Valdez, 1998).

46. Ibid., 130.

47. Carlos Monsiváis, *Mexican Postcards,* trans. John Kraniauskas (London: Verso, 1997), 45.

48. "Raul Canizares," 12 December 1996, Tepeyac, Mexico, videotaped interview by author in Spanish.

49. "Fernando Savera," 12 December 1996, Tepeyac, Mexico, videotaped interview by author in Spanish.

50. June Nash, "Gendered Deities and the Survival of Culture," in Sylvia Marcos, ed., *Genders/Bodies/Religions* (Cuernavaca, Mex.: ALER, 2000), 308.

51. Alan Sandstorm, "The Tonantso Cult of the Eastern Nahua," in James J. Preston, ed., *Mother Worship: Themes and Variations* (Chapel Hill: University of North Carolina Press, 1982), 5–24.

52. Giuriati and Kan, eds., *No temas yo soy tu madre,* 153.

53. John O. West, *Mexican American Folklore* (Little Rock, Ark.: August House, 1988), 159.

54. Richard Boudreaux, "Room for Ethnic Roots in the Church, Pope Says," *Los Angeles Times*, August 2, 2002.

55. John R. Chávez, *The Lost Land: The Chicano Image of the Southwest* (Albuquerque: University of New Mexico Press, 1984), 2.

56. Sandra Cisneros, "Tepeyac," in Cisneros, *Woman Hollering Creek* (New York: Vintage Books, 1991), 21–24. See also Luis Leal, "From Mango Street to Tepeyac," *No Longer Voiceless* (San Diego: Marin Publications, 1995), 127–34.

57. Cisneros, "Tepeyac," 22.

58. Ibid., 23.

59. James F. Smith and Margaret Ramirez, "Challenge to Sainthood Evokes Charges of Racism," *Los Angeles Times*, 11 December 2000.

CHAPTER 3. RELIGIOUS TRANSNATIONALISM

1. Quoted in Antonio Soto, "The Chicano and the Church in Northern California, 1848–1978: A Study of an Ethnic Minority within the Roman Catholic Church" (Ph.D. diss., University of California, Berkeley, 1978), 115.

2. "Señora Inés de la Cruz," 11 April 1993, East Los Angeles, interview conducted by author in Spanish. Tape recorded.

3. See especially Gary Reibe-Estrella and Timothy Matovina, eds., *Horizons of the Sacred: Mexican Religious Traditions in Twentieth-Century U.S. Catholicism* (Ithaca, N.Y.: Cornell University Press, 2002).

4. Lawrence J. Mosqueda, "Twentieth-Century Arizona, Hispanics, and the Catholic Church," *U.S. Catholic Historian* 9:1–2 (Winter–Spring 1990): 87–103, 90.

5. Manuel Gamio, *The Life Story of the Mexican Immigrant*, 2nd ed. (New York: Dover Publications, 1971 [1931]).

6. Soledad Sandoval, quoted in ibid., 63.

7. Ibid., 28.

8. Father Gregory Boyle, quoted in Margaret Ramirez, "The Gangs and Their God," *Los Angeles Times*, May 8, 1999.

9. "Yaquis of Mexico Join in Guadalupe Ceremony," *Los Angeles Times*, 12 December 1934; and *La Opinión* (Los Angeles), 16 December 1934, 3, 6.

10. See Francisco E. Balderrama, *In Defense of La Raza: The Los Angeles Mexican Consulate and the Mexican Community, 1929–1936* (Tucson: University of Arizona Press, 1982), 73–87.

11. See Rodolfo Acuña, *Occupied America: A History of Chicanos*, 3rd ed. (San Francisco: Harper and Row, 1988), 198–250. Acuña reports that over 500,000 Mexicans and Mexican-Americans were forcibly deported between the years 1929 and 1939. In 1931–34, the first three years of the Los Angeles County program, 12,668 were shipped to Mexico.

12. "Yaquis of Mexico Join in Guadalupe Ceremony," *Los Angeles Times*, 12 December 1934.

13. See Vicki L. Ruíz, *Cannery Women, Cannery Lives: Mexican Women,*

Unionization, and the California Food Processing Industry, 1930–1950 (Albuquerque: University of New Mexico Press, 1987).

14. Alden Buell Case, *Thirty Years with the Mexicans: In Peace and Revolution* (New York: Fleming H. Revell, 1917), 242, 243.

15. Guillermo Salorio, quoted in Gamio, *Life Story,* 129.

16. Evangeline Hymer, *A Study of the Social Attitudes of Adult Mexican Immigrants in Los Angeles and Vicinity* (San Francisco: R. and R. Research Associates, 1971 [1923]), 41.

17. See especially the descriptions in Vernon Monroe McCombs, *From over the Border: A Study of Mexicans in the United States* (New York: Council of Women for Home Missions, 1925), 131–33.

18. Michael E. Engh, "Companion of the Immigrants: Devotion to Our Lady of Guadalupe among Mexicans in the Los Angeles Area, 1900–1940," *Journal of Hispanic/Latino Theology* 5:1 (August 1997): 37–47, 41.

19. "Grupos católicos exponen los objectivos de la manifestación," *La Opinión,* 8 December 1934, 6.

20. Engh, "Companion of the Immigrants," 39.

21. Advertisement, *La Voz Guadalupana* (Los Angeles), 1 December 1936.

22. Robert O. Orsi, "The Center out There, in Here, and Everywhere Else," *Journal of Social History* 2 (Winter 1991): 213–32, 223.

23. See especially Mario T. Garcia, *Mexican Americans: Leadership, Ideology, and Identity, 1930–1960* (New Haven, Conn.: Yale University Press, 1989); and George J. Sánchez, *Becoming Mexican American: Ethnicity, Culture, and Identity in Chicano Los Angeles, 1900–1945* (New York: Oxford University Press, 1993).

24. P. A. Mendoza, "Los Estados Unidos se unen a la América Latina en su amor a la Santísima Virgen de Guadalupe," *La Voz Guadalupana,* March–May 1937, 9.

25. See Mike Davis, *City of Quartz: Excavating the Future in Los Angeles* (New York: Vintage Books, 1992), 325–72, 331.

26. Miguel de Zarraga, "México Afuera de México" and "Ofrenda a California," *La Voz Guadalupana,* March–May 1937, 12.

27. See Herbert Bolton, *The Padre on Horseback* (Chicago: Loyola University Press, 1963).

28. José Alvárez B., "The Mexicans in Los Angeles," *La Voz Guadalupana,* March–May 1937.

29. Antonio Pompa y Pompa, "El Padre Kino en las Californias," *La Voz Guadalupana,* July 1946, 10.

30. Manuel Tortolero, "Coronación de Nuestra Señora de Guadalupe," *La Voz Guadalupana,* June–August 1937, 6; emphasis original.

31. Alfonso Junco, "Seámos imperialistas," *La Voz Guadalupana,* September 1937, 35.

32. José Alvárez B., "La ciudad de Los Angeles, orgullo de California sur, atraccion del mundo, y centro de maravillas," *La Voz Guadalupana,* September 1937, 12.

33. *Los Angeles Times,* 6 June 1937.

34. Ibid., 18.

35. "Devout Hold Giant Parade," *Los Angeles Times,* 13 December 1938.

36. José Alvárez B., "The Triumph of Guadalupanism," *La Voz Guadalupana,* January 1947, 21; original in English.

37. Ibid.

38. Acuña, *Occupied America,* 251–306.

39. The 1950 census report in Los Angeles is unclear on this point. The enumeration added as a separate category for the first time "persons of Spanish surname," and determined how many of that group were either born in Mexico or had one or both parents born there. For a discussion of the 1950 census as it relates to ethnic Mexicans in Los Angeles, see Patrick H. McNamara, "Mexican Americans in Los Angeles County: A Study in Acculturation" (M.A. thesis, St. Louis University, 1957), 22–41.

40. McNamara, "Mexican Americans in Los Angeles County," 35, 39.

41. Lawrence J. Mosqueda has traced the positions espoused in various encyclicals and their potential impact on Chicano activism, beginning with Pope Leo XIII's 1891 *Rerum novarum* and ending in 1967 with Pope Paul VI's encyclical *Populorum progressio.* Mosqueda concludes that the documents "are not meant to overthrow capitalism but to save, humanize, and liberalize capitalism." Mosqueda, *Chicanos, Catholicism, and Political Ideology* (Lanham, Md.: University Press of America, 1986), 153.

42. For a discussion of César Chávez's movement, see especially Susan Ferriss and Ricardo Sandoval, *The Fight in the Fields: César Chavez and the Farmworkers Movement* (New York: Harcourt Brace, 1997).

43. Chávez, "The Mexican American and the Catholic Church," quoted in ibid., 215, 218; first ellipsis is original.

44. Cited in Alberto Pulido, "Are You an Emissary of Jesus Christ? Justice, the Catholic Church, and the Chicano Movement," *Explorations in Ethnic Studies* 14:1 (January 1991): 30.

45. *La Raza* (Los Angeles), 9 November 1969.

46. "Club-Swinging Mob Breaks into Church at Christmas Mass," *Los Angeles Times,* 25 December 1969.

47. Ibid.

48. Oscar Zeta Acosta, *The Revolt of the Cockroach People* (New York: Vintage Books, 1989), 18.

49. Lara Medina, "Las Hermanas: Chicana/Latina Religious-Political Activism, 1971–1997" (Ph.D. diss., Claremont Graduate School, 1998).

50. Juan Romero, "Charism and Power: An Essay on the History of PADRES," *U.S. Catholic Historian* 1–2 (Winter–Spring 1990): 147–63, 160.

51. See Edmundo Rodriguez, "Church Movements," in Jay P. Dolan and Allan Figueroa Deck, eds., *Hispanic Catholicism: Issues and Concerns* (Notre Dame, Ind.: University of Notre Dame Press, 1994), 130–54.

52. For a discussion of UNO, see Davis, *City of Quartz,* 325–72.

53. Cited in Rubén Martinez and Mike Davis, "The Church," *L.A. Weekly,* December 1989, 22–28.

54. Rubén Martinez, *The Other Side: Notes from the New L.A., Mexico City, and Beyond* (New York: Vintage Books, 1993), 27.

55. Ibid., 86.

56. Ibid., 87.

57. See Laura Pérez, *Altarities: Chicana Art, Politics, and Spirituality* (Durham, N.C.: Duke University Press, forthcoming).

58. For an extensive study of Mothers of East Los Angeles, see Mary Pardo, "Mexican American Women Grassroots Community Activists: Mothers of East Los Angeles," *Frontiers: A Journal of Women Studies* 1 (1990): 1–7; and Pardo, *Mexican American Women Activists: Identity and Resistance in Two Los Angeles Communities* (Philadelphia: Temple University Press, 1998).

59. Pardo, "Mexican American Women," 2.

60. "Señora Inés de la Cruz," 11 April 1993, East Los Angeles, interview conducted by author in Spanish. Tape recorded.

61. Kay Turner, "Subversive Views of the Virgin: Mexican American Women Altaring the Canon," privately circulated manuscript, 5. See also Turner, "Mexican American Women's Home Altars: The Art of Relationship" (Ph.D. diss., University of Texas at Austin, 1990); and Turner, "Mexican American Home Altars: Towards Their Interpretation," in *Aztlán: International Journal of Chicano Studies Research* 13 (1982): 309–26.

62. Turner, "Subversive Views of the Virgin," 2.

63. Ibid., 10.

64. Amalia Mesa-Bains, "Chicano Chronicle and Cosmology: The Works of Carmen Lomas Garza," in Carmen Lomas Garza, *Pedacito de mi Corazón* (Austin, Tex.: Laguna Gloria Art Museum, 1991), 28.

65. Amalia Mesa-Bains, "Site of Spiritual Geography: Translations of Lived Practice and Iconographic Gesture in Contemporary Art" (paper presented at the workshop on Sacred Images/Sacred Space, Getty Research Institute, Los Angeles, 24 January 2001). See also Mesa-Bains, "Spiritual Geographies," in Virginia M. Fields and Victor Zamudio Taylor, eds., *The Road to Aztlán: Art from a Mythic Homeland* (Los Angeles: Los Angeles County Museum of Art, 2002), 332–41.

66. Celeste Fremon, "Let No Child Be Left Behind," *Los Angeles Times Magazine,* 15 October 1995.

67. Ibid.

68. See Celeste Fremon, *Father Greg and the Homeboys: The Extraordinary Journey of Father Greg Boyle and His Work with the Latino Gangs of East L.A.* (New York: Hyperion, 1995).

69. Gregory J. Boyle, "Hope Is the Antidote," *Los Angeles Times,* 6 January 1995.

70. For more information about Father Boyle's work, write or call Reverend Gregory J. Boyle, S.J., Jobs for a Future, 1848 E. First Street, Los Angeles, Calif. 90033, (213) 526-1254.

71. Gregory J. Boyle, East Los Angeles, 11 June 1996, interview by author. All subsequent quotations of Father Boyle are from this interview.

72. Juan Sauvageau, *Stories That Must Not Die* (Austin: Oasis Press, 1976).

73. See Richard Flores, *Los Pastores: The Mexican Shepherd's Play in South Texas* (Washington, D.C.: Smithsonian Institution Press, 1995).

74. Mosqueda, *Chicanos, Catholicism, and Political Ideology,* 94.

75. Marta Weigle documents the *tinieblas* in *Brothers of Light, Brothers of Blood: The Penitentes of the Southwest* (Albuquerque: University of New Mexico Press, 1976).

76. See William A. Christian, Jr., *Local Religion in Sixteenth-Century Spain* (Princeton, N.J.: Princeton University Press, 1981).

77. See *Soul of the City,* prod. Adán M. Medrano (JM Communications, Houston, Tex., 1996), videocassette. A project of the Mexican-American Cultural Center, San Antonio.

78. Alberto Pulido, *The Sacred World of the Penitentes* (Washington, D.C.: Smithsonian Institution Press, 2000), 39.

79. Karen Mary Davalos, "La Quinceañera: Making Gender and Ethnic Identities," *Frontiers* 16 (1996): 121, 116.

80. Engh, "Companion of the Immigrants," 46.

81. On the transformation of foreign, hostile, and abstract "space" to familiar home "place" by means of memory, myth, and body, see Yi-Fu Tuan, *Space and Place: The Perspective of Experience* (Minneapolis: University of Minnesota Press, 1977).

82. Rodolfo F. Acuña, *Anything but Mexican: Chicanos in Contemporary Los Angeles* (London: Verso, 1996), x.

83. Javier Alva, "Los Angeles: The Sacred Spot," in Luis Valdez, ed., *Aztlán: An Anthology of Mexican American Literature* (New York: Vintage Books, 1972), 170–73.

84. See Mario T. García, *Ruben Salazar, Border Correspondent: 1955–1970* (Berkeley: University of California Press, 1995).

85. See Martinez, *The Other Side.*

86. Mesa-Bains, "Sites of Spiritual Geography"; see also Lara Medina, "Los Espíritus Siguen Hablando: Chicana Spiritualities," in Carla Trujillo, ed., *Living Chicana Theory* (Berkeley: Third Women Press, 1998), 189–213.

87. Jeffery S. Thies, *Mexican Catholicism in Southern California* (New York: Peter Lang, 1993), 10, 11.

88. Ibid., 9, 10.

89. Sandra Cisneros, *Woman Hollering Creek* (New York: Vintage Books, 1992), 117, 118.

90. William Madsen, *The Mexican Americans of South Texas,* 2nd ed. (New York: Henry Holt, 1973), 62–63.

91. Elaine K. Miller, *Mexican Folk Narrative from the Los Angeles Area* (Austin: University of Texas Press, 1973), 222.

92. Davíd Carrasco, *Religions of Mesoamerica: Cosmovision and Ceremonial Centers* (San Francisco: Harper and Row, 1990), 142.

93. Octavio Paz, *The Labyrinth of Solitude,* trans. Lysander Kemp (New York: Grove Press, 1985), 51.

94. Ibid., 52.

95. Ibid., 64.

96. Sybil Venegas, "The Day of the Dead in Aztlán: Chicano Variations on Life, Death, and Self-Preservation" (Los Angeles, published by author, 1995), 1. See also Juanita Garciagodoy, *Digging the Days of the Dead: A Reading of Mexico's Días de Muertos* (Boulder: University Press of Colorado, 1998).

97. Ibid; also, Paz, *Labyrinth of Solitude*, 64.

98. Juanita Garciagodoy, *Digging the Days of the Dead*, 144.

99. Lara Medina and Gilbert R. Cadena, "Días de los Muertos: Public Ritual, Community Renewal, and Popular Religion in Los Angeles," in Timothy Matovina and Gary Riebe-Estrella, eds., *Horizons of the Sacred: Mexican Traditions in U.S. Catholicism* (Ithaca: Cornell University Press, 2002).

100. Medina, "Los Espíritus Siguen Hablando," 189.

101. Ana Castillo, *Massacre of the Dreamers: Essays on Xicanisma* (New York: Plume, 1995), 152.

CHAPTER 4. *EL DON*

1. "Esperanza Perdida," 17 September 1999, East Los Angeles, interview by author.

2. *Curanderismo* comes from the Spanish verb *curar,* which means "to heal" or "to cure." The term *curanderismo* is used to describe a wide variety of practices, from herbal home remedies to spiritual healings. Generally, it is a community-based Mexican symbolic and spiritual system with antecedents in pre-Columbian Mexico; it blends Catholic rituals with those originating in pre-Columbian times. Today it is practiced in both Mexican and Chicano communities. For a discussion of *curanderismo,* see Robert Trotter and Juan Antonio Chavira, *Curanderismo: Mexican American Folk Healing,* 2nd ed. (Athens: University of Georgia Press, 1997).

3. Davíd Carrasco, "A Perspective for a Study of Religious Dimensions in Chicano Experience: *Bless Me, Ultima* as a Religious Text," *Aztlán: International Journal of Chicano Studies Research* 13 (1982): 195–222; and see also Isabel Lagárriga Attias, "Intento de caracterización del chamanismo urbano en Mexico con el ejemplo del espiritualismo Trinitario Mariano," in Attias, ed., *Chamanismo en Latinoamérica* (Mexico City: Plaza y Valdés, 1995).

4. Carlos Monsiváis, "The Boy Fidencio and the Roads to Ecstasy," in Monsiváis, *Mexican Postcards,* trans. John Kraniauskas (London: Verso, 1997), 121.

5. William Madsen, *The Mexican Americans of South Texas,* 2nd ed. (New York: Henry Holt, 1973), 70.

6. Fernando M. Trevino, ed., "Hispanic Health and Nutrition Examination Survey, 1982–1984: Findings on Health Status and Health Care Needs" (U.S. Department of Health and Human Services, 1992), 1.

7. Steven Lozano Applewhite, "Curanderismo," *Health and Social Work* 4 (November 1995): 247. This citation is taken from the author's abstract.

8. Beatrice Ann Roeder, "Chicano Folk Medicine from Los Angeles, California" (Ph.D. diss., University of California, Los Angeles, 1984), ix. Cf. Beatrice Ann Roeder, *Chicano Folk Medicine from Los Angeles, California* (Berkeley: University of California Press, 1988).

9. William Taylor, *Magistrates of the Sacred: Priests and Parishioners in Eighteenth-Century Mexico* (Stanford, Calif.: Stanford University Press, 1996), 71.

10. Bernardo Ortíz de Montellano, "Curanderos: Spanish Shamans or Aztec Scientists?" *Grito del Sol: A Chicano Quarterly* 2 (April–June 1976): 21–28, 22.

11. See Bernardo Ortíz de Montellano, "Mesoamerican Religious Tradition and Medicine," in Lawrence Sullivan, ed., *Healing and Restoring: Health and Medicine in the World's Religious Traditions* (New York: Macmillan, 1989), 359–94.

12. Ortíz de Montellano, "Curanderos," 27.

13. Sylvia Marcos, "Cognitive Structures and Medicine: The Challenge of Mexican Popular Medicines," *Concilium: Internation Review of Theology* 11 (1988): 87–96, 92.

14. Sylvia Marcos, "Sacred Earth: Mesoamerican Perspectives," *Concilium: International Review of Theology* 261, Leonardo Boff and Virgil Elizondo, eds. (October 1995): 27–37, 29, 30.

15. Hospitals in Los Angeles and in other Latina/o communities are incorporating *curanderismo*. See the recent report released by the Center for the Study of Religion and American Civic Culture: John Orr and Sherry May, "Religion and Health Services in Los Angeles: Reconfiguring the Terrain," December 1999, http://www.usc.edu/dept/LAS/religion_online/publications/civic_profile/CivicProfile_99.html.

16. "Luzina López," 10 December 1996, Mexico City, interviewed in Spanish by author.

17. See Trotter and Chavira, *Curanderismo*.

18. Eliseo Torres, *The Folk Healer: The Mexican-American Tradition of Curanderismo* (Kingsville, Tex.: Nieves Press, 1983), 6.

19. Ibid., 9.

20. Trotter and Chavira, *Curanderismo*, 92.

21. Torres, *The Folk Healer*, 23.

22. Ibid.

23. Doña Juanita, quoted in Trotter and Chavira, *Curanderismo*, 93.

24. On the theory of the gift as template and mechanism of social control, see Marcel Mauss, *The Gift: Forms and Functions of Exchange in Archaic Societies*, trans. Ian Cunnison (New York: W. W. Norton, 1967).

25. Madsen, *Mexican Americans of South Texas*, 90.

26. For discussion of the gift as temporal construct or "chronotype," see Jacques Derrida, *Given Time: 1. Counterfeit Money*, trans. Peggy Kamuf (Chicago: University of Chicago Press, 1992).

27. Max Weber, "The Prophet," in Weber, *The Sociology of Religion*, trans. Ephraim Fischoff (Boston: Beacon Press, 1963).

28. Madsen, *Mexican Americans of South Texas*, 90.

29. Ibid., 91.

30. Carrasco, "Perspective for a Study," 209.

31. See Ruth Dodson, "The Curandero of Los Olmos," in Wilson M. Hudson, ed., *The Healer of Los Olmos and Other Mexican Lore* (Dallas: Southern Methodist University Press, 1951), 9–70.

32. Octavio Romano, "Don Pedrito Jaramillo: The Emergence of a Mexican-American Folk-Saint" (Ph.D. diss., University of California, Berkeley, 1964).

33. Ibid., 18.

34. Ibid.; capitalization is original.

35. "Curandero Visits the City," *San Antonio Express*, 22 April 1894.

36. Ibid.

37. Juan Sauvageau, *Stories That Must Not Die* (Austin: Oasis Press, 1976), 21–22.

38. Ibid., 19.

39. "Curandero Visits the City," *San Antonio Express,* 22 April 1894.

40. See David Montejano, *Anglos and Mexicans in the Making of Texas, 1836–1965* (Austin: University of Texas Press, 1987).

41. To date, perhaps the best account of the life of Teresa Urrea in English remains Frank Putnam's article "Teresa Urrea, 'The Saint of Cabora,'" *Southern California Quarterly* 3 (September 1963): 245–64.

42. Helen Dare, "Santa Teresa, Celebrated Mexican Healer, Whose Powers Awe Warlike Yaquis in Sonora, Comes to Restore San Jose Boy to Health," *San Francisco Examiner,* 27 July 1900.

43. Putnam, "Teresa Urrea," 248.

44. Sources agree on the events of this story; however, some do not distinguish the two-week coma from the three-month, eighteen-day trancelike period that was to follow.

45. Mario Gill, "Teresa Urrea, la Santa de Cabora," *Historia Mexicana* (July 1956–June 1957): 626–44.

46. Barbara June Macklin and N. Ross Crumrine, "Three North Mexican Folk Saint Movements," *Comparative Studies in Society and History* 15 (1973): 89–105, 90.

47. Dare, "Santa Teresa."

48. William Curry Holden, *Teresita* (Owing Mills, Md.: Stemmer House, 1978), 106.

49. Ibid.

50. "Santa Teresa, the Yaqui Idol, *a Cause of Fierce Indian Uprisings,* Has Come to Heal Diseases," *San Francisco Examiner,* 9 September 1900 (italics in article title original).

51. According to Mexican anthropologist Sylvia Echániz, *espiritualistas* were present in Teresa's movement. Personal communication to author, Mexico City, June 1999.

52. Holden, *Teresita,* 76.

53. Ibid., 80.

54. Putnam, "Teresa Urrea," 253.

55. *San Francisco Examiner,* 29 July 1900.

56. Putnam, "Teresa Urrea," 254.

57. Public statement issued by Teresa Urrea, *El Paso Herald,* 11 September 1896.

58. Isabel Lagárriga Attias, personal communication to author, Mexico City, June 1999.

59. Holden, *Teresita,* 180.

60. Putnam has spoken of the lack of information on Teresa's life prior to her move to Cabora as a six-year "lapse," but he does not mention the relationship with María Sonora until Teresa is at Cabora. Holden discusses Teresa's mentor relationship with a *curandera* at Cabora, but he calls her "Huila," which is odd, given that Holden does not use pseudonyms in other parts of the text.

61. Holden, *Teresita,* 15. See also Carlos Larralde, "Santa Teresa: A Chicana Mystic," *Grito del Sol: A Chicano Quarterly* 2 (April–June 1978): 1–113. Larralde typically cites his earlier book, *Mexican American: Movements and Leaders* (Los Alamitos, Calif.: Hwong Publishing, 1976).

62. Carlos Castañeda, *The Teachings of Don Juan: A Yaqui Way of Knowledge,* 1st ed. (Berkeley: University of California Press, 1968).

63. Larralde, "Santa Teresa," 15.

64. Ibid., 92; emphasis added.

65. For a discussion of social segmentation through somatic training, see Norbert Elias, *The Civilizing Process* (New York: Pantheon, 1982).

66. Holden, *Teresita,* 103, 131.

67. See Manuel Terán Lira, *El Niño Fidencio* (Mexico City: Editorial Maconda, 1980); Fernando Garza Quiros, *El Niño Fidencio: Un personaje desconocido* (Monterrey, Nuevo León, Mex.: 1970); and especially June Macklin, "El Niño Fidencio: Un estudio del curanderismo en Nuevo León," in *Anuario humánitas* (Monterrey, N.L., Mex.: Universidad de Nuevo León, Centro de Estudios Humanísticos, 1967).

68. Quiros, *El Niño Fidencio,* 25.

69. Fidencio Constantino, cited in Barbara June Macklin and N. Ross Crumrine, "Three North Mexican Folk Saint Movements," *Comparative Studies in Society and History* 15 (1973): 89–105, 91.

70. Quiros, *El Niño Fidenco,* 96.

71. Macklin and Crumrine, "Three North Mexican Movements," 98.

72. Dr. Francisco Vela González, quoted in Monsiváis, *Mexican Postcards,* 125.

73. Monsiváis, *Mexican Postcards,* 127.

74. Ibid., 121.

75. Quiros, *El Niño Fidencio,* 34.

76. Ibid., 35.

77. Ibid., 37.

78. Ibid.

79. Lira, *El Niño Fidencio,* 19.

80. Ibid., 102, 103.

81. Tomás Eloy Martínez, *Santa Evita,* trans. Helen Lane (New York: Knopf, 1996), 52.

82. *We Believe in El Niño Fidencio* (Los Angeles: California State University, 1972), film.

83. Quoted in Quiros, *El Niño Fidencio,* 26.

84. Francisca Aguirre, quoted in Dore Gardner, *A Heart Thrown Open* (Albuquerque: Museum of New Mexico Press, 1992), 82.

85. I wish to thank June Macklin for generously sharing her extraordinary knowledge concerning Niño Fidencio with me, especially in Mexico City in June 1999.

86. For a discussion of the role of space and its Latina/o religious deconstruction, see Mary Davalos, "The Real Way of Praying: The Vía Crucis, Mexicano Sacred Space, and the Architecture of Domination," in Timothy Matovina and Gary Riebe-Estrella, eds., *Horizons of the Sacred: Mexican*

Traditions in U.S. Catholicism (Ithaca, N.Y.: Cornell University Press, 2002), 41–68.

87. Sagrado Corazón is located within the Boyle Heights region of East Los Angeles; historically, Boyle Heights has been the center of the region.

88. "Caridad," 17 September 1999, East Los Angeles, interview conducted by author.

89. Gloria Anzaldúa, *Borderlands/La Frontera: The New Mestiza,* 2nd ed. (San Francisco: Spinsters/Aunt Lute Press, 1999).

90. See Luis D. León, "*Soy una Curandera y Soy una Católica:* The Poetics of Religious Healing," in Matovina and Riebe-Estrella, *Horizons of the Sacred,* 95–118.

91. Monsiváis, *Mexican Postcards,* 125.

92. Rudolfo Anaya, *Bless Me, Ultima* (New York: Warner, 1972).

93. Carrasco, "Perspective for a Study," 212, 207.

94. Monsiváis, *Mexican Postcards,* 121.

CHAPTER 5. DIASPORA SPIRITS

1. Quoted in Isabel Lagárriga Attias, *Medicina tradicional y espiritismo: Los espiritualistas de Jalapa, Veracrus* (Mexico City: Instituto Nacional de Antropología e Historia, 1979), 25–26. Attias explains that this myth was told to her by a native informant, who claimed it was from the biography of Ovieda.

2. Attias, 1979, 53.

3. For an elaborate discussion on the differences between these groups, see June Macklin, "Belief, Ritual, and Healing: New England Spiritualism and Mexican American Spiritism Compared," in Irving I. Zaretsky and Mark P. Leone, eds., *Religious Movements in Contemporary America* (Princeton, N.J.: Princeton University Press, 1974), 383–417.

4. On American spiritualism, see Ann Braude, *Radical Spirits: Spiritualism and Women's Rights in Nineteenth-Century America* (Boston: Beacon, 1989).

5. See Kaja Finkler, "Spiritualism in Rural Mexico," in *International Congress of the Americanists: Proceedings September 2–10, 1976,* vol. 6 (1981): 99–105.

6. See Finkler, *Spiritualist Healers in Mexico: Successes and Failures of Alternative Therapeutics* (Salem, Wis.: Sheffield Publishing, 1994 [1985]).

7. "Espiritualismo mexicano," from the television series *Retorno a la espiritualidad,* Cine Testimonio, S.A. de C.V., 30 minutes.

8. See Enrique Krauze, *Francisco I. Madero: Místico de la Libertad México* (México, D.F.: Fondo de Cultura Económica, 1987).

9. Silvia Ortíz Echániz, *Una religiosidad popular: El espiritualismo trinitario mariano* (México, D.F.: Instituto Nacional de Antropología e Historia, 1990), 207; the sample is from 231 *espiritualistas.*

10. Echániz, "Gender Relations in the Spiritualist Ritual of the 'Marian Trinitarians,'" 347.

11. Ibid., 349.

12. This small booklet of 225 pages is sold privately by churches for a few dollars, and there is no publication information.

13. Jose Pacheco Domínquez, "Templo de 'La Fe'" (México, D.F., 1960), 1 page; reproduced in full in Echániz, "Espiritualismo en Mexico," app.; emphasis original.

14. See Echániz, "Espiritualismo en Mexico," xxx.

15. "Luzina López," Mexico City, 10 December 1996, interview conducted by author in Spanish.

16. Roque Rojas Esparza, *El ultimo testamento, revelado de los años 1861–1869* (Mexico City: n.p., n.d.), 216–17.

17. Diego Dúran, *Historia de las Indias de Nueva España e Islas de Tierra Firme* (México, D.F.: Consejo Nacional para la Cultura y las Artes, 1955).

18. Silvia Ortíz Echániz, "El espiritualismo en México," *America Indígena* 1 (January–March 1979): 147–50, 154.

19. "General Structure of the Mexican Patriarchal Church of Elías Founded by Roque Rojas in 1866," reproduced in full in Silvia Ortíz Echániz, *Espiritualismo en Mexico* (Mexico City: Distributed by Instituto Nacional de Antropología e Historia, 1977).

20. Quoted in Echániz, *Espiritualismo en Mexico,* 8.

21. Ibid., 15.

22. Echániz, *Una religiosidad popular,* 142.

23. "Luzina López," 10 December 1996, Mexico City, interview conducted by author in Spanish.

24. Echániz, *Espiritualismo en Mexico,* 18.

25. Conversation with temple guardian at Mediodía main temple, July 1999, Mexico City, conducted by author in Spanish.

26. Interview with two women outside the Mediodía main temple, 16 July 2001, Mexico City, conducted by author in Spanish.

27. 23 February 1997, Templo Mediodía Trinitario Mariano, Boyle Heights.

28. Ibid.

29. Srta. Celia Paredes Mandujano et al., *Libro del coro* (n.p, 1995), 21.

30. *Oraciones dadas al Sexto Sello,* no author (n.p., n.d.).

31. Ibid., 1.

32. Ibid., 9, 10.

33. Ibid., 9.

34. "Juana Cruz," 10 December 1996, Mexico City, interview conducted by author in Spanish.

35. "Sophia," 10 December 1996, Mexico City, interview conducted by author in Spanish.

36. "Dolores Pueblo," 10 December 1996, Mexico City, interview conducted by author in Spanish.

37. "Francisco Alvárez," 12 December 1996, Tepeyac, Mexico City, interview conducted by author in Spanish.

38. "Luzina López," 11 December 1996, Mexico City, interview conducted by author in Spanish. Subsequent quotations in this section are from this interview.

39. "Sister Ester," 1 March 1997, greater East Los Angeles area, interview conducted by author in Spanish.

40. Ibid.

41. Sylvia Marcos, "Cognitive Structures and Medicine: The Challenge of

Mexican Popular Medicines," *Concilium: International Review of Theology* 11 (1988): 87–96, 90.

42. Ronald Takaki, *Iron Cages: Race and Class in 19th Century America,* 2nd ed. (New York: Oxford University Press, 1990).

43. I. M. Lewis, *Ecstatic Religion: A Study of Shamanism and Spirit Possession* (London: Routledge, 1989).

44. See Michael Taussig, *Mimesis and Alterity: A Particular History of the Senses* (New York: Routledge, 1993).

45. Finkler, *Spiritualist Healers,* vii; emphasis added.

46. Ibid., 25.

CHAPTER 6. BORN AGAIN IN EAST L.A., AND BEYOND

1. "Fe," 11 April 1994, Boyle Heights, East Los Angeles, interview by author in Spanish.

2. Richard Rodriguez, *Days of Obligation: An Argument with My Mexican Father* (New York: Penguin, 1992), 176.

3. Andrew Greeley, "Defection among Hispanics," *America,* 30 July 1988, 61–62.

4. Gaston Espinosa, Virgilio Elizondo, and Jesse Miranda, eds., "Hispanic Churches in American Public Life: Summary of Findings," Interim Reports 2003.2 (January 2003): 1–28. For a copy of the summary, visit the HCAPL web page: HCAPL.org.

5. Ariela Keysar, Barry A. Kosmin, and Ego Mayer, eds., "Religious Identification among Hispanics in the United States/The American Religious Survey," 5. In partnership with the Program for the Analysis of Religion among Latinos (PARAL). Published by PARAL out of the Graduate Center of the City University of New York and Brooklyn College, 12 December 2002.

6. See *Epoca,* 16 October 1995, 15, 22.

7. See http://www.victoryoutreach.org.

8. See Harvey Cox, *Fire from Heaven: The Rise of Pentecostalism and the Reshaping of American Religion in the Twenty-First Century* (Reading, Mass.: Addison Wesley, 1995).

9. See Acts 2:1–22.

10. "Weird Babel of Tongues: New Sect of Fanatics Is Breaking Loose," *Los Angeles Times,* 18 April 1906.

11. Bartleman, *The Way of Faith,* 1 August 1906. See also Frank Bartleman, *Azusa Street* (Plainfield, N.J.: Logos International, 1980), a reprint of Bartleman's first account, printed in 1925 under the title *How "Pentecost" Came to Los Angeles—How It Was in the Beginning.*

12. Frank Bartleman, "Pentecost Has Come: Los Angeles Being Visited by a Revival of Bible Salvation and Pentecost as Recorded in the Book of Acts," *Apostolic Faith,* September 1906, 1.

13. Ibid.

14. Ibid.

15. On Protestant "cultural integration" of *mexicanos,* see Clifton Holland, *The Religious Dimension of Hispanic Los Angeles: A Protestant Case*

Study (Pasadena, Calif.: William Carey Library, 1974), 317. On the use of Guadalupe for evangelization, see Michael E. Engh, "Companion of the Immigrants: Devotion to Our Lady of Guadalupe among Mexicans in the Los Angeles Area, 1900–1940," *Journal of Hispanic/Latino Theology* 5:1 (August 1997): 45.

16. Manuel Gamio, *Mexican Immigration to the United States: A Study of Human Migration and Adjustment* (New York: Dover, 1971 [1930]), especially 108–27, 117.

17. Mrs. Mary Galmond, "The Pentecostal Baptism Restored," *Apostolic Faith,* October 1906, 2.

18. Bartleman, *The Way of Faith,* 1 August 1906, 64.

19. Ibid., 21; emphasis original.

20. William J. Seymour, "The Apostolic Faith Movement," *Apostolic Faith,* September 1906.

21. Ibid.

22. Bartleman, *The Way of Faith,* 1 August 1906.

23. On Latino Pentecostalism as a borderlands phenomenon, see Gaston Espinosa, "Borderland Religion: Los Angeles and the Origins of the Latino Pentecostalism Movement in the U.S., Mexico, and Puerto Rico, 1900–1945" (Ph.D. diss., University of California, Santa Barbara, 1999).

24. *Apostolic Faith,* November 1906, 1.

25. See Dañiel Ramirez, "Borderlands Praxis: The Immigrant Experience in Latino Pentecostal Churches," *Journal of the American Academy of Religion* 67:3 (September 1999): 573–96.

26. Grant Wacker, "Pentecostalism," in Charles H. Lippy and Peter W. Williams, eds., *The Encyclopedia of the American Religious Experience: Studies of Traditions and Movements,* 3 vols. (New York: Scribner's, 1988), 933–47.

27. Art Blajos, with Keith Wilkerson, *Blood In, Blood Out* (London: Monarch, 1996).

28. Ibid., 34, 35.

29. Ibid., 27.

30. Ibid., 28.

31. Ibid., 31.

32. Ibid., 150.

33. Ibid., 151, 152, 157; emphasis added.

34. Sonny Arguinzoni, *God's Junkie* (Plainfield, N.J.: Logos International, 1971); Arguinzoni, *Internalizing the Vision* (La Puente, Calif.: Victory Outreach Publications, 1995). The video- and audiotapes are called *The Testimony of Sonny Arguinzoni* and are distributed by Victory Outreach Publications, with no printed dates.

35. Sonny Arguinzoni and Julie Arguinzoni, *Treasures out of Darkness* (Green Forest, Ark.: New Leaf Press, 1991).

36. See Nicky Cruz, *Run, Baby, Run* (Plainfield, N.J.: Logos International, 1968).

37. Arguinzoni and Arguinzoni, *Treasures out of Darkness,* 99–100.

38. Ibid., 246.

39. *Victory Outreach Mission Statement* (n.p, n.d.), 1.

40. Rodriguez, *Days of Obligation*.

41. "Pastor Felix" and "Lola Felix," 11 April 1997, Boyle Heights, East Los Angeles, videotaped interview by author in English.

42. Eliodoro Esteves ("Pastor Lolo"), March 1995, East Los Angeles, interview by author.

43. See Luis D. León, "Somos un Cuerpo en Cristo: Notes on Power and the Body in an East Los Angeles Chicano/Mexicano Pentecostal Community," *Latino Studies Journal* 5 (September 1994): 60–86.

44. See Manuel H. Peña, *The Texas Mexican Conjunto: History of a Working-Class Music* (Austin: University of Texas Press, 1985); and Peña, *Barrio Rhythm: Mexican American Music in Los Angeles* (Urbana: University of Illinois Press, 1993).

45. Arlene Sanchez Walsh has powerfully described the cultural techniques deployed by AV and the more class- and culturally-diverse Vineyard Church. She does not consider the Spanish-language AV, which has become integral to the organization's success among Latino youth as a whole and fosters the middle-class constituency she claims the English churches lack. See "Slipping into Darkness: Popular Culture and the Creation of a Latino Evangelical Youth Culture," in Richard W. Flory and Donald E. Miller, eds., *Gen X Religion* (New York: Routledge, 2000), 74–91, 85.

46. "Brother Saul," 14 May 1996, East Los Angeles, interview by author.

47. "Kiko Chavez," 22 May 1995, Boyle Heights, East Los Angeles, interview by author.

48. "Jesse Garcia" ("Pastor Chuy"), 14 June 1995, El Sereno, Calif., interview by author. All his quotations come from this interview.

49. See Luis D. León, "Born Again in East L.A.: The Congregation as Border Space," in R. Stephen Warner and Judith Wittner, eds., *Gatherings in Diaspora: Religious Communities and the New Immigration* (Philadelphia: Temple University Press, 1998), 163–96.

50. "Manny Martinez," 30 April 1995, Boyle Heights, East Los Angeles, interview by author. All his quotations come from this interview.

51. "Magdalena Torres," 9 July 1996, Boyle Heights, East Los Angeles, interview by author in Spanish.

52. "Pastor Felix" and "Lola Felix," 11 April 1997, Boyle Heights, East Los Angeles, videotaped interview by author in English.

53. "Lulu," 30 April 1994, Boyle Heights, East Los Angeles, interview by author.

54. "Noé Garcia," 18 June 1995, East Los Angeles, interview by author.

55. Group interview by author, 5 June 1996, Boyle Heights, East Los Angeles. Subsequent quotations from this interview appear in this section.

56. "Señora Carmela," 16 May 1994, Boyle Heights, East Los Angeles, interview by author in Spanish.

57. Richard Rodríguez, "Evangelicos: Changes of Habit, Changes of Heart. The Crusade for the Soul of the Mission," *Image Magazine*, 26 October 1986.

58. Ty Tagami, "Body and Soul," *Los Angeles Times,* 30 November 1994.
59. See Victor Turner, *Dramas, Fields, and Metaphors: Symbolic Action in Human Society* (Ithaca, N.Y.: Cornell University Press, 1974).
60. Rodriguez, *Days of Obligation,* 198.
61. See especially Michel Foucault, *Discipline and Punish: The Birth of the Prison* (New York: Vintage Books, 1979).
62. Arguinzoni, *Internalizing the Vision,* 140.
63. *Victory Outreach Mission Statement,* 1.

CONCLUSION. *FIN DE SIGLO* IN THE BORDERLANDS

1. Homi Bhabha, *The Location of Culture* (New York: Routledge, 1994).
2. See Roberto S. Goizueta, *Caminemos con Jesús: Toward a Hispanic/ Latino Theology of Accompaniment* (New York: Orbis Press, 1995); and Alex García-Rivera, *A Community of the Beautiful: A Theological Aesthetics* (Collegeville, Minn.: Liturgical Press, 1999).
3. Rimbault-Dodderidge-Simon-El Vez, "Oralé," performed by El Vez, in *Boxing with God,* Graciasland Music BMI, n.d. Compact disc.
4. Quoted in June Nash, "Gendered Deities and the Survival of Culture," in Sylvia Marcos, ed., *Genders/Bodies/Religions* (Cuernavaca, Mex.: ALER, 2000), 308.
5. Anzaldúa, *Borderlands/La Frontera: The New Mestiza,* 2nd ed. (San Francisco: Aunt Lute Press, 1999), 102.
6. Davíd Carrasco, "The Sacrifice of Texcatlipoca: To Change Place," in Carrasco, ed., *To Change Place: Aztec Ceremonial Landscapes* (Boulder: University Press of Colorado Press), 33.
7. Enrique Dussel, "Europe, Modernity, and Eurocentrism," *Nepantla: Views from South* 1:3 (2000): 465–78, 474.
8. Lawrence Sullivan, "Bodyworks: Knowledge of the Body in the Study of Religion," *History of Religions* 30:1 (August 1990): 86–99, 87.
9. Michel Foucault, *Discipline and Punish: The Birth of the Prison,* trans. Alan Sheridan (New York: Vintage Books, 1979), 61.
10. Amalia Mesa-Bains, "Spiritual Geographies," in Virginia M. Fields and Victor Zamudio-Taylor, eds., *The Road to Aztlán: Art from a Mythic Homeland* (Los Angeles: Los Angeles Country Museum of Art, 2001).
11. Yolanda M. López, "The Virgin of Guadalupe on the Road to Aztlán" (paper presented at the Los Angeles County Museum of Art, Los Angeles, 4 August 2001).
12. See especially Ari Keiv, *Curanderismo: Mexican-American Folk Psychiatry* (New York: Free Press, 1968).
13. Michel Foucault, *Birth of the Clinic: An Archaeology of Medical Perception* (New York: Vintage, 1973), 166.
14. Isabel Lagarriga Attias, "Intento de caracterización del chamanismo urbano en Mexico con el ejemplo del espiritualismo Trinitario Mariano," in Attias, ed., *Chamanismo en Latinoamérica* (Mexico City: Plaza y Valdes, 1995), 85–102.
15. Kaja Finkler has documented this teaching in *Spiritualist Healers in Mex-*

ico: Successes and Failures of Alternative Therapeutics (Salem, Wisc.: Sheffield Publishing, 1994 [1985]).

16. Jonathan Z. Smith, *Map Is Not Territory: Studies in the History of Religions* (Chicago: University of Chicago Press, 1978), 143.

17. Carrasco, "Sacrifice of Texcatlipoca."

18. See Anita Brenner's now classic work, *Idols behind Altars* (New York: Biblo and Tannen, 1929).

19. Peter van der Veer, *Religious Nationalism: Hindus and Muslims in India* (Berkeley: University of California Press, 1994), 11.

20. Nash, "Gendered Deities," 309.

21. For a discussion of Fundamentalist dispensationalism, see George Marsden, *Fundamentalism and American Culture: The Shaping of Twentieth-Century Evangelicalism* (New York: Oxford University Press, 1980).

22. Karl Marx, *Capital: A Critique of Political Economy*, vol. 1, *The Process of Capitalist Production*, ed. Frederick Engels (New York: International Publishers, 1967), 51.

23. Marcel Maus, *The Gift: The Form and Reason for Exchange in Archaic Societies*, trans. by W. D. Haus (New York: Norton, 1990); Jacques Derrida, *Given Time: 1. Counterfeit Money*, trans. Peggy Kamuf (Chicago: University of Chicago Press, 1992).

24. See Leigh Schmidt, *Consumer Rites: The Buying and Selling of American Holidays* (Princeton, N.J.: Princeton University Press, 1995).

25. Richard Flores, "Religion and Gender," paper presented to the Program for the Analysis of Religion among Latinos, Symposium on Popular Religion, Chicago, 17 October 1996.

26. Ibid., 9.

27. See Harvey Cox: *Fire from Heaven: The Rise of Pentecostalism and the Reshaping of Religion in the Twenty-First Century* (Reading, Mass: Addison Wesley, 1995).

28. Max Weber, "The Prophet," in Weber, *The Sociology of Religion*, trans. Ephraim Fischoff (Boston: Beacon Press, 1963).

29. Catherine Bell, "Performance," in Mark C. Taylor, ed., *Critical Terms for Religious Studies* (Chicago: University of Chicago Press, 1998), 205–224, 208, 216; emphasis original.

30. For a discussion of the concept of misrecognition, see Catherine Bell, *Ritual Theory, Ritual Power* (New York: Oxford University Press, 1992).

31. Judith Butler, *Gender Trouble: Feminism and the Subversion of Identity* (New York: Routledge, 1990).

32. Ruth Behar, *Translated Woman: Crossing the Border with Esperanza's Story* (Boston: Beacon Press, 1993), 315, 316.

33. Michel Taussig, *Mimesis and Alterity: A Particular History of the Senses* (New York: Routledge, 1993).

34. Alberto Pulido, *The Sacred World of the Penitentes* (Washington, D.C.: Smithsonian Institution Press, 2000).

35. I. M. Lewis, *Ecstatic Religion: A Study of Shamanism and Spirit Possession* (London: Routledge, 1989).

36. Manuel Vasquez, "Pentecostalism, Collective Identity, and Transnation-

alism among Salvadorans and Peruvians in the U.S.," *Journal of the American Academy of Religion* 67:3 (September 1999): 617–36, 624.

37. The language of disembedding suggests Anthony Giddens's theory of modernity. However, Giddens's thesis focuses on disembedding *social relations* from their traditional contexts and embedding them in modernity, and hence is not apt for the present discussion. See Giddens, *The Consequences of Modernity* (Stanford, Calif.: Stanford University Press, 1990).

38. Chela Sandoval, "Mestizaje as Method," in Carla Trujillo, ed., *Living Chicana Theory* (Berkeley, Calif.: Third Woman Press, 1998).

39. Victor Turner and Edith Turner, *Image and Pilgrimage in Christian Culture: Anthropological Perspectives* (New York: Columbia University Press, 1978), 34–35.

40. Walter Benjamin, *Illuminations*, trans. Harry Zohn (New York: Schocken Books, 1968), 257.

41. Guillermo Gómez-Peña, in Guillermo Gómez-Peña, Enrique Chagoya, and Felicia Rice, *Codex Espangliensis: From Columbus to the Border Patrol* (San Francisco: City Lights Books, 2000), n.p.

42. Ibid.

43. Judith Butler, *Bodies That Matter: On the Discursive Limits of Sex* (New York: Routledge, 1993), 48–49.

44. See "The Return of the Dead," in Elaine K. Miller, ed., *Mexican Folk Narrative from the Los Angeles Area* (Austin: University of Texas Press, 1973), 55–109.

45. Ibid., 99; the translation is mine; ellipses are original.

46. Sandra Cisneros, *Woman Hollering Creek* (New York: Vintage Books, 1991), 51.

47. Ibid., 55.

48. Avery Gordon, *Ghostly Matters: Haunting and the Sociological Imagination* (Minneapolis: University of Minnesota Press, 1997), 8.

49. Edward W. Soja, *Postmodern Geographies: The Reassertation of Social Space in Critical Social Theory* (London: Verso, 1989), 217, 219.

50. Ana Castillo, *So Far from God* (New York: Norton, 1993).

51. Davíd Carrasco, "The Myth of the Chicano Borderlands: Shamanism and the Loco-Centric Imagination in the Work of Gloria Anzaldúa and Dr. Loco" (paper presented at the New Directions in Chicano Religions Conference, 17 February 1997, Santa Barbara, Calif.), 23.

52. Gloria Anzaldúa, interview with Karin Ikas, in Anzaldúa, *Borderlands/La Frontera: The New Mestiza*, 2nd ed. (San Francisco: Aunt Lute Books, 1999), 239.

53. Carlos Monsiváis, *Mexican Postcards*, trans. John Kraniauskas (London: Verso, 1997), 125.

54. Ibid., 127.

55. José Saldívar, *Border Matters: Remapping American Cultural Studies* (Berkeley: University of California Press, 1997), 148.

56. Guillermo Gómez-Peña, "The Two Guadalupes," in Ana Castillo, ed., *Goddess of the Americas, La Diosa de las Americas: Writings on the Virgin of Guadalupe* (New York: Riverhead Books, 1996), 178–83, 178.

57. Ibid., 181.

58. Ibid., 180.

59. Alurista, "Cultural Nationalism and Xicano Literature during the Decade of 1965–1975," *Melus* 8:2 (Summer 1981): 22–34.

60. Gloria Anzaldúa, interview in Louise Keating, ed., *Interviews/Entrevistas* (New York: Routledge, 2000), 73, 77.

Index

muina (anger sickness), 135
Muñoz, Carlos, 54
Murieta, Joaquín, 51–53, 284n97
mutualistas (mutual aid societies), 49, 96, 107
myths: anthropological studies of, 5; of apparitions, 88; as narrative, 270n3; sacred, 270n3. *See also* cosmology, Aztec; cosmology, Mesoamerican
myths, foundational: of Alcance Victoria, 215; of *espiritualismo*, 165, 167; of Los Angeles, 36; of *mestiza/os*, 61; of Victory Outreach, 215–16, 220; of Virgen de Guadalupe, 64

Nahuas: beliefs on death, 124; concept of truth, 244; cosmology of, 28, 29–30; Tonantzin's significance for, 87
Nash, June, 27–28, 32, 87
nationalism, Mexican: Virgen de Guadalupe in, 63
Native Americans: of California missions, 35–38; compulsory labor by, 37–38; conquistadors' assimilation of, 31; conversion of, 33, 37, 69; Jefferson on, 19; mimetic power of, 74; resistance to Christianity, 33; revolts by, 33, 34; slavery debate over, 32–33
nepantlaism, 265; of Aztec religion, 30; in borderland religions, 56–58, 259; of converts, 26–27; and *curanderismo*, 130; defined, 26–27; of evangelical congregations, 223–24; of Mexican immigrants, 47, 49; in mission system, 39–40; vs. syncretism, 27; of Virgen de Guadalupe, 62
New Mexico: lay Catholicism of, 45, 119–20; pueblos of, 37
Nietzsche, Friedrich: on return, 260; on transvaluation of morals, 4, 274n6
El Niño Fidencio, 130, 151–57, 161, 162; androgyny of, 156–57; biographies of, 155; body of, 155; channeling of, 156–57; as Christ figure, 155; collectives honoring, 156; conflict with Catholic Church, 154–55; death of, 155, 156; early life of, 152; *espiritualismo* of, 153; festivals of, 156; government investigation of, 155; healing by, 9, 152; photographs of, 155; and Plutarco Calles, 153; popularity of, 153; prophecies of, 154; "slaves" of, 154; as Virgen de Guadalupe, 157; visions of, 152–53
El Niño Fidencio (film), 154
nuns, Chicana, 111

obligation: of *curanderas*, 137; of *evangélicos*, 257; and exchange, 66–67; in Guadalupe devotion, 257
Olivares, Father Luis, 112–14; illness of, 113–14
ollin (movement), 28. *See also* movement
Ometéotl (god), 30, 132–33
Orsi, Robert, 99
Ortíz de Montellano, Bernardo, 132
Oviedo, Damiana, 165, 166, 176, 297n1; numerology of, 178

PADRES (organization), 111–12
Pardo, Mary, 114
Los Pastores (play), 118, 253
Patriarchal Mexican Church of Elías. *See* Mediodía
Paz, Octavio, 8, 124–25, 266; on border crossings, 125; on La Malinche, 10; on Mexican Catholicism, 11–12
penitents, 45; processions of, 119
Pentecostalism: body in, 210; as borderland religion, 200n23, 211; conversion to, 238; divine healing in, 210; local deployment in, 257; multiculturalism of, 211; rehabilitation in, 225; signs in, 209; theology of, 249; trance in, 210. *See also* evangelicalism
Pentecostals, 204; of Los Angeles, 207–8, 219–20. See also *evangélicos*
Perez, Emma, 4, 14
Pérez, Laura, ix, 6
Pérez-Torres, Rafael, 56
performance: agency during, 255; gifting of, 253; limits of, 255; mimetic, 256; the normative in, 244; and prophecy, 253–56; and rituals, 272n17; symbolic, 254; transgressive, 86
performance, religious, 253, 256; of *evangélicos*, 235–37, 239, 255; Tepeyac pilgrimage as, 86
Perón, Evita, 156
place, concepts of, 249–50. *See also* space
La Placita Church (East Los Angeles), 3, 96–97, 99, 274n1; civil disobedience in, 112–14; political refugees at, 113
Plan of Iguala (1821), 75
poetics: cultural, 14; *difrasismo*, 51; of identity, 49; of salvation, 16
poetics, religious: action in, 17; actors in, 5; body in, 246; border-crossing in, 58; of colonialism, 162; cross in, 245; cultural micropractices in, 272n16; of *curanderismo*, 130, 131, 158; of death, 21, 124–25; devil in, 14; of *espiritualismo*, 167, 181, 183; genealogy of, 25, 277n48; gifts in,

Text: 10/13 Sabon
Display: Sabon
Compositor: Binghamton Valley Composition, LLC
Printer and Binder: Sheridan Books, Inc.